Handbook of Transnational Governance

Handbook of Transnational Governance

Institutions and Innovations

Edited by
Thomas Hale and David Held

polity

Contents

Notes on Contributors   x
Preface   xxiii

1. Editors' Introduction: Mapping Changes in
   Transnational Governance   1
   Thomas Hale and David Held

Part I   **Transgovernmental Networks**
    Introduction   37

2. The Basel Committee on Banking Supervision   39
   Kevin Young

3. Financial Action Task Force   45
   Ian Roberge

4. Financial Stability Board   50
   Randall Germain

5. The Group of Twenty   55
   John Kirton

6. Global Forum on Transparency and Exchange
   of Information for Tax Purposes   61
   Tony Porter and Verónica Rubio Vega

7. International Accounting Standards Board   66
   Andreas Nölke

8. International Association of Insurance Supervisors   71
   Donato Masciandaro

9. International Competition Network   80
   Marie-Laure Djelic

10.   International Conference on Harmonization
of Technical Requirements for the Registration
of Pharmaceutical Products   88
Dimitrios Katsikas

11.   International Network for Environmental
Compliance and Enforcement   94
*Durwood Zaelke, Kenneth Markowitz
and Meredith R. Koparova*

12.   Joint Forum   101
Kevin Young

13.   Transnational Policing   106
Monica den Boer

Part II   Arbitration Bodies
Introduction   115

14.   Citizen Submission Process of the North American
Commission for Environmental Cooperation   117
Thomas Hale

15.   Independent Accountability Mechanisms at Regional
Development Banks   122
Daniel D. Bradlow and Andria Naudé Fourie

16.   Transnational Commercial Arbitration   138
Dirk Lehmkuhl

17.   World Bank Inspection Panel   148
Thomas Hale

Part III   Multistakeholder Initiatives
Introduction   155

18.   The Framework Convention Alliance   157
Ross MacKenzie

19.   Global Fund to Fight AIDS, Tuberculosis and Malaria 161
Johanna Hanefeld

20.   Global Polio Eradication Initiative   166
Mathias Koenig-Archibugi

21.   Internet Corporation for Assigned
       Names and Numbers   176
       Jonathan Koppell

22.   International Coral Reef Initiative   182
       Radoslav S. Dimitrov

23.   International Health Partnership and IHP+   189
       Anna Holzscheiter

24.   Multistakeholder Involvement in UN Conferences   195
       Kathrin Böhling

25.   World Commission on Dams   202
       Navroz K. Dubash

Part IV   Voluntary Regulations
       Introduction   211

26.   Carbon Disclosure Project   213
       Eun-Hee Kim and Thomas P. Lyon

27.   Codex Alimentarius Commission   219
       Tim Büthe and Nathaniel Harris

28.   The Equator Principles   229
       Christopher Wright

29.   Extractive Industries Transparency Initiative   236
       Helmut Weidner

30.   Fair Labor Association   243
       Kate MacDonald

31.   The Fair Trade System   252
       Kate MacDonald

32.   Clean Clothes Campaign   259
       Niklas Egels-Zandén

33.   Forest Stewardship Council   265
       Philipp Pattberg

34. Global Corporate Governance Principles   273
     Andrew Baker

35. Global Reporting Initiative   281
     Halina Szejnwald Brown

36. International Organization for Standardization   289
     Jonathan Koppell

37. International Organization for Standardization 14001   295
     Matthew Potoski and Elizabeth Elwakeil

38. Kimberly Process   302
     Carola Kantz

39. Marine Stewardship Council   308
     Thomas Hale

40. OECD Guidelines for Multinational Enterprises   314
     Elisa Morgera

41. Partnering against Corruption Initiative and
     the Business Principles for Countering Bribery   322
     David Hess

42. Responsible Care   328
     Ivan Montiel

43. Rugmark   333
     Mathias Koenig-Archibugi

44. Social Accountability International   338
     Rainer Braun

45. International Council of Toy Industries
     Code of Conduct   344
     Reinhard Biedermann

46. United Nations Global Compact   350
     Thomas Hale

47. Voluntary Principles on Security and Human Rights   357
     Chip Pitts

48.   Worker Rights Consortium   364
        Robert J. S. Ross

Part V   Finance Mechanisms
        Introduction   369

49.   Carbon Offsets   371
        Jessica F. Green

50.   Financing Mechanisms for Climate Change Mitigation   377
        Charlotte Streck

51.   Global Alliance for Vaccines and Immunisation   384
        Andrew Harmer and Carlos Bruen

52.   UNITAID   394
        Anna Holzscheiter

Index   400

Notes on Contributors

Andrew Baker is Senior Lecturer in Political Economy at the Queen's University of Belfast. He is one of the current editors of the *British Journal of Politics and International Relations* and researches in the field of International Political Economy, focusing on the politics of Global Financial Governance. He is the author of *The Group of Seven: Finance Ministries, Central Banks and Global Financial Governance* (2006) and co-author, with David Hudson and Richard Woodward, of *Governing Financial Globalization: International Political Economy and Multi Level Governance* (2007), both published by Routledge.

Dr Reinhard Biedermann is Assistant Professor at the Department of Global Politics and Economics at Tamkang University in Taiwan, and at the Graduate Institute of European Studies at the same university. He worked for the German nongovernmental origanization Misereor on globalization and was a post-doctoral researcher at the Law Institute of Academia Sinica in Taipei, Taiwan. Besides his research focus on globalization and corporate social responsibility, he also publishes on trade and security relations between the EU and East Asia.

Dr Kathrin Böhling, Assistant Professor in the Department of Forest and Environmental Policy at Munich Technical University, has developed a particular interest in the emergence and diffusion of multi-stakeholder arrangements as a standard in global governance. Currently, she looks at the role of these arrangements in the resolution of conflict in environmental governance. Prior to her work at Munich Technical University, Kathrin was a member of the Social Science Research Centre in Berlin.

Daniel D. Bradlow is SARCHI Professor of International Development Law and African Economic Relations at the University of Pretoria, South Africa, and Professor of Law at American University Washington

College of Law in Washington, DC. He is also the Chair of the Roster of Experts for the Independent Review Mechanism at the African Development Bank.

Rainer Braun is a political scientist in New York. He teaches at Columbia University and Long Island University, where he is the research coordinator for the graduate United Nations Program. His research interests are political development, human rights and corporate social accountability.

Rainer has worked as a consultant with various organizations in the field of corporate social responsibility. He is currently advising the Office of the New York State Comptroller on human rights related policies for its investment portfolio. In the past, his human rights related work included positions with the National Human Rights Commissioner of Honduras and the Friedrich Ebert Foundation. Rainer holds a BA in Political Science and Economics from the University of Bremen and an MA from the Free University of Berlin, where he is currently finishing his Ph.D. in International Political Economy.

Carlos Bruen is a researcher and Ph.D. candidate in the Division of Population Health Sciences, Royal College of Surgeons in Ireland. His research focuses on global health governance and policy, including the emergence and evolution of new global health initiatives, and the role of individuals, organizations and networks in shaping heath systems responses and institutional change. He also assists with coordination activities for the Global HIV/AIDS Initiatives Network (GHIN), a network of researchers from twenty-two countries (www.ghinet. org). Prior to this he completed an M.Sc. in Equality Studies in University College Dublin (UCD), after which he worked as a teaching and research fellow at the UCD Equality Studies Centre, responsible for modules on global politics and development.

Tim Büthe is Assistant Professor of Political Science at Duke University. His research focuses on institutional persistence and change, the interaction of domestic and international institutions, global private politics, and the regulation of product and financial markets. His work has been published in, *inter alia*, the *American Political Science Review*, the *American Journal of Political Science*, *World Politics*, *Governance*, and his co-authored book, *New Global Rulers: The Privatization of Regulation in the World Economy* (Princeton University Press, 2011).

Professor Dr Monica den Boer holds the Police Academy Chair on Comparative Public Administration, in particular the Internationalization of the Police Function, at the VU University Amsterdam, and is Professor at the College of Europe in Bruges. Her publications focus on European law enforcement cooperation, with a more recent focus on the ethical aspects of international counter-terrorism governance and surveillance. Within the European Commission-sponsored INEX project, she carries responsibility for international research on ethical values of security professionals.

Radoslav S. Dimitrov is Associate Professor of Political Science at the University of Western Ontario. He participates in UN environmental negotiations as government delegate for the European Union, UN rapporteur for the *Earth Negotiation Bulletin*, and consultant to the World Business Council for Sustainable Development. His research on global institutions, environmental regimes, the science–policy connection and norms in world politics is published in *Science and International Environmental Policy: Regimes and Nonregimes in Global Governance* (Rowman and Littlefield, 2006), and articles in *International Studies Quarterly, International Studies Review, Global Environmental Politics* and the *Journal of Environment and Development*.

Marie-Laure Djelic is Professor in Management at ESSEC Business School, France. She has published in many different outlets on capitalism and its transformation, and on the diffusion of practices, ideas and organizational forms, as well as on globalization and its governance. She is, in particular, the author of *Exporting the American Model* (Oxford University Press, 1998) – which obtained the 2000 Max Weber Award for the Best Book in Organizational Sociology from the American Sociological Association. She has also edited, together with Kerstin Sahlin-Andersson in 2006, *Transnational Governance*, and, in 2010, with Sigrid Quack, *Transnational Communities: Shaping Global Economic Governance* (both for Cambridge University Press).

Navroz K. Dubash works on climate change policy and politics, global environmental governance, the political economy of energy in India and Asia, and environmental governance in India. In addition to publishing in various journals, he is also active in Indian policy fora, has a long history of engagement with civil society in India and globally, and is on the editorial board of several international journals. Dr Dubash holds an AB in Public Policy from Princeton University, and MA and Ph.D. degrees from the University of California, Berkeley.

Niklas Egels-Zandén, Ph.D., is Director of the Centre for Business in Society at the School of Business, Economics and Law, University of Gothenburg, Sweden. His areas of research are international business and corporate social responsibility, especially in relation to multinational corporations in emerging economies. He has previously published in, for example, *Journal of Business Ethics, Business Ethics: A European Review, Business Strategy and the Environment* and *Journal of Corporate Citizenship*.

Elizabeth Elwakeil is a graduate student in the Department of Political Science at Iowa State University. Her research interests primarily involve international relations, with specific concentration on Middle East affairs.

Randall Germain is Professor of Political Science at Carleton University, Canada. His scholarly publications include *The International Organization of Credit: States and Global Finance in the World-Economy* (Cambridge University Press, 1997) and *Global Politics and Financial Governance* (Palgrave, 2010). He is also editor of *Globalization and Its Critics: Perspectives from Political Economy* (Palgrave, 2000), and co-editor, with Michael Kenny, of *The Idea of Global Civil Society: Politics and Ethics in a Globalizing Era* (Routledge, 2005). He is currently Chair of the Department of Political Science.

Professor Jessica F. Green is Assistant Professor of Political Science at Case Western Reserve University. She received her Ph.D. from the Woodrow Wilson School of Public and International Affairs at Princeton University. Her research focuses on the ways that private actors make rules and set standards in world politics, particularly in the environmental arena. She holds an MPA in Public Policy from Columbia University and a BA from Brown University. She has worked with the United Nations University in New York and Tokyo, the UN Framework Convention on Climate Change, and the World Resources Institute.

Thomas Hale is a Ph.D. candidate in the Department of Politics at Princeton University. His research focuses on the governance of transnational problems such as climate change and commercial dispute resolution. He has written on the role of private actors in global governance, the accountability of international organizations, East Asian regionalism, innovative governance mechanisms, and transnational democracy. He holds a Master's degree in Global Politics from the London School of Economics, and an AB in Public Policy from Princeton's Woodrow Wilson School.

Dr Johanna Hanefeld is an honorary research fellow in the Department for Global Health and Development at the London School of Hygiene and Tropical Medicine (LSHTM). There, she recently completed her Ph.D., a policy analysis focusing on policy implementation processes relating to the roll-out of antiretroviral treatment in Zambia and South Africa, taking a special interest in the role of global health initiatives. She has extensive research experience in Sub-Saharan Africa and the Caribbean, mainly focusing on HIV/AIDS, health and human rights in Africa. Prior to joining LSHTM, Johanna worked as a researcher at Amnesty International and the Coordinator of the Panos Global AIDS Programme. Johanna now works for the WHO EURO Region on Social Determinants of Health.

Andrew Harmer is a research fellow in the Department of Global Health and Development at the London School of Hygiene and Tropical Medicine (LSHTM). A political scientist by training, his research has focused primarily on global health partnerships and initiatives. He is a coordinator of the Global Health Initiatives Network (www.ghinet. org), a network of researchers exploring the effects of global health initiatives on scale-up of HIV/AIDS services at sub-national level in countries across Africa, Europe and Asia. His research also explores synergies between public health and international relations theory, particularly constructivist approaches to global health governance and globalization. His interest in ideas and discourse is reflected in publications in various journals.

Nathaniel Harris is a graduate student in the Department of Political Science at Duke University. His primary research interests include non-state actors in global politics, global governance, and international relations theory, as well as human security. Substantively, his current research focuses on the influence of international human rights instruments and the impact of conflict and violence on global health.

David Held is the Graham Wallas Chair in Political Science, and co-Director of LSE Global Governance, at the London School of Economics. Among his most recent publications are *Cosmopolitanism: Ideals and Realities* (2010), *Globalisation/Anti-Globalisation* (2007), *Models of Democracy* (2006), *Global Covenant* (2004), *Global Transformations: Politics, Economics and Culture* (1999) and *Democracy and the Global Order: From the Modern State to Cosmopolitan Governance* (1995). His main research interests include the study of globalization, changing forms of democracy and the prospects of regional and global governance. He is a director of

Polity Press, which he co-founded in 1984, and General Editor of *Global Policy*.

David Hess is an associate professor of Business Law and Business Ethics at the Ross School of Business at the University of Michigan. Professor Hess has a Ph.D. in Management from The Wharton School of the University of Pennsylvania and a JD from the University of Iowa College of Law. His work on corporate accountability has appeared in such journals as *Business Ethics Quarterly*, *Journal of Business Ethics*, *Journal of Corporation Law* and the *Michigan Law Review*.

Anna Holzscheiter is Lecturer in International Relations at the Free University Berlin. Her theoretical research focuses on the theory and analysis of discourse in the discipline of International Relations, on constructivist theories of power and on the role of nongovernmental actors in world politics. Empirically, she has focused on international law in the field of children's rights and on contending policy discourses and policy coordination in the global governance of HIV/AIDS.

Carola Kantz currently works as a consultant for stakeholder relations and sustainability issues in the energy and mobility sectors. Prior to this, she taught in the International Relations Department at the London School of Economics and worked as a freelance consultant on corporate social responsibility issues in the extractive industries. She received her Ph.D. from the London School of Economics. Her doctoral thesis is titled 'Precious Stones, Black Gold and the Extractive Industries: Accounting for the Institutional Design of Multi-stakeholder Initiatives'.

Dimitrios Katsikas is a 'Stavros Costopoulos' Research Fellow at the Hellenic Foundation for European and Foreign Policy. He has been recently elected Lecturer of International and European Political Economy at the University of Athens. His research interests include non-state actors, the institutions of global governance, political authority and democracy in the context of multilevel global governance, and transnational business and financial regulation.

Eun-Hee Kim is Assistant Professor of Strategic Management and Public Policy at the George Washington University. She received her Ph.D. from the University of Michigan, Ann Arbor, in 2009. Her work 'Strategic Environmental Disclosure' is forthcoming in the *Journal of Environmental Economics and Management* (with Tom Lyon). She is currently working on several topics including environmental regulation, renewable energy and symbolic management.

John Kirton is co-Director of the G20 Research Group and Director of the G8 Research Group, as well as co-Director of the Global Health Diplomacy Program, all based at Trinity College at the Munk School of Global Affairs at the University of Toronto, where he is a professor of Political Science.

Mathias Koenig-Archibugi is Senior Lecturer in Global Politics at the London School of Economics and Political Science and Research Fellow at LSE Global Governance. His work is published in the *European Journal of International Relations, International Organization, Philosophy & Public Affairs*, and other journals. He edited *New Modes of Governance in the Global System*, with Michael Zürn (Palgrave, 2006) and *Global Governance and Public Accountability*, with David Held (Blackwell, 2005).

Meredith R. Koparova is the Director of Programs at the INECE Secretariat. Mrs Koparova's main areas of work include communicating the importance of environmental compliance and enforcement, delivering capacity building programmes on performance measurement indicators, and supporting INECE projects on climate compliance and seaport environmental security.

Jonathan Koppell is Director of the School of Public Affairs at Arizona State University where he also holds the Lattie and Elva Coor Presidential Chair. He is the author of *World Rule: Accountability, Legitimacy and the Design of Global Governance* (University of Chicago Press, 2010), an empirical study of the structure of twenty-five global rule-making organizations, as well as *The Politics of Quasi-Government: Hybrid Organizations and the Dynamics of Bureaucratic Control* (Cambridge University Press, 2003).

Dirk Lehmkuhl is Professor of European Politics at the University of St Gallen in Switzerland. His teaching and research portfolio includes issues on European public policies and EU external governance, comparative regional integration, the contribution of non-state actors to global governance and the legalization of transnational relations. He is Academic Director of the BA and MA Programmes in International Affairs and Governance at the University of St Gallen.

Thomas P. Lyon is the Director of the Erb Institute for Global Sustainable Enterprise at the University of Michigan. He holds the Dow Chair of Sustainable Science, Technology and Commerce, with appointments in both the Ross School of Business and the School of Natural Resources and Environment. Professor Lyon is a leader in using economic analysis to understand corporate environmental strategy and how it is shaped by emerging government regulations, nongovernmental organizations and consumer demands. His book *Corporate Environmentalism and Public* Policy (2004), published by Cambridge University Press, is the first rigorous economic analysis of this increasingly important topic. His current research focuses on corporate environmental information disclosure, greenwashing, the causes and consequences of renewable energy policy, and voluntary programmes for environmental improvement.

Kate Macdonald is a lecturer at the University of Melbourne, having held previous positions at the London School of Economics and Political Science, the Australian National University, and Oxford University. Her current research focuses on social, labour and human rights governance arrangements and their implications for developing countries. She has carried out research and consultancy work on these topics for a range of nongovernmental organizations including Amnesty International, Action Aid Australia and the UK's Corporate Responsibility Coalition.

Ross MacKenzie is a lecturer in health studies at Macquarie University in Sydney. He has worked on tobacco control research projects at the School of Public Health, University of Sydney; the Cancer Council New South Wales; the Centre on Global Change and Health at the London School of Hygiene and Tropical Medicine; and Action on Smoking and Health (ASH) Thailand in Bangkok. He has published articles on topics ranging from tobacco industry operations in Southeast Asia to media influence on government subsidization of medicine.

Kenneth Markowitz is the Managing Director of the INECE Secretariat, President and founder of Earthpace LLC, and Senior Climate Change Consultant for Akin Gump Strauss Hauer & Feld. Mr Markowitz plays a central role in the management of INECE and has headed INECE initiatives to strengthen compliance, improve investor confidence and ensure environmental integrity in carbon markets, bringing together regulators, business and civil society around the world.

Donato Masciandaro, born in Italy in 1961, is Full Professor of Economics, Chair in Economics of Financial Regulation, at Bocconi University. He is head of the Department of Economics and Director of the Paolo Baffi Centre on Central Banking and Financial Regulation. He is a Board member of the SUERF (The European Money and Finance Forum). Formerly he served as a visiting scholar at the IMF Institute, as well as Consultant at the United Nations. He is Associate Editor of the *Journal of Financial Stability*. His work has covered three main topics: central banking, financial regulation and supervision, illegal financial markets. His two most recent books are: *Designing Financial Supervision Institutions: Independence, Accountability and Governance* (ed. with M. Quintyn, Edward Elgar, 2007) and *Black Finance: The Economics of Money Laundering* (with E. Takats and B. Unger, Edward Elgar, 2007).

Ivan Montiel is an assistant professor of Corporate Sustainability at College of Business Administration at Loyola Marymount University. He received his Ph.D. in Environmental Science & Management at the University of California. His research interests include how organizations can design socially responsible and sustainable strategies while remaining competitive. He is currently working on several research projects analysing environmental behaviour of firms in Mexico.

Dr Elisa Morgera is Lecturer in European Environmental Law at University of Edinburgh School of Law, UK. She specializes in European, international and comparative environmental law and has published in the area of environmental integration in the European Union external relations, biodiversity law, and corporate environmental accountability (including the monograph *Corporate Accountability in International Environmental Law* (Oxford University Press, 2009).

Andria Naudé Fourie is Assistant Professor of Public International Law at the Erasmus School of Law, Rotterdam, in the Netherlands. She completed her Ph.D. on the World Bank's Inspection Panel in 2009 (*cum laude*).

Andreas Nölke is Professor of Political Science, in particular International Relations and International Political Economy, at Goethe University Frankfurt. He is co-editor of *The Transnational Politics of Corporate Governance Regulation* (Routledge, 2007) and *Transnational Private Governance and its Limits* (Routledge, 2008), and has published in journals such as *World Politics*, *Review of International Political Economy* and *Journal of Common Market Studies*.

Philipp Pattberg is Associate Professor of Transnational Governance, Department of Environmental Policy Analysis, Institute for Environmental Studies (IVM), VU University Amsterdam, the Netherlands. He acts as the deputy-director and research coordinator of the international Global Governance Project, a joint research programme of leading European universities, and is currently Management Committee Chair of the European COST Action 'The

Transformation of Global Environmental Governance: Risks and Opportunities' (2008–12).

Chip Pitts is a lecturer in Law at Stanford Law School and Oxford University, and Professorial Fellow at the SMU Law Institute of the Americas. His teaching, research and writing focuses on ethical globalization, corporate social responsibility, sustainable development and business/human rights. Previously a partner at Baker & McKenzie global law firm, then Chief Legal Officer of Nokia, Inc., he is former Chair of Amnesty International USA, an Advisor to the UN Global Compact, and a frequent delegate to UN conferences. He is co-author and editor of the recent book *Corporate Social Responsibility: A Legal Analysis* (LexisNexis, 2009) (the royalties for which all go to sustainability and business/human rights charities).

Tony Porter is Professor of Political Science at McMaster University in Hamilton, Canada. His most recent books are *Globalization and Finance* (Polity Press, 2005) and *The Challenges of Global Business Authority: Democratic Renewal, Stalemate, or Decay?* (SUNY Press, 2010), co-edited with Karsten Ronit.

Matthew Potoski is a professor in the Department of Political Science at Iowa State University where he teaches courses on public management and policy. He has received Iowa State University LAS awards for Early and Mid-Career Achievement in Research. He is co-Editor of the *Journal of Policy Analysis and Management* and the *International Public Management Journal*. He is co-author with Aseem Prakash of *The Voluntary Environmentalists* (Cambridge, 2006) and co-Editor of *Voluntary Programs: A Club Theory Approach* (MIT, 2008).

Ian Roberge is Department Chair and Associate Professor in the Department of Political Science, Glendon College, York University, in Toronto, Ontario, Canada. Professor Roberge's research focuses on organized crime, money laundering and terrorism financing, as well as on financial services sector regulation. He holds a Ph.D. in Comparative Public Policy from McMaster University in Hamilton, Ontario.

Robert J. S. Ross is Professor of Sociology and Director of the International Studies Stream at Clark University, where he has been since 1972. He has held visiting positions at MIT, Harvard, Michigan and Wheaton. Ross is the author of *Slaves to Fashion: Poverty and Abuse in the New Sweatshops* (Michigan University Press, 2004) and numerous journal and magazine articles about the global apparel industry. With

Kent Trachte he is the author of an early analysis of global capitalism: *Global Capitalism: The New Leviathan* (SUNY Press, 1990).

Verónica Rubio Vega is a Global Governance Ph.D. student at Wilfrid Laurier University (Balsillie School of International Affairs). She holds an MA in Globalization Studies from McMaster University in Canada. Her academic interests focus on the political economy of Latin America regarding issues such as Latin American countries' scope for participation in global policymaking and in the ongoing reconfiguration of financial governance. She has previously conducted research on international labour and taxation mechanisms and also worked in the private telecommunications industry in Ecuador.

Dr Charlotte Streck is Director of Climate Focus and a former Senior Counsel with the World Bank in Washington, DC. Charlotte has been actively involved in climate change policy and carbon projects throughout her career and has worked on, among other things, the setting-up of several of the World Bank's carbon funds. Charlotte is an advisor to numerous governments, private companies, foundations and non-for-profit organizations, and is actively involved in the debate around the development of new carbon finance mechanisms in the area of reducing emissions from deforestation, climate-resilient agriculture, national and international climate frameworks, and a reform of the current Kyoto Mechanisms. She serves on several advisory and editorial panels and serves as lead counsel for climate change with the Center for International Sustainable Development Law at McGill University.

Halina Szejnwald Brown is Professor of Environmental Science and Policy at Clark University, Worcester, Massachusetts. Currently she works in the areas of environmental policy, socio-technical innovation for sustainability, the role of the corporate sector in sustainability transition, and sustainable consumption. Brown received a Ph.D. degree in Chemistry from New York University, and, prior to joining Clark University, she was a chief toxicologist at the Massachusetts Department of Environmental Protection. Brown has served on numerous advisory panels, including: the National Academy of Science; Environmental Protection Agency; Massachusetts Toxic Use Reduction Institute; National Science Foundation; and American Association for the Advancement of Science. She is a fellow of the International Society for Risk Analysis, a fellow of the American Association for the Advancement of Science, and a co-founder of Sustainable Consumption Research and Action Initiative (SCORAI).

Helmut Weidner, political scientist, is Senior Researcher at the Social Science Research Center (WZB) and Adjunct Professor at the Free University Berlin. His major topics of research include cross-national analysis of environmental policy and capacity building; climate policy and equity; mining and sustainable development. Selected publications include: 'Capacity Building for Ecological Modernization: Lessons from Cross-National Research' in *American Behavioral Scientist* (2002), and 'German Climate Change Policy: A Success Story with Some Flaws' in *The Journal of Environment & Development* (with Lutz Mez, 2008).

Christopher Wright is Senior Researcher at the Center for Development and Environment at the University of Oslo. His research interests are in the field of international political economy, focusing on the interplay between international finance and the global politics of human rights and the environment.

Kevin Young is LSE Fellow in Global Politics at the London School of Economics and Political Science (LSE) in the Department of Government. His research interests include global financial governance, interest group theory and international political economy. His empirical research focuses on the politics of financial regulation and financial sector lobbying, at the national and global levels. He teaches classes on globalization and international political economy.

Durwood Zaelke is founder and President of the Institute for Governance & Sustainable Development (IGSD) in Washington, DC, and Geneva; the founding Director of the Secretariat for the International Network for Environmental Compliance & Enforcement; co-founder of the Program on Governance for Sustainable Development at the University of California, Santa Barbara's Bren School of Environmental Science & Management; and co-founder of the Center for International Environmental Law. In 2005, Mr Zaelke published *Making Law Work: Environmental Compliance and Sustainable Development* (with Kaniaru and Kruíková), a two-volume analysis of the best literature on environmental compliance and enforcement; the publication includes 'What Reason Demands: Making Law Work for Sustainable Development' by Zaelke, M. Stilwell and O. Young. Mr Zaelke also directs IGSD's efforts to promote fast-action climate mitigation strategies, including: reducing black carbon, expanding the use of biochar, and continuing to strengthen the Montreal Protocol ozone treaty to protect the climate.

Preface

Our world is changing, and with it the institutions that govern us. Globalization has altered the social, economic and ecological relations between people around the world, creating a host of new policy challenges. Overambitious mortgages in the United States can take the livelihoods from people in Iceland. The health infrastructure in Indonesia can affect how many people will die of flu in Mexico. Rates of car ownership in China can affect national survival for the people of Tuvalu.

Policymakers and scholars have long recognized that our preeminent political institution, the sovereign state, is deeply challenged by problems that fall outside its territorial jurisdiction. Moreover, the traditional institutions that states use to address transborder problems – treaties and intergovernmental organizations – have also proven wanting. On a range of pressing global policy issues today – the Doha trade round, negotiations over climate change, financial regulation, nuclear non-proliferation, etc. – countries seem unable to cooperate effectively. The consequences of these stalemates for the lives of people around the world are severe.

But there is more to contemporary global governance than simply state, behaviour and the formal treaties and intergovernmental organizations they create. We live in a period of remarkable institutional innovation in global politics. States are engaging each other outside of traditional diplomatic channels, linking 'domestic' officials into transgovernmental policy networks. Private actors like nongovernmental organizations and companies are engaging in rule-making, implementation, monitoring, enforcement and service provision – that is, in governance – at all levels, either as the partners of states or intergovernmental organizations, or as private authorities in their own right. New modes of accountability and enforcement based on capacity building, transparency, market incentives or moral suasion are joining formal rules as key features of the governance architecture.

These and other new institutional forms are widely recognized in the literature but, in our view, remain poorly understood. They do not always fit comfortably with the leading academic theories of global politics. This is unfortunate, because in many areas these new institutions are increasingly important features of the political landscape with profound impacts on people's lives. From healthcare, to financial governance, to human rights, to the environment, some of the governance institutions that matter most are not the kind of state-to-state institutions imagined by the leading theories. This is a striking empirical development that students of global politics must account for.

Given the all-too-visible inadequacies of existing intergovernmental institutions, institutional innovation matters for normative reasons as well. To the extent institutional design affects policy outcomes – and we believe it often does – institutional innovation represents, potentially, an important means to confront the challenges of an increasingly globalized world. While by no means a panacea, institutional design is one of the few factors policymakers can control. It therefore behooves us to study emerging forms of transnational governance seriously.

The first step is to understand what, exactly, has changed. Despite widespread attention in the literature to broad trends and individual examples, no comprehensive map of new transnational political institutions exists. This volume aims to change that by providing an indicative sample of over fifty cases. Our goal is to promote further research on the causes behind these changes, as well as their implications.

This map was originally envisioned as an online wiki that would collect and update examples of innovative governance institutions in real time. However, as is often the case in global politics, the most functionally efficient solution was not the one that proved compatible with the incentives of the relevant actors, as the exigencies of academic life continue to favour words that appear on paper over words rendered in electrons. But happily, the project's central goal of providing an empirical baseline of innovative transnational governance mechanisms has not suffered in the transition from wiki to book. Indeed, we believe the entries that follow will give the reader an excellent understanding of what is new in transnational institutions.

Many individuals and institutions have proven invaluable along the way. Conceptual and practical guidance came from an advisory board to the initial wiki project, including Robert Keohane, Kelley Lee, Andrew Moravcsik, Tony Porter, Thomas Risse, Anne-Marie Slaughter, Gill Walt, Oran Young, Michael Zürn and, particularly, Mathias Koenig-Archibugi, who provided generous advice throughout the course of the project. Insights from Kevin Young also enhanced the project at various points along the way.

Financial support was provided by LSE Global Governance at the London School of Economics, the LSE Seed Fund, the Niehaus Center for Globalization and Governance at Princeton's Woodrow Wilson School of Public and International Affairs, and the Nuffield Foundation. We are grateful to Harriet Carter at LSE and Pat Trinity at Princeton for their administrative capacities, and to Exozet GmbH of Berlin for excellent web services. Above all, we are indebted to the contributors to this volume for sharing their expertise and insights. We hope the reader will learn as much from them as we have.

T. H. and D. H.
August 2010

Editors' Introduction: Mapping Changes in Transnational Governance
Thomas Hale and David Held

Governance institutions alter over time, often dramatically. Human societies have ruled themselves through tribes, city states, empires, kingdoms, leagues, confederations, nation states, and many variations thereon. The institutions that cut across and link these polities – transborder institutions – change as well. Records of treaties date back to the first permanent settlements (Tucker 1965). It was only in the last century, however, and especially since the Second World War, that the formal treaties and intergovernmental organizations we are familiar with became so numerous and authoritative.

But contemporary changes in global politics go beyond just the increasing number and importance of treaties and intergovernmental organizations. We live in a remarkable period of institutional innovation in transnational governance, with different types of institutions – some with historical antecedents, some unprecedented – playing a crucial role. This volume seeks to map these changes.

Consider a few examples. Following the 2008–9 global financial crisis, financial regulation has become a top concern of policymakers around the world. Much of this regulation is drawn up not simply by national politicians and diplomats, but by networks of government regulators, international bureaucrats and, in many cases, representatives of the regulated industries. Such networks, like the Basel Committee on Banking Supervision (chapter 2) or the International Association of Insurance Supervisors (chapter 8), develop technical standards that profoundly shape the global economy.

In the environmental realm, countries have frequently failed to negotiate and enforce the rules needed to sustain the ecosystems and natural resources on which we depend. But private groups have gone ahead and developed their own standards and regulations, 'enforcing' them through innovative techniques like labelling schemes that allow consumers to choose green products over damaging ones (chapters 33, 39).

Even the institutions governing such a basic concern as health have evolved. Developing countries' healthcare systems are increasingly guided by global initiatives like the International Health Partnership and its related initiatives (chapter 23), a multisectoral, expert-driven consortium of donor countries, international organizations and a private organization, the Bill and Melinda Gates Foundation. In order to receive funds from these sources – which can mean life or death for millions of people – countries must design their healthcare delivery systems according to the experts' directives.

Examples like these raise three fundamental questions. What has changed, why has it changed, and what are the implications of these changes? This volume, a survey of innovative transnational governance institutions, addresses the first of these questions with the hope of opening a path to further research on the other two. While many observers have recognized changes in transnational governance, never has such a broad sample of institutional innovations been gathered together. Such an empirical baseline is needed for sound theorizing of the causes and effects of innovations in transnational governance.

The Handbook's goal is to push forward a debate on institutional change at the transborder level that has been carried out predominantly in very broad or very narrow terms. On the broad end of the spectrum, some scholars have identified contemporary transnational governance institutions as partial or even complete replacements for national governments, predicting an epochal shift in political institutions (Strange 1996; Zürn and Leibfried 2005; Rosenau 2007). For example, a number of observers have declared a 'neo-medieval' period in politics, in which globalization renders political institutions increasingly overlapping and pluralistic (Korbin 1999). Others speak of a 'postnational constellation' (Habermas 2001) or of increasing sectoral autonomy and self-regulation (Teubner 1983) Slaughter (1997, 2004), in turn, identified transnational networks of government officials as a novel form of governance, but one that continued to rely on the state. By 'disaggregating' sovereignty and allowing the state – or parts of it – to act transnationally, 'transgovernmental' networks represented an alternative to intergovernmental institutions, and even a 'new world order' (Slaughter 1997, 2004). This work can take a deterministic flavour, implying that political institutions necessarily evolve with macro trends in society. There likely are causal relationships between institutions and structural changes, but the diversity of political institutions implies that these relationships are anything but straightforward and homogeneous. The 'broad' literature can only take us so far.

At the narrow end, numerous observers have identified specific changes within an issue area, noted the emergence of a new type of governance mechanisms across issue areas, or otherwise explored particular aspects of changes in global governance. Such work provides a detailed counterpoint to the broader discussions, but only rarely collects and synthesizes this information to illuminate larger trends in institutional evolution. Moreover, as discussed below, individual trends (e.g. complexity, the participation of transnational actors, private governance) are typically studied in isolation of each other.[1] For these reasons, the 'narrow' literature is often vulnerable to the charge that innovative institutions have had only a marginal impact on global politics.

We believe a synthesis of broad but detailed empirical work is the best way to advance our understanding of changes in transborder political institutions. The *Handbook* seeks to bridge this divide by collecting empirical examples that will allow the reader to consider a number of detailed cases in comparative perspective.

While the *Handbook* is intended as a social scientific resource, it is also relevant for readers more interested in action than analysis. Many observers have noted that contemporary globalization and interdependence pose enormous challenges to our current political institutions (Keohane 2001; Held and McGrew 2007). Without doubt, the modern nation state has been the most effective governance technology ever devised, securing, at its best, an unprecedented level of prosperity and security for its citizens. But in an interdependent world, no individual state, no matter how competent, can address transnational issues ranging from climate change, to financial regulation, to macroeconomic management, to extremist terrorist networks. Nor can it confront the moral challenges of our age like global poverty or disease. We are essentially using 17th-century institutional technology to confront 21st-century challenges.

The traditional tools of interstate cooperation – intergovernmental organizations and treaties – have also proven inadequate. From the Doha trade round, to climate negotiations, to debates over nuclear non-proliferation, to financial reform, multilateral institutions seem stalled. This is not just a product of the plodding negotiations, weak enforcement provisions, power imbalances between states, and other difficulties associated with intergovernmental processes. Because these institutions rely on the consent and participation of sovereign states, they often reflect the lowest common denominator of political ambition.

[1] In an exception to this fragmented literature, Koenig-Archibugi (2005) presents a helpfully general typology of new types of global governance institutions. He locates institutions in an issue space defined by three dimensions – publicness, delegation and inclusiveness – generating a number of ideal types ranging from global intergovernmental or even supranational institutions (like the World Trade Organization (WTO) or the European Union (EU)) to private, restricted institutions like the global diamond cartel.

We do not argue that new kinds of institutions are a panacea for these problems. The same interests, power imbalances and transaction costs that prevent traditional institutions from effectively managing globalization will beset any new ones as well. We do not, however, subscribe to the view that institutions are merely epiphenomenal to these underlying conditions. Instead, we contend that innovative institutions designed in a way sensitive to the constraints upon them stand the greatest chance of improving transnational governance. Indeed, precisely because transborder institutions are strongly restricted by other factors, intelligent institutional design and innovation are all the more crucial.

The institutions presented here do not necessarily rise to this challenge. As the entries show, their record is quite mixed. We do, however, argue that understanding recent institutional changes in transnational governance can help scholars and policymakers design and implement the kinds of institutions needed to manage globalization. We therefore give the new mechanisms in this volume the positive connotation of 'innovations' in an aspirational sense.

We focus on changes in transborder governance, even though, to be sure, innovation is not limited to the transnational realm. Scholars of domestic policy speak of 'the new public management' or the 'new governance' (Rhodes 1996). In many countries, institutions in fields as diverse as environmental regulation (Orts 1995) and welfare provision (Sørensen and Torfing 2006) now bear little resemblance to a traditional Weberian public bureaucracy. As discussed below, some of these domestic trends are no doubt relevant to changes in transborder relations as well. They also imply that globalization cannot be the *only* driver of institutional innovation in transborder governance. However, the *Handbook* focuses on innovations beyond state boundaries.

This chapter proceeds as follows. The next section situates contemporary innovations in governance in the larger literature, explaining what came before and highlighting several trends in global governance and our theoretical understanding of it. The following section describes the *Handbook* and its contribution to the study of global politics. The fourth and fifth sections extract some observations from the *Handbook*'s entries on the second and third questions raised above: why has governance changed, and what are the implications? The conclusion suggests how a research agenda on this topic might develop.

Before proceeding, it may be helpful to define some key terms. 'International' refers to state-to-state interactions in which one sovereign country deals with another. 'Transnational', in turn, is used to refer to interactions that cross national boundaries at levels other than sovereign-to-sovereign. 'Transborder' is used as a more general category to include all boundary-spanning interactions, while 'global' is used for transborder interactions that include (approximately) the entire world system.

The Rise and Evolution of Governance beyond the State

Transborder political institutions have taken many different forms throughout history. Some, like formalized agreements between independent polities (i.e. treaties), have always been part of politics. Some appear and disappear at different times and places – for example, merchants in Ancient China, medieval Europe, and everywhere today have formed a variety of non-state cross-border institutions to facilitate long-distance commerce (Milgrom, North et al. 1990; Cutler, Haufler et al. 1999; Hamilton 2006). And some once-prominent institutions are now extinct. For much of history, strategic marriage and kinship ties were used to cement alliances, gain influence and structure the anarchic world of state-to-state relations through the institution of the family. This practice seems to have disappeared in the modern era of de-personalized politics.

This volume focuses on contemporary changes, taking the postwar interstate system, characterized by formal treaties and intergovernmental organizations, as its baseline. We define this baseline in empirical terms – these were the kinds of institutions that dominated the international system – as well as theoretical ones – scholars understood international institutions nearly exclusively in formalistic, state-centred terms. Before proceeding to the innovations, it is important to first understand this starting point, which we present in somewhat stylized terms.

Beginning in earnest in the late nineteenth century, and then again after the Second World War, countries have built a growing infrastructure of intergovernmental institutions. By the end of the twentieth century, the number of intergovernmental organizations had grown from a handful to more than 2,000 (Held, McGrew et al. 1999). Multilateral and bilateral treaties have also increased, now standing at around 3,000 and 27,000, respectively (Simmons 2010).

In the decades after Second World War, students of politics became puzzled by the increasing organization and institutionalization of international politics. The expansion of transnational relations and interdependence that characterized the postwar global economy presented an anomaly to neorealism, the dominant theoretical position at that time. This theory doubted the possibility of enduring cooperation between countries given the lack of an overarching global authority and the imperative of each country to pursue survival in a world characterized by uncertainty (Waltz 1979). If each country must prioritize its own interests and cannot trust the promises of others, cooperation – which might make a country dependent on others, or help one country more than another – is unlikely. In the Realist analysis, these structural barriers make the idea of global governance either nonsensical, or at most epiphenomenal to the balance of power between states (Mearsheimer 1994; Gilpin 2002).

The seminal shift away from neorealist theories was Keohane and Nye's *Power and Interdependence* (1977), which put forth a novel theory of international organization as a rational response to growing interdependence between countries. This theoretical innovation was more fully developed by Keohane in *After Hegemony* (1984) and other work. Drawing on microeconomic theories of institutions, Keohane showed how, even maintaining the central assumptions of neorealism, states can and will cooperate under certain conditions (Keohane 1984). Institutions facilitate this process by allowing states to surmount the barriers to cooperation imposed by the anarchic international system. By providing information and structuring repeated interactions, institutions change the environment in which states operate, enabling them to structure incentives so as to make cheating less attractive. This theory of 'neoliberal institutionalism', or 'modified structural realism', quickly came to occupy the attention of numerous scholars and led to a series of debates between neorealists and institutionalists, which we do not summarize here (Baldwin 1993). The relevant point is that, by the early 1990s, the terms of this debate had shifted from *whether* international institutions matter to *how* they matter, with neoliberal institutionalism the dominant explanation.

But as this debate came to something of a resolution, new questions arose. In part, the end of the Cold War seemed to bring the world into an unprecedented era of globalization and institutional change, and new – and newly recognized – empirical facts exposed gaps in the existing institutionalist logic (Held, McGrew et al. 1999). Political institutions were evolving beyond the state-centric, formal treaties and intergovernmental organizations that had been the predominant subject of scholarly concern (Koenig-Archibugi 2005). Below we outline five key trends: the merging of 'domestic' and 'international' politics; the increased role of non-state actors in global politics; the emergence of private governance; the shift to new modes of eliciting compliance with transborder standards; and the growing complexity of the institutional landscape.

Domestic politics and transgovernmentalism

Traditionally, the study of international politics was separated from domestic issues for theoretical reasons. One of the central tenants of

Realism, shared by its institutionalist modification, held that the state could be studied as a 'unitary' actor with a coherent national interest. One of the most important developments of the 1990s was the relaxation of this assumption and the integration of domestic and interstate politics (Milner 1998).

One strand of this research looked at how domestic politics affect state behavior and intergovernmental organizations. The basic insight can be found in Putnam's concept of 'two-level games', and indeed in earlier work on transnationalism (Kaiser 1971) and strategic bargaining (Schelling 1960). Putnam pointed out that governments face a two-sided strategic interaction: a domestic one, vis-à-vis societal actors, and an international one, vis-à-vis other states. State behaviour is a function of both these interactions, he argued (Putnam 1988). The potential of this idea to explain global governance was more fully realized by later work (Evans, Jacobson et al. 1993). For example, Milner's Interests, Institutions, and Information, which modelled international cooperation (or lack thereof) as a strategic interaction between societal actors (acting through the legislature), a home government and a foreign government (Milner 1997). Moravcsik expands these insights into a general theory of international relations (Moravcsik 1997), consisting of three core assumptions: societal actors are the primary units of politics; states represent the preferences of the dominant societal group; the configuration of interdependent state preferences determines state behaviour. Variation in state preferences – a process determined by domestic politics – is the key explanatory variable, coming analytically prior to considerations of the distribution of state power and the availability of institutional strategies. These theories demonstrate how relaxing the unitary actor assumption can better explain the behavior of states and groups within them. They modify neoliberal institutionalism to explain why states might not even seek efficient cooperation, not only why they might fail to achieve it.

A second strand of research attacked the unitary actor assumption from the other side, examining how ostensibly 'domestic' actors became increasingly engaged in networks of transnational relations. First discussed by Keohane and Nye (1974), transgovernmental networks — informal, horizontal linkages between non-diplomatic government officials and their peers in other jurisdictions — were recognized by Slaughter as a new form of governance. The state is not receding, she contends, but rather changing the way it exercises sovereignty (Slaughter 2003, 2004a, 2004b, 2004c). As transnational problems impinge on what were previously considered domestic questions, domestic officials respond by working more and more at the transnational level. Rejecting the view that interdependence could only weaken the state (either through supranationalism or some variation of neo-medievalism), Slaughter argued that the state, though 'disag-gregated,' would remain the central actor in global governance. Though this offers an important corrective to the state-transnational governance dichotomy that pervades much of the literature, it is also true that many forms of transnational governance have emerged that do not center around public authority; we turn to these now.

Non-state transnational actors

Non-state actors – individuals, firms, nongovernmental organizations (NGOs), etc. – increasingly participate in transnational governance. International legal agreements have recognized them as holders of rights and obligations in contexts as diverse as human rights agree-ments and bilateral investment treaties. These actors provide techni-cal expertise (Haas 1991), set agendas (Betsill and Corell 2008), monitor compliance (Keck and Sikkink 1998), lobby decision makers (Mazey and Richardson 2006), make regulatory decisions (Büthe 2009), and even 'enforce' them by, for example, naming and shaming (Keck and Sikkink 1998; Hale 2008b). All of these actions may be taken either as the delegated agents of government entities, partners of government entities, or without any state involvement at all (Green 2010).

The 1970s work on transnationalism considered non-state actors central features of world politics. Nye and Keohane, for example, write that a key characteristic of complex interdependence are the transnational bonds that non-state actors create (Nye and Keohane 1971). Other writers go further, arguing that global politics should be conceived of not as a system of state-to-state relations at all, but rather as a 'complex conglomerate system' involving a variety of actors (Mansbach, Ferguson et al. 1976). Dependency theorists and other neo-Marxist approaches also focused attention on the political role of multinational corporations.

However, the rise of state-centric neoliberal institutionalism in the 1980s lessened interest in non-state actors. So lost from the debate did transnational actors become that, by the mid 1990s, it was possible for Risse-Kappen to edit a volume entitled *Bringing Transnational Relations Back In*, which sought to reassess the impact of non-state actors on state behaviour (Risse-Kappen 1995). In contrast to the domestic politics theories, Risse-Kappen argues these interactions are not merely part of the *domestic* process through which state preferences are formed, but an essential element of the *international* politics that determine state behaviour. This renewed interest in transnational actors led to more sophisticated theorizing. Keck and Sikkink (1998), for example, studied how transnational networks of activists could wield power in the international system by lobbying powerful states to join their cause. Kaldor and colleagues documented substantial growth in the engagement of civil society actors in global politics (Anheier, Kaldor et al. 2006). Still, while the 1990s work on transnational activism distinguished itself from its 1970s predecessors through its relative theoretical sophistication, much of it retained the assumption that the only way transnational actors might influence global politics, or at least the only important way, is by convincing states to support their cause.

In many issue areas, however, transnational actors influence international institutions directly, potentially subverting the principal–agent relationship that keeps ultimate power in the hands of member states. In this way they act not merely as 'inputs' to domestic political processes – though this function remains key – but also as direct influencers of global policy.

Environmental politics is one realm in which this phenomenon has become commonplace. Betsill and Corell (2008), for example, argue that in many international environmental fora NGOs are best thought of not as observers but as functionally equivalent, in many ways, to diplomats, in that they 'perform many of the same functions as state delegates: they represent the interests of their constituencies, they engage in information exchange, they negotiate, and they provide policy advice'. The entry on multistakeholder participation in United Nations (UN) summits in this volume (chapter 24) speaks exactly to this question.

The European Union (EU) is also cited as a common target of direct interest group lobbying. According to Mazey and Richardson (2006), 'the national preferences formation process is certainly "shaped through contention among domestic political groups" (Moravcsik 1998: 22) as intergovernmentalists argue, but ... domestic groups are also increasingly engaged *independently* at the supranational level and see that level as a venue where they can pursue their own goals'. Their analysis highlights the variety of strategies available to interest groups to lobby either through states or around them, and demonstrates how a 'promiscuous' strategy – forming relationships with all relevant actors, national and supranational – allows lobbyists to manage regulatory risk.

The literature on transnational actors' participation in intergovernmental fora leaves unresolved the issue of whether such engagement is 'allowed' by states and intergovernmental institutions (Tallberg 2008) or 'seized' by non-state actors (e.g. much of the literature on environmental regimes and the EU). Are NGOs equivalent to diplomats, as Betsill and Corell would have it, or does increasing NGO participation simply reflect efficient delegation by the state? Should we agree with Raustiala that the fact 'that NGOs are now more pervasive in international environmental institutions illustrates the expansion, not the retreat, of the state . . . ' (Raustiala 1997)?

Private governance

The divide between what Green (2010) calls 'delegated' and 'entrepreneurial' private authority also remains under-explored in governance mechanisms created by private actors themselves (Cutler, Haufler et al. 1999; Hall and Biersteker 2002; Falkner 2003; Kahler and Lake 2004; Mattli and Büthe 2004–5; Graz and Nölke 2008). Some of these exist with the acquiescence and assistance of public authorities; others are modern-day regulatory privateers.[2] Examples range from the de facto use of industry representatives to set the food sanitation standards that form the basis of WTO regulations (Büthe 2009, chapter 27), to private certification schemes that label products that meet certain ecological or social standards (Vogel 2008; part IV), to the way an initiative by the Gates Foundation, working with other major donors, has led to the standardization of health systems in developing countries (chapter 23).

Though Green's (2010) study of the environmental realm provides numerical evidence that private authority has grown significantly in that area, overall quantification of this trend remains elusive. Still, there seems to be a clear increase in the number of private actors performing transnational governance functions and in the scope of these activities. While a few observers in the 1970s and 1990s have claimed that the rise of private governance represents a fundamental shift in the nature of the global system, perhaps marking a return to a 'neo-medieval' world of patchwork authority (Mansbach, Ferguson et al. 1976; Mathews 1997; Rosenau 2007), other scholars believe these claims are exaggerated. Only recently have scholars begun to study the conditions under which private governance emerges and how it substitutes for or complements public governance (Cutler, Haufler et al. 1999; Graz and Nölke 2008; Green 2010).

The means and meaning of enforcement

Both private and public governance have also evolved with respect to the mode in which they elicit compliance with transnational rules. Under the traditional model, formal international laws – treaties, or the regulations of treaty-based organizations – are supposed to be enforced through the imposition of some sort of sanction on viola-

[2] For a description of this variation, see Abbott and Snidal (2009), and Mattli and Woods (2009).

tors. Increasingly today, rules are not necessarily formal, and enforcement does not necessarily occur through sanction. Consider each in turn.

First, transborder rules need not take the form of formal law based in treaty or custom. Increasingly, private actors promulgate their own regulations, which obtain varying degrees of recognition from other actors. Similarly, transgovernmental networks develop 'best practices' or recommendations that are voluntary in nature, but, like the Basel banking regulations (chapter 2), are required, *de facto*, for participation in the global economy. And sometimes these voluntary rules are later adopted into formal public international law, as with the food safety guidelines of the Codex Alimentarius, which now serve as a basis for WTO dispute resolutions judgements (chapter 27).

At the same time, the concept of regulation has evolved beyond a 'command and control' model in which standards are set and then enforced. The 'managerial' approach to compliance focuses instead on improving actors' ability and willingness to comply with international standards through capacity building, dissemination of best practices, and normative persuasion (Chayes and Chayes 1995). This tactic is employed by voluntary regulatory institutions like the UN Global Compact (chapter 46) or transgovernmental networks like the International Network for Environmental Compliance and Enforcement (chapter 11).

Transparency is another increasingly common approach to regulation (Hale 2008b). Instead of specifying regulations and punishing those who breach them, the transparency approach simply requires actors to disclose information about the governance question at hand. This approach can be seen in institutions as diverse as the Carbon Disclosure Project (chapter 26), the Global Reporting Initiative (chapter 35) or the North American Commission on Environmental Cooperation's Citizen Submission Process (chapter 14).

These changes in regulatory practices mirror patterns at the domestic level, where voluntary agreements between firms and government regulators (Carraro and Lévêque 1999), 'participatory regulation', and transparency-based initiatives (Fung, Graham et al. 2007) are increasingly common. However, there is an important distinction. While traditional international agreements can be considered somewhat analogous to the 'command and control' model (given that they set standards and try to enforce them), enforcement has always been more tentative at the transborder level.

Institutional complexity

The proliferation of actors and institutions at the transnational level has also disrupted a common, though often implicit, assumption of the 'traditional' literature on transborder institutions: that such institutions can be grouped into cohesive regimes or 'institutions possessing norms, decision rules, and procedures which facilitate a convergence of expectations' (Krasner 1983). While this canonical definition of an international regime is broad enough to encompass a great degree of institutional complexity, in practice scholars have often discussed regimes as if they were reducible to a single international organization or treaty.

In contrast, Victor and Raustiala argue that the expansion and overlap of international institutions require students of global politics to think in terms of 'regime complexes', defined as 'an array of partially overlapping and nonhierarchical institutions governing a particular issue area' (Raustiala and Victor 2004). Complexity draws attention to new kinds of problems in international politics (Young 1999; Oberthur and Gehring 2006; Alter and Meunier 2009). It allows actors to 'forum shop' between institutions; it makes it more difficult for actors to assess the costs and benefits of different strategies; it encourages institutions that include only like-minded actors instead of cross-cutting ones; and it potentially generates unforeseen interactions between different institutions (Alter and Meunier 2009).

Innovative transnational governance institutions contribute to this growing complexity of world politics. Not only are states creating more and more intergovernmental organizations and treaties, but they, and other actors, are creating new kinds of institutions with policymaking authority. This has led many regime complexes today to be truly multifarious amalgamations of institutions and actors. Sometimes these regime complexes – for example, around global health – are relatively cohesive around shared goals and understandings. Others, however, include institutions working at cross-purposes. The regime governing forestry practices, for example, includes a stalled public intergovernmental process; an innovative, multisectoral private labelling scheme, the Forest Stewardship Council (chapter 33); and numerous other innovative voluntary regulation schemes, some of which aim at conservation, others of which are simply industry public relations initiatives (Humphreys 2006).

Mapping Innovations in Transnational Governance

This volume presents more than fifty examples of innovations in transnational governance (see table 1.1). Each of these terms – innovative, transnational, governance – requires explanation. To begin with the last, we understand governance as the processes and institutions, formal and informal, whereby rules are created, compliance is elicited, and goods are provided in pursuit of collective goals. In this

Table 1.1 Transnational governance mechanisms by type and issue area

	Institution	Issue area(s)
Transgovernmental networks	Basel Committee on Banking Supervision	Economic regulation
	Financial Action Task Force	Economic regulation
	Financial Stability Board	Economic regulation
	G-20	Economic regulation
	Global Forum on Transparency and Exchange of Information	Economic regulation
	International Accounting Standards Board	Economic regulation, commerce
	International Association of Insurance Supervisors	Economic regulation, commerce
	International Competition Network	Economic regulation
	International Conference on Harmonization	Commerce, health
	International Network for Environmental Compliance and Enforcement	Environment
	Joint Forum	Economic regulation
	Transnational Policing	Security
Arbitration bodies	Citizen Submission Process of the North American Commission on Environmental Cooperation	Environment
	Regional development bank review mechanisms	Development, environment, human rights
	Transnational commercial arbitration	Commerce
	World Bank Inspection Panel	Development, environment, human rights
Multistakeholder initiatives	Framework Convention Alliance	Health
	Global Fund to Fight AIDS, Tuberculosis, and Malaria	Health
	Global Polio Eradication Initiative	Health
	Internet Corporation for Assigned Names and Numbers	Commerce
	International Coral Reef Initiative	Environment
	International Health Partnership and IHP+	Health
	Multistakeholder involvement in UN conferences	General
	World Commission on Dams	Development, environment, human rights
Voluntary regulations	Carbon Disclosure Project	Environment

(*Continued*)

Table 1.1 *(continued)*

	Institution	Issue area(s)
	Codex Alimentarius	Commerce, health
	Equator Principles	Development, environment, human rights
	Extractive Industries Transparency Initiative	Development, environment, human rights
	Fair Labor Association	Labour rights
	Fair Trade	Labour rights
	Clean Clothes Campaign	Labour rights
	Forest Stewardship Council	Environment
	Global corporate governance principles	Commerce
	Global Reporting Initiative	Environment, labour rights
	International Standards Organization	Commerce
	International Standards Organization 14001	Environment
	Kimberly Process	Development, human rights
	Marine Stewardship Council	Environment
	OECD Guidelines for Multinational Enterprises	Environment
	Partnering against Corruption Initiative and Business Principles for Countering Bribery	Commerce, development
	Responsible Care	Environment
	Rugmark	Labour rights
	Social Accountability International	Labour rights
	International Council of Toy Industries Code of Conduct	Labour rights
	United Nations Global Compact	Environment, human rights, labour rights
	Voluntary Principles on Security and Human Rights	Human rights
	Worker Rights Consortium	Labour rights
Finance mechanisms	Carbon offsets	Environment
	Financing mechanisms for climate change mitigation	Environment
	Global Alliance for Vaccines and Immunisation (GAVI Alliance)	Health
	UNITAID	Health

definition, government is the subset of governance that is performed by the state.

'Transnational' is often used to describe cross-border activities undertaken by non-state actors. This distinguishes such activities from state-to-state or 'international' relations. However, as the examples in this volume make obvious, such a clear distinction is often difficult to maintain in a world of hybrid governance (Nye and Keohane 1971). We therefore employ the term 'transnational' simply to describe activities, institutions, actors or processes that cross at least one national border, *especially* when actors other than national governments are involved. This open definition excludes purely domestic interactions and institutions.

'Innovative' is perhaps the most subjective of the criteria. The governance institutions presented here stand in contraposition to 'traditional' modes of cross-border governance that include state-to-state diplomacy, treaties that enshrine agreements in international law, and treaty-based intergovernmental organizations. These activities are traditional in both an empirical and theoretical sense. Empirically, they have been the predominant mode of transborder governance; theoretically, they have long been the central topic of scholarly attention.

These definitions are intentionally broad because our goal is to capture a wide sample of innovations in transnational governance. For example, we include the Group of Twenty (chapter 5), even though some aspects may seem quite traditional (e.g. summits of heads of state), because other aspects, for example the freestanding network of finance ministers, are not.

At the same time, some potential entries have been intentionally excluded. First, the *Handbook* does not include any of the state-to-state elements of the global human rights regime that emerged following the Second World War (though it does include other human rights institutions). Despite following the traditional structure of formal institutions between states, some human rights treaties and intergovernmental organizations could potentially be considered transnational because they address the rights of individuals *within* states. In some cases, like the International Criminal Court, a supranational prosecutor is charged with holding individuals to account for crimes they commit against other individuals. Such an institution is clearly innovative in global politics (though it does emerge from a long historical tradition of universal jurisdiction regarding, for example, pirates).

Second, we exclude regional organizations of states. Some of these (e.g. the North American Fair Trade Agreement (NAFTA)) are quite traditional, and so would not merit inclusion. The EU, in turn, is without doubt one of the most innovative transborder governance mechanisms ever to exist. While much of the politics of the EU follows a traditional intergovernmental logic (Moravcsik 1998), institutions like the European Central Bank and the European Parliament represent striking cases of supranational authority.

These cases fall somewhere in the grey zone around our criteria for inclusion; there are reasons both to include and to exclude them. We exclude them, in the end, for an important but ultimately non-theoretical reason: both are well studied elsewhere (Donnelly 2003; Richardson 2006). Given our goal of bringing scholarly attention to cases that lack it, we have chosen to spend precious pages elsewhere. We trust, however, that the reader will keep these cases in mind when thinking about the totality of innovations in transnational governance.

This volume aims to give the reader a comprehensive, yet not exhaustive sample of changes in transnational governance. This goal requires a broad taxonomy. We have grouped institutions by the form they take, identifying five types: transgovernmental networks, arbitration bodies, multistakeholder initiatives, voluntary regulations and finance mechanisms. These are not mutually exclusive or exhaustive categories, and in many cases the institutions in this volume could fall under more than one.

Transgovernmental networks: Transgovernmental networks bring 'domestic' government officials together with their peers around specific issues, often regulatory in nature (Keohane and Nye 1974; Slaughter 2004; Slaughter and Zaring 2006). Some, like the International Competition Network (chapter 9) or the International Network for Environmental Compliance and Enforcement (chapter 11) serve as fora for sharing best practices and information, while others, like the Basel Committee on Banking Supervision (chapter 2), perform an active regulatory function. The networks also differ in their degree of formalization, with some approximating formal intergovernmental organizations and others remaining loose and decentralized.

Arbitration bodies: A growing class of public and private arbiters has emerged to adjudicate various transnational conflicts. For example, private arbitration panels are now the main institution used to resolve transborder disputes between companies, and are increasingly common fora for disputes between investors and states (chapter 16). Also, review mechanisms have been created at international organizations that allow stakeholders affected by the organization's activities to petition for redress (chapters 14, 15, 17).

Multistakeholder initiatives: It is increasingly common for different types of actors, both public and private, to form partnerships to achieve some governance goal. Their activities can range from service provision (e.g. the Global Fund, chapter 19) to deliberative policymaking (e.g. the World Commission on Dams, chapter 25). Within this category, public–private partnerships have received significant attention in the literature (Schäferhoff, Campe et al. 2009).

Voluntary regulations: One of the most common new forms of global governance is informal regulation. Numerous codes of conduct for corporations have been created by NGOs, nation states, international organizations and corporations themselves, operating either alone or in partnership. Some are based on customary international law or even formal treaties (e.g. the Voluntary Principles, chapter 47). Others are based on principles negotiated between the various stakeholders (e.g. the Forest Stewardship Council, chapter 33), or simply promulgated by a single actor. They typically include mechanisms to monitor compliance with standards, and to enforce them either by 'naming and shaming' violators or by rewarding compliers through reputational benefits such as eco-labels. Some take a more 'command and control' regulatory approach, while others, like the UN Global Compact (chapter 46), aim to disseminate best practices and build capacity for compliance.

Finance mechanisms: Transnational public goods are costly. Traditionally, donations from national governments provided resources for these needs. Today, a variety of new ways have been developed to raise and disburse resources. For example, emissions trading markets are increasingly employed to channel private investment into emissions-reducing projects (chapters 49, 50). At the other end of the spectrum, UNITAID is a global tax on airline tickets between participating countries to raise funds for global health needs (chapter 52).

Observations from the *Handbook*: Why Has Transborder Governance Changed?

As mentioned above, the innovations catalogued in this volume raise three fundamental questions: what has changed, why has it changed, and what are the implications? Regarding the first, the entries in the *Handbook* confirm and expand on the trends identified above. The division between the 'international' and the 'domestic' has blurred. Non-state actors are increasingly important participants in global politics, sometimes creating their own private governance institutions. Institutions of all kinds are proliferating, generating complex systems of institutional interactions, and new modalities of rule-making and enforcement are expanding the nature of governance itself.

Below we offer some observations from the *Handbook* on the second and third of these questions: why has governance evolved in this way, and what are the implications? Full answers will require more detailed studies than is possible in this chapter, a programme to which we turn in the conclusion.

We can identify four classes of theories that seek to explain recent innovations in governance: functionalist theories, theories of competition between interests, ideational theories and historical theories. Each is presented below. Though they emphasize different variables and causal processes, these theories are not necessarily exclusive or rival explanations. We imagine that different innovations or aspects of innovations will be better explained by different theories, singularly or in combination, and that no one group of theories will provide a comprehensive explanation of institutional change in transnational governance. However, this does not imply that scholars should not seek to refine theories into rival testable hypotheses seeking to explain specific innovations, as we argue in the conclusion.

Functionalism

Functionalist theories draw a line between changes in the nature of political problems, such as interdependence or complexity, and institutional arrangements. The functional effectiveness of governance 'technologies' vis-à-vis a given issue is the key explanatory variable. Kolliker, for example, argues that as policy externalities become more transnational, governance arrangements will also spill across borders. Similarly, as 'cross-sectoral externalities' increase, institutions are more likely to be public, but highly specialized or autonomous social sectors will prefer private governance (Kolliker 2005).

Traditional intergovernmental processes tend to be characterized by face-to-face negotiations between diplomats representing national governments, legally binding treaties that must often be ratified by domestic legislatures, formal delegation to international bureaucracies, financial contributions from national governments, and a reliance on state authorities for enforcement of agreed standards and provisions. The innovations explored in this volume, in contrast, display a range of different features. Non-state actors are often key or even dominant participants in governance arrangements. Institutions need not encompass all the actors resident in a territorial state, but can organize themselves around common concerns or interests. Standards can be legally binding, but often are not. Enforcement rarely occurs through the coercive power of the state, taking forms as diverse as market incentives, naming and shaming, and capacity building.

In a functionalist view, each of these differences serves some purpose. For example, scholars of transgovernmental networks have argued they provide a more flexible and less costly format for state-to-state coordination than intergovernmental organizations (Slaughter 2004). Where the goal is simply to share information, networks may be more efficient than formal organizations. But if the goal were to bind countries to specific commitments, the cost of formal organizations to monitor and promote compliance may be worth paying.

Or, consider the example of private governance agreements. When the issue at hand only concerns a subset of actors, and does not require the coercive power of the state for enforcement, private governance may be an efficient institutional technology. This might be particularly true if the private actors possess specialized knowledge or other capacities to address the issue. For example, private commercial arbitration (chapter 16) has been described as a self-enforcing mechanism to resolve business disputes; because companies who flaunt arbitration decisions will lose their trustworthiness and ability to make contracts in the future, they may voluntarily comply even with decisions that are not juridically binding. Private arbitrators may also have much deeper knowledge about the business in question than state judges, facilitating a better decision (Cutler, Haufler et al. 1999; Mattli 2001).

In the functionalist perspective, institutions rise and fall through an evolutionary logic. Institutions that are well adapted to their socio-economic setting will survive and replicate, while institutions that do not match their settings must adapt or perish (Greif 2006). Scholars have argued that under conditions of economic globalization, it is natural to expect more global and transnational institutions to manage interdependence, leading to a relative decline of the nation state. This idea informs much of the neo-medieval literature (Korbin 1999). At the same time, the increasing complexity of politics necessitates institutions more closely tailored to policy problems than the society-wide institutions of the state.

Functionalism presents an intuitively compelling explanation for recent innovations in global governance, but also suffers some important limitations. At the extreme, functionalist explanations risk rendering institutions completely endogenous to the nature of the issues they address. As Mitchell notes, this approach would render institutions just as epiphenomenal as does Realism, which focuses solely on the distribution of power (Mitchell 2006). That we can observe different types of institutions governing the same types of issues suggests that functionalist explanations – though they may accommodate multiple institutional equilibria – may not be wholly convincing.

Most obviously, functionalist explanations ignore the question of *for whom* an institution is efficient. Political institutions are not simply rationally designed solutions to governance challenges. They almost always benefit some interests at the expense of others, leading to distributional struggles characterized by power politics. It is to these explanations that we next turn.

Competition between interests

This approach shares the idea that collective action problems create demand for institutions, but is less certain that institutional outcomes will solve such problems efficiently, highlighting distributional conflicts. The logic is as follows. Changes in interdependence connect the interests of groups to the actions of groups and governments across borders. These changes will lead them to prefer certain institutional arrangements – those that benefit them – to others, and to push both their society and others to adopt the institutions they prefer. Their ability to do so will be constrained by their power relative to other groups and states, which may have diverging interests, and also by the existing institutional environment. Institutions, then, are shaped by the consciously enacted strategies of self-interested actors, not the logic of evolution.

Consider the example of voluntary labour standards. Workers' rights advocates have pressed for strong global governance of working conditions through the International Labor Organization (ILO), aided by developed states that have adopted the same stance. Both normative and material interests motivate these groups and the states they influence. However, the developing countries that are typically the target of these campaigns are loath to cede sovereignty in this matter and wary of covert protectionism, ensuring that public global governance (e.g. the ILO) remains weak. Marginal improvements are possible only when labour rights are linked to other issues, for example in preferential trade agreements, in which developed countries can apply pressure (Hafner-Burton 2005). In response, private actors have created a proliferation of certification and labelling schemes to try to improve working conditions by changing market incentives (chapters 30, 31, 32, 43, 44, 45, 48).

This example suggests that institutional innovation is a product of competition over transnational policy. The ability of an interest group to control public governance is a key determinant of private governance or lack thereof. However, power is not just a question of controlling the state, as it might be in traditional governance. Bargaining occurs outside of state institutions as well, as private groups seek to bring other private groups to comply with their preferred institutions. As Keohane and Nye recognized in the context of international interdependence, if one actor depends on another to achieve some policy goal, the independent actor gains some power over the dependent one (Keohane and Nye 1977). As Abbott and Snidal argue, this 'go it alone power', is a key element of the politics of private governance as well (Abbott and Snidal 2009). A corporation seeking to enhance its reputation with credible voluntary regulation may need to make concessions to NGOs to achieve this goal, while a corporation that does not trade on its social credentials will not.

(Neo)Marxist theories also focus on the explanatory power of interest competition. These theories tend to see global governance as, to alter Marx's phrasing, the executive committee of the global bourgeoisie. Innovations in transnational governance, because they often give a role to transnational corporations, are particularly likely to represent the interests of capital. In this view, global capitalism creates power structures to facilitate the extraction of surplus from workers and the global periphery (Callinicos 2002). Some writers stress the role of capitalist actors – specifically multinational corporations – in this process (Bornschier and Chase-Dunn 1985), while more structural theories emphasize the abstract forces of global capitalist integration (Hardt and Negri 2000; Van Apeldoorn 2004). The growth of global capitalism in the postwar world thus explains the rise of global institutions and their bias toward the interests of powerful, Western economic actors and their Third World compradors. There is, of course, much variation this theory cannot account for – e.g. the differing form between, say, the trade regime and the finance regime, or the different levels of success achieved in regulating different environmental issues. It is insensitive to the potential divergence of interests between workers and capitalists in the North and in the South. Nonetheless, the central insight of these theories – that global governance tends to reflect the interests of the powerful economic interests in powerful states – is compelling.

Ideational theories

Ideational or constructivist theories ask what types of arrangements key actors believe to be normatively or functionally appropriate, and how these beliefs change (Ruggie 2004). These socially determined beliefs 'construct' the political reality in which actors operate, and so are the key variable for explaining political behaviour. Innovation, then, results from changing ideas about how political institutions should be organized.

Two mechanisms can link beliefs and ideas to institutional structures. First, institutional arrangements may reflect dominant ideologies regarding the appropriate way to solve collective action problems. For example, the rise of the democratic welfare state in the mid twentieth century, characterized by extensive public intervention in economic affairs, reflected the predominant statist mentality. The mid-century international organizations reflected a similar view that competent bureaucracies were the best way to solve governance challenges. This view then shifted just a generation later with the rise of neoliberal thinking that would seek to replace 'command and control' and 'tax and spend' with bottom-up or market-based solutions to collective action problems. The rise of private or informal institutions at the transnational level can be associated with this trend. However, ideological preferences for public versus private governance are interlaced with material interests, and thus may be difficult to distinguish from the competition model discussed above.

Another mechanism could be simply the development and 'discovery' of new ways of addressing certain problems. Just as innovations in technology are often emulated by competitors and diffused through the market, so too have innovations in governance been copied and spread. Dingwerth and Pattberg argue that microsocial processes of learning and norm diffusion are a key driver of new governance arrangements in the environmental field (Dingwerth and Pattberg 2009). As new governance technologies, including transnational ones, are developed and diffused through learning, global governance and its various forms can be understood as a learned behaviour.

Learning can also occur across levels of governance. A number of the transnational governance mechanisms exhibit striking institutional similarities with each other and with domestic cognates (Rhodes 1996). For example, the global carbon trading system is directly modelled on the sulphur dioxide market created to address air pollution in the United States. The same is true for product labelling schemes (Abbott and Snidal 2009), public–private partnerships and transgovernmental networks (Sørensen and Torfing 2006). That all these mechanisms have grown more common both domestically and transnationally during the same period suggests that interdependence is not their only driver.

Ideational theories often seek to identify and describe the discourse surrounding governance institutions as a way to understand the meaning they hold for social actors (Risse 2007). Such beliefs – e.g. regarding how legitimate or appropriate an institution is – are seen as key drivers of the processes that lead to institutional change. Scholars have also argued that Habermasian discursive politics can make global governance more legitimate by exposing transnational policymaking to reasoned deliberation (Dryzek 1996; Payne and Samhat 2004). Several of the innovations in this volume, such as the 'info-courts', seek to create precisely this effect (Hale 2008a).

Historical approaches

Historical approaches connect the nature of governance arrangements to contingent shifts in society and the economy. They often rely on variables and causal processes similar to the theories listed above, but emphasize the specific historical pathways in which these factors play out. In this view, changes in governance come as part of a 'great transformation'. For example, Polanyi's landmark book of that title describes the evolution of modern capitalism and the modern state out of the feudal system that preceded them. He argues that both the modern nation state and modern capitalism required each other in order to function, and should not be thought of as 'market' and 'state' but rather as an integrated social structure (Polanyi 1944).

Along these lines, Murphy (1994) gives a neo-Gramscian interpretation of the evolution of global governance. In his view the world passes through successive 'historical blocs' in which both governance structures and civil society operate through similar logics – based in the nature of the contemporary economy – and exhibit similar characteristics. Thus he argues, for example, that the nineteenth-century international public unions (e.g. the Universal Postal Union; the International Telegraph Union) reflected the experiences and ideologies of the technocratic, nation-building elites of that time. These 'system builders' had first confronted these issues while designing institutions for the new national industrial economies that were emerging in places like the United States and Germany, and the international unions they built directly reflected these domestic experiences. Today, in contrast, Murphy argues that changes in technology are shifting the world from a Fordist historical bloc to a historical bloc defined by the information economy. Domestic institutions and transborder ones alike are thus reforming into a new pattern or organization (Murphy 1994).

Like the ideational theories described above, Murphy's approach allows the analyst to make sense of the parallel shifts in transborder and domestic political institutions. However, it is less clear on why institutional diversity persists even within a single historical bloc. While undoubtedly helpful as a heuristic for interpreting long-term trends, historical approaches are perhaps less useful for distinguishing contemporary cases, or for institutional design.

Observations from the *Handbook*: What Are the Implications?

The innovations in transnational governance presented in this volume strongly affect global politics. Below we consider the implications for policy effectiveness, geopolitics and the legitimacy of global governance.

Effectiveness

Like most political institutions, the innovative mechanisms surveyed in this volume rarely entirely satisfy the hopes of their creators, but some are more effective than others. Among the more successful we might list private commercial arbitration (chapter 16), the technical standard-setting bodies (chapters 10, 36), the GAVI Alliance (chapter 51), the financial transgovernmental networks (chapters 2–9, 12) or the Global Polio Eradication Initiative (chapter 20). It is perhaps unsurprising that many of these institutions operate in issue areas where the relevant actors all have an interest in smooth-functioning institutions.

Less effective endeavours include many of the voluntary regulatory mechanisms. Institutions like the Extractive Industries Transparency Initiative (chapter 29), which has yet to be widely implemented, or the Marine Stewardship Council (chapter 39), which has reached only about 5 per cent of the commercial fish market, have not yet managed to change the way natural resource companies operate in the developing world, or to slow the precipitous decline in global fish stocks, respectively. There are good reasons to expect universal adoption and compliance to be unlikely for these institutions. They would impose significant costs on specific actors, while the beneficiaries and the supposed enforcers of these programmes (often, socially minded consumers or investors) are on average far less invested and more dispersed.

Of course, the effectiveness of a given mechanism should not be compared only to some hypothetical ideal. The more pertinent assessment of an institution's impact is to consider how the governance outcome differs from the *status quo ante*, and how it differs from the likely outcomes of politically feasible alternatives. For example, given that strong global agreements on many environmental issues or rigorous enforcement of labour protections are unlikely in the near future, we might consider voluntary regulatory programmes at least partially effective stand-ins. A voluntary labour rights initiative that only helps some workers at some participating factories may be considered a success even if it does not solve the larger issue of exploitation. That said, it is also important to consider the possible unintended consequences of these programmes, including reduced job opportunities for poor populations, the shifting of production to even more exploitative factories, or the possible sapping of political will for more comprehensive solutions.

Such assessments present methodological difficulties for social scientists, because they require us to imagine how the case might have differed under another governance institution. We can gain some empirical traction on this counterfactual only when an institution can be compared to other, similar examples. However, this is often not the case in global politics, as truly comparable examples are few. Accordingly, thoughtful, context-rich, and theoretically guided analysis is typically the best way to assess effectiveness.

Participation in transnational governance in the global South

One of the clearest observations to emerge from the *Handbook* is the 'governance gap' between North and South. To put the issue starkly, while many of the programmes rely on Southern participation and serve the interests of Southern stakeholders, almost none of the innovations in transnational governance gathered here have been led by Southern actors. Instead, institutional innovation has been led by Northern states, NGOs, corporations and international organizations. While some of the innovative institutions (e.g. the World Commission on Dams, chapter 25) have been careful to try to ensure Southern participation, and many of the programmes target policies in the global South, Southern leadership remains limited.

This North–South governance gap in innovative institutions is larger than in traditional institutions. While Southern actors certainly tend to be marginalized in treaties and intergovernmental organizations, they frequently initiate and actively participate in such governance mechanisms. Consider, for example, the concerted efforts of developing countries to build a 'New International Economic Order' in the 1970s through a range of new intergovernmental bodies and agreements (Hart 1983).

Amongst the innovative institutions studied here, Southern actors have shown comparable initiative only regarding the financial governance architecture. These calls have led to moderate progress. The creation of the G-20 (chapter 5) in 1999 was a significant step toward giving the developing world a greater say in global governance. More recently, the 2008 global financial crisis brought forward a series of changes. In 2008 the entire G-20 was invited to join the Financial Stability Board (chapter 4), in 2009 the Basel Committee on Banking Supervision (chapter 2) also welcomed the G-20 members into its governing body, along with Hong Kong and Singapore, and the

International Organization of Securities Commissions added several new members to its leadership. These changes paralleled the reform of voting rights in the traditional international financial institutions, the World Bank and the International Monetary Fund (IMF). It should be noted, however, that these changes were less about including the 'have-nots' in global governance, and more about recognizing the fact that the number of 'haves' had expanded.

The question thus remains: why have Southern actors not taken or demanded greater leadership in many of the innovative mechanisms studied here? The theoretical approaches outlined above offer some insights. Functionalism would argue that actors from the South are on average less interdependent than their Northern counterparts, and so have less need for various governance mechanisms beyond the nation state. Competition theories might say that the dominant interests in the South are well served by the institutional status quo – their control of the state ensures their interests are defended in intergovernmental fora – and thus frown on innovative governance mechanisms. Alternatively, they might argue that Northern interests have shifted decision-making away from intergovernmental fora in which all states have a right to participate (if not necessarily on equal terms), and toward more decentralized and flexible mechanisms precisely because doing so allows them to control Southern access and influence. Ideational theories would argue it is Northern actors that have developed the organizational techniques and belief systems these innovative governance mechanisms require. And historical theories might argue, along the lines of modernization theory, that the South has simply not reached a level of development at which these kinds of mechanisms emerge, perhaps because Southern actors simply lack the material resources to create innovative governance tools.

These difficulties aside, it seems that Southern actors could employ many of the types of mechanisms studied in this volume more proactively to serve their interests. For example, private voluntary regulation of environmental or labour standards is typically seen as the concern of Northern consumers and groups, but there is no reason why Southern actors might not also use them. More labelling schemes could be used to differentiate export products for socially minded consumers willing to pay a premium. Or, in an inversion of the usual logic, 'development labels' could be used to encourage multinational corporations that sell to the global South to take a more pro-development stance.

Global power shifts and transnational governance mechanisms

Given that innovative transnational governance mechanisms are dominated by the West, how will these institutions change as non-

Western countries and non-Western transnational actors become increasingly important for global politics? We might think that current institutions are a product of Western hegemony. Certainly, they seem to reflect the interests of various Western actors, though these are often not homogeneous. While we lack detailed empirical information, it also seems likely that these types of institutions – networks, multistakeholder partnerships, market-oriented regulation, etc. – are more common in Western domestic politics than in other countries. The pluralistic, non-state characteristics that many of the innovative mechanisms share also tend to be more associated with Western political contexts. To the extent innovative governance mechanisms are based on Western practice, a decrease in Western power in global politics may mean a return to more traditional, formal and state-centred forms of global governance. To take just one example, Chinese state-owned natural resource companies have yet to engage in innovative governance mechanisms like the Extractive Industries Transparency Initiative (chapter 29).

At the same time, transborder political institutions do sometimes outlast changes in the power relationships that underlie them. As Keohane (1984) argued in *After Hegemony*, global institutions created under the leadership of the United States after the Second World War persisted even after the United States declined in economic importance relative to Europe and Japan. While some institutions – such as the gold standard – did not survive the global economic dislocations of the 1970s, many did because the newly arisen powers derived functional benefits from them.

Of course, China, India and other emerging economies are not the same as postwar Europe and Japan. However, the evidence to date does not point toward a fundamental upheaval. As noted above, the 2008–9 financial crisis has led to a moderate strengthening and expansion of participation in global economic governance, though more will be needed to place the global economy on a sure footing (Held and Young 2011). Interestingly, however, rising powers have chosen to join the financial transgovernmental networks, not fight against them or ignore them. Indeed, the shift in economic power from the developed countries to emerging markets is arguably an important cause behind innovative governance mechanisms like the G-20.

This engagement bodes well for innovative transnational governance mechanisms, which in turn may actually have some comparative advantages in facilitating cooperation between current and rising powers. The informal, networked nature of institutions like the G-20 may allow for more fluid adjustment of responsibilities and obligations than, for example, traditional institutions like the World Bank or the IMF (see Kirton, chapter 5; Slaughter and Hale 2010). Given the wide range of crucial policy impasses between existing and rising powers – e.g. the Doha trade round, global climate negotiations, non-proliferation, etc. – any contribution innovative governance mechanisms make to easing international cooperation between established and rising powers should be seized by policymakers.

Of course, many of the innovative governance mechanisms studied in this volume do not address the core interests of emerging countries and the actors within them, and thus stand an increased risk of becoming marginalized. We mentioned the case of the Extractive Industries Transparency Initiative above. It is also telling that consumer-driven sustainability labelling schemes like the Forest Stewardship Council (chapter 33) and the Marine Stewardship Council (chapter 39) have done relatively well in Europe and North America, but remain marginal in many other markets. This divide must shrink if these and other schemes are to achieve their goals, which would require a significant change in consumer behaviour. Economic development in emerging economies is likely to facilitate such a transition, but it seems such governance schemes will have to find new ways to educate consumers en masse if they are to continue and succeed.

The legitimacy of global governance

Each of the innovations studied in this *Handbook* raises questions about the normative legitimacy of transborder governance. If political legitimacy is defined in broadly democratic terms – political institutions should be responsive to the interests of the people whose lives they affect – then traditional international organizations are already potentially problematic in the democratic calculus because they attenuate the chain of delegation between citizen and policy, creating a potential 'democratic deficit' (Nye 2001).

The new institutions presented here both alleviate and exacerbate these difficulties. Many of the innovations aim – with varying degrees of success – to give individuals a greater say in transnational governance. For example, the 'info-courts' at the World Bank (chapter 17) and the regional development banks (chapter 15) allow individuals to challenge traditional international organizations through a quasi-judicial procedure. Some voluntary regulatory schemes like the Forest Stewardship Council (chapter 33), which self-consciously seeks to give strong representation to the full range of affected interests, achieve a level of participatory decision-making that exceeds what has been possible through traditional intergovernmental institutions. And even many traditional intergovernmental processes are much more participatory than ever before, as this volume's chapter on stakeholder participation in UN summits shows (chapter 24).

Some observers have found in these and similar institutional innovations the seeds of a new kind of cosmopolitan democracy (Payne and Samhat 2004). Such democracy does not occur through voting and legislatures, as in the nation state model, but rather in the plurality of decentralized governance institutions in which interests are represented and decisions made. For example, voluntary regulation is a way for non-state actors to make progress toward policy goals like labour or environmental standards even when traditional intergovernmental processes stall. To the extent this increases the ability of individuals to influence the policies that affect their lives, it may be considered democracy-enhancing.

But in the same innovations in which some see democratic promise, others see peril. Many of the innovative institutions collected in this volume shift decision-making authority away from formal political representatives and to private actors, technocrats, or both. Such delegation is of course a common feature of any modern nation state that must confront complex challenges (think of central banks or scientific commissions) and so is not problematic per se (Keohane, Macedo et al. 2009). A crucial difference, however, is that at the domestic level a government that at least nominally represents society as a whole has ultimate responsibility for all governance decisions, and can usually intervene when necessary. No such ultimate safeguard exists for transborder institutions, though individual states can of course choose the extent to which they participate in such institutions in the first place.

Given these opposite but linked trends – greater participation for specific stakeholders, but also less oversight in the general interest – it is not possible to say whether, on balance, innovation has been good or bad for the democratic legitimacy of transnational governance. Certainly, it suggests that legitimacy questions matter in transnational politics, no matter what institutions are involved. Innovative mechanisms for accountability are thus needed. The Global Administrative Law project, which seeks to apply the logic of domestic administrative law (through which public bodies are held accountable) to global governance, has made some steps in this direction, thinking about how accountability standards developed for national bureaucracies might apply to the increasingly diverse range of transnational institutions (Krisch and Kingsbury 2006).

Conclusion: Much to Learn

The chapters in this volume demonstrate that transnational governance is evolving. As we have described above, observers have begun to explain why this is and what implications it holds for global politics. In the pages that follow, the contributors address these issues in the context of specific examples. Much remains to be done, however.

First, from an empirical perspective, significant opportunities exist to test rival causal hypotheses. Above we have outlined several theoretical logics – functionalism, interest competition, ideational mechanisms and broad historical shifts – each of which, we believe, gives insight into some aspects of change in transnational governance. However, this theoretical ecumenicism does not imply it is unimportant for scholars to understand which factors and causal processes are more or less central for which innovations. Indeed, the fact that several theoretical logics are at play means that it is crucial for social scientists to outline the conditions under which each does and does not matter for governance outcomes. We suggest that significant insights can be gained by subjecting innovations in transnational governance to more theory-testing research designs than has thus far been common in the literature.

Second, we have presented the institutions collected in this volume as innovations, and they certainly differ significantly from formal, state-centric modes of global governance that have dominated global politics. However, one can find mechanisms similar to some of those presented in the pages that follow throughout history. For example, contemporary transnational commercial arbitration has been compared to the courts medieval merchants formed to adjudicate disputes at the fairs that dominated long-distance trade at that time. It is common to frame transnational governance as a post-Cold War phenomenon, and there is no doubt that this period has been particularly dynamic. But this does not mean scholars should ignore the long historical record of cross-border governance institutions.

Third, it is important for scholars of transnational governance to study domestic cognates. The fact that many of the institutional forms found at the transnational level also appear in local, regional or national politics implies that they may respond to similar logics, or that institutional forms diffuse between political spheres. It would be shortsighted for students of innovative governance mechanisms to repeat the bifurcation of the international and domestic politics that international relations scholars have moved away from.

Last, the insights this research agenda seeks matter for more than just academic reasons. The world is undergoing a period of profound transformation as globalization raises new policy problems faster than political institutions adapt to address them. Innovations in global governance are not just an observable fact; they are imperative if the public goods on which society relies are going to be available in a globalized world.

The chapters in this volume paint a picture of what innovation there has been in transnational governance, but more will certainly be needed. The final task of scholars and policymakers, then, is to imagine ourselves also as inventers and entrepreneurs. Just as new devices can be designed and deployed, new political technologies can be imagined and promoted. The process is inevitably more constrained and messy in the social world, and especially difficult for many traditional global governance institutions because of the scale at which they operate; in principle there can be only one UN or World Bank, so we cannot test various alternatives. However, many of the innovations studied in this volume operate at a smaller scale, making them ripe laboratories for experimentation. Indeed, we can think of the map of innovations gathered in this volume as a version of what Dorf and Sabel call 'democratic experimentalism' – the idea that policymaking should be distributed across small, dynamic institutions that try new methods and share their results with others in a continual process of learning and reform (Dorf and Sabel 1998). Scholars and policymakers have an important role to play, then, in learning about the new institutions of transnational governance and improving them.

References

Abbott, K. W., and D. Snidal (2009). 'The Governance Triangle: Regulatory Standards Institutions and the Shadow of the State'. *The Politics of Global Regulation*, ed. W. Mattli and N. Woods. Princeton: Princeton University Press.

Alter, K. J., and S. Meunier (2009). 'The Politics of International Regime Complexity'. *Perspectives on Politics* 7(1): 13–24.

Anheier, H. K., M. Kaldor et al., eds. (2006). *Global Civil Society 2006/7*. London: SAGE.

Anne-Marie Slaughter, 'The Real New World Order,' Foreign Affairs, September/ October 1997.

Baldwin, D. A., ed. (1993). *Neorealism and Neoliberalism: The Contemporary Debate*. New York: Columbia University Press.

Betsill, M. M., and E. Corell, eds. (2008). *NGO Diplomacy: The Influence of Nongovernmental Organizations in International Environmental Negotiations*. Cambridge, MA: MIT Press.

Bornschier, V., and C. K. Chase-Dunn (1985). *Transnational Corporations and Underdevelopment*. Santa Barbara: Greenwood Publishing.

Büthe, T. (2009). 'The Politics of Food Safety in the Age of Global Trade: The Codex Alimentarius Commission in the SPS-Agreement of the WTO'. *Import Safety: Regulatory Governance in the Global Economy*, ed. C. Coglianese, A. Finkel et al. Philadelphia: University of Pennsylvania Press.

Callinicos, A. (2002). 'Marxism and Global Governance'. *Governing Globalization: Power, Authority, and Global Governance*, ed. D. Held and A. McGrew. Cambridge: Polity.

Carraro, C., and F. Lévêque (1999). *Voluntary Approaches in Environmental Policy*. New York: Springer.

Chayes, A., and A. H. Chayes (1995). *The New Sovereignty: Compliance with International Regulatory Agreements*. Cambridge, MA: Harvard University Press.

Cutler, A. C. C., V. Haufler et al., eds. (1999). *Private Authority and International Affairs*. Albany: State University of New York Press.

Dingwerth, K., and P. Pattberg (2009). 'World Politics and Organizational Fields: The Case of Transnational Sustainability Governance'. *European Journal of International Relations* 15: 707–43.

Donnelly, J. (2003). *Universal Human Rights in Theory and Practice*. Ithaca: Cornell University Press.

Dorf, M. C., and C. F. Sabel (1998). 'A Constitution of Democratic Experimentalism'. *Columbia Law Review* 98(2): 267–473.

Dryzek, J. S. (1996). *Deliberative Global Politics: Discourse and Democracy in a Divided World*. Cambridge: Polity.

Evans, P. B., H. K. Jacobson et al. (1993). *Double-Edged Diplomacy: International Bargaining and Domestic Politics*. Berkeley: University of California Press.

Falkner, R. (2003). 'Private Environmental Governance and International Relations: Exploring the Links'. *Global Environmental Governance* 3(2): 72–87.

Fung, A., M. Graham et al. (2007). *Full Disclosure: The Perils and Promise of Transparency*. Cambridge: Cambridge University Press.

Gilpin, R. (2002). 'A Realist Perspective on International Governance'. *Governing Globalization*, ed. D. Held and A. McGrew. Cambridge: Polity.

Graz, J.-C., and A. Nölke, eds. (2008). *Transnational Private Governance and Its Limits*. New York: Routledge.

Green, J. (2010). 'Private Authority, Public Goals: Non-state Actors in Global Environmental Politics'. Politics Department dissertation. Princeton University.

Greif, A. (2006). *Institutions and the Path to the Modern Economy: Lessons from Medieval Trade*. Cambridge: Cambridge University Press.

Haas, P. M. (1991). 'Policy Responses to Stratospheric Ozone Depletion'. *Global Environmental Change* 1(224–34).

Habermas, J. (2001). *The Postnational Constellation*. Cambridge, MA: MIT Press.

Hafner-Burton, E. M. (2005). 'Trading Human Rights: How Preferential Trade Agreements Influence Government Repression'. *International Organization* 59(3): 593–629.

Hale, T. (2008a). '"Info-Courts" and the Accountability of International Organizations: Evidence from the World Bank Inspection Panel'. Paper presented at the Fourth Global Administrative Law Seminar, Viterbo, Italy, 13–14 June 2008.

Hale, T. N. (2008b). 'Transparency, Accountability, and Global Governance'. *Global Governance* 14: 73–94.

Hall, R. B., and T. J. Biersteker, eds. (2002). *The Emergence of Private Authority in Global Governance*. New York: Cambridge University Press.

Hamilton, G. G. (2006). 'Why No Capitalism in China?' *Commerce and Capitalism in Chinese Societies*, ed. G. G. Hamilton. New York: Routledge.

Hardt, M., and A. Negri (2000). *Empire*. Cambridge, MA: Harvard University Press.

Hart, J. A. (1983). *The New International Economic Order: Conflict and Cooperation in North–South Economic Relations, 1974–77*. London: Macmillan.

Held, D., and A. McGrew (2007). *Globalization/Anti-globalization: Beyond the Great Divide*. Cambridge: Polity.

Held, D., A. McGrew et al. (1999). *Global Transformations: Politics, Economics, and Culture*. Palo Alto: Stanford University Press.

Held, D., and K. Young (2011). *The Financial Crisis and Global Governance*. Forthcoming.

Humphreys, D. (2006). *Logjam: Deforestation and the Crisis of Global Governance*. London: Earthscan.

Kahler, M., and D. A. Lake (2004). 'Governance in a Global Economy: Political Authority in Transition'. *Political Science and Politics* 37(3): 409–14.

Kaiser, K. (1971). 'Transnational Politics: Toward a Theory of Multinational Politics'. *International Organization* 25: 790–817.

Keck, M. E. and K. Sikkink (1998). *Activists beyond Borders*. Ithaca: Cornell University Press.

Keohane, R. O. (1984). *After Hegemony*. Princeton: Princeton University Press.

Keohane, R. O. (2001). 'Governance in a Partially Globalized World: "Presidential Address", American Political Science Association, 2000'. *The American Political Science Review* 95(1): 1–13.

Keohane, R. O., and J. S. Nye (1974). 'Transgovernmental Relations and International Organizations'. *World Politics* 27(1): 39–62.

Keohane, R. O., and J. S. Nye (1977). *Power and Interdependence: World Politics in Transition*. New York: Little, Brown, and Co.

Keohane, R. O., S. Macedo et al. (2009). 'Democracy-Enhancing Multilateralism'. *International Organization* 63: 1–31.

Koenig-Archibugi, M. (2005). 'Introduction: Institutional Diversity in Global Governance'. *New Modes of Governance in the Global System: Exploring Publicness, Delegation and Inclusiveness*, ed. M. Koenig-Archibugi and M. Zürn. Basingstoke: Palgrave.

Kolliker, A. (2005). 'Conclusion I: Governance Arrangements and Public Goods Theory: Explaining Aspects of Publicness, Inclusiveness and Delegation'. *New Modes of Governance in the Global System: Exploring Publicness, Delegation and Inclusiveness*, ed. M. Koenig-Archibugi and M. Zürn. Basingstoke: Palgrave.

Korbin, S. (1999). 'Back to the Future: Neomedievalism and the Postmodern Digital World Economy'. *Globalization and Governance*, ed. A. Prakash and J. Hart. New York: Routledge.

Krasner, S., ed. (1983). *International Regimes*. Ithaca: Cornell University Press.

Krisch, N., and B. Kingsbury (2006). 'Introduction: Global Governance and Global Administrative Law in the International Legal Order'. *The European Journal of International Law* 17(1): 1–13.

Mansbach, R., Y. H. Ferguson et al. (1976). *The Web of World Politics: Nonstate Actors in the Global System*. Englewood Cliffs, NJ: Prentice-Hall.

Mathews, J. (1997). 'Power Shift'. *Foreign Affairs* (January/February): 50–66.

Mattli, W. (2001). 'Private Justice in a Global Economy: From Litigation to Arbitration'. *International Organization* 55(4): 919–47.

Mattli, W., and T. Büthe (2004–5). 'Global Private Governance: Lessons from a National Model of Setting Standards in Accounting'. *Law and Contemporary Problems* 68: 225–62.

Mattli, W., and N. Woods, eds. (2009). *The Politics of Global Regulation*. Princeton: Princeton University Press.

Mazey, S., and J. Richardson (2006). 'Interest Groups and EU Policy-making: Organisational Logic and Venue Shopping'. *European Union: Power and Policy-making*, ed. J. Richardson. New York: Routledge.

Mearsheimer, J. (1994). 'The False Promise of International Institutions'. *International Security* 13(3): 5–49.

Milgrom, P., D. North et al. (1990). 'The Role of Institutions in the Revival of Trade: The Law Merchant, Private Judges, and the Champagne Fairs'. *Economics and Politics* 2: 1–23.

Milner, H. (1997). *Interests, Institutions, and Information*. Princeton: Princeton University Press.

Milner, H. (1998). 'Rationalizing Politics: The Emerging Synthesis of International, American, and Comparative Politics'. *International Organization* 52(4): 759–86.

Mitchell, R. B. (2006). 'Problem Structure, Institutional Design, and the Relative Effectiveness of International Environmental Agreements'. *Global Environmental Politics* 6(3): 72–89.

Moravcsik, A. (1997). 'Taking Preferences Seriously: A Liberal Theory of International Relations'. *International Organization* 51(4): 513–33.

Moravcsik, A. (1998). *The Choice for Europe: Social Purpose and State Power from Messina to Maastricht*. Ithaca: Cornell University Press.

Murphy, C. (1994). *International Organization and Industrial Change: Global Governance since 1850*. Cambridge: Polity.

Nye, J. S. (2001). 'Globalization's Democratic Deficit – How to Make International Institutions More Accountable'. *Foreign Affairs* 80(2): 2–6.

Nye, J. S., and R. O. Keohane (1971). 'Transnational Relations and World Politics: An Introduction'. *International Organization* 25(3): 329–49.

Oberthur, S., and T. Gehring, eds. (2006). *Institutional Interaction in Global Environmental Governance*. Cambridge: MIT Press.

Orts, E. W. (1995). 'Reflexive Environmental Law'. *Northwestern University Law Review* 89: 1227–1340.

Payne, R. A., and N. H. Samhat (2004). *Democratizing Global Politics: Discourse Norms, International Regimes, and Political Community*. Albany: SUNY Press.

Polanyi, K. (1944). *The Great Transformation: The Political and Economic Origins of Our Time*. Boston: Beacon Press.

Putnam, R. D. (1988). 'Diplomacy and Domestic Politics: The Logic of Two-Level Games'. *International Organization* 42(3): 427–60.

Raustiala, K. (1997). 'States, NGOs, and International Institutions'. *International Studies Quarterly* 41: 719–40.

Raustiala, K., and D. G. Victor (2004). 'The Regime Complex for Plant Genetic Resources'. *International Organization* 58: 277–309.

Rhodes, R. A. W. (1996). 'The New Governance: Governing without Government'. *Political Studies* 44: 652–67.

Richardson, J., ed. (2006). *European Union: Power and Policymaking*. London: Routledge.

Risse, T. (2007). 'Social Constructivism Meets Globalization'. *Globalization Theory: Approaches and Controversies*, ed. D. Held and A. McGrew. Cambridge: Polity.

Risse-Kappen, T. (1995). *Bringing Transnational Relations Back In: Non-State Actors, Domestic Structures and International Institutions*. Cambridge: Cambridge University Press.

Rosenau, J. N. (2007). 'Governing the Ungovernable: The Challenge of a Global Disaggregation of Authority'. *Regulation and Governance* 1: 88–97.

Ruggie, J. (2004). 'Reconstituting the Global Public Domain – Issues, Actors, and Practices'. *European Journal of International Relations* 10: 499–531.

Schäferhoff, M., S. Campe et al. (2009). 'Transnational Public–Private Partnerships in International Relations: Making Sense of Concepts, Research Frameworks, and Results'. *International Studies Review* 11(3): 451–74.

Schelling, Thomas C. (1980). *The Strategy of Conflict*. Cambridge, MA: Harvard University Press.

Simmons, B. (2010). 'Treaty Compliance and Violation'. *Annual Review of Political Science* 13: 273–96.

Slaughter, A.-M. (2004). *A New World Order*. Princeton: Princeton University Press.

Slaughter, A.-M., and T. Hale (2010). 'Transgovernmental Networks and Emerging Powers'. *Rising States; Rising Institutions: Can the World Be Governed?* ed. A. S. Alexandroff and A. F. Cooper. Washington, DC: Brookings Institution Press.

Slaughter, A.-M., and D. Zaring (2006). 'Networking Goes International: An Update'. *Annual Review of Law and Social Science* 2: 211.

Slaughter, Anne-Marie, *Sovereignty and Power in a Networked World Order*, 40 STANFORD JOURNAL OF INTERNATIONAL LAW 283-328 (2004).

Slaughter, Anne-Marie (2004). *Disaggregated Sovereignty: Toward the Public Accountability of Global Government Networks* in GOVERNMENT AND OPPOSITION 39 (2): 159–190.

Slaughter, Anne-Marie, *Global Government Networks, Global Information Agencies, and Disaggregated Democracy*, 24 MICHIGAN JOURNAL OF INTERNATIONAL LAW 1041-1075 (2003).

Sørensen, E., and J. Torfing (2006). *Theories of Democratic Network Governance*. New York: Palgrave.

Strange, S. (1996). *The Retreat of the State: The Diffusion of Power in the World Economy*. Cambridge: Cambridge University Press.

Tallberg, J. (2008). 'Explaining Transnational Access to International Institutions'. Paper presented at the Annual Convention of the International Studies Association, San Francisco, 26–29 March.

Teubner, G. (1983). 'Substantive and Reflexive Elements in Modern Law'. *Law and Society Review* 17(2): 239–85.

Tucker, G. M. (1965). 'Covenant Forms and Contract Forms'. *Vetus Testamentum* 15(4): 487–503.

Van Apeldoorn, B. (2004). 'Theorizing the Transnational: A Historical Materialist Approach'. *Journal of International Relations and Development* 7: 142–76.

Vogel, D. (2008). 'Private Global Business Regulation'. *Annual Review of Political Science* 11: 261–82.

Waltz, K. (1979). *Theory of International Politics*. New York: McGraw Hill.

Young, O. R. (1999). *Governance in World Affairs*. Ithaca: Cornell University Press.

Zürn, M., and S. Leibfried (2005). 'A New Perspective on the State: Reconfiguring the National Constellation'. *European Review* 13(1): 1–36.

Part I
Transgovernmental Networks

Introduction

Transgovernmental networks bring together 'domestic' government officials from various national jurisdictions to coordinate policy on a given issue. Instead of employing professional diplomats and formal intergovernmental organizations, states sometimes link other types of public servants – regulators, enforcers, technocrats, etc. – with their counterparts abroad. The resulting networks range from more informal groupings (e.g. the International Competition Network), which may lack a permanent secretariat or official by-laws, to more institutionalized organizations that share some of the characteristics of traditional intergovernmental organizations (e.g. the Basel Committee on Banking Supervision). In many cases a process of gradual institutionalization occurs. Though acknowledged by scholars in the 1970s (Keohane and Nye 1974), transgovernmental networks have only recently become a topic of sustained academic interest (Slaughter 2004; Slaughter and Zaring 2006; Slaughter and Hale 2010).

Slaughter (2004) notes that transgovernmental networks tend to serve one of three functions. Some, like the International Network for Environmental Compliance and Enforcement (INECE), aim to share information and best practices concerning challenges that all governments face – in the case of INECE, environmental regulation. Others seek to coordinate and harmonize policy across jurisdictions. The International Conference on Harmonization of Technical Requirements for the Registration of Pharmaceutical Products (ICH), for example, standardizes the regulation of pharmaceutical products across Europe, the United States and Japan, simplifying the global regulatory framework. A third type of transgovernmental network increases countries' enforcement capacities regarding transnational problems like organized crime or terrorism by pooling resources and information and carrying out joint operations (e.g. the Financial Action Task Force).

Networks offer both advantages and disadvantages relative to more traditional international organizations. The lack of formality can allow them to respond more quickly to policy challenges because the transaction costs are lower. Informality can also help to accommodate heterogeneous preferences. And for issues that require technical expertise, it is often simpler to let specialized officials interact rather than generalist diplomats. The flipside of these benefits is that networks are often ill suited for states to make credible commitments to one another and enforce them. Their very flexibility means that states cannot lock one another into binding agreements, as traditional treaties do.

References

Keohane, R. O., and J. S. Nye (1974). 'Transgovernmental Relations and International Organizations'. *World Politics* 27(1): 39–62.

Slaughter, A.-M. (2004). *A New World Order*. Princeton: Princeton University Press.

Slaughter, A.-M., and T. Hale (2010). 'Transgovernmental Networks'. *The Handbook of Governance*, ed. M. Bevir. London: SAGE.

Slaughter, A.-M., and D. Zaring (2006). 'Networking Goes International: An Update'. *Annual Review of Law and Social Science* 2: 211.

2

The Basel Committee on Banking Supervision
Kevin Young

The Basel Committee on Banking Supervision (BCBS) is a transgovernmental institution that facilitates cooperation between agencies that supervise and regulate banks. While it serves a variety of purposes, its principal function has been to construct an internationally agreed-upon set of standards by which banks are to be regulated. It is consistently identified as the archetypal example of a transnationally organized technical institution setting the pace of financial regulation, and is considered central to the system of global financial governance (Alexander, Dhumale et al. 2006: 34–78). Its primary stated objective is to 'enhance understanding of key supervisory issues and improve the quality of banking supervision worldwide'. Despite this extensive remit, it is composed of only a small secretariat and representatives from central banks and banking regulatory agencies from twenty-two countries.

The output of the BCBS has far-reaching consequences in terms of how financial regulation is conducted all over the world. In addition to establishing agreed-upon regulatory standards for the Committee members themselves, there are strong incentives for states outside the BCBS to emulate the standards it generates (Ho 2002; Delonis 2004: 579–81; Kerwer 2006). International capital markets have also used BCBS-based standards to evaluate the financial soundness of banks; and international institutions, such as the IMF, have used BCBS standards as a crucial metric (Alexander, Dhumale et al. 2006: 41–2). Because of these far-reaching consequences, its output has been regarded as a prime example of 'soft law', as its standards are enforced, but not through legal, sovereign authority (Abbott and Snidal 2000; Delonis 2004; Panourgias 2006).

History

As an informal group within the Bank for International Settlements in Basel, Switzerland, the BCBS was established in 1974 after it was becoming evident that the re-emergence of global finance was causing governance dilemmas which could not be addressed at the national level alone. Principal among these was the infamous 'Herstatt Crisis' of that year in which the failure of a German bank operating in several different jurisdictions highlighted the limitations national regulation faced in handling an increasingly international banking business. The 'Basel Concordat' of 1975 (later refined in 1983) set up, for the first time, a framework of agreed rules to ensure a clear international division of labour between regulatory authorities in regard to how international banks were supervised. While the BCBS has produced a large number of reports, observations and standards ever since, arguably its most significant achievements are the first and second Basel Accords, produced in 1988 and 2004, respectively (see BCBS 1988; BCBS 2004). These Accords have sought to construct a common international regime for the regulation of banks by drawing up a series of minimum standards for the assessment of the amount of capital adequacy that banks should hold.

For most of its history, formal participants within the BCBS have been drawn from what is known as the 'G-10': Belgium, Canada, France, Germany, Italy, Japan, Luxembourg, the Netherlands, Sweden, Switzerland, the United Kingdom and the United States. In 2001, Spain was added as a participant, following recognition that its banks had substantial exposures and expertise in Latin America. Following the call by the G-20 in November 2008 to examine participation in the global standard-setting bodies, the BCBS was expanded dramatically in March 2009 to include Australia, Brazil, China, India, Mexico, South Korea and Russia. Following the April G-20 London Summit, the BCBS was expanded a second time to include the entire G-20, along with Hong Kong and Singapore (see Helleiner and Pagliari 2010).

Governance

The BCBS does not possess any formal supranational regulatory authority; in other words, its standards do not have legal force (see BCBS 2006: 1). At the same time, the particular institutional design of the BCBS has meant that its decisions are several steps removed from national authority as well. The participants within the BCBS are not elected representatives, and in most cases they have not even been formally delegated to make decisions within the BCBS on behalf of governments. Rather, participants are bureaucrats within regulatory agencies and central banks – institutions which are typically very independent from elected legislatures and executives of governments. Additionally, the decisions of the BCBS itself are not subject to formal approval by any national government or external authority. The G-10 Governors within the Bank for International Settlements approve major policy outputs of the BCBS, but this role is largely ceremonial, and in any case is composed of some of the same institutions as the BCBS itself (see Davies and Green 2008: 218–19). As Underhill and Zhang have correctly asserted, the BCBS is characterized 'by virtual separation from any accountable political process' (Underhill with Zhang 2006: 29). Most decisions are made on the basis of technical discussion in a manner commensurate with 'deliberation', meaning that most engagement is informal in character, and the de facto decision-rule is implicit consensus (see Slaughter 1997; Slaughter 2004: 160; Kussin and Kette 2006). This norm, however, has not meant that power dynamics are absent from the BCBS. Indeed, the formation of both the 1988 Capital Accord and the 2004 Capital Accord featured important geopolitical conflicts. In the late 1980s, for example, regulators from Japan were effectively coerced into a global agreement that damaged their banks' business strategies at the time (see Kapstein 1992; Singer 2004). Throughout the formation of the second Basel Capital Accord, 'Basel II', there were significant disagreements between German and US members of the BCBS on the appropriate shape and content of various regulatory policies as they were being designed (see Wood 2005; Young 2009).

Structure and Activities

The BCBS operates with a very small secretariat. While some of the secretariat is the official staff of the BCBS itself, most are on temporary secondment from the regulatory agencies that compose the BCBS. The secretariat fulfils a number of roles. It conducts the secretarial work for the BCBS as a whole, both in its day-to-day capacity and in the organization of special projects. It also guides and organizes the BCBS's subcommittees, which should be distinguished from its 'full committee'. While the 'full committee' approves the major decisions, sets the agenda and deliberates on major decisions, it is the subcommittees of the Basel Committee that often engage in the important detailed work, including research for special purposes, the drafting of proposals, and engagement with outside groups. Subcommittees and the sub-groups within them are typically assigned on an informal basis and engage in both formal in-person meetings and informal communication within the group.

   While the BCBS has largely operated as a closed informal group for the vast majority of its engagements, since the late 1990s it has increasingly engaged in consultative processes with outsiders (see below). These have included engagement with regional groupings of financial supervisory authorities as well as its biannual conferences of supervisors from all over the world (Porter and Wood 2002: 245; see also BCBS 2006: 4–5). Such outreach has also taken the form of technical consultative papers which are open for public comment – a process characterized by a great deal of private sector involvement, but which has also featured feedback from non-BCBS country regulators, academics and international institutions like the International Monetary Fund (IMF). The Basel Committee also formally engages with other institutions of transnational governance. It is a prominent member of the Joint Forum on Financial Conglomerates, which is also composed of the International Association of Insurance Supervisors and the International Organization of Securities Commissions (see chapters 8 and 12).

Impact

The Basel Committee has been heralded for its transcendence of many of the problems that have beleaguered regulatory initiatives at the international level. Because of its particular institutional structure and the informal character of its agreements, it is usually able to draw on a network of specialists organized at the transnational level without being encumbered by national political constraints. At the same time, the BCBS has attracted criticism for the extent to which it engages with outside groups, for two reasons.

First, the BCBS has attracted criticism on the basis of its consultation with business groups. Since the late 1990s in particular, the BCBS has met with internationally organized groups such as the Institute of International Finance and the International Swaps and Derivatives Association. Because these institutions are seen by many to represent the interests of large banks, the recent output of the BCBS – principally the 2004 Basel Accord – has been called into question. Indeed, the work of the BCBS has been widely regarded as an example of 'regulatory capture' at the transnational level, whereby the content of regulations has been systematically influenced by the very banks it seeks to regulate (see, for example, Helleiner and Porter 2009: 20; Ocampo 2009: 10; Goldin and Vogel 2010: 13; Tsingou 2010: 24).

Second, the BCBS has attracted widespread criticism for the composition of its membership – which until 2009 was limited to developed countries only (specifically, regulators and central bankers from the 'G-10' states – Belgium, Canada, France, Germany, Italy, Japan, Luxembourg, the Netherlands, Sweden, Switzerland, the United Kingdom and the United States). This has led many to challenge the legitimacy of the BCBS as an institution of global governance, on the grounds that its output did not take into account the particularities of less-developed countries (Claessens, Underhill et al. 2008; Griffith-Jones and Persaud 2008). For a long period BCBS operated as an exclusive club despite the increased importance of its work and despite calls from the UN's Monterrey Consensus that participation within such bodies should be widened (see Davies 2005; Kregel 2006). Though Spain was added to the BCBS in 2001, no developing countries were included, despite the widely recognized impacts of the BCBS's work. This changed following the call by the G-20 in November 2008 for international standard-setting bodies to review their country composition as part of the multilateral initiatives to reform global financial governance. The subsequent expansion of the BCBS, noted above, dramatically increased the international diversity of its membership: by March 2009 the BCBS invited regulators and central bankers from Australia, Brazil, China, India, Mexico, South Korea and Russia to join (BCBS 2009a). The second round of expansion in June 2009 further widened the membership to include the entire G-20, as well as Hong Kong and Singapore (BCBS 2009b).

References

Abbott, K. W., and D. Snidal (2000). 'Hard and Soft Law in International Governance', *International Organization* 54(3): 421–56.

Alexander, K., R. Dhumale et al. (2006). *Global Governance of Financial Systems: The International Regulation of Systemic Risk*. Oxford: Oxford University Press.

BCBS (1988). *International Convergence of Capital Measurement and Capital Standards*. Basel: BCBS.

BCBS (2004). *International Convergence of Capital Measurement and Capital Standards: A Revised Framework*. Basel: BCBS.

BCBS (2006). *History of the Basel Committee and its Membership*. Basel: BCBS.

BCBS (2009a). 'Expansion of Membership Announced by the Basel Committee'. Press release, 13 March.

BCBS (2009b). 'Basel Committee Broadens its Membership'. Press release, 10 June.

Claessens, S., G. R. D. Underhill et al. (2008). 'The Political Economy of Basle II: The Costs for Poor Countries'. *The World Economy* 31(3): 313–460.

Davies, H. (2005). 'A Review of the Review'. *Financial Markets, Institutions & Instruments* 14(5): 247–52.

Davies, H., and D. Green (2008). *Global Financial Regulation: The Essential Guide*. Cambridge: Polity.

Delonis, R. P. (2004). 'International Financial Standards and Codes: Mandatory Regulation Without Representation'. *NYU Journal of International Law and Politics* 36 (Winter/Spring): 563–634.

Goldin, I., and T. Vogel (2010). 'Global Governance and Systemic Risk in the 21st Century: Lessons from the Financial Crisis', *Global Policy* 1(1) (January): 4–15.

Griffith-Jones, S., and A. Persaud (2008). 'The Pro-cyclical Impact of Basle II on Emerging Markets and its Political Economy'. *Capital Market Liberalization and Development*, ed. J. Stiglitz and J. A. Ocampo. Oxford: Oxford University Press.

Helleiner, E., and S. Pagliari. (2010). 'Crisis and the Reform of International Financial Regulation'. *Global Finance in Crisis: The Politics of International Regulatory Change*, ed. E. Helleiner, S. Pagliari et al. London: Routledge.

Helleiner, E., and T. Porter (2009). 'Making Transnational Networks More Accountable'. *Re-Defining the Global Economy* (Occasional Paper no. 42), ed. S. Burke. New York: Friedrich Ebert Stiftung. Available at http://library.fes.de/pdf-files/iez/global/06293.pdf (accessed 23 February 2010).

Ho, D. (2002). 'Compliance and International Soft Law: Why Do Countries Implement the Basel Accord?' *Journal of International Economic Law* 5: 647–48.

Kapstein, E. B. 1992. 'Between Power and Purpose: Central Bankers and the Politics of Regulatory Convergence'. *International Organization* 46: 265–87.

Kerwer, D.)2006). 'Governing Financial Markets by International Standards'. *New Modes of Governance in the Global System: Exploring Publicness, Delegation and Inclusiveness*, ed. M. Koenig-Archibugi and M. Zürn. London: Palgrave.

Kregel, J. (2006). 'From Monterrey to Basel: Who Rules the Banks?' *Social Watch* 26–8.

Kussin, M., and Kette, S. (2006). 'Making Use of Cognitive Standards: On the Logic of a New Mode of Governance in International Finance'. *Toward a Cognitive Mode in Global Finance: The Governance of a Knowledge-Based Financial System*, ed. T. Strulik and H. Willke. Frankfurt: Campus Verlag.

Ocampo, J. A. (2009). '7-Point Plan For Development-Friendly Reform'. *Re-Defining the Global Economy* (Occasional Paper no. 42), ed. Sara Burke. New York: Friedrich Ebert Stiftung.

Panourgias, L. E. (2006). *Banking Regulation and World Trade Law*. Oxford: Hart Publishing.

Porter, T., and D. Wood (2002). 'Reform without Representation? The International and Transnational Dialogue on the Global Financial Architecture'. *Debating the Global Financial Architecture*, ed. L. E. Armijo. Albany: SUNY Press.

Singer, D. A. (2004). 'Capital Rules? The Domestic Politics of International Regulatory Harmonization'. *International Organization* 58 (Summer): 531–65.

Slaughter, A.-M. (2004). 'Disaggregated Sovereignty: Towards the Public Accountability of Global Government Networks', *Government and Opposition* 39(2): 159–90.

Slaughter, A.-M. (1997). 'The Real New World Order'. *Foreign Affairs* 183: 76.

Tsingou, E. (2010). 'Regulatory Reactions to the Global Credit Crisis: Analyzing a Policy Community Under Stress'. *Global Finance in Crisis: The Politics of International Regulatory Change*, ed. E. Helleiner, S. Pagliari et al. London: Routledge.

Underhill, G., with X. Zhang (2006). 'Norms, Legitimacy, and Global Financial Governance'. Working Paper no. WEF0013, World Economy and Finance Research Programme of the UK Econ. and Soc. Res. Council, September. Available at www.worldeconomyandfinance.org/working_papers_publications/wpdetail0013.html.

Underhill, G., and X. Zhang (2008). 'Setting the Rules: Private Power, Political Underpinnings, and Legitimacy in Global Monetary and Financial Governance'. *International Affairs* 84(3): 535–54.

Wood, D. (2005). *Governing Global Banking: The Basel Committee and the Politics of Financial Globalization*. Aldershot: Ashgate.

Young, K. (2009). 'Financial Governance and the Limits to Transnational Risk Regulation'. *Risk and Regulation* (Summer): 12.

3

Financial Action Task Force
Ian Roberge

The Financial Action Task Force (FATF) is the principal organization for dealing with money laundering and terrorist financing at the international level. Created in 1989, it has made a significant contribution to global governance through its 40+9 recommendations elaborated to tackle the threat of illicit finance. The FATF is a flexible organization that facilitates policy diffusion across members and the broader global community. Critics will highlight the mixed results of the fight against illicit finance. Despite some drawbacks the FATF is generally perceived as a success by members of the international community.

History

The FATF was created in 1989 to respond to the challenges posed by money laundering. It followed the adoption by the United Nations of the Convention against Illicit Narcotic Drugs and Psychotropic Substances, which for the first time in international law criminalized the laundering of proceeds of crime monies. The FATF emerged from a direct initiative of the G-7 and came to be located, despite its status as an independent entity, in the offices of the Organisation for Economic Co-operation and Development (OECD) in Paris. In 1990, the FATF elaborated forty recommendations to tackle money laundering. States around the world were strongly encouraged to adopt the new standards. The recommendations were revised in 1996 and 2003. Following the events of 11 September 2001, the FATF was also tasked with addressing terrorist financing. It elaborated nine special recommendations to deal with this particular issue. At the 2009 Pittsburg Summit, the G-20 directed the FATF to address problems relating to proceeds of corruption. The Task Force, at the time of writing, has thirty-six members, including thirty-four jurisdictions and two regional organizations, remaining small enough to ensure cohesion. The FATF operates through a temporary mandate; the current one, to be renewed, is set to expire in 2012. There are FATF-style regional bodies which contribute to the dissemination of anti-money laundering standards and norms across the globe.

Compliance Mechanisms

The FATF's contribution to global governance is most evident through its 40+9 recommendations which serve as minimum requirements for states to meet in facing the threat of money laundering and terrorist financing (Gilmore 2004). The Task Force has elaborated four distinct mechanisms to ensure the compliance of members. The first mechanism is that of self-assessment, through which states are sent a yearly questionnaire asking them to note their progress in the fight against illicit finance.

The second process is that of mutual evaluation, whereby FATF-selected assessors determine the level of compliance of a member state with the FATF guidelines. In case of extreme non-compliance the FATF can invoke Recommendation 21, which is used to warn the financial community of the threat potentially posed by intermediaries in the targeted jurisdiction. Counterparties need to give 'special attention' to their business dealings in that country, thus potentially impacting financial and economic opportunities. Recommendation 21 was applied, for instance, against Turkey in the mid-1990s, and later against Austria, whose membership was temporarily suspended in February 2000. Practices of mutual evaluations, as first elaborated by the FATF, are now also widely used by FATF-style regional bodies.

Third, the FATF can use cross-country reviews, a little-used mechanism, to supervise the implementation of a recommendation by the membership as a whole.

The fourth and the most controversial FATF compliance mechanism has been that of the so-called 'name and shame' strategy. As part of the Non-Cooperating Countries and Territories Initiative, the FATF, beginning in 2000, identified twenty-three states (non-FATF members) largely non-compliant with the international anti-money laundering standards and norms. The FATF used public admonition to force these states to put in place or reform counter-money laundering systems. Most identified states were offshore centres in the Caribbean and the Pacific, though Israel, the Russian Federation (now a Task Force member) and the Philippines also found themselves on the initial list. The initiative was contentious since it seemed to particularly target small states that had chosen to allow for the existence of various financial products to foster domestic economic growth. The list fell into disuse in 2006 with all states once named having been removed; the FATF selected at that time a more low-key approach to incite hesitant states to take appropriate legislative and regulatory action. Responding to the request of the G-20, the FATF elaborated in February 2010 two new lists of high-risk jurisdictions, focusing on states which pose a serious threat, and on states which – despite some deficiencies – have shown a political commitment to cooperating with the international community.

Strengths

The FATF is often considered an example of successful international collaboration. First, it stands as the focal point of the regime tackling illicit finance. There are many organizations, such as the United Nations (UN), the International Monetary Fund (IMF), the World Bank, Interpol, the Egmont Group (representing financial intelligence units – national organizations that collect and analyse financial intelligence), the Bank for International Settlements, and others that are all working in dealing with the issue of money laundering. There are also regional organizations involved in this field, such as the Council of Europe. It should also be noted that private sector organizations play a role as well, most notably the Wolfsberg Group of Banks, representing some of the largest financial intermediaries on the planet. Many of these organizations have observer status at the FATF. The FATF has raised awareness globally, including in the developing world, regarding the threats and damages resulting from illicit financial activities; its recommendations serve as the basis for action worldwide. The organization has succeeded in placing an issue that had largely been ignored up until the 1990s at the forefront of the international political agenda.

Second, the FATF operates as a forum for discussion facilitating policy innovation and policy diffusion. The FATF operates through two principal working groups. The Working Group on Money Laundering and Terrorist Financing provides, through interpretive notes and best-practices analysis, common guidance to states on the implementation of recommendations and on general steps to be taken to minimize threats from illicit finance. The working group also supports the 'annual typologies' exercise providing a forum for the exchange of information on money laundering cases and operations. The Working Group on Evaluation and Implementation supports the assessment procedures and fosters cooperation with the private sector. There are many examples that support the idea that the FATF acts as an instrument for policy diffusion. For instance, the 1996 recommendations expanded the target of money laundering offences to all crimes of significance, a view now accepted worldwide. The FATF also encouraged states to develop reporting mechanisms by creating financial intelligence units.

Third, the FATF's organizational structure is flexible, allowing for quick action when needed. The FATF has a yearly revolving presidency and its business is conducted through an annual plenary. The FATF's flexibility was shown, most importantly, when less than a month after the terrorist attacks in the United States in 2001, it agreed to review its mandate and integrate more fully the task of tackling terrorist financing. In recent years, the FATF has also further opened its deliberations to private sector actors. Whereas many international organizations are bogged down by rules and procedures, the FATF's restricted membership allows it to reach consensus and agreement more easily through focused dialogue.

Concerns

The FATF is not, however, without its critics. It can be seen as an instrument of the G-7, or more directly of the United States. Does the FATF represent anything more than the legitimization of the American approach toward illicit finance? Through its 'War on Drugs' the United States pushed strongly to place money laundering on the international agenda. In the late 1990s, the American government, under pressure from a Republican Congress concerned about privacy rights, seemed to distance itself from the fight against illicit finance. The trend continued during the first few months of the Bush presidency. During this time, the FATF was perceived as largely moribund. The events of 11 September 2001 reinvigorated the international regime by expanding the fight to cover terrorist financing, a new

American priority. Small states, especially offshore financial centres, have felt bullied by both the FATF and the United States in this policy field. Clearly though, the FATF is able to foster support for its agenda because it is backed by the might of major powers.

The performance of the FATF-led regime, or more specifically of states' counter-money laundering policies, is also of concern. Johnson and Lim (2002) tried to assess the vulnerability of states to money laundering and noticed incremental benefits when governments started to take the issue of illicit finance seriously. Reuter and Truman's (2004) assessment of American policies against money laundering and terrorist financing raised serious issues of efficiency and effectiveness. Part of the problem is methodological. There are no accurate data on illegal financial transfers. The often-cited IMF number is that such transfers amount to 2–5 per cent of global GDP or higher. The FATF attempted to address methodological questions in the mid-1990s, but it failed to come to any sort of an agreement on how to measure the pool of laundered funds.

There are, finally, researchers for whom money laundering is a constructed, or at the very least an exaggerated, threat. Most notably, R. T. Naylor argues that money laundering is a fictive crime since it involves the use of the financial system for its stated purpose: that is, to make more money (2004). Hülsse (2007) refers to the central role of the FATF in the 'problematization' of money laundering. There are concerns about the ability, or willingness, of financial firms to combat illicit finance, and, as well, about the negative externalities of public and private sector measures especially on dispossessed and alienated communities (for a discussion above and beyond money laundering, please see Amoore and de Goede 2008).

Conclusion

Despite serious concerns, the FATF remains an important organization for transnational governance. Money laundering, terrorist financing and corruption are perceived by policymakers, especially in the West, as issues that are critical and that must be addressed to further circumscribe threats posed by transnational organized crime and terrorism, and to ensure the soundness of the international financial system. The FATF is generally seen as a successful organization, one that is flexible enough to adjust to changing circumstances. As such, the FATF will most likely continue to play an important role in international policymaking.

References

Amoore, L., and M. de Goede (2008). *Risk and the War on Terror*. Abingdon: Routledge.

Gilmore, W. C. (2004). *Dirty Money: The Evolution of International Measures to Counter Money Laundering and the Financing of Terrorism*. Strasbourg: Council of Europe Publishing.

Hülsse, R. (2007). 'Creating Demand for Global Governance: The Making of a Global Money Laundering Problem'. *Global Society* 21(2): 155–78.

Johnson, J., and Y. C. D. Lim (2002). 'Money-Laundering: Has the Financial Action Task Force Made a Difference?' *Journal of Financial Crime* 10(1): 7–23.

Naylor, R.T. (2004). *Wages of Crime: Black Markets, Illegal Finance, and the Underworld Economy*. Ithaca: Cornell University Press.

Reuter, P., and E. M. Truman (2004). *Chasing Dirty Money: The Fight against Money Laundering*. Washington, DC: Institute for International Economics.

4

Financial Stability Board
Randall Germain

Introduction

The Financial Stability Board (FSB) is part of the growing network of transgovernmental organizations that comprise the global framework for financial governance. Historically, financial governance has emerged at the national level within the context of market–state interaction. As banks and other financial institutions grew in terms of the complexity of their organization and the scope and range of their activities, states developed different regulatory frameworks to try to balance the competing demands of efficiency and stability (Kindelberger 1993). These efforts remained focused primarily at the national level until the breakdown of the postwar Bretton Woods period, most critically during the decade of the 1970s (Herring and Litan 1995). But as national financial markets became increasingly integrated, and as new and distinctly international markets developed in the absence of clear national oversight, a number of international efforts were initiated to develop a cooperative and integrated regulatory support structure that paralleled how financial institutions were organized and operated (Wood 2005). The FSB is associated with this latter period, and therefore should be seen as part of the growing global framework that reinforces how states govern financial activity.

The Origins and Structure of the Financial Stability Board

The origins of the FSB date back to the Asian financial crisis of 1997/8 and the international community's response to it (Eichengreen 2008). A series of reports were commissioned in 1998 by different bodies including the G-7 and a new grouping of finance ministers that was then identified as the G-22 (but which eventually became the G-20). The G-7 asked the then President of Deutsche Bundesbank, Hans Tietmeyer, to consider ways of strengthening the international structure or architecture of financial governance in light of the lessons being learned from the Asian crisis. One such lesson was the vexed problem of how to effectively coordinate the way in which states were monitoring systemic vulnerabilities – in other words, how to ensure that, as far as possible, all of the relevant regulatory officials were aware of the overall level of systemic risk and how they might work together to reduce it. One recommendation that came out of the Tietmeyer Report was the creation of a new cross-national body designed to bring together on a regular basis key regulators responsible for systemic risk and vulnerability. This new body was called the Financial Stability Forum (FSF), and it began to operate in 1999 (Porter 2005).

The central idea behind the FSF was to provide a forum where the principal regulatory officials could interact and communicate as a cohesive whole. It was therefore composed of high-level representatives from G-7 central banks, ministries of finance and financial regulators, as well as representatives from other international institutions and committees involved in financial governance, among them the IMF, the (newly established) European Central Bank (ECB), the Basel Committee on Banking Supervision (BCBS), the International Association of Insurance Supervisors (IAIS) and the International Organization of Securities Commissions (IOSCO). Shortly after its inaugural meeting in April 1999, it expanded its membership beyond the G-7 to include formal representation from four other systemically significant (but non-G-7) financial markets: the Netherlands, Australia, Singapore and Hong Kong, bringing the total to thirty-five members. This number did not change until the global credit crisis of 2008/9.

The FSF met on a regular basis to consider and share information about ongoing and emerging vulnerabilities and risks associated with the global operation of financial institutions and markets. The FSF operated by monitoring issues and developments within the global financial system and alerting member countries where appropriate. If consensus existed, the FSF formed committees of interested parties to explore particular problems in more depth. It also undertook to develop and codify a growing body of international standards that various regulatory agencies were deliberating upon and advancing. The FSF met formally twice a year, and more infrequently as specific consultative exercises demanded. One of the innovative features of the FSF that emerged out of its regulatory mandate was an outreach programme that engaged with private sector institutions, including hedge funds and banks based in emerging market economies. The FSF was from its origins a surprisingly nimble governance organization that uniquely spanned both the public and private sectors, even if ultimately it has to be viewed as an organ of public authority (Davies and Green 2008).

In its operations, the FSF followed in the path of previous transgovernmental governance organizations that sought to bring together national regulators into some type of international forum, such as the BCBS and Joint Forum (Baker 2006). The critical theme to note here is that the FSF could not *mandate* states to undertake particular courses of action. When the FSF became seized of an issue – such as with prudential safeguards involving highly leveraged institutions – it could only suggest a suitable course of action for its members to adopt, in the belief that if this course of action became the consensus view, then it would eventually become embodied in the regulatory practices of all members. In this way, the FSF inserted itself into the global framework of financial governance through a consensus-oriented *modus operandi*.

The FSF operated as above from its inauguration in 1999 until the global credit crisis of 2008/9. Its main achievements were to coordinate more effectively the development of international standards across a wide variety of financial issue areas, to strengthen the regulatory links between emerging market and highly developed financial systems, and to foster extended awareness of the changing patterns of systemic risk among the world's major financial systems. These achievements are not inconsiderable, and they reflect the long, evolutionary development of global finance since the end of the Second World War (Helleiner 1994; Langley 2002; Eichengreen 2008). At the same time, precisely because of the way in which the FSF exercised its mandate – without any recourse to coercive powers to ensure compliance of its benchmark practices – and because at bottom the FSF, like every other transgovernmental governance organization, is able to move no farther or faster than its most powerful member states (in this case the US and UK), it was unable to retard the growth of either financial asset bubbles or unsustainable capital account imbalances among its member states. In the end, a global framework of financial governance can only support nation states and national regulators in their efforts, and where they refuse to tread governance organizations like the FSF cannot lead.

The 2008/9 global credit crisis has neither changed nor challenged the roles played by transgovernmental governance organizations. In the case of the FSF, however, there has been an interesting development, which is a move to align its membership more closely with the upgraded version of the G-20 that emerged as a central component of the international community's response to the crisis. Whereas the Asian crisis of 1997/8 resulted in the creation of the G-20 at the level of finance ministers, by 2008 – after a decade of strong economic growth among several emerging market economies, especially Brazil, China, India and Russia (the so-called 'BRIC economies') – an argument had emerged calling for it to be hardened into a heads-of-state group. This idea crystallized during the tumultuous autumn of 2008, and it was only a small leap to consider how the FSF might also parallel this new configuration of political authority. Thus it was that the new Leaders G-20 directed the FSF to expand its membership and rename itself as a Board from April 2009, exactly ten years after the FSF was first created.

The mandate of the FSB, however, has not changed in any important respect from that of the FSF. It is still involved in developing international standards and monitoring systemic vulnerabilities. It has also been charged by the G-20 to work closely with the IMF to develop better surveillance efforts to forestall the emergence of global financial risks. In this respect, it remains to be seen whether the FSB will be any more (or less) successful than the FSF, given that none of its fundamental attributes has changed.

The FSB and Financial Governance

Among scholars, there are many who appreciate the efforts of transgovernmental organizations such as the FSB, but who nevertheless doubt whether any kind of consensus-oriented governance organization can actually rein in the speculative practices of private financial institutions (Underhill and Zhang 2003), especially where there are arbitrage opportunities to exploit within the context of unclear lines of national accountability. Others are even more sceptical that governments will ever protect their citizens from the worst excesses of global capitalism (Soederberg 2004; Panitch and

Konings 2009). If the FSB is an exemplar of the kind of governance possible for globalized finance, these scholars echo Susan Strange's argument that things will need to get much worse before they can get better (Strange 1998).

However, in important respects this is a worst-case scenario. Financial governance has no choice but to work within two important sets of conditions. One condition is the system of international or global politics currently in place, which operates through the twin matrices of state-based sovereignty and an asymmetrical balance of economic and financial power. As long as the juridical reach of government is limited by the international system of states, financial governance will be limited by the extent of consensus and cooperation that can be achieved between sovereign states. The second condition is the evolving balance between private and public authority, most often associated with the tug-of-war between states and markets. The history of finance and financial governance is replete with alterations in this balance, when the extent and capacities of one form of authority outrun the other, only to be checked and capped when crisis occurs. The 2008/9 global financial crisis is one such occurrence, with the result that national regulation of financial activity is being strengthened on the back of direct actions by national authorities (Germain 2010). The FSB fits into this picture as a mechanism that supports the national regulatory policies of states by helping to develop consensual policies concerning financial regulation, and by facilitating more effective coordination among states. It is part of the global framework of financial governance, but only a subordinate element.

References

Baker, A. (2006). *The Group of Seven: Finance Ministries, Central Banks and Global Financial Governance*. London: Routledge.

Davies, H., and D. Green (2008). *Global Financial Regulation*. Cambridge: Polity Press.

Eichengreen, B. (2008). *Globalizing Capital: A History of the International Monetary System*, 2nd edn. Princeton: Princeton University Press.

Germain, R. (2010). *Global Politics and Financial Governance*. Basingstoke: Palgrave.

Helleiner, E. (1994). *States and the Re-emergence of Global Finance*. Ithaca: Cornell University Press.

Herring, R. J., and R. E. Litan. (1995). *Financial Regulation in the Global Economy*. Washington, DC: Brookings Institution Press.

Kindelberger, C. (1993). *A History of Finance in Western Europe*, 2nd edn. Oxford: Oxford University Press.

Langley, P. (2002). *World Financial Orders: An Historical International Political Economy*. London: Routledge.

Panitch, L., and M. Konings, eds. (2009). *American Empire and the Political Economy of Global Finance*. London: Palgrave.

Porter, T. (2005). *Globalization and Finance*. Cambridge: Polity Press.

Soederberg, S. (2004). *The Politics of the New International Financial Architecture*. London: Zed Books.

Strange, S. (1998). *Mad Money*. Manchester: University of Manchester Press.

Wood, D. (2005). *Governing Global Banking: The Basel Committee and the Politics of Financial Globalization*. Aldershot: Ashgate.

Underhill, G. R.D., and X. Zhang, eds. (2003). *International Financial Governance under Stress: Global Structures versus National Imperatives*. Cambridge: Cambridge University Press.

5

The Group of Twenty
John Kirton

Speed, flexibility, adaptability, learning and innovation are critical components of effective governance in today's complex, intensely interconnected, fast-moving, globalized world. Global challenges require responses that can mobilize and coordinate work with a variety of international, regional and national actors, processes and structures. Responses need to be adjustable, innovative and forward-looking to anticipate and address evolving challenges, circumstances and evidence. They require resilient, adaptable governance structures that can adjust their membership, agenda and actions as necessary. Thus transgovernmental networks, including those operating within and through intergovernmental institutions, are becoming an increasingly attractive, utilized and effective mechanism of global governance (Slaughter 2000, 2004, 2009; Slaughter and Hale 2010).

History and Structure of the G-20

One such horizontal network arising recently with a global reach is the Group of Twenty (G-20) (Germain 2001; Kirton 2001a, 2008, 2010;

Alexandroff and Kirton 2010).[1] It was first created through the leadership of Canadian finance minister Paul Martin and United States treasury secretary Lawrence Summers at the finance ministers and central bank governors level in 1999, in response to the Asian-turned-global financial crisis of the preceding two years. Since first meeting on 15–16 December that year, the finance ministers and central bank governors from the nineteen most systemically significant countries from the developed and developing worlds plus the European Union have met annually in the autumn as equals to address financial, economic and related issues. Their agenda has expanded to embrace issues of terrorism, development, energy, education and the environment.

To provide leadership, this 'G-20 finance' body developed a rotating *troika* of the incoming, current and outgoing chairs. Each year the current chair develops a work programme focused on the chair's priorities and existing and emerging global challenges. The G-20 finance forum immediately took up terrorist financing in 2001, and later moved on to migration, international financial institution reform, trade, energy and climate change.

The G-20 is distinct from the 'hard', legalized organizations of the United Nations – Bretton Woods system born in the 1940s. The G-20 was established because these older bodies could not govern the financial challenges of a globalizing world (Kirton 2001a, 2001b, 2005). Unlike in the UN system, G-20 members have the flexibility to decide how often to meet, what to address and how to adapt their institution to deal with the crises at hand, as well as longer-term issues.

On 14–15 November 2008, after the American-turned-global financial crisis emerged, US president George W. Bush convened the first meeting of G-20 leaders in Washington, adding a higher-layer network over the finance ministers. The leaders committed to tackling the crisis in a coordinated manner through macroeconomic stimuli, domestic financial regulation, trade, development assistance and reform of the international financial institutions. Overall, the elevation of the G-20 to the leaders' level was welcomed, especially by those who had long called for this (De Brouwer and Yeaman 2007; Martin 2008). The G-20 leaders met for a second time on 1–2 April 2009, in London, where they pledged to implement all necessary measures to end the crisis. They promised $1.1 trillion in new money, beyond their massive domestic fiscal and monetary stimulus, rejected protection-

[1]The G-20 includes Argentina, Australia, Brazil, Canada, China, France, Germany, India, Indonesia, Italy, Japan, Korea, Mexico, Russia, Saudi Arabia, South Africa, Turkey, the United Kingdom, the United States and the European Union. The International Monetary Fund and World Bank also participate.

ism, and pledged assistance to the most vulnerable peoples and states. They met for a third time on 24–25 September 2009, in Pittsburgh. Here they discussed climate financing options and coordinated strategies for easing economic stimulus plans. They agreed that this new G-20 Summit would become the permanent, premier forum for international economic cooperation.

The G-20 has a flexible format similar to the Group of Eight (G-8), which has been operating since 1975 (Fues 2007).[2] However, the G-20 includes a broader, more diverse range of members, which many have argued make it a more credible and legitimate global governor (Porter 2000; Bergsten 2004; Boyer and Truman 2005; De Brouwer 2007). Many observers now argue that the G-20 will and should continue to expand its agenda just as the G-20 finance ministers had done after the Asian financial crisis began to wane (Samans, Uzan et al. 2007).

Critiques

Yet several observers have noted weaknesses. First, they ask if G-20 leaders can appropriately govern some of the detailed financial challenges that require technical expertise that many leaders lack (Kirton 2008).

Second, others argue that the right twenty countries are not included, or that, like the G-8, the G-20 is too elitist (Sohn 2005; Taylor 2005; Beeson and Bell 2009; Kirton and Guebert 2009). While the G-20 has included participants outside its twenty members since the November 2008 Summit, many feel that African participation is particularly weak and European representation too strong, especially with the involvement of Spain and the Netherlands at the first three summits. Hopefully, should the need arise, the G-20, as a flexible informal institution, can readily expand its membership and network, just as the older G-7 did when it added Russia in 1998. This is much easier to do than in formal multilateral organizations, such as the United Nations Security Council, International Monetary Fund (IMF) and World Bank executive boards, where membership changes require major negotiations that take place all at once only every few decades or so.

Last, some observers argue that the G-20 is simply a tool of the less legitimate and still dominant G-8, which serves in practice as the G-20's steering committee (Soederberg 2002; Martinez-Diaz 2007). Despite these concerns, the G-20 has now shown five times at the

[2] The G-8 includes Canada, France, Germany, Italy, Japan, Russia, the United Kingdom, the United States and the European Union.

summit level that it can come to consensus, make balanced decisions, undertake coordinated actions and implement harmonized responses.

The latest debate concerns what the roles and relationships of the G-8 and G-20 will be (Kirton 2009). The G-8 and G-20 could continue to meet separately, could combine their meetings, or could fade away. Some argue that that the G-8 adds something that the G-20 cannot – the shared values of open democracy, individual liberty and social advance. With non-democratic Saudi Arabia and China as full members of the G-20, it is poorly positioned to take political action on North Korea, Darfur, Zimbabwe, Myanmar and elsewhere, as the G-8 long has. The G-20 also has yet to address in a serious way many issues on the G-8's agenda, such as global health and biodiversity.

Future Directions

The G-8 and the G-20 will probably coexist, much like the G-20 and Group of Seven (G-7) finance ministers have since 1999.[3] The G-20 would focus on core financial and economic issues, while the G-8 would address social and political ones. The two groups could meet around the same time and place – as they did in Canada in June 2010 – or they could spread out with the G-8 summit still taking place in the summer and the G-20 in the autumn as in 2011.

The G-20 could conceivably replace the G-8 (Martin 2008). There would need to be agreement on how this would happen, what format it would follow, who would host and in what order, and what the agenda would be. Since 2003, the G-8 has included a wider number of participants, including many members of the G-20. If these countries are included and treated as equals, they might be more willing to collaborate on global priorities. It would be necessary for the G-20's agenda to expand quickly, allowing it to make large, cross-issue package deals. By taking over as the only 'G' group, the G-20 could add some of the legitimacy that the G-8 lacks. But some of the G-8's compact, club-like ability to come to a consensus and resulting effectiveness could be lost.

It remains to be seen how the G-20 Summit will evolve and how effective it will be. Thus far, in its crisis phase, the summit has proven to be a successful and effective governor. Its ability to be flexible, adaptive and innovative has allowed it to function effectively – even if not perfectly – in the face of the economic crisis. And its ability to expand its membership and agenda will allow it to evolve.

[3] The G-7 includes all the members of the G-8 except Russia.

References

Alexandroff, A. S., and J. Kirton (2010). 'The "Great Recession" and the Emergence of the G20 Leaders' Summit'. *Rising States, Rising Institutions: The Challenge of Global Governance*, ed. A. S. Alexandroff and A. F. Cooper. Washington DC: Brookings Institution Press.

Beeson, M., and S. Bell (2009). 'The G20 and International Economic Governance: Hegemony, Collectivism or Both?' *Global Governance* 15: 67–86.

Bergsten, C. F. (2004). '"The G20 and the World Economy". Statement to the Deputies of the G20. Leipzig, Germany, March 4'. *World Economics* 5(3): 27–36.

Boyer, J. E., and E. M. Truman (2005). 'The United States and Large Emerging Market Economies: Competitors or Partners'. *The United States and the World Economy: Foreign Economic Policy for the Next Decade*, ed. C. F. Bergsten and the Institute for International Economics. Washington, DC: Institute for International Economics.

De Brouwer, G. (2007). 'Institutions to Promote Financial Stability: Reflections on East Asia and an Asian Monetary Fund.' *The International Monetary System, the IMF and the G20: A Great Transformation in the Making*, ed. R. Samans, M. Uzan et al. Houndmills: Palgrave Macmillan.

Fues, T. (2007). 'Global Governance beyond the G8: Reform Prospects for the Summit Architecture'. *Internationale Politik und Gesellschaft* 2: 11–24.

Germain, R. (2001). 'Reforming the International Financial Architecture: The New Political Agenda'. Paper presented at the annual convention of the International Studies Association, Chicago, IL, 20–24 February. Available at www.g8.utoronto.ca/scholar/germain2001/Germain_G20. pdf (accessed February 2010).

Kirton, J. (2001a). 'The G20: Representativeness, Effectiveness and Leadership in Global Governance.' *Guiding Global Order: G8 Governance in the Twenty-First Century*, ed. J. Kirton, J. Daniels et al. Aldershot: Ashgate.

Kirton, J. (2001b). 'Guiding Global Economic Governance: The G20, the G7 and the International Monetary Fund at Century's Dawn'. *New Directions in Global Economic Governance: Managing Globalisation in the Twenty-First Century*, ed. J. J. Kirton and G. M. von Furstenberg. Aldershot: Ashgate.

Kirton, J. (2005). 'Toward Multilateral Reform: The G20's Contribution'. *Reforming Multilateral Institutions from the Top: A Leaders 20 Summit*, ed. J. English, R. Thakur et al. Tokyo: United Nations University Press.

Kirton, J. (2008). 'Prospects for the G20 Leaders Summit on Financial Markets and the World Economy'. *The G20 Leaders Summit on Financial Markets and the World Economy*, ed. J. Kirton. Toronto: G20 Research Group. Available at www.g20.utoronto.ca/g20leadersbook/g20leaders-kirton-081111.pdf (accessed February 2010).

Kirton, J. (2009). 'Coexistence, Cooperation, Competition: G Summits', *Aspenia* 43–4: 156–62.

Kirton, J. (2010). 'The G20 Finance Ministers: Network Governance'. *Rising States, Rising Institutions: The Challenge of Global Governance*, ed. A. S. Alexandroff and A. F. Cooper. Washington, DC: Brookings Institution Press.

Kirton, J., and J. Guebert (2009). 'A Summit of Substantial Success: The Performance of the G20 in Washington in 2008'. G20 Research Group. Available at www.g20.utoronto.ca/analysis/2008performance090307. pdf (accessed February 2010).

Martin, P. (2008). 'Time for the G20 to Take the Mantle from the G8'. *Growth, Innovation, Inclusion: The G20 at Ten*, ed. J. Kirton and M. Koch. London: Newsdesk Communications.

Martinez-Diaz, L. (2007). *The G20 after Eight Years: How Effective a Vehicle for Developing-Country Influence?* (Global Economy and Development Working Paper no. 12). Washington, DC: Brookings Institution Press. Available at www.brookings.edu/papers/2007/1017development.aspx (accessed February 2010).

Porter, T. (2000). 'The G7, the Financial Stability Forum, the G20 and the Politics of International Financial Regulation'. Paper presented at the annual convention of the International Studies Association, Los Angeles, 15 March. Available at www.g8.utoronto.ca/g20/biblio/porter-isa-2000.pdf (accessed February 2010).

Samans, R., M. Uzan et al. (2007). 'The International Monetary Convention Project: A Public–Private Exploration of the Future of the International Monetary System'. *The International Monetary System, the IMF and the G20: A Great Transformation in the Making?* ed. R. Samans, M. Uzan et al. Houndmills: Palgrave Macmillan.

Slaughter, A.-M. (2000). 'Governing the Global Economy through Government Networks'. *The Role of Law in International Politics: Essays in International Relations and International Law*, ed. M. Byers. Oxford: Oxford University Press.

Slaughter, A.-M. (2004). *A New World Order*. Princeton: Princeton University Press.

Slaughter, A.-M. (2009). 'America's Edge'. *Foreign Affairs* 88(1): 94–113.

Slaughter, A.-M., and T. Hale (2010). 'Transgovernmental Networks and Emerging Powers'. *Rising States, Rising Institutions: The Challenge of Global Governance*, ed. A. S. Alexandroff and A. F. Cooper. Washington, DC: Brookings Institution Press.

Soederberg, S. (2002). 'On the Contradictions of the New International Financial Architecture: Another Procrustean Bed for Emerging Market Economies?' *Third World Quarterly* 23(4): 607–20.

Sohn, I. (2005). 'Asian Financial Cooperation: The Problem of Legitimacy in Global Financial Governance'. *Global Governance* 11 (October–December): 487–504.

Taylor, I. (2005). 'South Africa: Beyond the Impasse in Global Governance'. *Reforming Multilateral Institutions from the Top: A Leaders 20 Summit*, ed. J. English, R. Thakur and A. F. Cooper. Tokyo: United Nations University Press.

6

Global Forum on Transparency and Exchange of Information for Tax Purposes
Tony Porter and Verónica Rubio Vega

The Global Forum on Transparency and Exchange of Information for Tax Purposes (GFTEITP), established in 2000 by the Organisation for Economic Co-operation and Development (OECD), had by 2010 become the primary transnational venue for combating tax evasion. Tax evasion is a huge public policy problem. An estimated $6.2 trillion is held offshore by wealthy individuals from developing countries, resulting in tax losses to those countries of $64–124 billion per year, potentially exceeding the $103 billion per year that developing countries receive in foreign aid (Oxfam 2009). Developed countries similarly experience massive tax losses: the US government has estimated that tax havens cost $123–153 billion in forgone tax revenue annually (Addison 2009: 707). The combination of the globalization of finance and the persistence of the sovereign state system has made control of tax evasion extraordinarily difficult. Yet, as OECD Secretary-General Angel Gurría stated in his 2009 address to the GFTEITP in Mexico City, a meeting at which the institutionalization of the GFTEITP took a dramatic step forward: 'What has happened in the tax area over the past 10 months is nothing less than a revolution! . . . The threshold of tolerance for tax evasion has dropped to zero.' The GFTEITP is interesting not just for its important practical effects in combating tax evasion, but also for what it can tell us about transnational governance innovation. Five lessons stand out.

Network Structure

First, the GFTEITP is a quintessential example of a transnational policy network, using policy instruments such as best-practice standards, and yet it has been remarkably effective – challenging more traditional state-centric perspectives that see only the more formally organized structures of states, intergovernmental organizations or treaty law as having any significance. The OECD has been a pioneer of some of the organizational innovations that have now become widespread in transnational governance. These include peer review, the fostering of informal transnational interactions among officials, and the creation of mechanisms to include nongovernmental actors such as business and labour, all of which have been part of the OECD since its founding in 1961. More recently the OECD has sought to strengthen its relations with actors other than its member states by sponsoring Global Forums, networks devoted to disseminating best practices in various policy areas. The GFTEITP operated as one such Global Forum from 2000 to 2009, when it was further institutionalized. It developed international standards, especially the Model Agreement on Exchange of Information on Tax Purposes in 2002. For many years the OECD and the GFTEITP have put pressure on countries to accept standards on transparency and exchange of information by creating lists of compliant and non-compliant jurisdictions. These reports have become more detailed and specific over time, covering 87 countries by 2009, and compliance has increased significantly. By 2009 over 100 tax information exchange agreements had been signed and dozens more were under negotiation (Gurría 2009). All 87 jurisdictions surveyed had committed to the internationally agreed tax standard, but 22 jurisdictions, from Andorra to Uruguay, had not yet substantially implemented it. However, even many of those were moving quickly toward compliance.

The meeting in Mexico in 2009, attended by 178 delegates from over 70 jurisdictions and international organizations, dramatically strengthened the GFTEITP. Delegates agreed to make the organization more independent from the OECD, to establish self-financing mechanisms based on member contributions, to invite new members committed to implementing its standards, and to establish a Steering Group, a permanent secretariat (which the OECD will host) and a Peer Review Group to develop plans for mandatory peer reviews with publication and follow-up, providing the GFTEITP with a more institutionalized structure than the other Global Forums. While seeking consensus, the peer review process will aim to ensure 'that no one jurisdiction can block the adoption or publication of a review' (OECD Council 2009a: 2). The GFTEITP's own decision to institutionalize itself was reinforced by a Decision of the OECD Council establishing the GFTEITP in its new form on a three-year basis (OECD Council 2009b).

Legitimacy and Inclusion

The second lesson from the GFTEITP experience is how its greater attentiveness to legitimacy and inclusion than previous OECD initiatives has contributed to its success. Beginning in the 1990s, the OECD, building on its long experience in tax issues, began to become heavily involved in addressing tax evasion and 'harmful tax competition'. The early initiatives provoked harsh criticisms from offshore centres, especially in the Caribbean, which argued that tax policies were the sovereign prerogative of each individual state. The offshore centres accused the OECD of hypocrisy for targeting them when many OECD countries had similar tax policies. This criticism, combined with the G. W. Bush administration's hostility toward the idea of harmful tax competition and the legacy of the OECD's reputation as a club of wealthy states, seriously hindered the OECD's campaign. However, in sponsoring the GFTEITP the OECD was careful to integrate developing country actors and issues, for instance stressing the damage done by tax evasion in the global South and the need to help developing country tax administrations with capacity building. The Steering Group and Peer Review Group of the GFTEITP include non-OECD countries as Vice-Chairs. This inclusiveness is an important ingredient of the GFTEITP's success.

Continuing Role of the State and Intergovernmental Organizations

The third lesson from the GFTEITP experience is that, despite the GFTEITP's networked character, state power and traditional institutions are still important – but in interaction with the relatively informal GFTEITP. The OECD is a formal intergovernmental organization (IGO) with powerful member states, and its initial support for the GFTEITP was crucial. The changes from Clinton to Bush to Obama had a large impact on the governance of transnational tax matters, reflecting the ongoing power of the US. The G-20's strong endorsement of the GFTEITP's work bolstered it, especially when the G-20 leaders' meeting in April 2009 agreed to 'develop a toolbox of effective counter measures' such as imposing stricter requirements on transactions with non-cooperative jurisdictions, and tying foreign aid and investment policies to compliance with GFTEITP standards. This stance was reinforced later in the year in Pittsburgh, where the G-20 stated they 'stand ready to use countermeasures against tax havens from March 2010'. This greatly increased the effectiveness of the threat that powerful states could take measures to penalize transactions with non-cooperative jurisdictions.

The significance of differentials in power is evident not just in the pressure on small tax havens to comply, but also in the unfortunate asymmetry of specific provisions of the standards. The standards require countries to sign twelve or more tax information exchange agreements to be compliant, and since these have tended to be bilateral they favour powerful countries that have a greater capacity to negotiate favourable agreements.

However, all these examples of power politics are either mitigated by or entangled with other more transnational aspects of the GFTEITP. Although the OECD is a formal IGO, the GFTEITP itself is a network involving many types of actors. As such, powerful states do not always get their way. For example, changes in the US administration affected transnational tax governance but not decisively – the OECD's work continued even during the Bush years (Ault 2009: 770–2). The GFTEITP involves commitments that work against power differentials, such as explicit commitments to 'ensure that its members participate on an equal footing' (OECD Council 2009a: 1), and to assist weaker states with capacity building.

Crisis and Innovation

The fourth lesson is how the GFTEITP experience reinforces the long-recognized connection between crisis and policy innovation, since the global economic crisis of 2008 played an important part in the strengthening of global commitments against tax evasion. In addition to the enhanced opportunities for mobilizing political support for structural change that are typical in crises of all types, there were more specific effects of this crisis. Governments were facing extraordinarily difficult fiscal challenges in having to reduce the debt incurred by stimulus spending at a time when their economic recoveries were fragile. Popular anger at bank bailouts and bonuses had focused attention on the perceived unfairness of the relationship between personal incomes and corporate revenues, on the one hand, and fiscal policy on the other. As the G-8 leaders noted in their July 2009 Declaration: 'In this difficult time, the protection of our tax base and the efforts to combat tax fraud and tax evasion are all the more important, especially given the extraordinary fiscal measures adopted to stabilize the world economy and the need to ensure that economic activity is conducted in a fair and transparent manner.' Although the crisis had not originated in the offshore centres, their lack of transparency and light regulation were easy to connect rhetorically with the crucial role that these had played in bringing about the crisis. All these aspects of the crisis greatly increased the political pressures supporting the strengthening of the GFTEITP.

Future Reforms

The fifth lesson is that, while weaknesses persist in the GFTEITP, its organizational form has certain advantages in addressing these. The major weakness in the standards is the requirement that tax authorities requesting information from another jurisdiction must have a good documented reason to suspect an individual or firm and must limit their request to that case. This has been characterized by the OECD (2009: 13) as prohibiting 'fishing expeditions'. However, this compromise greatly weakens the regime since tax evasion usually involves concealment of exactly the type of information that the authorities would need to document suspicions sufficiently to request assistance.

At the same time, the organizational character of the GFTEITP provides opportunities for further innovation to address these weaknesses. The GFTEITP and the institutions associated with it have produced a subtle alteration in shared transnational norms about tax sovereignty (Christians 2009). Much as in other issue areas, such as the environment or war crimes, there is an emergent understanding that states have responsibilities to the global community and to citizens in other states that go beyond their obligation to not interfere with the sovereignty of other states. The character of the GFTEITP will allow this emergent understanding to be strengthened more effectively than treaty negotiations and other more formalized mechanisms, which tend to freeze existing understandings. Additionally, the flexibility of the GFTEITP provides opportunities for sub-sets of states to go beyond existing standards and require higher standards for their own taxpayers, thereby putting upward pressure on the global standards (Kudrle 2009). Finally, forward momentum is evident in the GFTEITP, for instance in its commitment to continue to expand the number of agreements on the exchange of tax information, including through the development of new types of unilateral and multilateral measures, in addition to the bilateral ones that initially were most important. Moreover, the OECD has made clear that a jurisdiction cannot simply stop at the minimum twelve bilateral agreements to be compliant but must 'continue to sign agreements even after it has reached this threshold' (OECD 2009: 10).

References

Addison, T. V. (2009). 'Shooting Blanks: The War on Tax Havens'. *Indiana Journal of Global Legal Studies* 16(2, Summer): 703–27.

Ault, H. J. (2009). 'Reflections on the Role of the OECD in Developing International Tax Norms'. *Brooklyn Journal of International Law* 34: 757–81.

Christians, A. (2009). 'Sovereignty, Taxation and the Social Contract'. *Minnesota Journal of International Law* 18(Winter): 99–143.

Gurría, A. (2009). 'Remarks at the Global Forum on Transparency and Exchange of Information'. Available at www.oecd.org/document/7/0,33

43,en_2649_33745_43596999_1_1__1_1,00.html (accessed 17 December 2009).

Kudrle, R. T. (2009). 'Ending the Tax Haven Scandal'. *Economy Journal* 9(3): 1–11.

OECD (2009). 'Overview of the OECD's Work on Countering International Tax Evasion: A Background Brief'. Available at www.oecd.org/dataoecd/32/45/43757434.pdf (accessed 17 December 2009).

OECD Council (2009a). 'Summary of Outcomes of the Meeting of the Global Forum on Transparency and Exchange of Information for Tax Purposes Held in Mexico on 1–2 September 2009'. Available at www.oecd.org/dataoecd/44/39/43610626.pdf (accessed 17 December 2009).

OECD Council (2009b). 'Decision of the Council Establishing the Global Forum on Transparency and Exchange of Information for Tax Purposes'. Available at www.olis.oecd.org/olis/2009doc.nsf/ENGDATCORPLOOK/NT00004F8E/$FILE/JT03270334.PDF (accessed 17 December 2009).

Oxfam (2009). 'Tax Haven Crackdown Could Deliver $120 Bn a Year to Fight Poverty'. Available at www.oxfam.org/pressroom/pressrelease/2009-03-13/tax-haven-could-deliver-120bn-year-fight-poverty (accessed 24 February 2010).

7

International Accounting Standards Board
Andreas Nölke

Overview

As of 2005, all listed companies within the European Union (EU) have had to base their accounts on International Financial Reporting Standards (IFRS). Since 2008, these standards have also been accepted by the US regulators. Beside the twenty-seven EU member states, about ninety other countries use IFRS. These standards are devised by the International Accounting Standards Board (IASB), a private organization with fifteen full-time members that is located in London and directed as well as funded by the International Accounting Standards Committee Foundation (IASCF), a private company registered in the US state of Delaware. The IASCF is traditionally financed by the Big Four accounting companies (PricewaterhouseCoopers, KPMG, Deloitte & Touche, and Ernst & Young), although the IASCF funding basis has become much broader during the last few years. The IASB features some interesting procedural innovations. It publishes drafts of its proposed accounting standards as well as other programmatic documents on its homepage, usually for ninety days. During this period everyone can submit a comment letter that will be published on the IASB site and will be taken as an input in the deliberative process within the IASB committee network. All meetings of the IASB, as well as most meetings of the IASCF bodies, are held in public and are webcast. Every five years, the IASCF Trustees have to undertake a formal public review of its Constitution.

Given that IFRS replace public regulations in many countries – in Germany, for example, the accounting standards contained in the *Handelsgesetzbuch* – we may consider this recent development as one of the most wide-ranging delegations of public authority to a private body within international politics. Like securities and corporate governance principles, IFRS are one of the twelve Standards for Sound Financial Systems overseen by the Financial Stability Board.

Development

From the perspective of innovations in transnational governance, the IASB somewhat surprisingly has been able to develop nearly globally accepted norms, whereas several earlier attempts by more established international organizations such as the United Nations and the European Union failed. A number of authors have highlighted the institutional entrepreneurship of the International Accounting Standards Committee / IASC, the predecessor of the IASB, within this process. In 1973, the IASC was initially formed to ease British accession to the European Union. British accounting bodies were afraid that accession would lead to a transfer of continental standards to the UK (Hopwood 1994: 243). While this fear never materialized (the EU accounting directives became a mixture of British and German features; Katsikas 2008: 137), the IASC still gradually strengthened its position, most notably by concluding agreements with institutional partners (Martinez-Diaz 2005). These partners include the International Federation of Accountants / IFAC (1982) and the International Organization of Securities Commissions / IOSCO (1995), as well as the members of the Financial Stability Board. The endorsement by IOSCO and, later, by other international organizations (IOs) such as the World Bank and the IMF were crucial steps in the rise of the IASB toward becoming a nearly global standard-setter (Martinez-Diaz 2005). For these IOs, the empowerment of the IASC/IASB proved to be an effective way of reaching their regulatory targets.

Two other key players behind the rise of the IASC/IASB were the US Securities and Exchange Commission (SEC) and the European Union. While the European Union cemented this process with its endorsement of IASB standards as a formal requirement for listed European companies, it was the SEC that had a major influence on the early structures and procedures of the IASC/IASB (Martinez-Diaz 2005; Katsikas 2008). While some suggested the IASB be based on equal representation of its most important geographic constituencies, it has instead been modelled according to the US Financial Accounting Standards Board (FASB), which prioritizes independence and technical skills. Although not all officials were entirely happy with the US blueprint for the work of the IASB, the EU was nervous that more and more European corporations would follow the lead of Daimler-Benz and shift to the US Generally Accepted Accounting Principles (GAAP) because the adoption of these standards are a basic pre-condition for being listed on the US stock exchange (Katsikas 2008: 154). In order not to become a pure regulation-taker, the European Commission rather preferred to adopt IASB, and to retain a minimum influence (Dewing and Russell 2004: 293–4).

Competition over Standards

Although the EU has provided a crucial endorsement for the IASB, both its mode of operation and the substance of its accounting standards are strongly influenced by Anglo-Saxon models. Here we can juxtapose Continental European and Anglo-Saxon modes of accounting standard setting. The Anglo-Saxon mode, as exemplified by the US FASB, is based on private professional expertise, whereas the European mode relies on national representation and an important role for public actors. These competing models led to a major confrontation between the SEC and the European Commission over the constitution of the IASB (Martinez-Diaz 2005: 19). In the end, the IASB has moved clearly toward a US model, as demonstrated by an institutional analysis of the 2000 and 2005 constitutional changes within the IASB (Botzem 2008).

From this perspective, the 2000 constitutional reform of the IASB was based on the Anglo-American approach of self-regulation, strongly resembling the US FASB. Furthermore, the reform replaced a part-time decision-making body that was geared toward representation of the different strands of the profession with an expert-driven organization that is only open to those with the necessary analytical resources, particularly those with experience within one of the Big Four auditing firms.

Correspondingly, an analysis of all comment letters between 1 April 2002 and 5 August 2004 – a total of 1,910 letters written by 900 organizations and individuals – demonstrated a clear bias in representation. The most prominent actors were the Big Four accounting firms. In general, the comment letter process is dominated by corporations from the financial sector, whereas non-financial corporations play a minor role. The only active international organization is IOSCO. Moreover, social groups such as labour do not participate at all (Perry and Nölke 2005). A similar picture evolves from a network analysis of IASB committee memberships. Again, the Big Four occupy the most central positions, accompanied by influential financial sector actors and the complete absence of broad social constituencies such as labour. In terms of nationality, organizations with a background in the United Kingdom are most prominently represented, amplified by the predominantly Anglo-Saxon character of the Big Four (Perry and Nölke 2005). These observations are also broadly in line with other recent studies on the decision-making within the IASB. Other authors highlight the dominance of representatives from Anglo-Saxon countries (Botzem 2008) and of IOs that are close to the preferences held by these representatives (Dewing and Russell 2007).

Impact

Globally accepted accounting standards clearly indicate a major problem-solving contribution, since they substantially ease financial transactions across borders. In contrast to many other cases of transnational private governance, such as corporate social responsibility schemes, IASB norms are not only very broadly accepted, but also comprehensively implemented and enforced (although the latter relies on public authority). However, the substantive impact of the evolution of global accounting standards is more controversial (Perry and Nölke 2006). In particular, the Fair Value approach to accounting as utilized by the IASB has come under fire. Fair Value accounting, in contrast to the Historical Cost accounting traditionally prevailing in Continental Western Europe, values an asset according to its current market price. On the one hand, the Fair Value approach strongly favours a short-term-investor perspective toward the corporation, conflicting with the more prudent long-term perspective of lenders and management in Continental Western Europe. Moreover, Fair Value accounting of current market prices has significantly contributed to the severity of the 2008–9 sub-prime crisis, since it forced banks and other companies to write down their assets, frequently forcing them to emergency sales, and thereby leading to additional write-downs. The IASB, however, has so far been unwilling to revise its stance on Fair Value, and instead proposes only minor modifications to the standards that determine the value of financial assets (Nölke 2009). However, one result of the sub-prime crisis was the creation of a Monitoring Board that links the IASCF Trustees to a number of public capital market authorities. Whether this modification substantially increases public oversight over the private IASB remains to be seen.

References

Botzem, S. (2008). 'Transnational Expert-driven Standardization: Accountancy Governance from a Professional Point of View'. *Transnational Private Governance and its Limits*, ed. J.-C. Graz and A. Nölke. London and New York: Routledge.

Dewing, I. P., and P. O. Russell (2004). 'Accounting, Auditing and Corporate Governance of European Listed Companies: EU Policy Developments before and after Enron'. *Journal of Common Market Studies* 42(2): 289–319.

Dewing, I. P., and P O. Russell (2007). 'The Role of Private Actors in Global Governance and Regulation: US, European and International Convergence of Accounting and Auditing Standards in a Post-Enron World'. *The Politics of Corporate Governance Regulation* (Routledge/RIPE Studies in Global Political Economy), ed. A. Nölke, H. Overbeek et al. London and New York: Routledge.

Godfrey, J M., and K. Chalmers, eds. (2007). *Globalisation of Accounting Standards*. Cheltenham: Edward Elgar.

Hopwood, A. (1994). 'Some Reflections on "The Harmonization of Accounting within the EU"'. *European Accounting Review* 3(2): 241–52.

Katsikas, D. (2008). 'Transnational Regulatory Authority and Global Economic Governance'. Thesis submitted for the Degree of Ph.D. in International Relations, London School of Economics.

Martinez-Diaz, L. (2005). 'Strategic Experts and Improvising Regulators: Explaining the IASC's Rise to Global Influence, 1973–2001'. *Business and Politics* 7(4): Article 3.

Nölke, A. (2009). 'The Politics of Accounting Regulation: Responses to the Subprime Crisis'. *Global Finance in Crisis. The Politics of International Regulatory Change*, ed. E. Helleiner, S. Pagliari et al. London and New York: Routledge.

Perry, J., and A. Nölke (2005). 'International Accounting Standard Setting: A Network Perspective'. *Business and Politics* 7(3): 1–32.

Perry, J., and A. Nölke (2006). 'The Political Economy of International Accounting Standards'. *Review of International Political Economy* 13(4): 559–86.

8

International Association of Insurance Supervisors
Donato Masciandaro[1]

Introduction

Established in 1994, the International Association of Insurance Supervisors (IAIS) is an international forum for supervisors of the insurance industry that aims to set global standards in this field. Until roughly twenty years ago, the international shape of the insurance supervisory architecture was considered irrelevant. Since then, financial market development and the growing importance of insurance – as well as securities and pension fund sectors – have made supervision of non-bank financial intermediaries, as well as the investor protection dimension of supervision, increasingly important.

The international forum for insurance supervision was born in a period of intense reform. In the last two decades, many countries have reformed the structure of their financial regulation. If we consider a dataset with 102 countries belonging to all continents from 1998 to 2009, 69 per cent of the countries included in the sample chose to reform their financial supervisory structure (Masciandaro and Quintyn 2009). The trend of reforms is even more evident when we add a regional and country-income perspective. Providing a breakdown by country groups, the result shows that the European, the EU and OECD countries make up, respectively, 82 per cent, 77 per cent and 73 per cent of the countries that have undertaken reforms.

The first ten years of the IAIS's history were mainly dedicated to building up the structure of the organization, which largely reflects the close interconnection of the IAIS with similar standard-setting bodies and with international fora in the financial sector. The IAIS standards have become a globally recognized cornerstone for the insurance sector, widely utilized also by other institutions, including the IMF and the World Bank, when assessing financial systems across the world. By 2003, with the issuance of revised standards, the essential regulatory framework was developed. Since then a major effort has been made to implement the rules set by the IAIS. Because IAIS

[1] The author wishes to thank Antonio Riso for helpful assistance in collecting information.

instruments are not legally binding, providing assistance to those members which need it to comply correctly with the standards has been an issue of particular importance.

History

The IAIS was founded in 1993 at a Chicago meeting of insurance supervisory officials from fifty-three countries, it was then established in 1994 as a non-profit association under Swiss law, and its secretariat has been hosted by the Bank of International Settlements, in Basel, since 1998 (IAIS 2009).

The stated objectives of the IAIS are: (a) to contribute to improved supervision of the insurance industry for the protection of policy holders; (b) to promote the development of well-regulated insurance markets; (c) to contribute to global financial stability (IAIS 2009). This last objective was added in 1999 after the creation of the Financial Stability Forum.

The IAIS membership has broadened its coverage since the foundation and now covers 97 per cent of the world's insurance premiums across some 190 jurisdictions in 140 countries.[2] Moreover, since 1999, subjects other than regulators and supervisors – currently more than 120 – have been admitted to the IAIS as Observers, including industry associations, professional associations, insurers and reinsurers, consultants and international financial institutions.[3]

Full Membership is, however, reserved only to domestic insurance supervisors. The IAIS holds an Annual Conference where supervisors, industry representatives and other professionals discuss developments in the insurance sector and topics affecting insurance regulation. Moreover, the IAIS develops training materials and organizes a

---

[2] IAIS (2009). The reason for this discrepancy is that in the US insurance regulation is a state competence, and therefore there are fifty separate jurisdictions. The National Association of Insurance Commissioners (NAIC) is merely a voluntary federation of the fifty separate Commissions or Superintendencies.

[3] International institutions having the status of Observer are: the Asian Development Bank (ADB), the Association of Mutual Insurers and Insurance Cooperatives (AMICE), the Comité Européen des Assurances (CEA), the Federación Interamericana de Empresas de Seguros (FIDES), the International Actuarial Association (IAA), the International Insurance Foundation (IIF), the International Cooperative and Mutual Insurance Federation, the Institute of International Finance (IIF), the Geneva Association, the World Federation of Insurance Intermediaries (WFII).

number of training programmes and regional training seminars for insurance supervisors.

The IAIS closely cooperates with other financial sector standard-setting bodies and international organizations to promote financial stability. In 1996, IAIS, the International Organization of Securities Commissions and the Basel Committee established under their aegis the Joint Forum for the purpose of facilitating the exchange of information between supervisors within their own sectors, enhancing supervisory coordination, and developing principles for a more effective supervision of financial conglomerates.[4]

The IAIS has also been a member of the Financial Stability Board (FSB) – previously the Financial Stability Forum (FSF) – since its foundation in 1999. The arrival of the FSF had a broader impact on the activity of the IAIS; its standards and codes began to be used by the IMF in its Financial Sector Assessment Programs (FSAPs), and the IAIS contributes to assessments of jurisdictions' observance of standards in close collaboration with the IMF and World Bank.

The FSF report of April 2008 on Enhancing Market and Institutional Resilience contains a series of recommendations which ask the IAIS to focus its work on three main areas identified as critical to the IAIS and its members: monocline insurers and financial guarantors, risk disclosures, and international colleges of supervisors. The IAIS conducted surveys on these issues, which will be used to determine future standard-setting and to put initiatives in place in these areas (IAIS 2008).

Within the solvency and accounting area the IAIS also closely cooperates with the International Accounting Standards Board (IASB), monitoring developments and providing input. The IAIS also recently conducted a survey jointly with the OECD and the World Bank in the area of corporate governance (IAIS 2008). Finally, the IAIS continuously cooperates with other international organizations such as the Financial Stability Institute (FSI), the FIRST Initiative, the Geneva Association, the International Insurance Foundation, and the Toronto Centre.

Structure

The governance structure of the IAIS is founded on three main organs: (a) the General Meeting of the Members, (b) the Executive Committee, (c) the Secretariat.

[4]For more details on the Basel Committee and the Joint Forum, refer to chapters 2 and 12.

The ultimate authority is held by the General Meeting, which is presided over by the Chair of the Executive Committee. Convened at least once a year, it is open to all Members and Observers; however, the Executive Committee may restrict part of the proceedings to Members only. Essential decisions such as those concerning the structure of the Association (e.g. the amendment of the By-laws) and those regarding the adoption of Principles, Standards and Guidance are taken by the Meeting with a two-thirds majority vote, whereas a simple majority is required for other decisions, including those on applications for participation in the Association and on the membership status.

The Executive Committee is elected by the General Meeting and is composed of nine to twenty-four voting members,[5] chosen from people employed by the Members of the IAIS. It is responsible for the sound functioning and the furtherance of the objectives of the Association; it prepares amendments to the By-laws, calls General Meetings, prepares the programme of activities of the Association and the Annual Report, and recommends to the General Meeting decisions concerning the business and affairs of the Association. The Executive Committee is supported by the Technical Committee, the Implementation Committee, and the Budget Committee, each of them forming subcommittees and working parties to accomplish their objectives.

The Technical Committee is the core structure of the Association, since it develops international principles, standards, guidance and other documents related to insurance supervision through its subcommittees. The Implementation Committee works on issues related to assistance in implementation of IAIS Principles, Standards and Guidance; it, in particular, supports emerging markets in establishing sound insurance regulatory and supervisory systems. The Budget Committee proposes an annual budget and annual fees for Members and Observers to the Executive Committee, and reports periodically to the latter on the financial situation of the Association. There is also an Audit Committee which reviews the internal controls of the Association and monitors whether its activities achieve their objectives through effective and efficient operations and are compliant with applicable procedures and resolutions. The Secretariat carries out any other task which is needed to facilitate the smooth operation of the association.

---

[5] The Chair of the Technical Committee, the Chair of the Implementation Committee and the Chair of the Budget Committee are non-voting members when they are not members with voting rights already.

Operation

The main objective of the IAIS is to set out a Framework for Insurance Supervisors consisting of a series of non-binding instruments (Principles, Standards and Guidance papers) which represent best practices, or targets, for supervisors, that can be implemented in a flexible manner depending on the circumstances within each jurisdiction.

These instruments concern the 'preconditions' (Level 1 of the Framework) – i.e. the basic principles for the effective functioning of the insurance supervisory authority – the regulatory requirements (financial requirements, and those relating to governance and market conduct: Level 2), and the supervisory action (supervisory assessment and intervention: Level 3).

Principles identify areas in which the insurance supervisor should have authority or control and cover basic rules which need to be in place in order for a supervisory system to be effective. They are the basis of Standards, which focus instead on specific issues and describe best practices. Some are directly aimed to supervisory authorities, whereas others describe the practices that a well-managed insurer should follow and thereby assist supervisors in assessing the practices that companies in their jurisdictions have in place. Guidance papers are designed in addition to Principles and Standards to assist supervisors and raise the effectiveness of supervision.

The basic framework for insurance supervision is shaped in the Insurance Core Principles and Methodology (ICPs), formulated in 1997 and revised in October 2003. It contains twenty-eight essential Principles that need to be in place for a supervisory system to be effective, divided into eight main areas. Another important set of principles is contained in the Insurance Concordat, approved in 1997 and amended in 1999, which aims to improve the supervision of internationally active insurance companies, stating that authorization involving cross-border activities should be subject to consultation between the relevant supervisors, and that provision should be made for external audits and for information sharing.

After having developed the ICPs and other key Principles and Standards, since 2002 the IAIS has mainly focused on four areas. A special effort has been made with respect to capital adequacy and solvency, one example being the Principles on Capital Adequacy and Solvency of January 2002, in which fourteen Principles were elaborated for evaluating the solvency of life and non-life insurance undertakings.

The lack of a common standard for capital adequacy and solvency requirements by which insurers could be measured induced the IAIS to work toward convergence between different jurisdictions. The IAIS has worked on this issue in close cooperation with the European Commission, the IAA, the Basel Committee, the OECD and the World Bank. Consistency is also essential for insurers, reinsurers and other stakeholders in the field of accounting, where the IAIS approach in setting a common basis for regulatory reporting by insurers has been coordinated with IASB Standards. A third area in which the IAIS has focused its activity of standard-setting is reinsurance, a sector which has been not sufficiently supervised up until now in many jurisdictions. Finally, Standards in the field of transparency and disclosure were also set by the IAIS. It should be noted that the IAIS has also started working on the areas of anti-money laundering and the financing of terrorism.

So far seventeen Standards have been issued by the IAIS on different issues, mainly with the aim of describing the best practices of compliance with the underlying Principles and Standards. Guidance papers are mainly used by the IAIS, in addition to Principles and Standards, as an instrument to assist supervisors to raise the effectiveness of their system. They mainly provide guidance for compliance with Principles and Standards; some of them also offer models for enhancing cooperation among supervisors.

With the aim of fostering coordination and information sharing among insurance supervisors, the IAIS also drafted in February 2007 a Multilateral Memorandum of Understanding (MMoU) which covers all issues related to the supervision of insurance companies where cross-border aspects arise; it must be observed, though, that the signatories of the MMoU are currently only six.[6]

Impact

The implementation of Principles and Standards by the members of the IAIS is a crucial question for the organization's effectiveness. Since the above-mentioned instruments are not legally binding, members are responsible for compliance within their jurisdictions. Data provided by the IAIS regarding compliance are unfortunately partial and incomplete due to the irregular nature of the

---

[6] Australia Prudential Regulation Authority, Australia; Bermuda Monetary Authority, Bermuda; Financial Supervisory Commission, Chinese Taipei; Autorité de Contrôle des Assurances et des Mutuelles, France; Bundesanstalt für Finanzdienstleistungsaufsicht (BaFin), Germany; De Nederlandsche Bank, the Netherlands. Information current as of November 2009.

control on the implementation of its instruments, i.e. Principles and Standards.

The most important initiative, in this respect, is the ICPs self-assessment programme, which was initiated in October 2000. The exercise is conducted by each member of the IAIS in its jurisdiction, and is based on the Assessment Methodology, a document produced by the IAIS to assist the assessor in performing the task. Accordingly, each ICP is accompanied by a set of essential and advanced criteria, on whose basis the assessment is carried out.

The most recent survey on the results of this exercise is the *Report on Insurance Core Principles Self-Assessment Exercise 2004/2005* (IAIS 2006b), of February 2006. Fifty-eight members completed their self-assessment on observance of the ICPs as of 1 December 2005, representing about two-thirds of the jurisdictions involved in the IAIS at that time[7] and providing a quite representative (although not statistically valid) sample.

Some key findings to note: among the respondents there were more integrated supervisors compared to the previous self-assessment of 2001.[8] The finding reflects a general trend: in the 1990s an increasing number of countries have consolidated supervisory responsibilities, which has resulted in the establishment of unified supervisors in a number of countries (Masciandaro and Quintyn 2009).

Thirty nine jurisdictions out of fifty-eight reported a high level of observance with IAIS Insurance Core Principles, all twenty-eight Principles having been observed (or largely observed) by eight jurisdictions, and twenty-five or more Principles having been observed by thirty-one jurisdictions (Masciandaro and Quintyn 2009).

The most interesting finding, perhaps, is that several respondents have suggested that technical assistance is necessary to enable them to implement the ICPs. However, the IAIS states in the same report that it does not have the means to meet these requests, and therefore sought assistance for this matter from the IMF and World Bank, without receiving any commitment from them up until the report's publication.

Another important source for the overall assessment of the most important instrument issued by the IAIS, the ICPs, is provided by the Financial Sector Assessment Program (FSAP) conducted on a country basis jointly by the IMF and the World Bank. Assessment of the

---

[7] The NAIC took part in the self-assessment exercise on behalf of the fifty US jurisdictions.

[8] Unfortunately this statement is not supported by any numerical evidence. See IAIS (2006b: 8).

insurance supervisory system began in 1999 and is based on the evaluation of the ICPs, which is then integrated in Fund surveillance through the Financial System Stability Assessment (FSSA) and the Reports on the Observance of Standards and Codes (ROSCs).

Three documents on the overall experience with this assessment exercise were produced by the IMF and the World Bank in 2001, 2003 and 2005; they can be useful in providing some other details on the implementation of the ICPs and its progress.

The findings of the first report, in which twenty ICP assessments had been completed, showed some weaknesses in meeting the preconditions for effective insurance supervision, divergent accounting and actuarial practices, and the absence of internationally acceptable standards relating to capital. Also, transparency practices followed by insurance supervisors needed strengthening, according to the assessors. It was recalled, though, that in many countries, including some industrial ones, effective insurance regulation had emerged only in the 1980s, and that international cooperation among insurance supervisors began only ten years later.

However, it must be highlighted that the stage of development of the insurance sector in the assessed countries varied substantially, and the degree of observance of the ICPs also changed accordingly, being significantly higher in those countries having a more developed insurance sector than in those having a less developed one. Another interesting finding was that the self-assessment consistently gave supervisors better marks than the IMF and World Bank assessments. As of December 2002, forty-five assessments had taken place, which still revealed common weaknesses in a number of areas. The 2005 report is of particular importance, since it was produced after the revision of the ICPs in 2003 and because it still represents the most complete survey with respect to the overall implementation of these insurance standards at a global level. At that moment a weaker level of observance of international standards than in the banking sector could still be observed. However, differences in the level of observance emerged across the Principles, the major weaknesses being in the areas of organization of the supervisor and asset risk management.

Besides these surveys on the ICPs' implementation the IAIS has also conducted surveys on the implementation of other standards, in the areas of cross-border and cross-sector cooperation and information exchange (2005), implementation of International Financial Reporting Standards (IFRS – 2006), preventing, detecting and remedying fraud in insurance (2007) and disclosure standards (2008). A general impression which may be derived from the analysis of these reports is that there is still a broad difference among countries in respect of the level of implementation of the international standards, and that much effort is still required in this respect, in particular in emerging markets.

Conclusion

In conclusion, it must be noticed that the process of internationalization of the insurance industry has noticeably increased the role of the IAIS and its function of standard-setting. In today's global market, international regulatory efforts start directly at the international level, so that a top-down approach is gradually replacing the former bottom-up process of regulation. Several areas have been deeply influenced by this process of internationalization.

As noted above, from the first MoUs in 1997 to the more recent MMoU, supervisors have found it increasingly necessary to cooperate across borders to solve complicated regulatory challenges.

Because the IAIS is a relatively young organization, the request by some emerging markets to be assisted in implementing its Principles and Standards seems to suggest a positive experience, up until now. However, the lack of capacity to provide this assistance at the moment, reflected in the partial or inefficient application of its rules by some members, might end up decreasing confidence in the framework as a whole. Therefore the issue of implementation seems to be the real challenge the IAIS has to face in the next years.

References

For details on the history and the main features of the IAIS, as well as its annual reports, Principles, Standards and Guidance Papers, see the IAIS website: www.iaisweb.org. See also the Financial Sector Assessment Program (FSAP) and the Reports on Observance of Standards and Codes (ROSCs) undertaken by the IMF and by the World Bank, available at the websites: www.imf.org/external/NP/fsap/fsap.asp and http://www1.worldbank.org/finance/html/fsap.html.

IAIS (2006). *Report on Insurance Core Principles Self-Assessment Exercise 2004/2005.* IAIS.

IAIS (2008). *Survey on Implementation of IAIS Disclosure Standards – Report on Responses.* IAIS.

IAIS (2009). 'About the IAIS'. Available at www.iaisweb.org (accessed 7 January 2010).

Masciandaro, D., and M. Quintyn (2009). 'Reforming Financial Supervision and the Role of the Central Banks: A Review of Global Trends, Causes and Effects (1998–2008)'. *CEPR Policy Insight* 30: 1–11.

9

International Competition Network
Marie-Laure Djelic

The International Competition Network (ICN) was officially set up in October 2001. The founding members were thirteen national anti-trust agencies and the European Union competition agency.[1] Membership was open from the beginning to all national, regional or multinational antitrust agencies and, in fact, the numbers rose fast. By the spring of 2002, there were already fifty members. Today, the ICN is close to having a global reach – ninety-six jurisdictions are represented that together account for more than 90 per cent of world Gross Domestic Product (GDP) (ICN 2009). From its early days, the ICN defined and positioned itself as a transnational 'community of interest' structured around issues of competition and antitrust. The founding document indicated that the 'ICN w[ould] provide antitrust agencies from developed and developing countries a stronger and broader network for addressing practical competition enforcement and policy issues' (ICN 2002).[2] As years have passed, it has become clear that the ICN is much more than an informal club of like-minded organizations and individuals sharing problems, information and solutions. The ICN is not only a platform for discussion around topics of common interest. It is also a 'self-disciplining' transnational community (Djelic and Quack 2003). Through time, the ICN has become an influential transnational governance forum (Djelic and Sahlin-Andersson 2006). As such, it produces collective rules and standards, monitors their diffusion and implementation and helps members as they familiarize themselves with those rules. The objective of the ICN, ultimately, is to reach 'procedural and substantive convergence at the global level' (ICN 2002).

[1] The thirteen countries were Australia, Canada, France, Germany, Israel, Italy, Japan, Korea, Mexico, South Africa, the United Kingdom, the United States and Zambia.
[2] Unless otherwise indicated, factual information on the ICN comes from the ICN website.

The ICN – A Fluid Network with Broad Reach

The ICN is a 'project-oriented, consensus-based, informal network of antitrust agencies from developed and developing countries' (ICN 2002). The focus of the ICN is competition – 'all competition all the time' (von Finckenstein 2003). As a network, the ICN has three main characteristics – it is virtual, inclusive and open.

The ICN is a virtual network – with no offices, legal status, employees or even budget. Members pay for themselves and cover the costs of their involvement with the ICN – for example, participation in yearly conferences or in working groups. The ICN does not have a geographic hub or a permanent secretariat. A Steering Group sets agendas and work plans, identifying priorities that then have to be approved by ICN members during the yearly conference. The Steering Group consists of fifteen members (recommended by former Steering Group members and confirmed by the membership at the conference) to which are added the representatives of the country organizing the annual conference. The agency chairing the Steering Group takes on, for a year, on a rotating basis, secretarial tasks and bears the costs associated with them. At the beginning, members of the Steering Group were representatives from those countries 'that [we]re committed to going forward with the mission of the ICN' (ICN 2002). All in all, in fact, the Steering Group has been and remains dominated by representatives from the more established antitrust agencies – with an overwhelming weight for developed countries.[3] The work itself is done within ad hoc and temporary working groups that each focus on particular issues and meet rarely, instead relying on modern technology. Initially, three main working groups were set up. The Merger Review working group, coordinated by the US, was supposed to address the challenges of merger review in a multi-jurisdictional context. The Advocacy working group, coordinated by Mexico, was in charge of identifying the means to champion and advocate antitrust and competition, particularly in developing countries. The Capacity Building and Competition Policy Implementation working group, co-chaired by the EU and South Africa, was working on the rationalization and systematization of technical assistance to help countries stabilize, entrench and implement competition regimes. Today, the first two working groups are still active; the Merger group is still

[3] In 2008, the list of countries represented in the Steering Group was quite telling and not very different from the list of founding members: US (two representatives), UK, Mexico, Japan, Canada, Russia, Brazil, Australia, Korea, Germany, Turkey, the Netherlands, France, EU, South Africa, Italy, Switzerland.

chaired by the US and the Advocacy group is co-chaired by the UK and Russia. The third initial working group was wound down and essentially replaced, in 2009, by the Agency Effectiveness working group (co-chaired by Brazil and Turkey). Two more working groups have been added since 2002 – Cartel (co-chaired by the EU and Hungary) and Unilateral Conduct (co-chaired by the US and Germany). Here again, the weight of large and developed countries is unmistakable.

The ICN is an inclusive network, based on voluntary membership. Any national or multinational competition authority can easily become a member without having to fit any particular criteria. The website shows very clearly that there is no barrier to membership for national, regional or multinational agencies that are involved in competition policy in the broad sense of the term. The speed at which membership has increased is another sign of this ease. The ICN has gone from 14 founding members in 2001 to 107 members (competition agencies) from 96 jurisdictions in 2009 (ICN 2009).

The ICN, finally, is an open network. While membership in the full sense of the term is restricted to competition agencies, the ICN keeps a number of doors open to other parties interested in or connected to issues of competition and antitrust. In principle, the ICN wants to 'maximize cooperation with non-governmental antitrust experts from the relevant international, industry, consumer, legal, economic and academic communities' (Ugarte 2002). In practice, this means that member agencies and in particular members of the Steering Group can invite nongovernmental experts to the annual ICN conferences. Working group members can also call upon some of those experts to help them in their tasks. The list of nongovernmental advisors that were invited to the First Conference in Naples, in 2002, is telling. Out of forty-eight experts, five were from international fora (e.g. the United Nations Conference on Trade and Development (UNCTAD), Organisation for Economic Co-operation and Development (OECD), World Bank, World Trade Organization (WTO)). Only two could be said to represent a 'consumer' constituency. There were three representatives of industry and nine from the academic community. All the rest were private lawyers and, more precisely, partners from large Anglo-Saxon law firms. The overrepresentation of large Anglo-Saxon law firms unmistakably creates a bias in the 'openness' of the network, and it certainly is not without consequences for the ICN's development.

The ICN – From a Network Intent on Spreading a Culture . . .

At its creation, the ICN was an initiative to foster dialogue amongst antitrust officials and beyond, with a view to bringing about common understandings and a common culture. The ICN was a looser alternative, championed by American agencies, to a European initiative within the WTO that had been calling for a strict and binding transnational competition frame (Djelic 2005). The objective behind the ICN had been to create, deepen and spread, worldwide, a 'culture' of antitrust and competition – which, as key actors recognized, was part of a 'broader mosaic' and came together with a culture of 'markets' (Kolasky 2002: 3–5). A forum for dialogue, exchange and collaborative work would generate a common culture around competition policy. It would also build up in time a dense social space and, hopefully, a real 'community of interest' (Von Finckenstein 2002).

The idea behind the ICN was to create an inclusive and tight network of insiders and to combine and articulate it with a number of weaker external networks reaching out to important constituencies within society. Such a combination would be likely to increase the scale and scope of the double effort at transnational culture-building and transnational culture-spreading. That one of the three original working groups focused on 'advocacy' says enough about the centrality of that double project. The Advocacy working group defined its mission in the following way: 'Competition advocacy refers to those activities conducted by the competition authority related to the promotion of a competitive environment for economic activities by means of non-enforcement mechanisms, mainly through its relationships with other governmental entities and by increasing public awareness of the benefits of competition' (AWG 2002).

The Advocacy working group (AWG) began with a systematic comparison of the situation of member agencies and with an exploration of their embeddedness in unique national institutional contexts. The AWG sent a questionnaire to each ICN member to build up the empirical base for such a comparison and exploration. The first report it presented, during the 2002 Naples conference, underscored different perceptions of the importance of advocacy in each member agency as well as variation in the types of obstacles and challenges that member agencies face in their competition advocacy activities. As a consequence of this analysis, the AWG gave itself the mission of 'recommending best practices to ICN members and providing them with information to support their advocacy tasks', with a consideration for the variability of national institutional conditions and local politics (AWG 2002).

Toward a Transnational Community of Governance

The ICN does not define itself as a regulatory actor in the way, for example, its members are regulatory actors in their respective jurisdictions. Still, its role and impact since 2001 show an ambition that goes well beyond dialogue, information and exchange. The ICN has made it clear that it wants to have a real impact on national competition regimes. More precisely, the ICN wants to drive progressive homogenization not only of formal rules, but also of practices and understandings. As David Lewis, Chairman of the ICN Steering Group, said in his introductory remarks to the 2009 Zurich conference, 'we [the ICN] are clearly in the business of making "soft law" and this is what we must continue' (Lewis 2009). 'Soft law', he made clear, is qualitatively different from 'hard law' – and not just a 'less blinding, pale version' of it (see also Mörth 2006). The ICN does not follow a logic of constraint or coercion. 'Soft law', Lewis continues, 'is rooted in consensus rather than majority; in persuasion through shared experience rather than coercion; in understanding and celebrating differences rather than suppressing them' (Lewis 2009).

The notion of a 'community of governance' fits quite well the contemporary history of the ICN (Djelic and Quack 2003; Djelic and Sahlin-Andersson 2006). In such a scenario, there is no differentiation between rule-makers and purported rule-followers. The community – in the wide sense of the term – of those who are likely to be concerned by a particular set of rules take it upon themselves to define and agree upon those rules. The logic or mode by which rules are made in this scenario is one of negotiation but with the ultimate objective of reaching a situation of 'communion'. The link between rule-making and rule-following is the mechanism of socialization, with associated processes, in particular, of 'naming and shaming' (Boli 2006). The impact of this type of mechanism may be gradual. But, in the long term, it may be better suited than external constraint or coercion to bringing about effective homogenization and coordination of standards and practices.

While the ICN community tends to be inclusive, and at first sight rather democratic, the process of negotiation is nevertheless likely to reflect imbalances in terms of resources, clout, power and influence. In the case of the ICN, it has been shown that negotiations have been and will be biased in favour of developed countries and regions with a longer tradition of antitrust. This was visible from the start and has led – including within the ranks of the ICN – to some powerful reactions. Already at the first annual conference in 2002 in Naples, the Chairman of the Italian Competition Authority, Giuseppe Tesauro, strongly warned of this problem in his opening speech as main organizer of the conference:

> So far it was indeed necessary for the Steering Committee to act rapidly and with no frills. Now, I personally consider that it may be useful to ponder on some modification and improvement concerning

the number of members of the Steering Committee, its composition and its working methods in order to achieve a better balance between the biggest and the smallest economic and political entities. It must be clear that all members of the competition family are the actors of the initiative and that they all play an equal role. (Tesauro 2002)

These types of warnings, though, have ultimately had limited impact and, as we showed above, the Steering Group has remained to this day clearly dominated by developed countries. Leading members of the ICN Steering Group are defending themselves and protesting that 'of course, consistently sound antitrust enforcement policy cannot be defined and decreed for others by the US and Canada – not that you would presume to do such a thing' (Kolasky 2002: 3). Naturally, the imbalance of power in the structure and functioning of the ICN makes this 'neutrality' a discourse more than a reality. Power relations are very much at work but they play out in the guise of hegemonic processes (Foucault 1994) that are more subtle and more complex to identify and counter.

The ICN, and in particular members of the Steering Group, are well aware of and dedicated to their transnational governance agenda. They seek two forms of impact that have elsewhere been called 'trickle-down' and 'trickle-up' trajectories (Djelic and Quack 2003). Regarding the first, members of the Steering Group hope that ICN work will come to reflect upon national competition regimes in a direct way, through the involvement of representatives from member agencies. The idea is not that members comply with recommended practices right from the outset. Rather, the hope is that they will 'consider them as aspirational goals in the context of evolving national competition frameworks' (Von Finckenstein 2003: 13). Members are, in other words, under no obligation to ensure that domestic laws reflect ICN guidelines and recommendations. Each agency will decide whether and how to implement the recommendations – adapting its strategies to local politics and constraints (Fingleton 2009b: 21). Still, members of the ICN Steering Group expect, on a practical level, that 'as best practice proposals are acted upon by members, a natural peer influence will come to bear on other jurisdictions to do the same' (Von Finckenstein 2002: 4).

The ICN Steering Group hopes that such trickle-down trajectory will combine with a trickle-up one. By opening the network of insiders to representatives of relevant and important constituencies, the Steering Group hopes to build bridges toward those constituencies. Nongovernmental experts are co-opted and involved in the work of the ICN at many different stages, with the idea that they will then become important agents in the fight for competition and antitrust in their respective constituencies. Once a number of local constituencies – or parts thereof – become champions of competition and antitrust, they can push those ideas back up to the governmental level and thus reinforce the impact and influence of competition authorities.

Since its beginnings in 2001, the ICN has proven to be much more than a simple 'community of interest', fostering dialogue and exchange. It clearly is also a 'community of governance' – and belongs as such to the dense web of contemporary transnational governance activity (Djelic and Sahlin-Andersson 2006; Djelic and Quack 2010). Members of the Steering Group are conscious of – and claim in fact – such a broadening of their ambitions. The ICN is not an arena for policymaking or for working together on any particular antitrust case. The type of influence the ICN is hoping for is rather quite parallel to mechanisms of diffusion associated with and attributed to 'epistemic communities' (Haas 1989). The ICN is hoping to bring closer together a loosely coupled 'epistemic community' or 'community of interest'. It aims at closing the ranks of that community both by deepening its common culture and by helping to strengthen its local or national position and power. This should translate in time into greater convergence and a degree of homogenization of practices and policy application locally.

At the same time, though, it seems that members of the ICN have come to realize through the years the limits of this ambition and the complexities of transnational 'soft' governance. As Lewis recently acknowledged, 'the evidence is that "best practices", even in relatively uncontroversial areas, usually have to be tailored to national circumstances and so implementation will always be uneven at best' (Lewis 2009). The ICN, hence, while still claiming a broad governance ambition has had to revise somewhat its ultimate objectives. The Steering Group appears to have come to the realization that 'convergence is not possible' and is now talking about 'informed divergence' instead, as a less ambitious, more realist but also more complex goal (Fingleton 2009a: 6). 'Informed divergence' implies identifying the 'nature and sources of divergence and to understand and respect the divergent underlying rationale' in each national jurisdiction (Fingleton 2009b: 27).

References

AWG (2002). 'Advocacy and Competition Policy'. Report prepared by the Advocacy Working Group for the First ICN Conference, Naples. Available at www.internationalcompetitionnetwork.org/uploads/library/doc358.pdf.

Boli, J. (2006). 'The Rationalization of Virtue and Virtuosity in World Society'. *Transnational Governance*, ed. M. L. Djelic and K. Sahlin-Andersson. Cambridge: Cambridge University Press.

Djelic, M. L. (2005). 'From Local Legislation to Global Structuring Frame: The Story of Antitrust'. *Global Social Policy* 5: 55–76.

Djelic, M. L., and S. Quack (2003). 'Globalization as a Double Process of Institutional Change and Institution Building'. *Globalization and Institutions: Redefining the Rules of the Economic Game*, ed. M. L. Djelic and S. Quack. Cheltenham: Edward Elgar.

Djelic, M. L., and S. Quack, eds. (2010). *Transnational Communities: Shaping Global Economic Governance*. Cambridge: Cambridge University Press.

Djelic, M. L., and K. Sahlin-Andersson (2006). 'A World of Governance: The Rise of Transnational Regulation'. *Transnational Governance*, ed. M. L. Djelic and K. Sahlin-Andersson. Cambridge: Cambridge University Press.

Fingleton, J. (2009a). 'Closing Speech to International Competition Network Conference, Zurich'. Available at www.oft.gov.uk/shared_oft/speeches/2009/spe0909.pdf.

Fingleton, J. (2009b). 'Competition Agencies and Global Markets: The Challenges Ahead'. www.oft.gov.uk/shared_oft/speeches/2009/spe0909paper.pdf.

Foucault, M. (1994). *The Order of Things*. New York: Random House.

Haas, P. (1989) 'Do Regimes Matter? Epistemic Communities and Mediterranean Pollution Control'. *International Organization* 43(3): 377–403.

ICN (2002). 'Memorandum on the Establishment and Operation of the International Competition Network'. Available at www.international-competitionnetwork.org/uploads/library/doc579.pdf.

ICN (2009). 'International Competition Network Moves Forward with a New Chair and New Challenges'. Available at www.internationalcompetitionnetwork.org/uploads/2009%20news/newsrelease-icnconference-final.pdf.

Kolasky, W. (2002). 'International Convergence Efforts: A US Perspective'. Address by the Deputy Assistant Attorney General, Antitrust Division, US Department of Justice, before the International Dimensions of Competition Law Conference, Toronto, 22 March 22. Available at www.justice.gov/atr/public/speeches/10885.pdf.

Lewis, D. (2009). 'Introductory Address to ICN Conference, Zurich'. Available at www.internationalcompetitionnetwork.org/news-and-events/newsroom-2009/intro-address.aspx.

Mörth, U. (2006). 'Soft Regulation and Global Democracy'. *Transnational Governance*, ed. M. L. Djelic and K. Sahlin-Andersson. Cambridge: Cambridge University Press.

Tesauro, G. (2002). Opening Speech at the International Competition Network First Annual Conference, Naples, 28 September.

Ugarte, F. S. (2002). 'International Competition Network'. Speech in Cape Town, South Africa, 18 March.

von Finckenstein, K. (2002). 'Introductory Remarks' at the First ICN
    Conference, Naples, 28–29 September. Available at www.
    bureaudelaconcurrence.gc.ca/eic/site/cb-bc.nsf/vwapj/ct02433e.
    pdf/$file/ct02433e.pdf.
von Finckenstein, K (2003). 'Recent Developments in the Internat-
    ional Competition Network'. An address to the Forum in International
    Competition Law, New York, 6 February.

10

International Conference on Harmonization of Technical Requirements for the Registration of Pharmaceutical Products
Dimitrios Katsikas

The International Conference on Harmonization of Technical
Requirements for the Registration of Pharmaceutical Products (ICH)
is a transnational body that brings together regulators and industry
associations from Europe, Japan and the United States. The ICH issues
Harmonized Tripartite Guidelines which aim to provide common
guidance in the three jurisdictions on how to conduct the evaluation
of applications for new medicines for human use. The ICH has issued
more than fifty guidelines which have been adopted by the regulators
of the three jurisdictions and have been incorporated in the national/
regional regulatory framework alongside other guidelines and regulations, often replacing the latter.

Pharmaceutical Harmonization and the ICH

The pharmaceutical industry is one of the most heavily regulated
industries. This is deemed necessary in order to protect public health,
which, due to considerable negative market externalities (e.g. the
time lag before a bad drug is identified, which can lead to loss of
human life) cannot be safeguarded by market mechanisms alone. This
has been demonstrated repeatedly since most regulatory interventions have followed public health crises. Perhaps the most significant
of these, in terms of regulatory consequences, was the 1961–2 thalido-
mide crisis, which spurred governments to intervene in the research
and development process of new drugs by introducing significant
pre-marketing regulation. In recent years, national drug approval and
registration regulatory measures have increased significantly, result-

ing in a multitude of different national regulations. This regulatory diversity creates significant costs for the industry, while also posing potentially significant public health risks by delaying the introduction of new drugs and creating disincentives for research and development. These problems became evident early on, and efforts to harmonize pharmaceutical regulations began in the 1970s, shortly after the introduction of national pharmaceutical regulations. These efforts originally took place in the context of the World Health Organization (WHO), a United Nations specialized agency set up to address health issues. However, since the late 1980s, the WHO's role in this issue area has diminished significantly, and the ICH has become the dominant forum for the harmonization of national drug approval and market registration procedures.

The ICH comprises the pharmaceutical regulatory authorities of the EU, the United States and Japan – which are the European Commission (EC), the Food and Drug Administration (FDA), and the Japanese Ministry of Health, Labour and Welfare (MHLW), respectively – as well as their industry associations, the European Federation of Pharmaceutical Industries and Associations (EFPIA), the Pharmaceutical Research and Manufacturers of America (PhRMA) and the Japan Pharmaceutical Manufacturers Association (JPMA). The aim of the ICH has been the harmonization of national drug approval and registration regulatory procedures in the three jurisdictions. The idea for the ICH originated in 1988, in a meeting between Japan and the EU, part of a series of bilateral meetings on pharmaceutical harmonization between Europe, the US and Japan that took place during the 1980s (Braithwaite and Drahos 2000; Abraham and Reed 2001). The first ICH conference was held in Brussels in 1991 and achieved the first concrete harmonization results, such as a 'minimum data blueprint' that defined control conditions for testing, a reduction of long-term toxicity tests to six months, and the abolition of the 'Lethal Dose 50' toxicity test (Jordan 1992).[1] ICH2 took place in 1993 in Orlando, Florida. Progress was again made in the area of safety, and agreement was reached for issuing draft guidelines covering various aspects of Good Clinical Practices (Kidd 1997), while a third, equally successful conference, took place in Japan in 1995 (Vogel 1998). The success of the conferences turned the ICH into a continuing harmonization process despite the fact that it was originally designed to be a six-year project. As a result, further conferences were held in Brussels in 1997, San Diego in 2000 and Osaka in 2003. In

---

[1] This was a very costly and ethically questionable toxicity test as it entailed increasing doses to laboratory animals until 50 per cent of the animals died.

2007, it was decided that the ICH would hold more frequent and smaller 'regional public meetings', instead of large international conferences (Uzu et al. 2009). Four such meetings have taken place to date. The ICH has been very productive, having completed over fifty guidelines, while a number of new guidelines are currently at a development stage.[2]

Structure and Operation of the ICH

The ICH comprises six parties, the three regulatory authorities and the three industry associations from the EU, Japan and the US, respectively. This composition is reflected in the ICH Steering Committee (SC), which is the organ that determines the policies and procedures of the ICH, selects topics for harmonization, and monitors the progress of harmonization initiatives. Each of the six parties holds two seats on the SC and their votes carry equal weight. The International Federation of Pharmaceutical Manufacturers and Associations (IFPMA) provides the organization's Secretariat, and participates as a non-voting member, as do the ICH Observers (WHO, Canada and the European Free Trade Area – EFTA).

The topics selected for harmonization are divided into Safety, Quality, and Efficacy in order to reflect the three criteria needed for approval and authorization to market new drugs in most countries, while a fourth topic refers to multidisciplinary issues that do not fit exclusively into one of the other categories. The product of the ICH harmonization process is a set of technical guidelines, which are developed in five steps. First, a Concept Paper for a new topic is adopted by the SC, and an Expert Working Group (EWG) made up of experts from the six parties is established. When consensus is reached among all six parties, the EWG signs the Experts Document, which, following the SC's approval, proceeds in the form of a draft guideline to the stage of regulatory consultation. At this stage the draft guideline becomes the subject of the normal regulatory consultation process of each of the three regulatory authorities. After obtaining all consultation results, the original EWG resumes, and releases the Step 4 Experts Document. Following agreement in the SC, the SC regulatory parties sign off the agreed document as an ICH Harmonized Tripartite Guideline. The final step is regulatory implementation. This is carried out according to the national/regional procedures that apply to other regulatory guidelines and requirements in the three

[2] See ICH website, www.ich.org (accessed 18 January 2010).

jurisdictions.[3] In recent years, to ensure better updating and implementation of the guidelines, similar procedures have been established for the creation of explanatory Q&A sections, revisions and maintenance of the guidelines.

Impact of the ICH

The guidelines are implemented in each jurisdiction according to the national or regional procedures that apply for other similar regulatory guidelines. The exact legal nature of the guidelines, therefore, depends on the legal and regulatory framework of each region and/or state. Nonetheless, the ICH guidelines enjoy an authoritative status in the three jurisdictions, since they have been added to the government rulebook for medicinal product registration and approval, and enjoy the same status as other guidelines adopted through the respective national regulatory procedures. Moreover, some of the ICH guidelines have become legally binding in the EU and in Japan, while others enjoy a more binding status than is the case with usual regulatory guidelines.

Beyond their legal impact in the participating jurisdictions, the ICH guidelines' impact is also growing in other jurisdictions.[4] To a large degree, this is due to the dominant position of the three players in the global pharmaceutical industry. Of the top forty R&D spending companies in the world, only one is located outside the US, Europe or Japan, while approximately 90 per cent of all new chemical and biological entities introduced in the world market come from the 'triad' (EFPIA 2006). The harmonization of these markets therefore, leads to a de facto global harmonization, based on the ICH guidelines, since they are adopted by transnational pharmaceutical companies operating in both developed and less-developed countries. Moreover, the appeal of gaining access to the large pharmaceutical markets of Europe, US and Japan often prompts new pharmaceutical companies from large emerging markets (e.g. India) to adopt the ICH guidelines as a matter of strategy (WHO 2002). The spread of the ICH guidelines beyond the triad has also been facilitated by the creation, in the context of the ICH, of the Global Cooperation Group (GCG) in 1999, whose objective is to help developing countries to understand and implement the ICH guidelines. In order to better promote the adoption and implementation of the guidelines, the ICH decided in 2003

---

[3] Ibid.
[4] The guidelines have also been adopted by Canada and the EFTA countries which are Observers in the ICH process.

to invite Regional Harmonization Initiatives (RHIs)[5] to participate in the GCG, while in 2007 the decision was taken to also invite certain individual Drug Regulatory Agencies (DRAs).[6]

Controversies

While harmonization creates considerable efficiency gains for pharmaceutical companies, and brings potentially important public health benefits through timely introduction of new medicines and lower prices, the process of harmonization in the context of the ICH, and its impact beyond the three ICH jurisdictions, have also raised significant concerns and criticism. First, the ICH has been repeatedly criticized for its lack of accountability and transparency (Hodgkin 1996; Abraham and Reed 2001; Abraham 2002). The ICH process, with the sole exception of the industry, excludes all other interested stakeholders. Thus, medical associations and patient or consumer organizations do not participate in the process except at the stage of public consultation. The close and exclusive cooperation between regulators and industry in the ICH has led critics to argue that the agenda of the ICH is to a large degree determined by the industry, primarily aiming to reduce the regulatory burden for companies (Hodgkin 1996; Abraham and Reed 2001; WHO 2002), even if that could lead to a weakening of safety standards for new medicines (Abraham and Reed 2001, 2003; Abraham 2007). On the other hand, ICH participants have always maintained that, beyond diminishing duplicate regulatory requirements, their work raises the quality of regulation and thus promotes the protection of public health (D'Arcy and Harron 1992, 1994). Moreover, they have justified the exclusion of other actors on the grounds that other stakeholders lack the necessary technical expertise to participate meaningfully in the ICH proceedings (D'Arcy and Harron 1992, 1994; Abraham and Reed 2001).

A second significant criticism relates to the use of ICH guidelines in the developing world. The ICH guidelines often require considerable technological capabilities in order for them to be properly applied. These requirements are largely driven by technological developments in production, and the assessment of their benefits is not always based on concrete scientific evidence (WHO 2002; Timmermans 2004). These requirements create significant costs for the small and

---

[5]These include regional initiatives in Asia-Pacific, Southeast Asia, the Persian Gulf, the Americas and South Africa.
[6]These are the DRAs of Australia, Brazil, China, Chinese Taipei, India, Russia, Singapore and South Korea.

generic manufacturers that operate in developing countries.[7] These manufacturers often lack the required resources for the implementation of the ICH guidelines, which means that the latter could become regulatory 'barriers to entry' for these companies, with consequences for the economies of developing countries, and also for the availability of low-priced essential medicines (WHO 2002). ICH participants defend the guidelines by arguing that scientific and technological developments are transforming the pharmaceutical research and development process, and work on harmonization needs to keep up with these developments (D'Arcy and Harron 1992, 1994; ICH 2000).

In view of the public health aspect of ICH's work, the debate concerning the benefits of harmonization provided by the ICH and the critique related to ICH's process and impact beyond the 'triad' is likely to continue.

References

Abraham, J. (2002). 'The Pharmaceutical Industry as a Political Player'. *The Lancet* 360: 1498–502.

Abraham, J. (2007). 'Drug Trials and Evidence Bases in International Regulatory Context'. *BioSocieties* 2: 41–56.

Abraham, J., and J. Reed (2001). 'Trading Risks for Markets: The International Harmonization of Pharmaceuticals Regulation'. *Health, Risk and Society* 3(1): 113–28.

Abraham, J., and J. Reed (2003). 'Reshaping the Carcinogenic Risk Assessment of Medicines: International Harmonization for Drug Safety, Industry/Regulator Efficiency or Both?' *Social Science and Medicine* 57(2): 195–204.

Braithwaite, J., and P. Drahos (2000). *Global Business Regulation*. Cambridge: Cambridge University Press.

D'Arcy, P. F., and D. W. G. Harron (1992). *Proceedings of the First International Conference on Harmonisation Brussels 1991*. Geneva: IFPMA.

D'Arcy, P. F., and D. W. G. Harron (1994). *Proceedings of the Second International Conference on Harmonisation Orlando 1993*. Geneva: IFPMA.

European Federation of Pharmaceutical Industries and Associations (2006). *The Pharmaceutical Industry in Figures*. Brussels: EFPIA.

Hodgkin, C (1996). 'International Harmonisation – The Need for Transparency'. *International Journal of Risk and Safety in Medicine* 9: 195–9.

[7] Not all pharmaceutical companies conduct original research; many firms produce generics, which are usually produced by a manufacturer who is not the inventor of the original product and are marketed when intellectual property protection rights of the original product are exhausted (EFPIA 2006).

International Conference on Harmonization (2000). *The Future of ICH – Revised 2000. Statement by the ICH Steering Committee on the Occasion of the Fifth International Conference on Harmonization, 9–11 November 2000, San Diego*. Available at www.ich.org (accessed 18 January 2010).

Jordan, D. W. (1992). 'International Regulatory Harmonization: A New Era in Prescription Drug Approval'. *Vanderbilt Journal of Transnational Law* 25: 471–507.

Kidd, D. (1997). 'The International Conference on Harmonization of Pharmaceutical Regulations, the European Medicines Evaluation Agency, and the FDA: Who's Zooming Who?' *Indiana Journal of Global Legal Studies* 4: 183–206.

Timmermans, K. (2004). 'Harmonization, Regulation, and Trade: Interactions in the Pharmaceutical Field'. *International Journal of Health Services* 34(4): 651–61.

Uzu, S. et al. (2009). *Proceedings of ICH Public Meeting: ICH Japan Symposium 2009*. Geneva: IFPMA. Available at www.ich.org (accessed 18 January 2010).

Vogel, D. (1998). 'The Globalization of Pharmaceutical Regulation'. *Governance: An International Journal of Policy and Administration* 11(1): 1–22.

World Health Organization (2002). *The Impact of Implementation of ICH Guidelines in Non-ICH Countries. Report of a WHO Meeting*. Geneva, World Health Organization.

11

International Network for Environmental Compliance and Enforcement
Durwood Zaelke, Kenneth Markowitz and Meredith R. Koparova

Overview

Over the past few decades, considerable efforts have been made to improve management of human relationships with nature. Countries have created environmental agencies, negotiated multilateral agreements, and undertaken new initiatives at the local, national and international levels to protect human health, limit greenhouse gas emissions, conserve biodiversity and wildlife, and manage natural resources. These efforts have involved leaders in government agencies, parliaments, and the judiciary, and in international organizations, businesses and civil society.

These achievements are significant, but global assessments of ecosystem health show growing challenges. The United Nations Environment Programme's (UNEP's) GEO-4 Report recognizes that environmental 'issues transcend borders. Protecting the global environment is largely beyond the capacity of individual countries. Only concerted and coordinated international action will be sufficient. The world needs a more coherent system of international environmental governance' (UNEP 2007: xvi).

Transgovernmental networks, such as the International Network for Environmental Compliance and Enforcement (INECE), enable informal cooperation among government regulators, other governmental actors, international and nongovernmental organizations (NGOs), civil society and the regulated community. Informal cooperation on common environmental concerns can help resolve transboundary environmental problems, create efficiencies in the development of tools and programmes, create a level playing field for the regulated industries among countries, and ultimately foster the political will needed to reform weak implementation of environmental standards.

The Contribution of Transgovernmental Networks to Strengthening Environmental Compliance and Enforcement

Transgovernmental networks can enhance environmental regulation. As Slaughter observes, 'we need global rules without centralized power but with government actors who can be held to account through a variety of political mechanisms. In this context, a world order based on government networks, working alongside and even in place of more traditional international institutions, holds great potential' (Slaughter 2004: 10).

Figure 11.1   Environmental compliance and enforcement are the foundation for the rule of law, good governance, and sustainable development.

INECE provides a case in point. In 1990, thirteen countries and international organizations attended the first Workshop for Environmental Compliance and Enforcement in Utrecht, the Netherlands. The Workshop resulted in other, broader conferences and ultimately in an agreement to launch INECE, a unique transgovernmental network dedicated to a tri-fold mission of:

- raising awareness of the importance of environmental compliance and enforcement;
- strengthening capacity throughout the regulatory cycle to implement and secure compliance with environmental requirements;
- developing networks for enforcement and compliance cooperation.

INECE is now a global network of more than 4,000 compliance and enforcement professionals from more than 140 countries who are working in governmental organizations, the judiciary, international institutions, NGOs and academia. What unites the INECE community is the shared commitment among participants to the importance of assuring compliance with laws designed to protect human health and the environment.

INECE is governed by an Executive Planning Committee (EPC) which defines INECE's cooperative efforts and makes decisions to realize the INECE mission. The EPC is composed of no more than thirty persons with balanced representation among regions of the world, primarily government/public officials, representatives from international organizations including UNEP and the World Bank, the Organisation for Economic Co-operation and Development (OECD), the European Commission, and NGOs.

Since INECE is an informal partnership, the INECE Secretariat is not a formal international organization, but rather a partnership activity supported by a nongovernmental host convener, the Institute for Governance & Sustainable Development. The INECE Secretariat provides technical, administrative, publications, and communications support for EPC functions and helps to implement the INECE work programme.

INECE participants help define and communicate about mutual work programme activities and facilitate resources to advance shared goals. INECE activities are voluntary and build upon related duties and job responsibilities of contributing individuals and institutions. INECE members and partners participate in and pursue support for the general goals and specific work programme of INECE, as resources, priorities and laws governing such exchanges permit.

Raising Awareness

INECE has demonstrated to the international community and policy-makers in each country the importance of compliance with and enforcement of environmental laws at all levels to achieving rule of law, good governance and environmentally sustainable development. International environmental mandates, including Agenda 21, have recognized and incorporated INECE's message on the relationship between compliance with environmental laws and sustainable development.

INECE continues to raise awareness of the importance of compliance and enforcement through its participation in meetings of the UN Convention on Climate Change and the Basel Convention Secretariat, as well as through its work with American University's Washington College of Law; the Bren School of Environmental Science & Management at the University of California, Santa Barbara; and Tsinghua University in Beijing.

The INECE website, www.inece.org, is one of the Network's most important tools for raising awareness. It is the only one of its kind to provide the global environmental community with comprehensive coverage of environmental compliance and enforcement issues and materials to assist practitioners with problems in their home countries. INECE publications such as *Making Law Work: Environmental Compliance & Sustainable Development* (Zaelke, Kaniaru et al. 2005) are also critical resources for Network participants. *Making Law Work* is a compilation of the best literature on topics related to compliance with and enforcement of laws to protect the environment and promote sustainable development, and provides insights into a framework for diagnosing what currently ails international and domestic environmental governance, offers suggestions for making improvements, and raises questions for further exploration.

Strengthening Capacity

INECE participants have affirmed the importance of providing capacity building activities across the network. Similar to its efforts to support the development of regional networks, INECE also supports the development of networks among practitioner communities.

INECE's climate compliance network

Assuring compliance with existing and emerging domestic climate-related policies and measures is an essential activity for countries seeking to meet emissions reduction targets. Domestic climate poli-cies include direct greenhouse gas emissions restrictions; environ-mental laws with climate co-benefits, such as those designed to reduce black carbon emissions or promote energy conservation; and adapta-tion measures, such as those to protect forests. Improving compliance with existing multilateral environmental agreements (MEAs) also can enhance climate co-benefits, including MEAs addressing shipping, regional air pollution, and protection of the stratospheric ozone layer.[1]

At the same time, the complexity of the emissions markets makes it difficult for regulators to detect non-compliance, provide technical assistance for the regulated community, and take meaningful enforce-ment against violators. As these markets proliferate and attract new investment, there is a need to strengthen their environmental and financial integrity through improved monitoring, reporting, verifica-tion and communications. INECE's Climate Compliance Network brings together experts to analyse and respond to these challenges.

INECE's international network for environmental compliance training professionals

INECE supports the activities of the International Network for Environmental Compliance Training Professionals, a practitioner knowledge community that shares information and best practices, supports trainer education and exchanges, and promotes the impor-tance of effective environmental compliance training.

A priority activity of the Network for Environmental Compliance Training Professionals has been the delivery of INECE flagship capac-ity building programmes on the Principles of Environmental Compliance and Enforcement and on Performance Measurement Indicators for Environmental Compliance Programs. The environ-mental compliance and enforcement indicators methodology devel-oped by INECE assists programme managers and decision makers in realizing efficiencies and cost savings in the implementation of envi-ronmental policies. Environmental compliance and enforcement indicators are management tools for measuring and communicating the results achieved by environmental compliance and enforcement programmes. Identifying, designing and using performance indica-tors can help managers better evaluate how effectively environmental

---

[1]For more details see the INECE Special Report on Climate Comp-liance, available online at http://inece.org/climate/SpecialReportClimate-Compliance.pdf.

compliance and enforcement programmes bring about behavioural change and respond to priority environmental problems (INECE 2008).

Seaport environmental security network

Despite the existence of international, regional and bilateral agreements designed to ensure the safe and environmentally sound treatment and transport of hazardous waste through seaports, the illegal trade in hazardous waste remains a significant problem throughout the world (INECE Seaport Environmental Security Network 2009). Obstacles to effective international efforts to detect and deter illegal shipments of hazardous waste may vary, but together they affect the ability of enforcement authorities to ensure that international shipments comply with hazardous waste management requirements and customs and port obligations. INECE's Seaport Environmental Security Network (SESN) is an operational network of professionals building capacity for facilitating international enforcement collaboration to improve the inspection and monitoring of transboundary movements of hazardous waste through seaports.

Regional Networks

INECE has a long history of supporting the development of regional compliance and enforcement networks. Its first international conference in 1990 inspired the creation of the first network for environmental law implementation and enforcement for member states of the European Union (IMPEL) and, using this model as a basis, regional compliance and enforcement networks and partnerships have developed among practitioners in the European accession countries (ECENA); the Eastern Europe, Caucasus and Central Asia region (REPIN); Australasia (AELERT); Asia (AECEN); North America (CEC and its Expert Group on Compliance); and Central America, through the Central American Commission for Environment and Development (CCAD).

As a result of the 8th international conference in Cape Town in 2008, investigations into the potential for establishing an East Africa regional network are now being spearheaded by the National Environment Management Authority of Kenya. A regional conference was held in May 2010 to formally launch the East African Network for Environmental Compliance and Enforcement (EANECE), with participants from environmental management government entities in all five East African countries (Kenya, Uganda, Tanzania, Burundi and Rwanda).

The 7th international conference in 2005 had a similar effect, significantly increasing awareness and action on environmental compliance and enforcement in the Maghreb region. The Network for Environmental Compliance and Enforcement in the Maghreb (NECEMA) was launched at the 7th conference by Morocco, Tunisia, Algeria and Mauritania, and continues to be an active environmental partner in the region. INECE also provides support for an environmental compliance and enforcement network in the Arab region (ANECE), which held its first meeting in 2009 in Jordan.

Impact

INECE has grown significantly over the last two decades to become the leading voice on international environmental compliance and enforcement. Beginning with a small group of countries working to build capacity on the basic 'principles' of environmental compliance and enforcement, INECE has expanded its scope of work to encompass complex international partnerships responding to sophisticated transboundary issues, including those related to seaport environmental security and compliance with climate-related policies and measures. Much of INECE's successful infrastructure and many of its projects have been made possible by INECE's informal operating structure, the dedication of INECE's participants to raising awareness of the importance of environmental compliance and enforcement, and the long-term commitments of many organizations to providing technical support to the network.

While working within the framework of an informal transgovernmental network, the cooperative activities among INECE's more than 4,000 participants have resulted in formal impacts on national and local environmental compliance and enforcement. The network has produced eight major international conferences, a wealth of materials to help raise awareness and build capacity among environmental compliance and enforcement practitioners, established key regional and topic-specific environmental networks, and worked to strengthen existing ones.

As INECE looks back over its past twenty years of history, the network must recognize its challenges alongside its successes. Key challenges for INECE include securing a sustainable and long-term funding base, identifying new audiences for the Network's messages, and continuing to evolve to remain relevant to an increasingly sophisticated environmental compliance and enforcement practitioner community.

References

INECE (2008). *INECE Performance Measurement Guidance for Environmental Compliance and Enforcement Practitioners*. Available at http://inece.org/indicators/guidance.pdf.

INECE Seaport Environmental Security Network (2009). *International Hazardous Waste Trade Through Seaports Working Paper*. Available at http://inece.org/seaport/SeaportWorkingPaper_24November.pdf.

Slaughter, A. (2004). *A New World Order*. Princeton: Princeton University Press.

United Nations Environment Programme (UNEP) (2007). *Global Environment Outlook: Environment for Development (GEO-4)*. Nairobi: UNEP.

Zaelke, D., D. Kaniaru et al. (2005). *Making Law Work: Environmental Compliance & Sustainable Development*. London: Cameron May.

12

Joint Forum
Kevin Young

The Joint Forum on Financial Conglomerates – 'the Joint Forum', as it is widely known – is an informal transgovernmental forum for financial sector supervisors in the banking, insurance and securities markets. The Joint Forum is the child of its 'parent organizations' – the Basel Committee on Banking Supervision (BCBS), the International Organization of Securities Commissions (IOSCO) and the International Association of Insurance Supervisors (IAIS). Officially the Joint Forum works as a cooperative forum between the three organizations, with the heads of each of these organizations meeting regularly. Equal numbers of senior banking, insurance and securities supervisors from Australia, Belgium, Canada, France, Germany, Italy, Japan, the Netherlands, Spain, Sweden, Switzerland, the United Kingdom and the US meet three times a year. Representatives from the European Commission also attend meetings of the Joint Forum, but only as observers, while representatives of the BCBS, IOSCO and IAIS attend meetings as well.

The focus of the Joint Forum's work is twofold. First, the Forum focuses on facilitating the flow of information related to the regulation and supervision of financial conglomerates. Financial conglomerates are large financial firms with complex organizational and management structures whose scale transgresses both national borders and normally conceived boundaries within the financial sector. The Joint Forum attempts to improve supervision of these institutions by facilitating cooperation across each of the financial sectors that these conglomerates span (Joint Forum 1997). The aim especially since the late 1990s has been to compare the core supervisory principles across sectors in order to identify common principles and to understand differences when they arise (Joint Forum 1999d). The Forum's second primary role is to provide policy research and advice. For the most part, this consists of issuing detailed reports reflecting research and recommendations regarding common standards on the supervision of financial conglomerates. This has taken the form of general principles as well as detailed recommendations for specific regulatory areas of risk assessment (Joint Forum 1999d). Both of these functions are regarded as having a broad value for facilitating transnational and cross-sectoral cooperation. However, the main effort of the Joint Forum is to provide recommendations to its 'parent organizations' – the IOSCO, the BCBS and the IAIS.

History

While the Joint Forum has existed since 1996, its origins actually lie in an earlier organization called the Tripartite Group. This group was established in 1993 at the initiative of the BCBS in order to address the growing concern with financial conglomerates. The rise of this form of activity raised two challenging questions for financial sector supervisors in North America and Europe at the time. On the one hand, the rise of large internationally active financial conglomerates challenged the boundaries that existed in the regulation and supervision of banking, insurance and securities markets generally. Large firms like JP Morgan and Citigroup, for example, were increasingly engaging in all three of these activities, and in many different country contexts on an unprecedented scale. On the other hand, the size of large financial conglomerates raised questions about the level of risk that these institutions posed (Porter 2005: 36–7). Thus while transgovernmental cooperation existed in the banking, insurance and securities markets already, there was no institution in place to facilitate communication among these new groups.

Despite the benefit of increased cooperation that the Tripartite Group brought, it was decided in 1995 that its progress would be restricted by the informal nature of the group (Tripartite Group 1995: 9). The Joint Forum was established shortly thereafter, in 1996. The Joint Forum's more formal structure also meant a change in representation – with supervisors from Australian financial markets joining the group and Luxembourg no longer attending meetings. The more formal institutional structure of the Joint Forum has also ensured a more equal number of participants. While within the Tripartite Group some countries only had one representative (such as Canada) and others had four (such as the United States), the Joint Forum ensures an equal three representatives for each country (see Tripartite Group 1995: 67–8).

Institutional Structure

The Joint Forum is led by a Chair appointed for a two-year term, who seeks to steward the process of transgovernmental cooperation and facilitate meetings. Past Chairs have been drawn from the Bank of the Netherlands, the Australian Securities and Investments Commission, the Financial Inspection Agency of Sweden, the Bank of Spain, the UK Financial Services Authority (FSA), the Hong Kong Securities and Futures Commission and the US Office of the Comptroller of the Currency. Representatives from the Bank of the Netherlands and the Australian Securities and Investments Commission have chaired the Joint Forum twice. Each 'member country' participant in the Joint Forum comprises an equal number of bank, insurance and securities supervisors. Because the supervision of banking, insurance and securities markets in each of these countries is sometimes organized through the same institution, some member countries have only one institution – but different departments – participating. In the UK and Germany, for example, one central institution oversees the supervision of these different areas – the FSA in the UK, and the Bundesanstalt für Finanzdienstleistungsaufsicht (BaFin) in Germany. Each of these institutions has three seats at the Joint Forum, however. In countries like the United States and France, where banking, insurance and securities are supervised through different institutions, a representative from each of these institutions has a seat. In countries without a consolidated national supervisory system of securities regulation, the participation within the Joint Forum is split. For example, for Canada the securities commissions of the Province of Ontario and the Province of Quebec are different. In this case, they share the seat at the Joint Forum on a rotational basis.

Unlike many other transgovernmental networks, the Joint Forum does not have its own secretariat, but rather utilizes the small secretariat within the Basel Committee, which itself is based in the Bank for International Settlements building in Basel, Switzerland. In fact, the Joint Forum has traditionally utilized only half a secretarial staff member from the BCBS (Davies and Green 2008: 82). In a similar manner to the BCBS, in the late 1990s the Joint Forum began releasing drafts of its supervisory standards to the public, in the effort to seek feedback and engage in a 'consultative process' not only with other public agencies but also with industry groups (see Joint Forum 1999a). Since then it has held roundtables with industry participants to discuss regulatory differences in the insurance, securities and banking sectors in 2006 (Joint Forum 2006).

Governance

The Joint Forum has been regarded as an example of transgovernmental cooperation (Slaughter 1997: 191), and as an instance of important cross-sectoral collaboration between different areas of financial regulation (Porter 2005: 36–7). Because of this peculiar structure, the Joint Forum arguably facilitates the communication of information not only at the transnational level, but also at the national level – i.e. across different national sectors of financial supervision. The principles of the Joint Forum have been used by the G-7 finance ministers, and have more recently been part of the initiative of the G-20 to encourage a more robust international regulatory system as well (see Joint Forum 1999c: 105, 112–14; Joint Forum 2010a).

The Joint Forum's impact on financial regulation should not be overstated, however. The sharing of information is voluntary, and its output is largely confined to making recommendations to its 'parent bodies', the IOSCO, the BCBS and the IAIS (Joint Forum 1999d). Despite these limitations, the standards that the Joint Forum produces have been used in concrete regulatory actions. In 2000, for example, the European Commission took the initiative to implement the Joint Forum's recommendations by setting out specific legal requirements for financial conglomerates in the Directive on Financial Conglomerates (see Joint Forum 1999b, 1999e; European Commission Internal Market Directorate General 2000: 4, 7). Some have also criticized the composition of the Joint Forum's membership, which they believe hampers its effectiveness. According to Davies and Green, concrete progress on conglomerate supervision at the global level has proved elusive mainly 'due to political resistance in the US in particular and the long-standing resistance of the large US investment banks to group supervision of any kind' (Davies and Green 2008: 84). Similarly, Porter (2003: 538) has argued that despite the collaboration that the Joint Forum represents, it has been limited by its narrow mandate.

Some have proposed granting the Joint Forum more authority. Davies and Green (2008: 224), for example, have argued that the Joint Forum should be subsumed within the organizational auspices of the Financial Stability Forum (now the Financial Stability Board (FSB)). While this has not occurred, the Joint Forum has taken some of its recent cues from the FSB. Through an initiative of the G-20 following the recent global financial crisis, the FSB tasked the Joint Forum with carrying out a comprehensive review of differences and gaps in the regulation of financial markets (Joint Forum 2010a). The emphasis has been on unregulated or 'lightly regulated' entities and activities in particular, with the aim of addressing potential issues of systemic risks which may not be captured in the current framework, such as activities related to mortgage origination, hedge funds and credit default swaps (Joint Forum 2010b).

References

Davies, H., and D. Green (2008). *Global Financial Regulation: The Essential Guide*. Cambridge: Polity Press.

European Commission Internal Market Directorate General (2000). *Towards an EU Directive on the Prudential Supervision of Financial Conglomerates*. Brussels: European Commission.

Joint Forum (1997). 'Mr Cameron Appointed Chairman of the Joint Forum'. Press release, 27 November.

Joint Forum (1999a). 'Basle Committee, IOSCO and IAIS Release Final Documents on the Supervision of Financial Conglomerates'. Press release, 19 February.

Joint Forum (1999b). *Joint Forum Paper on the Supervision of Financial Conglomerates*. Basel: Joint Forum.

Joint Forum (1999c). *Supervision of Financial Conglomerates: Papers Prepared by the Joint Forum on Financial Conglomerates*. Basel: Joint Forum.

Joint Forum (1999d). 'New Mandate and Appointment of New Chairman of Joint Forum'. Press release, 4 December.

Joint Forum (1999e). *Concentration Principles and Intra-Group Transactions and Exposures Principles*. Basel: Joint Forum.

Joint Forum (2006). 'Joint Forum Issues Paper on Regulatory and Market Differences'. Press release, 3 May.

Joint Forum (2010a). 'Review of the Differentiated Nature and Scope of Financial Regulation Released by the Joint Forum'. Press release, 8 January.

Joint Forum (2010b). *Review of the Differentiated Nature and Scope of Financial Regulation – Key Issues and Recommendations*. Basel: Joint Forum.

Porter, T. (2003). 'Technical Collaboration and Political Conflict in the Emerging Regime for International Financial Regulation'. *Review of International Political Economy* 10(3): 520–51.

Porter, T. (2005). *Globalization and Finance*. Cambridge: Polity Press.

Slaughter, A.-M. (1997). 'The Real New World Order'. *Foreign Affairs* September/October: 183–97.

Tripartite Group (1995). *The Supervision of Financial Conglomerates: A Report by the Tripartite Group of Bank, Securities, and Insurance Regulators*. Basel: Tripartite Group.

13

Transnational Policing
Monica den Boer

The term 'policing' encompasses several practices of social order regulation and supervision, often labelled 'law enforcement'. Usually, the police organization is seen as a particular institutional expression of state sovereignty, and for this purpose it is endowed with the monopoly of violence.

However, given the vast mobility of crime and the growing opportunities that new technology provides to criminal entrepreneurs, crime, like migration, finance and tourism, now moves around the world like water. In response, governmental and law enforcement authorities have taken several initiatives. Police organizations often complain about the lack of flexibility as a consequence of legislation that makes it more difficult for them to reach beyond the national borders of their jurisdiction. As a result, most of the recent efforts in the transnationalization of policing are aimed at improving cross-border information and intelligence exchange, operational investigations, good practices and training.

In describing transnational crime and policing, the emphasis in this article lies on transnational crime and policing practices in Europe. Moreover, the focus is less on the institutional shaping of international police cooperation, and more on practices that are more networked and informal in character, and have a potential to interlink actors from a variety of sectors. This choice implies that we will not take into account the practices and procedures of international law enforcement agencies, such as Interpol and Europol. It should be underlined that these intergovernmental bodies possess network characteristics, particularly in their liaison officer and information architecture; however, it should be emphasized that their governance relationships are vertical in character and authorized by national authorities in the relevant member states.

The Globalization of Crime

Arguably, globalization plays an important role in increasing mobile and transnational crime (Berdal and Serrano 2002: 24; Fijnaut and Paoli 2006; Den Boer 2010). Transnational crime necessitates information exchange and operational cooperation between police authorities at different levels of governance. Serious transnational crime includes fraud, forgery, money laundering, people-smuggling, trafficking in human beings, drug trafficking, stolen vehicle trafficking, environmental crime, cyber-crime, child pornography, illegal arms trafficking, and even terrorism. Global connections are seen as a major explanatory factor behind the increasing mobility of crime. Associations which have been consolidated across large distances, bundled around demographic shifts and diasporas, and migratory movements across the world are also key factors.

Transnational crime exploits technology abundantly. Virtual crime and cyber-crime, such as phishing, hacking, password-theft, electronic child pornography, industrial espionage, software piracy, fraudulent e-commerce transactions, digital money laundering, cyber-stalking, electronic infringement of intellectual property and several other crimes are enabled by computers and the Internet. Moreover, innovations in communication technology are widely exploited by criminal groups to facilitate their exchanges (Thomas and Loader 2000). The recent introduction of several international legal instruments has facilitated the cross-border prosecution of these types of criminal offences; however, criminal activity in cyberspace is still vast and complex (Den Boer 2002: 436).

When analysing market dynamics as a crucial variable in mobile crime, opportunity structures (Klerks, 2003: 99), market structures, 'criminogenic asymmetries' (Wright 2006: 206), or the 'proximity to source countries' (Von Lampe 2008: 9) are certainly factors to take into account. Globalization has thus far not eroded the wide regional variation in illegal markets within particular countries. However, the regional criminal networks have developed mutual relationships, revolving around infrastructure and supply and demand opportunities. Infrastructure (transport, roads, harbours, airports, communication infrastructure) is a crucial variable in the mobility of crime. Economic liberalization has reduced transportation costs, has encouraged improvement in transportation infrastructures, and has expanded worldwide distribution networks, e.g. through the use of containers (Andreas 2002: 40). Sources, markets and criminal activities can be combined in corridors (Köppel and Székely 2002; Netherlands Police Agency 2004: 14).

Legal loopholes (Passas 2002: 27) facilitate 'jurisdiction shopping' and thus benefit criminal entrepreneurship. Criminal organizations target jurisdictions which are lenient or tolerate conduct which has been criminalized in another state. Mutual connections between crime structures are symbiotic in nature, and this may also apply to criminal groups that become 'the crucial bases of support for governments and elites determined to hold on to power' (Berdal and Serrano 2002: 199).

Transnational organized crime is hard not only to quantify but also to qualify. Its volatile, chameleon-like, networked and mobile character makes it a phenomenon hard to grasp (Mitsilegas 2003; Sheptycki 2003) or operationalize (Von Lampe 2008: 7). Several (competing) paradigms have been used to conceptualize transnational organized crime, including the hierarchy (also the Mafia paradigm), the Octopus, the Enterprise Paradigm, the Ad Hoc Coalition, and the Network Paradigm (Wright 2006: 144ff.). Moreover, it has been argued that a global web of criminal networks continues to build cooperative ventures (Williams 2002: 80).

The dominant assessment is that transnational organized crime (not only in Europe, but worldwide) has gained a more fluid and networked character. The 'crime landscape' in Europe can be characterized by its 'patchwork character' (Von Lampe 2008: 9; see also Galeotti 2007). The diversification of contacts, relationships and criminal activities make criminal groups less permeable, and makes it more difficult for law enforcement to crack codes of communication, to identify membership, to establish evidence of a durable criminal enterprise, to delineate criminal activities within a geographically neatly delineated space, and to find evidence of structured organized crime groups (Klerks 2003: 100). To challenge the relative immunity of these groups to law enforcement interventions, there is mounting pressure to focus less on 'easily discernible organizational entities with some degree of formalization' and more on 'less easily recognizable collectives, such as local criminal milieus or cliques of individuals who share the same deviant values and socialize on a more or less continuous basis' (Von Lampe 2008: 12).

The European Police Office Europol states that criminal groups evolve into 'oriented clusters', also called crime hubs, and that they strategically join each other in a temporary fashion (Europol 2007: 9). In response, law enforcement strategies are increasingly built on the Network Paradigm, which regards transnational crime as predominantly fluid and mobile. The new discourse about transnational crime acknowledges the existence of criminal hierarchies, but at the same time diagnoses transnational crime as being intermeshed with ordinary social and economic life. Such discourse provides law enforcement organizations with a justification to move from targeted intelligence-gathering to catch-all strategies (Edwards and Gill 2003: 270; Grieve 2008: 19).

The flexible character of crime continuously challenges the political authorities and law enforcement organizations (Anderson, den Boer et al. 1995). First, the vast volume of serious and organized transnational crime makes it difficult for law enforcement organizations to allocate their material and human resources to complex cross-border investigations (Den Boer and Spapens 2002). In many countries, political pressure has been such that the more visible, tangible and local crimes have been targeted at the expense of attention to transnational law enforcement cooperation. This explanation relates to a second issue, namely that international cooperation obscures the efforts performed by professional individuals within the national systems. In the recent past, it has been difficult to establish cross-border joint investigation teams or a mutual legal assistance system, because they did not always enjoy sufficient priority within the law enforcement organization (Rijken and Vermeulen 2006), and because there were conflicts and misunderstandings about the leadership and location of these transnational initiatives.

Strategies for Transnational Policing

Despite these challenges, transnational law enforcement efforts can be successful. Several transnational joint ventures illustrate that countries have benefited from each other's intelligence, knowledge, analysis and strategic insight. One major strategy is international information exchange, which is seen by many as the core of transnational law enforcement cooperation. For each police organization, knowledge and information about the criminal, his movements, his contacts, his suppliers and his market is a crucially important condition for a successful investigation. Hence, several law enforcement organizations have embraced intelligence-led policing as their dominant *modus operandi*. In terms of police governance, this requires agreement about the distribution of funds that are to be invested in intelligence and surveillance systems, but, more importantly, about the exchange of information (which is appreciated as a valuable or even precious commodity) between different organizations in the public and private sector. Mutual trust between public and private actors remains a challenge, as privacy regulation is not always seen as a guarantee that data will be handled correctly.

Another related strategy has been to adopt networked operating structures. Frequently operating on the fringes of traditional legitimacy, law enforcement agencies have embraced networked structures as well as instruments and procedures that focus on the ability to interlink information that reveals criminal patterns of operation. The adoption of a networked governance system does not automatically lead to the abolition of typical law enforcement bureaucracies. However, networked features are encouraged by transnational liaison officers, mobile or nodal policing, and the creation of international information and intelligence architectures.

In particular, the secondment of law enforcement liaison officers to locations that harbour crime hubs is noteworthy in this respect (Den Boer 2005). Liaison officers are usually police officers stationed in a foreign jurisdiction who act as intermediaries between the law enforcement authorities of two countries. Their role can be quite ambiguous, because they can also 'fix things' and facilitate mutual legal assistance requests (Nadelmann 1993). Usually, liaison officers are stationed by one country in another, or placed within an organization like Europol, but the Nordic Union model allows liaison officers to act on behalf of a number of countries. This relatively flexible form – in which a liaison officer is seconded to another country for a few years – had its precedent in the United States (Andreas and Nadelmann 2006). Gradually, the activities of liaison officers have widened from drugs trafficking to other forms of crime, and also counter-terrorism (Bigo 2000: 74; Block 2008: 77).

A few examples of these strategies may be illustrative. It has been acknowledged that various methods of surveillance and data collection fold into a 'surveillance assemblage' (Shelley, Picarelli et al. 2005; Ericson 2007: 2). Among these surveillance methods is the Automatic Number Plate Recognition (ANPR), which entails that road cameras record all licence plates of vehicles that pass a certain location (e.g. tunnel, bridge, motorway) which is placed under continuous surveillance (Corbett 2008: 137). The volumes of data retention are enormous as there can be 50 million 'reads' on just one day in a country like the United Kingdom. The monitoring of traffic makes retrospective revisiting by the police possible (2008: 138). Large-scale data collection and data storage allows for data mining, text mining and pattern detection. At the level of the European Union, new legislation has been adopted to allow for extensive data-retention, as well as for the communication of Passenger Name Records (PNR) to some third countries (USA, Canada and Australia) (Kuipers 2008). The exchange of intelligence between law enforcement authorities may lead to transports of illegal goods being interrupted (Dorn 2003: 230), seized, or simply 'choked off' (Sheptycki 2003: 63).

With the creation of a 'surveillance assemblage' (Ericson 2007) and the convergence of intelligence systems, 'conjoining information across the categories of criminal law, disruption, administrative action and regulation of markets' (Dorn 2003: 237), there is a growing need for oversight and accountability (Passas 2002: 33). Moreover, reflection is required as to whether transnational intelligence-exchange and criminalization simply causes criminals to adapt or merely displaces them to other areas (Stelfox 2003: 120). In sum, transnational crime represents a vast and complex world of criminal contacts, which can profit from a range of variables, such as communication, infrastructure and market opportunities. The response of law enforcement is to adopt a transnational, networked character, thereby seeking to reduce the chances for transnational criminals to escape through jurisdictional mazes. In light of these patterns, Findlay (2008: xxi) advances the thesis that crime and terrorism are fundamental aspects of the new globalization.

References

Anderson, M., M. den Boer et al. (1995). *Policing the European Union*. Oxford: Clarendon Press.

Andreas, P. (2002). 'Transnational Crime and Economic Globalization'. *Transnational Organized Crime and International Security: Business as Usual?* ed. M. R. Berdal and M. Serrano. Boulder: Lynne Rienner Publishers.

Andreas, P., and E. Nadelmann (2006). *Policing the Globe: Criminalization and Crime Control in International Relations*. Oxford: Oxford University Press.

Berdal, M., and M. Serrano (2002). 'Transnational Organized Crime and International Security: The New Topography'. *Transnational Organized Crime and International Security: Business as Usual?* ed. M. R. Berdal and M. Serrano. London: Lynne Rienner Publishers.

Bigo, D. (2000). 'Liaison Officers in Europe: New Officers in the European Security Field'. *Issues in Transnational Policing*, ed. J, Sheptycki. London: Routledge.

Block, L. (2008). 'Combating Organized Crime in Europe: Practicalities of Police Cooperation'. *Policing: A Journal of Policy and Practice* 2(1): 74–81.

Corbett, C. (2008). 'Roads Policing: Current Context and Imminent Dangers'. *Policing: A Journal of Policy and Practice* 2(1): 131–42.

Den Boer, M. (2002). 'Cybercrime'. *Strategies of the EU and the US in Combating Transnational Organised Crime*, ed. B. de Ruyver, G. Vermeulen et al. Antwerp and Apeldoorn: Maklu.

Den Boer, M. (2005). 'Copweb Europe. Venues, Virtues and Vexations of Transnational Policing'. *Transnational European Union: Towards a Common Political Space*, ed. W. Kaiser and P. Starie. Abingdon: Routledge.

Den Boer, M. (2010) 'New Mobile Crime'. *The Routledge Handbook of New Security Studies*, ed. P. Burgess. Abingdon: Routledge.

Den Boer, M., and T. Spapens (2002). *Investigating Organised Crime in European Border Regions*. Tilburg: IVA / Tilburg University.

Dorn, N. (2003). 'Proteiform Criminalities. The Formation of Organised Crime as Organisers' Responses to Developments in Four Fields of Control'. *Transnational Organised Crime: Perspectives on Global Security*, ed. A. Edwards and P. Gill. New York: Routledge.

Edwards, A., and P. Gill (2003). 'After Transnational Organised Crime? The Politics of Public Safety'. *Transnational Organised Crime: Perspectives on Global Security*, ed. A. Edwards and P. Gill. New York: Routledge.

Ericson, R. V. (2007). *Crime in an Insecure World*. Cambridge: Polity Press.

Europol (2007). *Organised Crime Threat Assessment*. The Hague: Europol.

Fijnaut, C., and L. Paoli (2006), *Organised Crime in Europe: Concepts, Patterns and Control Policies in the European Union and Beyond*. Dordrecht: Springer.

Findlay, M. (2008). *Governing through Globalised Crime: Futures for International Criminal Justice*. Cullompton: Willan Publishing.

Galeotti, M., ed. (2007). *Global Crime Today – The Changing Face of Organized Crime*. London: Routledge.

Grieve, J. (2008). 'Lawfully Audacious: A Reflective Journey'. *The Handbook of Intelligent Policing: Consilience, Crime Control and Community Safety*, ed. C. Harfield, A. MacVean et al. Oxford: Oxford University Press.

Klerks, P. (2003). 'The Network Paradigm Applied to Criminal Organizations: Theoretical Nitpicking or a Relevant Doctrine for Investigators? Recent Developments in the Netherlands', *Transnational Organised Crime: Perspectives on Global Security*, ed. A. Edwards and P. Gill. New York: Routledge.

Köppel, T., and A. Székely (2002). 'Transnational Organized Crime and Conflict in the Balkans'. *Transnational Organized Crime and International Security: Business as Usual?* ed. M. Berdal and M. Serrano. London: Lynne Rienner Publishers.

Kuipers, F. (2008). *No Dream Ticket to Security: PNR Data & Terrorism*. Clingendael Security Paper No. 5. The Hague: Clingendael Institute.

Mitsilegas, V. (2003). 'Countering the Chameleon Threat of Dirty Money: "Hard" and "Soft" Law in the Emergence of a Global Regime against Money Laundering and Terrorist Finance'. *Transnational Organised Crime. Perspectives on Global Security*, ed. A. Edwards and P. Gill. New York: Routledge.

Nadelmann, E. (1993). *Cops across Borders: The Internationalization of US Law Enforcement*. University Park, PA: Pennsylvania State University Press.

Netherlands Police Agency (2004). *National Threat Assessment of Serious and Organised Crime in The Netherlands*. Zoetermeer: National Criminal Intelligence Department.

Passas, N. (2002). 'Cross-border Crime and the Interface between Legal and Illegal Actors'. *Upperworld and Underworld in Cross-Border Crime*, ed. P. van Duyne, K. von Lampe et al. Nijmegen: Wolf Legal Publishers.

Rijken, C. R. J. J., and G. Vermeulen (2006). 'The Legal and Practical Implementation of JITs: The Bumpy Road from EU to Member State Level'. *Joint Investigation Teams in the European Union*, ed. G. Vermeulen and C. Rijken. The Hague: T. M. C. Asser Press.

Shelley, L., J. T. Picarelli et al. (2005). *Methods and Motives: Exploring Links between Transnational Organized Crime and International Terrorism*.

Washington, DC: US Department of Justice (unpublished research report Award. No. 2003-IJ-CX-1019). Available at www.ncjrs.gov/pdf-files1/nij/grants/211207.pdf.

Sheptycki, J. (2003). 'Global Law Enforcement as a Protection Racket: Some Sceptical Notes on Transnational Organised crime as an Object of Global Governance'. *Transnational Organised Crime: Perspectives on Global Security*, ed. A. Edwards and P. Gill. New York: Routledge.

Stelfox, P. (2003). 'Transnational Organised Crime: A Police Perspective'. *Transnational Organised Crime: Perspectives on Global Security*, ed. A. Edwards and P. Gill. New York: Routledge.

Thomas, D., and B. D. Loader, eds. (2000). *Cybercrime: Law Enforcement, Security and Surveillance in the Information Age*. London and New York: Routledge.

Von Lampe, K. (2008). 'Organized Crime in Europe: Conceptions and Realities'. *Policing: A Journal of Policy and Practice* 2(1): 7–17.

Williams, P. (2002). 'Cooperation among Criminal Organizations'. *Transnational Organized Crime and International Security: Business as Usual?* ed. M. Berdal and M. Serrano. London: Lynne Rienner Publishers.

Wright, A. (2006). *Organised Crime*. Cullompton: Willan Publishing.

Part II
Arbitration Bodies

Introduction

World politics is increasingly legalized (Goldstein, Kahler et al. 2000). From the World Trade Organization's dispute procedures to the International Criminal Court, many important global governance functions have been given over to courts and lawyers. The innovative institutions studied in this section exemplify this trend, but also demonstrate how legalization need not imply formal law and institutions. Indeed, while the arbitration bodies presented here take the form of courts, none relies wholly on law per se, neither as a basis for adjudication nor as a means of coercion.

The accountability mechanisms at the World Bank and its regional counterparts, for example, aim to ensure these international organizations uphold their own social and environmental standards, but have no way to force them to do so. Instead, they count on transparency and exposure to bring the banks' behaviour into compliance. The same dynamic underlies the environmental side-agreement to the North American Free Trade Agreement, part of which allows individuals to expose countries' failures to enforce their own environmental laws. These so-called 'info-courts' (Hale 2008) have all the trappings of legal institutions, but their authority is based on information and persuasion, not law.

In contrast, private commercial arbitration, in which companies resolve their disputes in private courts, has a closer relationship to formal law. Most major economies have opted to make the decisions these private courts issue enforceable in state courts. Only rarely, however, does a dispute end up in a 'real' court of law. Instead, companies rely almost entirely on private arbitrators to resolve disputes transnationally.

References

Goldstein, J. L., M. Kahler et al. (2000). 'Introduction: Legalization and World Politics'. *International Organization* 54(3): 385–99.

Hale, T. (2008). '"Info-Courts" and the Accountability of International Organizations: Evidence from the World Bank Inspection Panel'. Paper presented at the Fourth Global Administrative Law Seminar, Viterbo, Italy, 13–14 June. Available at www.iilj.org/GAL/documents/Hale.pdf.

14

Citizen Submission Process of the North American Commission for Environmental Cooperation
Thomas Hale

The North American Commission for Environmental Cooperation (CEC) is a trilateral international organization based in Montreal that emerged from the environmental side-agreement to the North American Free Trade Agreement (NAFTA). It aims to ensure the NAFTA member states – Mexico, the United States and Canada – do not violate their own national environmental laws. The main enforcement mechanism is a citizen submission process that allows citizens in North America to challenge states' compliance through an independent review process. This process generates a factual record of state behaviour in a given case that, while lacking legal force, aims to pressure states to improve their environmental performance through publicity. This 'info-court' has led to some improvements in environmental enforcement in North America in specific cases, but its impact remains limited in scope.

Origin

When NAFTA was signed in December 1992, it became clear that the agreement would not pass the US Congress unless substantial concessions were made to unions and environmentalists. Uncommon bedfellows, these groups opposed NAFTA for similar but importantly distinct reasons. Both groups feared that free trade would allow production to shift from the US and Canada, where labour and environmental regulations are relatively strict, to Mexico, where standards were generally lower and enforcement spottier.

To address these concerns, the Clinton administration began negotiations with the other NAFTA parties in March of 1993 to create side-agreements to NAFTA on environmental and labour concerns. In addition to being a campaign pledge, these side-agreements were, as the administration knew, necessary in order to ensure Congressional ratification of the trade agreement.

The three countries began negotiating from very different positions. US unions and environmentalists wanted substantial enforcement provisions, or 'real teeth'. Mexico, however, was deeply suspicious of the side treaties, seeing them as infringements on its sovereignty and a hidden form of protectionism. A Mexican negotiator described the US proposition as 'infamous, imperialistic, and aggressive', colourfully portraying his government's response: '*nosotros los mandamos a la chingada*' (Cameron and Tomlin 2000: 188). At the same time Mexican officials knew that NAFTA would not be passed without the side-agreements, and that the longer the negotiations lasted, the more time NAFTA opponents would have to organize against ratification. These political constraints strengthened the US position, though the final outcomes were substantially weaker than the original US goal of legally binding environmental commitments. Instead, the resulting North American Agreement on Environmental Cooperation (NAAEC) included a new mechanism relying on transparency-based enforcement.

How the CEC Citizen Submission Process Works

Section 5(1) of the NAAEC requires each country to 'effectively enforce its environmental laws and regulations through appropriate governmental action'. This provision is somewhat unusual for an international treaty; it does not create new substantive obligations, but merely commits governments to enforce their existing laws. That is, it makes domestic enforcement a subject of international concern. This uncommon arrangement reflects the nature of the political controversy surrounding NAFTA's environmental impacts: Northern environmentalists were concerned that weak enforcement in Mexico would undermine any environmental accord. Implementation, not written law, was the most worrying problem.

The NAAEC contains two mechanisms to enforce this broad mandate. One is a 'hard', traditional intergovernmental process that relies on formal sanctions; the other is a 'soft' multistakeholder process that relies on civil society and transparency. The hard element is the dispute settlement procedure found in Articles 22 through 36. If one country finds in another 'a persistent pattern of failure by that other Party to effectively enforce its environmental law', it may request consultations with the alleged offender. Should these talks not resolve the matter, it is put to mediation and then, if there is still no result after sixty days, an arbitral panel of technical experts. This panel has the authority to determine whether a lack of enforcement has indeed occurred, and to recommend solutions. If the parties do not comply with the panel's findings, the panel may impose monetary fines. Countries that fail to pay such fines are subject to retaliatory tariffs of equivalent value to the fines.[1]

The NAAEC's 'soft' enforcement mechanism is the citizen submission process administered by the CEC, the focus of this chapter. Under Article 14 of the NAAEC any organization or individual in North America may submit a brief to the CEC Secretariat 'asserting that a Party is failing to effectively enforce its environmental law'. The Secretariat determines whether the submission merits a response from the country, considering:

- whether the submitter is being harmed by the alleged non-enforcement;
- whether further study of the issue would further the goals of the NAAEC;
- whether the submitter has pursued domestic legal remedies;
- whether the information is based entirely on mass media reports.

If the Secretariat decides to forward the request to the relevant member government, that country has thirty days to offer a response. If the matter in question is currently the subject of a judicial or administrative proceeding, the inquiry ends. However, if, after receiving the country response, the Secretariat believes more discussion of the issue is merited, it will request that the council of environment ministers allow a factual record to be created. This report, drafted by a panel of independent experts, draws from a wide range of technical expertise, including that of nongovernmental organizations (NGOs), governments and the Secretariat itself, to create an objective picture of the country in question's enforcement or lack thereof. The factual record is then shown to the countries' environment ministers, who may, by a two-thirds vote, decide to release it publicly. The end result of the entire process is a report on enforcement behaviour.

This type of accountability mechanism has been described as an 'info-court', because it follows many of the processes of judicial procedure, but substitutes transparency for legal remedies (Hale and Slaughter 2006; Hale 2008a, 2008b). Just as with courts, individuals adversely affected by a member state's non-compliance may challenge the member before a board of adjudicators. These adjudicators issue

---

[1] Canada refused to accept these hard sanctions, and managed to negotiate exceptions for itself. See Annex 36A of the NAAEC. Mexico, despite its virulent opposition to the NAAEC, knew that US environmental groups would never give it the same benefit of the doubt as they gave Canada, and recognized that some form of hard sanctions was the price of ratification in the US Congress.

a definitive statement as to whether or not the defendant has complied with the law.

The main difference is that this statement does not automatically coerce compliance from the guilty party as a legal ruling does. Rather, it relies on the 'soft' sanctions generated by transparency. Hale (2008a) identifies two types of pressure transparency can bring to bear. First, it forces states to reflect upon their own compliance record. States may not always explicitly realize they are not in compliance with the NAAEC, and so the citizen submission process functions as a 'fire alarm'. Second, transparency may increase external pressures on non-compliant states by strengthening the arguments of civil society. Activists pushing for changes in state behaviour can cite a CEC factual record as powerful evidence of the validity of their arguments.

Are these mechanisms sufficient? On paper, the intergovernmental dispute settlement mechanism seems significantly more robust than the CEC citizen submission process. The arbitral panel's ability to levy monetary fines and authorize retaliatory sanctions gives the NAAEC real teeth, while the CEC factual records are, in the words of two observers, merely 'soft teeth in the back of the mouth' (DiMento and Doughman 1998). This weakness is reinforced by the restrictions placed even on this 'soft' mechanism. Before a submission can become a factual record it must clear a number of hurdles. While the case winds through the decision process, the political momentum surrounding it may evaporate. If it does reach the final stage, at least two of the member states must vote to make it public.

Even then, the CEC can only state the substantive facts of the case; it is not allowed to draw any conclusions about member states' compliance. Moreover, it is difficult to see how independent the CEC truly is, given that member states appoint – and fire – its staff. Victor Lichtinger, the CEC Executive Director behind the *Cozumel Reef* case, resigned shortly after the case was decided, reportedly because Mexican and US officials thought him to be 'too environmental' (Stanton Kibel 2001).

At the same time, however, the CEC has been far more active than the dispute settlement process. While over seventy-two citizen submissions have been processed by the CEC as of February 2010, not a single action had been brought forward under the intergovernmental mechanism.

Still, scholars, activists and government officials disagree over how effective the citizen submissions have been in ensuring country compliance with the NAAEC. Mickey Kantor, the US Trade Representative who negotiated the side-agreements, argues: 'The mere fact of making problems public usually persuades the government to react properly'

(Davis 1993). But has exposing the NAFTA countries' lack of enforcement altered their behaviour?

Effectiveness of the CEC Citizen Submission Process

Dorn (2008) finds that while the CEC has not had a positive effect on law enforcement in Mexico, it has helped the Mexican environment by inducing companies and environmental regulators to take corrective actions before law enforcement becomes involved. Fear of publicity and shame, Dorn argues, drives this process, as these corrective actions are often take before a factual record is even published.

Still, transparency is no guarantee of environmental protection. In the *Cozumel Reef* case, the CEC factual record found that Mexican authorities had violated environmental law by approving the building of a pier for cruise ships in protected waters off the island of Cozumel. The pier was built anyway. Fear of publicity and shame do not always provide sufficient incentives for environmental protection.

Dorn (2008) notes several procedural difficulties with the CEC process. Petitions submitted by NGOs tend to advance much further through the process than those submitted by individuals, suggesting a certain threshold of technical and administrative capacity is needed to file a successful complaint. Reviews can also drag on for years; the average time for publication of the six factual records Dorn studies was 53 months. And when a factual record does emerge, the defendant can declare parts of it confidential on very discretionary grounds.

Hale (2008a) finds that those submissions with high levels of activism around them tend to generate stronger environmental outcomes than those that do not. While only about 15 per cent of all cases yielded high results in this study, this rate was double for those cases with high levels of activism. He further finds that over two-thirds of all CEC investigations led to some policy change.

In light of the restrictions placed on the process by disclosure-shy member states, the CEC is surprisingly effective. Given its limitations, that substantial changes have been achieved in *any* of the cases is remarkable. To extend the metaphor further, it seems the CEC's bite is not so much soft as muzzled. Even when restricted, the mechanism seems to place real pressure on nation states.

References

Cameron, M. A., and B. W. Tomlin (2000). *The Making of NAFTA: How the Deal Was Done.* Ithaca: Cornell University Press.

Davis, B. (1993). 'U.S. Urges Curbs on Power of Panels on North American Environment, Labor'. *Wall Street Journal*: 10 March.

DiMento, J. F., and P. M. Doughman (1998). 'Soft Teeth in the Back of the Mouth: The NAFTA Environmental Side Agreement Implemented'. *Georgetown International Environmental Law Review* 10: 651.

Dorn, J. (2008). 'NAAEC Citizen Submissions against Mexico: An Analysis of the Effectiveness of a Participatory Approach to Environmental Law Enforcement'. *Georgetown International Environmental Law Review* 20: 129–60.

Hale, T. N. (2008a). 'Transparency, Accountability, and Global Governance'. *Global Governance* 14(January–March): 73–94.

Hale, T. N. (2008b). '"Info-Courts" and the Accountability of International Organizations: Evidence from the World Bank Inspection Panel'. Paper presented at the Fourth Global Administrative Law Seminar, Viterbo, Italy, 13–14 June. Available at http://www.iilj.org/GAL/documents/Hale.pdf.

Hale, T. N., and A.-M. Slaughter (2006). 'Transparency: Possibilities and Limitations'. *Fletcher Forum on International Affairs* (Winter): 153–63.

Stanton Kibel, P. (2001). 'The Paper Tiger Awakens: North American Environmental Law and the Cozumel Reef Case'. *Columbia Journal of Transnational Law* 39: 470–1.

15

Independent Accountability Mechanisms at Regional Development Banks
Daniel D. Bradlow[1] and Andria Naudé Fourie

Introduction

Historically, the accountability of international organizations (IOs)[2] was limited to a few specific scenarios. Primarily, IOs were accountable to their member states, based on the treaty establishing the organization and any other agreements that may exist between the organization and its member states (Shihata 2000: 8–16). In prin-

---

[1] The views expressed in this chapter are his own and should not be attributed to the Independent Review Mechanism.

[2] The accountability of an IO is defined as 'the duty to account' for the exercise of its 'authority and power' – see International Law Association Report (2004: 5).

ciple, IOs could also be accountable to other subjects of international law, based on either international agreements between the organizations and these actors, or on customary international law (Reinisch 2001: 136). Finally, IOs were accountable to those non-state actors with whom they had entered into contractual arrangements.[3] As a general rule, IOs were not accountable to those individuals who may be adversely affected by their operations and activities but with whom they did not have a contractual relationship (Bradlow, 2005: 406). The exclusion of this last group of actors was not necessarily problematic as long as IOs limited their direct interactions to their member states, and their decisions and actions did not have substantial direct adverse effects on individuals and other non-state actors. However, over time, some IOs began to have more complex direct interactions with individuals and communities in their member states. The significance of these direct interactions first became clear in the case of the international financial institutions (IFIs), although it is not limited to them (Berger 1993–4; French 1994; Reinisch 2001; Bradlow 2003; Head 2003–4; Darrow 2006).

The significance of these interactions can be seen most clearly in the case of the multilateral development banks (MDBs). Their intense involvement in the large and high impact development projects they finance highlights that, *de facto* if not *de jure,* their operations can have a profound direct impact on non-state actors in the borrowing country and that they should be held accountable for these impacts. Moreover, it has been increasingly recognized that the relationship between the MDBs and individuals adversely affected by their operations is 'legally relevant' even though there is no formal legal relationship between the two actors (Hey 1997: 61).

The recognition of the significance of this relationship has resulted in an important innovation in transnational governance, namely the creation of independent accountability mechanisms (IAMs) at all major MDBs.

The World Bank (WB)[4] led the way when it established an Inspection Panel in 1993, followed by the establishment of comparable bodies at the Inter-American Development Bank (IDB) in 1994, the Asian Development Bank (AsDB) in 1995, the International Finance Corporation (IFC) in 1999, the European Bank for Reconstruction and Development (EBRD) in 2003, and the African Development Bank (AfDB) in 2004.

[3] Although this scenario is not without difficulties – see Institut de Droit International Report (1995).
[4] International Bank for Reconstruction and Development and the International Development Association. Hereafter, 'World Bank'.

Subsequently, the AsDB in 2003 and 2010,[5] the IDB in 2009, and the EBRD in 2009 and 2010 substantially revised their mechanisms.

This chapter will provide a brief comparative overview of these IAMs, followed by an assessment of their significance for governance at the MDBs. The chapter will conclude with a reflection on the broader significance of these mechanisms for transnational governance.

The Functions of the IAMs

While there are important distinctions between the IAMs at the different MDBs, there are certain characteristics that are shared by all IAMs. This section will discuss both their common characteristics and their most important functional differences.[6]

The independence of all IAMs from the MDBs' management is ensured through various formalities.[7] Except for the World Bank's Inspection Panel (IP),[8] the IAMs are mandated to undertake compliance reviews and problem-solving exercises related to the operations of the institution – spanning their planning and implementation.[9] In the case of compliance reviews, the IAMs are responsible for receiving and processing complaints from a group (usually two or more people) who allege that they have been harmed or threatened with harm by the failure of the particular MDB to act in compliance with its own internal operating policies and procedures. These policies and procedures effectively outline how the MDB staff and management should execute their operational responsibilities, and include a set of policies designed to prevent or mitigate various social and environmental risks (Kingsbury 1999). The compliance review, usually conducted by a panel of independent experts appointed for a fixed, non-renewable term and assisted by a secretariat, focuses on whether or not the MDB complied with its applicable

[5] Review expected to be completed in 2011.
[6] For a schematic but more detailed comparative overview, see the appendix to this chapter.
[7] E.g., IAM members are appointed by and are responsible to the MDB's Board of Directors; they can only be removed for good cause; their remuneration is determined by the Board, on recommendation from the MDB's president; and they often cannot be employed by the MDB (in any capacity) after the end of their term.
[8] *The WB Inspection Panel can only undertake compliance reviews.*
[9] IAM mandates do not cover 'completed' development projects as these typically fall under MDB departments responsible for retroactive evaluation. Project 'completion' is usually defined as disbursement of 95 per cent of the MBD loan.

policies and procedures in a particular project or transaction. The review aims to establish whether or not any act of non-compliance resulted in the (potential) harm that the complainant (often called a 'requester') suffered. It is important to recognize that the compliance review mandate of the IAMs is limited to investigating the acts and omissions of the MDB itself and that it has no power to investigate the actions of other parties, such as the borrower country (Shihata 2000: 13–14).[10]

The IAM's problem-solving function is usually undertaken by a full time official of the mechanism who is not a member of the compliance review panel. This official, similar to an ombudsperson, is typically empowered to follow whatever procedures he/she deems appropriate in attempting to resolve the problem. The official works with both the complainant and the MDB and, if appropriate, other stakeholders – for example the project sponsor, the borrowing state, and private or public companies involved in the implementation of the project – in resolving those aspects of the project or transaction that caused the complainant to approach the IAM.

While the circumstances leading to the filing of a complaint at the different IAMs of the MDBs are almost identical, and while the basic institutional designs contain many similarities, there are meaningful functional differences between so-called 'first-generation' IAMs (the WB's IP and, until recently, the IDB's Independent Investigation Mechanism[11]), and 'second-generation' mechanisms established by the IFC and other regional development banks.

First-generation IAMs focus solely on compliance review, and do not have a mandate to make any formal recommendations on how to remedy the situation. Instead, the MDB's management is required to develop a remedial action plan in the light of the IAM's compliance review findings. Second-generation IAMs are often empowered to make specific recommendations to the MDB's Board on ways to correct the items of non-compliance that they find in the course of their compliance reviews or, in some cases, on how to correct systemic problems relating to the operations or the policies and procedures of the MDB. Significantly, most first- and second-generation IAMs do not provide complainants with any formal role in the development of

[10] However, determining whether a particular action or omission can be attributed to the MDB or the borrower might be problematic in practice.
[11] In February 2010, the IDB announced the re-establishment of its IAM as the 'Independent Consultation and Investigation Mechanism'.

remedial action plans.[12] Finally, all second-generation IAMs offer complainants both problem-solving and compliance review options. In some cases, the complainant can select which of these options to follow.[13] In other cases, the complainant is either encouraged or required to first engage in a problem-solving exercise before requesting a compliance review.[14]

It is important to recognize that, for both first- and second-generation IAMs, the focus is on holding the institution accountable and not on assigning blame. IAMs aim to improve the quality of the MDB's projects and programmes by either seeking to improve compliance with MDB policies and procedures or by correcting problems that have arisen in the course of the institutions' projects and programmes. IAMs therefore also help stimulate institutional learning at the MDB, both enhancing its development effectiveness and, over time, improving its policies and procedures. Thus, some second-generation IAMs are specifically empowered to make recommendations relating to the specific compliance issues they investigated, and to policies and procedures in general, and are required to explicitly address the lessons learned in their annual reports to the Board of the MDB.[15] In no instances, however, are the IAMs specifically required to make findings of fault or to identify officials who may have contributed to the problems in the projects being investigated. In fact, to date no IAM has made such a finding – partly because the IAMs recognize that the projects they investigate are complex and that the acts of non-compliance may be more attributable to the complexity of the project or to weaknesses in the internal operating practices of the MDB than to the fault of any particular official.

[12] This situation has led to frequent criticism of the IAM model, and several IAMs have started to address the issue. E.g., the IDB's Ombudsperson has to consult with complainants about 'monitoring measures' required to implement agreements reached during the problem-solving phase, while the IDB's Compliance Review Panel also submits the first draft of its report to requesters for their input, and also has to obtain requester input on monitoring measures associated with the remedial action plan. The AfDB's IAM provides copies of its reports to the complainant at the same time as they are provided to the Board, so that complainants can comment before the Board actually considers the IAM report.

[13] E.g., the EBRD's Independent Recourse Mechanism.

[14] E.g., the IDB's Independent Consultation and Investigation Mechanism.

[15] E.g., the AfDB's Independent Review Mechanism.

Critical Appraisal of Independent Accountability Mechanisms

The establishment of the IAMs has been significant in several respects. As indicated above, they are the first mechanisms through which non-state actors in a non-contractual relationship with an IO can directly hold the organization accountable for its actions. Thus, they are an eloquent and meaningful recognition that at least some IOs exercise substantial influence over the lives of non-state actors, and, like any entity with power, need to be accountable to those over whom they exercise their authority. Given the novelty of this mechanism, it is not surprising that the IAMs are viewed with some hesitation by both the governments of the states in which these non-state actors reside and by the MDBs' management and staff.

Second, despite continuing criticism that the MDBs are not fully responsive to the findings and recommendations of the IAMs, there is evidence that the Banks do make adjustments to projects in response to the IAM reports. For instance, the World Bank suspended loan payments to the India Mumbai Urban Transport Project as a result of its IAM's findings of significant project non-compliance,[16] and it has publicly launched inquiries into allegations of corruption among its staff as a result of the IAM report in the Albania Coastal Zone Management Project (World Bank Press Release, 17 February 2009: 2). In other cases, such as the Bangladesh Jamuna Multipurpose Bridge Project (Eligibility Report, paras. 51–6) and Uganda Bujagali Hydropower Project, project plans have been altered in response to concerns that not all affected people were receiving the compensation required under the applicable MDB policies.

Third, the IAMs have caused MDB management and staff to become more aware of the significance of the institutions' policies and procedures, resulting in the MDBs following more transparent and participatory procedures in drafting their operational policies,[17] as well as in drafting the rules applicable to the IAMs themselves.[18] In addition,

[16] See World Bank (2004). The Bank suspended financing of project components, and laid down conditions for lifting the suspension. Note that the Board consistently refused to exercise such legal remedies during the IP's early years, despite repeated recommendations to do so.

[17] E.g., the WB has recently revised its Access to Information Policy, after receiving widespread input from civil society and other stakeholders, while the IFC has launched an extensive overhaul – with wide stakeholder input – of its entire 'sustainability framework' (see www. ifc.org/policyreview).

[18] See, e.g., the WB's effort to include stakeholder input during the two Board reviews of the IP function in 1996 and 1999 (Bradlow 1999; Shihata 2000).

MDB management and staff have begun to pay closer attention to the application of their operating policies and to ensuring that MDB operations comply with the applicable policies in order to avoid having projects become the target of IAM proceedings (a process known as 'panel proofing') (Roos 2001: 520).

The precedent established by the creation of the IAMs is beginning to have an impact beyond the MDBs. For example, a number of national agencies (such as the US government-owned Overseas Private Investment Corporation (OPIC) and the Japanese Bank for International Cooperation (JBIC)) have created their own versions of IAMs. In addition, the European Investment Bank's Complaints Mechanism is applicable to projects outside of Europe. To date, other IOs, such as the International Monetary Fund (IMF) and the United Nations, have not implemented the IAM model but have made some limited efforts to enhance their accountability to non-state actors adversely affected by their operations.[19] The IMF has also followed the example set by the MDBs of following more transparent and participatory procedures in formulating its new operational policies, for example on IMF conditionality.

On the other hand, despite various institutional design improvements implemented at several of the bodies, the IAM model has some important limitations. First, the symbolic, physical and psychological distance between affected people and the MDBs remains a significant barrier to the filing of complaints, and to their effective resolution. While local civil society (often aided by international civil society) plays an important role in bridging this gap (Clark, Fox et al. 2003), it nevertheless remains significant, and may be exacerbated by the personal risks involved in bringing complaints to the MDB.[20] Another important barrier to bridging this gap is the relative complexity of the compliance review procedures of the IAMs and attempts to unnecessarily 'legalize' the process (Hunter 2003: 208–10). In this regard, it is important to note that the actual number of complaints

[19] E.g., the IMF's Independent Evaluation Office conducts post facto evaluations of IMF operations, providing some scope for individuals to make suggestions for evaluations (see, e.g., Independent Evaluation Office 2004; and see Bradlow 2005: 447); regarding the UN, see, e.g., Reinisch (2001: 136–7); and Bradlow (2005: 448–9).

[20] These risks are particularly relevant because in most cases the government is a participant in the project. Note instances of physical harm coming to complainants – e.g., in the WB *Chad Pipeline* case, filed by an opposition leader who was tortured for his opposition to the project. Also see Clark (1999: 2).

filed with the IAMs, which have been relatively low, although not insignificant,[21] is not the best indicator of the need for these mechanisms.

Second, IAMs have a limited capacity for ensuring that their MDBs actually correct the acts of non-compliance that they have identified, and that the suggested solutions to the problems that they have sought to resolve are actually implemented. While some IAMs are authorized to monitor implementation of these solutions, all of them lack enforcement powers. Consequently, at most, the IAMs can inform the respective Boards of the MDBs about failures of implementation. This limitation on their powers weakens the IAMs' efficacy as instruments of transnational governance (Dunkerton 1995: 241).

Third, IAMs are only mandated to deal with the development projects of the MDB that created them. This is problematic because many projects involve co-financing by more than one MDB as well as other public and private funders. Consequently, a growing number of complaints concerning the same development project have been filed simultaneously at more than one IAM.[22] While the problems concerning the filing of complaints in 'multiple jurisdictions' have become a familiar issue in international law (ILC 2006), there are no clear rules or procedures for the IAMs to follow in coordinating these 'multiple jurisdictional' complaints. To date, there has only been one case of IAMs formally cooperating with a compliance investigation (*Uganda Bujagali*) and so it is too early to reach firm conclusions on how effectively IAMs can meet this challenge.[23]

---

[21] Number of complaints registered at the IAMs as of Dec. 2009: WB (49); IDB (5); IFC (68); AsDB (new IMA) (11); EBRD (5); AfDB (4).

[22] E.g., WB and IDB, *Paraguay/Argentina, Yacyretá* I (1996) and II (2003); EBRD and WB, *Albania, Power Sector Generation & Restructuring* (2007); WB and AfDB, *Uganda, Private Power Generation (Bujagali)* (II) (2007).

[23] The WB and IDB's mechanisms cooperated informally on both *Yacyretá* investigations, but the *Bujagali* case was the first joint investigation – i.e., the IAMs used the same consultants, conducted investigation jointly but issued separate reports. Also note that the IDB's new IAM specifically empowers its Ombudsperson and Compliance Review Panel to collaborate with another 'international financial institution or entity' in these situations. Moreover, in case of 'parallel co-financing by other institutions', the EBBD's new Project Complaint Mechanism specifically instructs its PCM Officer to notify the relevant IAMs of the complaint, and to 'communicate and cooperate' with them so as to 'avoid duplication of efforts and/or disruption or disturbance to common parties' (EBRD's PCM Rules of Procedure, para.16).

Conclusion

In conclusion, it can be confidently stated that, while the IAM model has some limitations, its creation has empowered individuals and civil society in a manner not seen before in transnational governance. It has given these non-state actors a mechanism that ensures 'recourse' – if not yet 'redress' in all instances (Horta 2002) – and which, in the process, is defining new standards for public participation and accountability in governance at the international level (Boisson de Chazournes 1999).[24]

Appendix: Comparative Overview of Independent Accountability Mechanisms at International and Regional Multilateral Development Banks

(as on 28 February 2011)[25]

---

[24] Note that several international environmental treaties and soft law do allow for public participation at the national level (and might even actively encourage it), but public participation at the international level (akin to 'deliberative democracy' in national constitutional systems) remains thinly conceived. See in general Ebbesson (2007).

[25] For more detail, see www.inspectionpanel.org; www.cao-ombudsman. org/; www.iadb.org/aboutus/iii/independent_invest/independent_invest. cfm?language=english; www.adb.org/accountability-mechanism/; www. ebrd.com/pages/project/pcm.s/html; www.afdb.org/portal/page?_pageid= 473,5848220&_dad=portal&_schema=PORTAL.

Institutional design element	First-generation IAM	Second-generation IAM				
	World Bank Inspection Panel	IFC & MIGA[26] Compliance Advisor/ Ombudsperson	IDB Independent Consultation and Investigation Mechanism	AsDB Accountability Mechanism	EBRD Project Complaint Mechanism	AfDB Review Mechanism
Structure	Three-member Compliance Review Panel; Chair full-time; fixed non-renewable-term; permanent staff	Compliance Advisor and Ombudsperson (CAO); permanent staff; fixed 3- to 5-year term, renewable by mutual consent	Project Ombudsperson, 3- to 5-year term, renewable; five-member Roster of Experts; 5-year term, non-renewable; permanent staff	Board committee; Compliance Review Panel, Special Project Facilitator (SPF); fixed term, non-renewable?; permanent staff	Chief Compliance Officer (CCO); ten-member (max.) Roster of PCM Experts (three-year term, renewable) non-renewable PCM Officer (five-year term, renewable)	Director of Compliance Review & Mediation Unit (CRMU); three-member Roster of Experts; Term is five years, non-renewable
Appointment	Panel appointed by Board on recommendation by World Bank Group (WBG) President and committee	CAO appointed by President of WBG	Project Ombudsperson and Panel appointed by Board	SPF appointed by President; Panel appointed by Board	PCM Expert Roster appointed by Board on recommendation of Bank President; CCO and PCM Officer appointed by President	Director appointed by President, in consultation with Board; Roster appointed by Board on recommendation by Bank President

(Continued)

[26] MIGA = Multilateral Investment Guarantee Agency

Institutional design element	First-generation IAM	Second-generation IAM				
	World Bank Inspection Panel	IFC & MIGA[26] Compliance Advisor/Ombudsperson	IDB Independent Consultation and Investigation Mechanism	AsDB Accountability Mechanism	EBRD Project Complaint Mechanism	AfDB Review Mechanism
Scope	Public sector development projects only	Private sector development projects; social and environmental policies only	Public and private sector development projects	Public and private sector development projects	Public and private sector development projects; environmental and public information policies only	Public sector projects: all policies; private sector projects: environmental and social policies only
Exclusion	Procurement; substantially disbursed loan (> 95%); fraud and corruption	'Sufficient and specific grounds' for the complaint; complaint is genuine (i.e., not malicious, trivial/ designed to gain competitive advantage)	Procurement; fraud and corruption; filed > 24 months after last disbursement; complaint without substance / to gain competitive business advantage; complaints before other judicial or review bodies	Procurement; substantially disbursed loan (> 95%); fraud and corruption	Problem solving: filed > 12months after last disbursement, or if dealt with by PCM or satisfactorily by other IAM Procurement; fraud and corruption; main purpose to seek competitive business advantage; complaints pending before other judicial bodies or IAMs might be cause to exclude; claim concerning 'adequacy or suitability of EBRD policies';	Procurement; fraud or corruption; complaints before other judicial or review bodies

Accepts complaints from affected people	Yes (two or more people)	Yes; compliance review can arise from complaint	Yes (one or more people)	Yes (two or more people)	Yes; problem solving: one or more people in project area, or who have economic interest; compliance review: one or more people or organizations	Yes (two or more people)
Complaint must allege violation of operating policies and procedures	Yes	No – CAO decides during compliance review	Yes	Yes – only for compliance review	Yes – only for compliance review	Yes – only for compliance review
Representative can file request on behalf of affected people	Local representative: yes; foreign representative: in exceptional circumstances with Board approval; Board Director can also file Request	Yes – with Ombudsperson	Yes, but local representative only	Yes, but local representative only	Yes, any 'authorized representative'	Yes
Requirement of prior approach to institution's management	Yes	No – Ombudsperson checks with management	Yes	Yes	Yes	Yes
Formal procedures established that include fixed timelines	Yes	Ombudsperson process – minimal (limited rules on closing case)	Yes	Yes	Yes	Yes

(Continued)

Institutional design element	First-generation IAM	Second-generation IAM				
	World Bank Inspection Panel	IFC & MIGA[26] Compliance Advisor / Ombudsperson	IDB Independent Consultation and Investigation Mechanism	AsDB Accountability Mechanism	EBRD Project Complaint Mechanism	AfDB Review Mechanism
Decision to authorize problem-solving exercise	Not applicable	CAO determines eligibility of request and makes decision to conduct problem-solving exercise	Ombudsperson determines eligibility of request, and decision to conduct problem-solving exercise requires consent of all involved parties	SPF determines eligibility of request; SPF decides to conduct problem-solving exercise, but final recommendations must be approved by Bank President	Eligibility assessors (PCM Experts) decide eligibility; requires Board approval (President for project not yet approved by Board) if recommendation not to authorize; President ultimately authorizes actual problem-solving exercise	Director of CRMU determines eligibility; and decides if problem-solving exercise is necessary
Decision to authorize compliance review	Panel recommends compliance review (based on recommendation of eligibility); and Board authorizes it (but Board's discretion limited after 1999)	CAO has discretion, after closing out the problem-solving exercise	Eligibility: Panel Chairperson; investigation authorized by Board / Bank President (for projects not yet approved)	Panel determines eligibility; Panel recommends investigation to Board committee, which recommends to Board; Board makes ultimate decision	Eligibility assessors (PCM Experts) decide eligibility; requires Board approval (President for project not yet approved by Board) if recommendation not to authorize; no further approval required	Director of CRMU recommends compliance review to Board; if recommends against review, he/she may refer request to chair of Roster for review, who may recommend compliance review to Board

Powers to investigate	Yes – guaranteed access to Bank documents and staff	Yes – guaranteed access to Bank documents and staff	Yes – guaranteed access to Bank documents and staff	Yes – guaranteed access to Bank documents and staff	Yes – guaranteed access to Bank documents and staff; while processing complaint, PCM Officer can make interim recommendation to relevant body to suspend Bank payments	Yes – guaranteed access to Bank documents and staff
Instrument of Board oversight, or management tool	Board oversight	Partial management tool, but independent since CAO reports to WBG President	Board oversight – except for projects not yet approved by Board	Board oversight	Board oversight – except for projects not yet approved by Board	Board oversight – except for projects not yet approved by Board
Investigation results in fact finding and/or recommendations	Fact finding	Fact finding and recommendation	Fact finding and recommendation	Fact finding and recommendation	Fact finding and recommendation; compliance review: can also recommend remedies (in line with what policies provide)	Fact finding and recommendation
Formal follow-up to problem-solving or compliance review reports	None; Board requests ad hoc Panel monitoring involvement in exceptional circumstances	Yes – Ombudsperson responsible	Problem solving: yes, Ombudsperson responsible; compliance review: only at request of the Board	No	Yes – PCM Officer monitors agreements reached as part of problem-solving and compliance review	Yes, there is follow up in both problem-solving and compliance review processes. In problem solving, this may be part of the agreement reached by parties

(Continued)

Institutional design element	First-generation IAM	Second-generation IAM					
	World Bank Inspection Panel	IFC & MIGA[26] Compliance Advisor/ Ombudsperson	IDB Independent Consultation and Investigation Mechanism	AsDB Accountability Mechanism	EBRD Project Complaint Mechanism	AfDB Review Mechanism
Contribution to institutional learning	Annual Report	Annual Report, but has advisory role	Annual Report; information for IDB staff and clients about the mechanism procedure	Annual Report	Annual Report; PCM Officer's Compliance Review Monitoring reports (at least bi-annually); regular Board review of IAM function mandatory	Annual Report – trends and lessons learnt
Publication of reports and decisions	Yes – including WB management monitoring reports on implementation of remedial action plans	Yes	Yes, including monitoring reports	Yes	Yes	Yes
Focus on compliance review and/or problem solving (dispute resolution), and policy advice	Compliance review – Bank management responsible for problem solving; Limited problem solving facilitated by IP during Eligibility Phase	Ombudsperson – problem solving, but also compliance and (limited) advisory role	Problem solving and compliance, limited advisory role	Problem solving and compliance	Problem solving and compliance	Problem solving and compliance

References

Reports

Institut de Droit International (1995). *The Legal Consequences for Member States of the Non-fulfilment by International Organizations of their Obligations toward Third Parties.*

International Law Association (2004). *Accountability of International Organisations.*

International Law Commission (2006). *Fragmentation Of International Law: Difficulties Arising from the Diversification and Expansion of International Law, Report of the Study Group.* UN Doc. A/CN.4/L.702, 18 July.

Books and articles

Berger, T. R. (1993–4). 'The World Bank's Independent Review of India's Sardar Sarovar Projects'. *American University Journal of International Law & Policy* 9(1): 33.

Boisson de Chazournes, L. (1999). 'Public Participation in Decision-Making: The World Bank Inspection Panel', *ASIL Studies in Transnational Legal Policy* 31: 84.

Bradlow, D. (1999). 'Precedent-Setting NGO Campaign Saves the World Bank's Inspection Panel'. *Human Rights Brief* 6: 7.

Bradlow, D. (2003). 'The Governance of the International Financial Institutions: The Need for Reform'. *Indian Journal of International Law* 43: 533.

Bradlow, D. (2005). 'Private Complainants and International Organizations: A Comparative Study of the Independent Inspection Mechanisms in International Financial Institutions'. *Georgetown Journal of International Law* 36: 403.

Clark, D. (1999). *A Citizen's Guide to the World Bank Inspection Panel.* Washington, DC: Centre for International Environmental Law.

Clark, D., J. Fox et al., eds. (2003). *Demanding Accountability: Civil-Society Claims and the World Bank Inspection Panel.* Oxford: Rowman & Littlefield Publishers Inc.

Darrow, M. (2006). *Between Light and Shadow: The World Bank, the International Monetary Fund and International Human Rights Law.* Portland, Oregon: Hart Publishing.

Dunkerton, K. J. (1995). 'The World Bank Inspection Panel and its Affect on Lending Accountability to Citizens of Borrowing Nations'. *University of Baltimore Journal of Environmental Law* 5: 226.

Ebbesson, J. (2007). 'Public Participation'. *The Oxford Handbook of International Environmental Law*, ed. D. Bodansky, J. Brunnée et al. Oxford: Oxford University Press.

French, H. F. (1994). 'The World Bank: Now Fifty, but How Fit?' *World Watch* 7: 10.

Head, J. W. (2003). 'For Richer or For Poorer: Assessing the Criticisms Directed at the Multilateral Development Banks'. *University of Kansas Law Review* 52: 241.

Hey, E. (1997). 'Towards the Recognition of a New Legally Relevant Relationship in International Law'. *The Hofstra Law & Policy Symposium* 2: 61.

Horta, K. (2002). 'Rhetoric and Reality: Human Rights and the World Bank'. *Harvard Human Rights Journal* 15: 227.

Hunter, D. (2003). 'Using the World Bank Inspection Panel to Defend the Interests of Project-Affected People'. *Chicago Journal of International Law* 4: 201.

Independent Evaluation Office (2004). 'Report on the Evaluation of the Role of the IMF in Argentina, 1991–2001'. Washington, DC: IMF. Available at www.imf.org/external/np/ieo/2004/arg/eng/index.htm.

Kingsbury, B. (1999). 'Operational Policies of International Institutions as Part of the Law-Making Process: The World Bank and Indigenous Peoples'. *The Reality of International Law: Essays in Honour of Ian Brownlie*, ed. G. S. Goodwin-Gill and S. Talmon. Oxford: Oxford University Press.

Reinisch, A. (2001). 'Securing the Accountability of International Organizations'. *Global Governance* 7: 131.

Roos, S. R. (2001). 'The World Bank Inspection Panel in its Seventh Year: An Analysis of its Process, Mandate, and Desirability with Special Reference to the China (Tibet) Case'. *Max Planck Yearbook of the United Nations Law* 5: 473.

Shihata, I. F. I. (2000). *The World Bank Inspection Panel: In Practice*. Oxford: Oxford University Press.

World Bank (2004). 'India Mumbai Urban Transport Project'. Press release, 29 March.

16

Transnational Commercial Arbitration
Dirk Lehmkuhl

As international trade has continued to expand, commercial arbitration has become the universally accepted method for addressing commercial disputes. Transnational commercial arbitration allows for contracting parties to choose to resolve any disputes that may emerge by reference to a private arbitral tribunal rather than through litigation in public courts. As the most compelling member of the family of alternative dispute resolution methods, it has the advantage of rendering binding decisions that are enforceable in foreign courts.

History

Any cross-border economic contract faces the problem that penalties for opportunistic behaviour are lower in the international realm than in a domestic legal system. However, the absence of a strong international legal framework has neither today, nor in the past, prevented economic actors from engaging in commerce across borders. In the early modern period, the more that merchants from up-coming cities such as Barcelona, Genoa, Venice and other ports in Southern Europe began to explore new markets around the Mediterranean and enter into trade with merchants from Flanders, France, Germany or England, the more devices were developed by the merchant community itself to mitigate problems of contractual commitment and enforcement. The expansion of commerce led not only to the evolution of a body of custom, mores and trade usages known as *lex mercatoria*, but also to new devices such as credit forms or the reputation-based mechanisms of Maghribi traders, both of which were employed to ensure contractual compliance. In this context, arbitration became very important as a mechanism of self-regulation, i.e. conflict resolution by merchant or commercial judges.

For instance, the establishment of courts specialized in the quick resolution of commercial disputes was absolutely necessary to ensure the functioning of trade fairs, which united buyers and sellers from far-away markets. Examples of such commercial courts are the Champagne fairs or guild courts, all of which were non-professional community tribunals. Other interesting examples include the local maritime courts in seaport towns ('admiralty courts') with jurisdiction over both commercial and maritime cases involving carriage of goods by sea; the so-called 'courts of staples' in England, Wales and Ireland, handling trade disputes in certain 'staple' products such as wool, leather or lead; and urban mercantile courts in Northern Italy, which were gradually granted jurisdiction over all mercantile cases within the cities. Adjudicators in these courts were generally selected from the ranks of merchants on the basis of their commercial experience, objectivity and seniority. It was expected that a merchant judge was able to assess mercantile custom, appreciate the needs of merchants and, in particular, understand the relevance of the facts surrounding a transaction in the context of changing trade dynamics (see, e.g., Trakman 1980, 1981; Berman 1983; Sachs 2006).

The use of arbitration to resolve private disputes has gained increasing practical importance over the last few decades of the twentieth century. It has been estimated that about 90 per cent of all cross-border contracts contain an arbitration clause, even reaching 100 per cent of cases in some industries, such as engineering (Bernstein 1996).

Table 16.1 Transnational arbitration cases received: top arbitration centres 1992–2007

	'92	'93	'95	'96	'98	'99	'00	'02	'03	'04	'05	'06	'07
CIETAC	267	486	902	778	645	609	543	684*	709*	850*	979*	981*	1118*
AAA	204	207	180	226	387	453	510	672	646	614	580	586	621
ICC	337	352	427	433	466	529	541	593*	580*	561*	521	593*	599*
HKIAC	185	139	184	197	240	257	298	320	287	280	281	394	448
LCIA	21	29	49	37	70*	56*	81*	88*	104*	87*	118*	133	137
SIAC	7	15	37	25	67	67	83	114	100	129	103	119	119
Stockholm	44	78	70	75	92	104	73	55	82	50	56	141	84
Vancouver	44	52	40	57	49	60	88	71	76	84	77	76*	82*
KCAB	30	28	18	36	59	40	40	47	38	46	53	47	59
Vienna	100	100	100	100	100	100	100	33	45	50	N/A	N/A	40

CIETAC China International Economic and Trade Arbitration Commission
AAA American Arbitration Association
ICC International Chamber of Commerce
HKIAC Hong Kong International Arbitration Centre
LCIA London Court of International Arbitration
SIAC Singapore International Arbitration Centre
Stockholm Arbitration Institute of the Stockholm Chamber of Commerce
Vancouver British Columbia International Commercial Arbitration Centre
KCAB The Korean Commercial Arbitration Board
Vienna International Arbitral Centre of the Austrian Federal Economic Chamber
These statistics include domestic and transnational arbitration.
Source: adapted from Hong Kong International Arbitration Centre, December 2008.

However, any effort to quantify the importance of arbitration is hampered by the fact that institutionalized arbitration – which is arbitration that is based on an arbitration clause in the contract between the parties and that involves an arbitration centre – can be registered, while ad hoc arbitration – which is arbitration that is agreed upon after the event of a dispute – cannot be accounted for. In general, commercial arbitration is most frequently associated with the International Court of Arbitration of the International Chamber of Commerce (ICC). Since the early 1920s, the ICC's Court of Arbitration has been the best-known forum for transnational commercial arbitration. As table 16.2 indicates, however, the world of arbitration is much more diverse, as evidenced by the multitude of cases resolved by top arbitration centres worldwide.

Operation

The advantages of arbitration over litigation in national courts are best highlighted by a few major features of the arbitration process.

Foremost among these is the high degree of procedural flexibility regarding the choice of location and nomination of arbitrators. Arbitrators may be appointed by the parties, designated by an independent appointing authority (such as an arbitration centre or a trade association) or selected by a list system (for example, both parties compile a list of three to four persons, exchange the lists, and eliminate names from the other party's list). Alternatively, a tribunal may be formed. In this case each party nominates one arbitrator each. These two party-nominated arbitrators jointly select a third arbitrator as a neutral president.

The neutrality and expertise of the arbitrators, as well as the speed and confidentiality of the proceedings, are further important features of commercial arbitration. Arbitration guarantees greater secrecy than litigation, as neither the procedures nor the awards are released as public information. Therefore, companies that must protect commercially sensitive information are more apt to choose arbitration than litigation due to the greater protection of private information. A final important aspect is the enforceability of arbitral awards. Signed in 1958, the New York Convention on the Recognition and Enforcement of Foreign Arbitral Awards significantly restricts the capability of national courts to annul or set aside a foreign arbitral award. Today, the New York Convention is signed by more than 137 countries. The result is that, between member countries, arbitral awards rendered in a foreign country are more likely to be accepted and enforced domestically than are decisions of foreign courts, even if the same foreign procedural and substantive provisions are the basis of both decisions.

Sceptical Voices

Today, there are critical voices from both practitioners and academics concerning the traditional advantages of transnational commercial arbitration. To begin with, Dezalay and Garth have noted that the traditionally amicable nature of dispute resolution is being replaced by a strong commercial attitude brought forth by the increasingly prominent role of transnational Anglo-Saxon law firms in international business relations. The adversarial nature of US-style litigation has begun to spill over into the international realm because American law firms consider transnational arbitration to be merely another form of litigation, and thus approach it with the same professional attitude (Dezalay and Garth 1996: 55). Forum-shopping activities and recourse to any legal means available – including the purposeful use of national courts to prevent the recognition and enforcement of arbitral awards – characterize this new tactical approach toward the resolution of transnational commercial disputes. The adverse effect is an increase in juridification, causing arbitration to become more complex, time-consuming and more expensive. Estimates of the distribution of costs in arbitration proceedings tend to confirm these assessments: of the overall costs, 82 per cent goes to the lawyers representing the parties, 16 per cent goes to the arbitrators and 2 per cent goes to the arbitration institutions.

Similarly, two factors put at risk the traditional advantage of confidentiality. First, there is an increasing tendency to publish arbitral awards either by arbitration centres or by arbitrators, who, in their function as lawyers or law professors at universities, contribute publications to specialized journals. Second, there is the obligation of listed companies to comply with increasingly detailed public reporting requirements, including the obligation to disclose, in a timely manner, reliable and comprehensive information on the existence and scope of arbitration proceedings to their shareholders.

Finally, there are normative critiques of private, out-of-court dispute settlement. Some of these criticisms refer to asymmetries between parties in traditional commercial arbitration (Kronstein 1963; Cutler 2003). More often, the critiques address the forms of private dispute settlement in specific areas such as investment disputes between states and private investors at the International Centre for Settlement of Investment Disputes under the auspices of the World Bank in Washington (Besson 2005; van Haarten 2005), or in the area of Internet domain names according to the Uniform Domain Name Dispute Resolution Policy of the Internet Corporation of Assigned Names and Numbers (Geist 2002; Mueller 2000).

Academic Scholarship

In sharp contrast to its actual importance, the transnational arbitration of cross-border economic interactions has received only limited attention in academic circles, with a significant variety of issues that are debated across different disciplines.

Historical

Apart from some research on the *historical* background and development of arbitration, either per se or in the context of the development of the Western world (Condliffe 1951; North and Thomas 1973; Trakman 1980, 1981; Rosenberg and Birdzell 1986; Munro 2001; Sachs 2006) and an outstanding *sociological portrait* (Dezalay and Garth 1996), *legal* contributions are by far the most frequent. They typically focus on either the legal quality of trade codes and empirical study of the existence of the *lex mercatoria*, or on arbitration as a private device allowing parties to opt out of state-enforced legal codes (Berman and Kaufman 1978; Berman and Dasser 1990; Bernstein 1992; Bernstein 1996; Bernstein 2001; Berger et al. 2001). More recently, scholars of the 'law and society' tradition have presented inspiring approaches that interpret the *lex mercatoria* and commercial arbitration as part of societal self-regulation, or even societal constitutionalism, in world society (Teubner 1997; Teubner 2001; Calliess 2002; Zumbansen 2002).

Economic

In the realm of *economic* analysis, two perspectives can be distinguished. On the one hand, trade codes and arbitration are described as institutionalized solutions to reduce transaction costs in long-distance economic exchange relations. Historical examples include the Champagne fairs or Maghribi traders' coalition that emerged to cope with commitment problems or other problems related to the resolution of disputes and the enforcement of judgements (Greif 1989, 1992, 1993; Milgrom, North et al. 1990; Greif, Milgrom et al. 1994). On the other hand, other scholars interpret the *lex mercatoria* and arbitration as intriguing cases of private ordering in which communities and markets overcome collective action problems. Both communities and markets may provide private alternatives to public legal systems by developing rule systems and the institutions for their application without recourse to public actors and organizations (Ostrom 1990; Ellickson 1991, 1994; Casella 1996; Benson 1998; Benson 1999).

Political science

The *political science* literature on arbitration is much more limited. With a rational-institutionalist framework, Walter Mattli attributes the choice of arbitration over litigation to the 'varying institutional needs of different types of disputes and disputants'. He argues that 'these needs can be explained in terms of the severity of the enforcement problem, uncertainty about the preferences or behaviour of contractual partners, and uncertainty about the state of the world'

(Mattli 2001). Picking up the idea of private justice in international affairs, arbitration has been described as a form of societal self-regulation and the *lex mercatoria* has been praised as a truly transnational solution (e.g. Higgott and Weber 2005). Along similar lines, Claire Cutler's pioneering work interprets trade norms and commercial arbitration from a historical materialist perspective. Taking arbitration as a *pars pro toto* form of transnational self-regulation, Cutler links up to the work of Kronstein by emphasizing asymmetries in business relations and the potential normative implications of self-regulation (Kronstein 1963; Cutler 1995, 2003).

Arbitration has also been interpreted with respect to its embeddedness into a more broadly evolving sociopolitical context. Arguing in the systems-theoretical tradition of Niklas Luhman, Mathias Albert conceptualizes private dispute resolution and private legal arrangements such as the *lex mercatoria* as expressions of a legalization process, framed in terms of co-evolution of the political and the legal systems of world society. Doing so implies shifting the focus toward the operation of law as a complex, self-referential, autopoietic social system and away from addressing debates on the underlying ontological assumptions concerning its 'nature' or the 'core of law'. Also, the systems-theoretical perspective implies that one must give up the 'assumption that "international relations" can be treated as an empirically or conceptually isolated realm within world society, giving analytical preference to the internal *functional differentiation* of that society (into a political system, a legal system, an economic system etc.) instead' (Albert 2007; also Albert 2002).

Finally, arbitration has been addressed within the research on transnationalized governance and its perspective on institutional change and institution-building (Djelic and Quack 2003; Djelic and Sahlin-Andersson 2006). In particular, the interest in institutionalized linkages between the national and the transnational level operates with the assumption that the institutions that have been established to facilitate trade and to provide legal certainty are products of the social, political and economic fabric of our contemporary period and are interwoven into it (cf. e.g. Greif 1992; Hasenclever, Mayer et al. 1997). This perspective also implies that actors who operate within and organize institutions are not merely constrained by them but rather also contribute to changing them. This general focus has also been applied to transnational dispute resolution. Operating explicitly with an interdisciplinary ambition, the attention herein shifts to the dynamics resulting from the parallel existence of competing claims of jurisdiction (Lehmkuhl 2003, 2006).

References

Albert, M. (2002). *Zur Politik der Weltgesellschaft: Identität und Recht im Kontextinternationaler Vergesellschaftung*. Weilerswist, Germany: Velbrück.

Albert, M. (2007). 'Beyond Legalization: Reading the Increase, Variation and Differentiation of Legal and Law-like Arrangements in International Relations through World Society Theory'. *Law and Legalisation in Transnational Relations*, ed. C. Brütsch and D. Lehmkuhl. London: Routledge.

Benson, B, L. (1998). 'How to Secede in Business Without Really Leaving: Evidence of the Substitution of Arbitration for Litigation'. *Secession, State & Liberty*, ed. D. Gordon. New Brunswick and London: Transaction Publishers.

Benson, B, L. (1999). 'To Arbitrate or to Litigate: That is the Question'. *European Journal of Law and Economics* 8: 91–151.

Berger, K. P., ed. (2001). *The Practice of Transnational Law*. New York: Kluwer Law International.

Berman, H. J. (1983). *Law and Revolution: The Formation of the Western Legal Tradition*. Cambridge, MA: Harvard University Press.

Berman, H. J., and C. Kaufman (1978). 'The Law of International Commercial Transactions (Lex Mercatoria)'. *Harvard International Law Journal* 19(1): 221–77.

Berman, H. J., and F. J. Dasser (1990). 'The "New" Law Merchant and the "Old" Sources, Content, and Legitimacy'. *Lex Mercatoria and Arbitration*, ed. T. E. Carbonneau. Dobbs Ferry, NY: Transnational Publisher.

Bernstein, L. (1992). 'Opting Out of the Legal System'. *Journal of Legal Studies* 21: 115–57.

Bernstein, L. (1996). 'Merchant Law in Merchant Court: Rethinking the Code's Search for Immanent Business Norms'. *The University of Pennsylvania Law Review* 144: 1756–821.

Bernstein, L. (2001). 'Private Commercial Law in the Cotton Industry: Creating Cooperation through Rules, Norms, and Institutions'. John M. Olin Law & Economics Working Paper. Chicago: The University of Chicago.

Besson, S. (2009). 'Le légitimité de l'arbitrage international d'investissement'. 25 July 2005. *Jusletter*. Available at www.weblaw.ch/jusletter/Artikel.asp?ArticleNr=3932&Language=1 (accessed 25 January 2009).

Calliess, G.-P. (2002). 'Reflexive Transnational Law. The Privatization of Civil Law and the Civilization of Private Law'. *Zeitschrift für Rechtssoziologie* 23(2): 185–216.

Casella, A. (1996). 'On Market Integration and the Development of Institutions: The Case of International Commercial Arbitration'. *European Economic Review* 40: 155–86.

Condliffe, J. B. (1951). *The Commerce of Nations*. London: Allen & Unwin.

Cutler, A. C. (1995). 'Global Capitalism and Liberal Myths: Dispute Settlement in Private International Trade Relations'. *Millennium: Journal of International Studies* 24(3): 377–97.

Cutler, A. C. (2003). *Private Power and Global Authority: Transnational Merchant Law and the Global Political Economy*. Cambridge: Cambridge University Press.

Dezalay, Y., and B. Garth (1996). *Dealing in Virtue: International Commercial Arbitration and the Construction of a Transnational Legal Order*. Chicago: The University of Chicago Press.

Djelic, Marie-L., and S. Quack, eds. (2003). *Globalization and Institutions: Redefining the Rules of the Economic Game*. Cheltenham, Glos.: Edward Elgar.

Djelic, M.-L., and K. Sahlin-Andersson (2006). *Transnational Governance in the Making: Regulatory Fields and their Dynamics*. Cambridge: Cambridge University Press.

Ellickson, R. C. (1991). *Order Without Law: How Neighbors Settle Disputes*. Cambridge, MA: Harvard University Press.

Ellickson, R. C. (1994). 'The Aim of Order without Law'. *Journal of Institutional and Theoretical Economics* 150: 97–100.

Geist, M. (2001). 'Fair.com? An examination of the allegations of systemic unfairness in the ICANN UDRP'. Available at www.udrpinfo.com/resc/fair.pdf (accessed 25 January 2009).

Geist, M. (2002). 'Fundamentally Fair.com? An Update on Bias Allegations and the ICANN UDRP'. Available at http://aix1.uottawa.ca/~geist/fairupdate.pdf (accessed 25 January 2009).

Greif, A. (1989). 'Reputation and Coalitions in Medieval Trade: Evidence on the Maghribi Traders'. *Journal of Economic History* 49: 857–82.

Greif, A. (1993). 'Contract Enforceability and Economic Institutions in Early Trade: The Maghribi Traders' Coalition'. *American Economic Review* 83(3): 525–48.

Greif, A. (1992). 'Institutions and International Trade: Lessons from the Commercial Revolution'. *American Economic Review* 82(2), *Papers and Proceedings of the Hundred and Fourth Annual Meeting of the American Economic Association (May, 1992)*: 128–33.

Greif, A., P. Milgrom et al. (1994). 'Coordination, Commitment, and Enforcement: The Case of the Merchant Guild'. *Journal of Political Economy* 102(4): 745–76.

Hasenclever, A., P. Mayer et al. (1997). *Theories of International Regimes*. Cambridge: Cambridge University Press.

Higgott, R. A., and H. Weber (2005). 'GATS in Context: Development, an Evolving Lex Mercatoria and the Doha Agenda'. *Review of International Political Economy* 12(3): 434–55.

Hong Kong International Arbitration Center. www.hkiac.org (accessed December 2008).

Kronstein, H. (1963). 'Arbitration is Power'. *New York University Law Review* 38: 661–700.

Lehmkuhl, D. (2003). 'Structuring Dispute Resolution in Transnational Trade: Competition and Co-evolution of Public and Private Institutions'. *Globalisation and Institutions: Redefining the Rules of the Economic Game*, ed. M.-L. Djelic and S. Quack. Cheltenham Glos.: Edward Elgar.

Lehmkuhl, D. (2006). 'Resolving Transnational Disputes: Commercial Arbitration and Linkages between Multiple Providers of Governance Services'. *New Modes of Governance in the Global System*, ed. M. König-Archibugi and M. Zürn. Basingstoke: Palgrave/Macmillan.

Mattli, W. (2001). 'Private Justice in a Global Economy: From Litigation to Arbitration'. *International Organization* 55(4): 919–48.

Milgrom, P. R., D. C. North et al. (1990. 'The Role of Institutions in the Revival of Trade: The Law Merchant, Private Judges, and the Champagne Fairs'. *Economics & Politics* 2: 1–23.

Mueller, M. (2000). 'Rough Justice. An Analysis of ICANN's Uniform Dispute Resolution Policy'. *Convergence Center*. Available at http://dcc.syr.edu/miscarticles/roughjustice.pdf (accessed 25 January 2009).

Munro, J. H. (2001). 'The New Institutional Economics and the Changing Fortunes of Fairs in Medieval and Early Modern Europe: The Textile Trades, Warfare, and Transaction Costs'. *Vierteljahrschrift für Sozial- und Wirtschaftsgeschichte* 88(1): 1–47.

North, D. C., and R. P. Thomas (1973). *The Rise of the Western World: A New Economic History*. Cambridge: Cambridge University Press.

Rosenberg, N., and L. E. Birdzell, Jr (1986). *How the West Grew Rich: The Economic Transformation of the Industrial World*. New York: Basic Books.

Sachs, S. E. (2006). 'From St Ives to Cyberspace: The Modern Distortion of the Medieval "Law Merchant"'. *American University International Law Review* 21(5): 685–812.

Teubner, G., ed. (1997). *Global Law without a State*. Aldershot: Dartmouth Publishing Company.

Teubner, G. (2001). 'Global Private Regimes: Neo-spontaneous Law and Dual Constitution of Autonomous Sectors in World Society?' *Public Governance in the Age of Globalization*, ed. K.-H. Ladeur. Aldershot: Ashgate.

Trakman, L. E. (1980). 'The Evolution of the Law Merchant: Our Commercial Heritage. Part I: Ancient and Medieval Law Merchant'. *Journal of Maritime Law and Commerce* 12(1): 1–24.

Trakman, L. E. (1981). 'The Evolution of the Law Merchant: Our Commercial Heritage. Part II: The Modern Law Merchant'. *Journal of Maritime Law and Commerce* 12(2): 153–82.

van Haarten, G. (2005). 'Private Authority and Transnational Governance: The Contours of the International System of Investor Protection'. *Review of International Political Economy* 12(4): 600–23.

Zumbansen, P. (2002). 'Piercing the Legal Veil: Commercial Arbitration and Transnational Law'. *European Law Journal* 8(3: September): 400–32.

17

World Bank Inspection Panel
Thomas Hale

The World Bank Inspection Panel is an independent review body that assesses the World Bank's compliance with its environmental and social safeguard policies. Anyone affected by a Bank project may bring a complaint before the Panel. If the complaint is deemed worthy of concern, the Panel investigates the alleged violations and publishes its findings as a public factual record. This process aims to use transparency to make the Bank more accountable to the people its projects affect.

Origins

During the 1980s and early 1990s the Bank faced a growing chorus of criticism over its lending policies. Critics alleged that Bank loans were perversely harming the very people and places they aimed to help, a problem exacerbated by the irresponsiveness, secrecy, and general unaccountability of Bank officials. The Bank adopted a number of policies in response to these charges. In 1987, the Bank adopted a number of 'operational directives' (ODs) designed to guide staff toward best practices. In 1992 the Bank reshuffled these directives into 'operational policies' (OPs) and 'bank procedures' (BPs), which are binding on Bank staff, and 'good practices' (GPs) which serve to disseminate information and highlight successes. These regulations created a body of social and environmental restrictions on staff behaviour. In 1993, in the wake of controversy over the Bank's Narmada dam project in India, the Bank created an information release policy under which important Bank documents and decisions were to be made public. It also created the Inspection Panel to act as an independent watchdog and ombudsperson (Bradlow 2003; Shahata 2004).

How the Inspection Panel Works

The Inspection Panel is a forum for people affected by Bank projects to bring forward claims that the Bank has violated its own environmental and social regulations. As such it seeks to increase the World Bank's accountability to its stakeholders. The Panel assesses these complaints and, if it finds them valid, investigates and publishes its findings as a public record.

The Panel's reports have no legal standing, and are not binding on the Bank in any way. Rather, they aim to correct errors in Bank behaviour via transparency.

The rules governing the Panel are laid out in its 1993 founding resolution and two subsequent 'clarifications' in 1996 and 1999. The Panel is composed of three independent development experts, one of whom is designated as the Chairperson. These individuals are nominated by the Bank President and appointed by the Board. A small secretariat, also independent of Bank management, provides logistical support.

The Panel entertains requests for investigation from project-affected people or their appointed representative, who may, in exceptional circumstances, be from a different country. An Executive Director of the Bank – that is, the country-appointed overseers who make up the Bank's top governing body – may also request an inspection. According to the rules governing the Panel, complaints must allege that an 'actual or threatened material adverse effect on the affected party's rights or interests' has resulted 'directly out of an action or omission of the Bank to follow its own operation policies and procedures during the design, appraisal, and/or implementation' of the project in question. Complaints may not pertain to alleged violations by the borrowing country, Bank procurement practices, or projects which have been more than 95 per cent completed. Complainants must also demonstrate that they have previously raised the issue with Bank staff and received unsatisfactory results. The Inspection Panel may only hear complaints pertaining to two of the Bank's five sub-sections, the International Bank for Reconstruction and Development and the International Development Association.

When the Chairperson receives a request, she considers whether it meets the basic eligibility requirements and then either requests more information or officially registers it. Once the request is registered, Management must submit a response within twenty-one days, at which point the Panel performs an initial eligibility review. The purpose of this review is to decide whether or not the case merits a full investigation. Typically this review is completed within twenty-one days, but the Panel may extend the deadline if it needs to gather further information.

The Panel's decision at this stage – to investigate or not – is only a recommendation. The Bank's Board then decides whether to adopt or reject the Panel's suggestion. It has fully rejected the Panel's recommendation to investigate in only two cases. Should the Panel recommend an investigation and the Board approve, the request is made public and the Panel is empowered to investigate the substance of the claim. Among other methods, it may hold public hearings and make site visits. Furthermore, 'any member of the public' may provide the Panel with relevant supplemental information.

After the Panel finishes its investigation it submits its report to the Executive Directors and the Bank staff, which has six weeks to prepare a reply 'indicating Management's recommendations in response to the Panel's findings'. The Board then considers the Panel report and Management's response, and must decide within two weeks whether or not to take any action on the matter – that is, whether to address the requesters' concerns or not. The Panel report, Management response and Board decision are then made public.

The Politics of the Inspection Panel

The tendency of states to support or oppose the Panel seems driven by their status as Bank creditors or borrowers. Among the creditors, the US has been a vocal defender of the Panel. This stance is largely a result of the pressure US-based environmental groups place on the US Congress, which must periodically authorize replenishments of the Bank's capital (Bowles and Kormos 1994–5). Borrower countries, especially Brazil, India, and China, which have been the indirect subjects of several investigations, oppose the Panel and have sought to limit it (Fox 2000). In the *China Western Poverty Reduction* case, for example, the Panel revealed an attitude amongst Bank staff that China's 'social and political systems' prohibited meaningful consultation with and involvement of affected stakeholders. It recommended that the Bank consult affected ethnic minorities and incorporate their concerns into the project's implementation. In response, the Chinese government declared the Panel a threat to its sovereignty and suggested the Board substantially reform it (World Bank 2000).

Bank Management has also resisted the Panel's activities. For example, in the first *Lesotho Highlands* case, Management received, disseminated and discussed with Executive Directors an unauthorized copy of the request application which made known the names of the requesters – information that was supposed to be confidential. The Panel admonished that 'such serious disregard of the Panel process threatens its integrity' and amounted 'to a serious abuse of reasonable due process'. Management also refused to provide a substantive response to the request (as the Panel's operating procedures require), arguing that because it believed the request did not meet the eligibility criteria, Management was under no obligation to respond.

The Panel vigorously rejected this claim and recommended an investigation into Management's objection. A more subtle form of disregard for the Panel has come in the form of 'panel proofing', the name the Bank staff has given to cosmetic adjustments intended to shield projects from Panel scrutiny (Fox and Brown 1998). In the *China Western Poverty Reduction* case, the Panel was disturbed to find Bank staff not just admitting to, but also seeking to justify 'this' 'check-list' or 'process' approach to compliance'. Fox (2000) notes this process can be helpful when it leads to higher compliance, but also runs the risk of promoting 'the pro forma fulfilment of administrative requirements rather than focusing on actual changes on the ground'.

Nongovernmental organizations have been quick to defend the Panel against attacks from Management and borrowers and have simultaneously pushed for the expansion of the Panel's scope and power (Clark, Fox et al. 2003; Hunter 2003). The Panel itself, however, has perhaps been its own most effective advocate. In various rulings the Panel has narrowly interpreted the restrictions on its mandate, even going so far as to violate them in letter in order, it claimed, to obey them in spirit. While some of these creative readings are most likely the inevitable growing pains associated with any new quasi-judicial body, in several instances the Panel's interpretations have broadly expanded its reach (Carmody 1999–2000). For example, the Panel's guidelines explicitly prohibit it from investigating loans that are more than 95 per cent disbursed. In the *Itaparica Resettlement and Irrigation* case, however, the Panel decided that, even though more than 95 per cent of the loan had been disbursed, the request was eligible for investigation because the project had only been approximately 50 per cent completed.

Evaluating the Inspection Panel

As of the beginning of 2010, the Panel had received sixty-four requests for inspection, forty-three of which it chose to pursue. Eighteen of these resulted in investigations. A full case history is available on the Panel's website.

Academic observers find it difficult to judge the Panel's effect on Bank decision-making given the lack of counterfactual examples (i.e., what would have happened in a specific case had a complaint not been brought before the Panel). Fox (2000) argues the Inspection Panel offers a useful illustration of how transnational advocacy networks can promote accountability at international institutions. However, he finds the Panel's impact on actual Bank practices an ambiguous mix of success and failures. He also notes that the states that control the Bank's Board remain a significant obstacle to the Panel's work.

Hale and Slaughter (2006) calculate that out of twenty-eight Inspection Panel cases studied, seven led to 'high' levels of policy change, and four led to 'medium' levels, with the remainder leading to small or no changes. Furthermore, Hale and Slaughter find that cases that attract more attention from civil society and the media stand a significantly higher chance of leading to policy changes.

Hale (2008) builds on these results with quantitative analysis of an expanded dataset that allows him to test competing explanations for the Panel's effectiveness. The results provide an important qualification to earlier findings that civil society activism drove the effectiveness of the Panel. While it is true that more publicized cases have a higher chance of coming before the Panel, once a case is being reviewed, the level of activism surrounding a case has little effect on Bank behaviour. Instead, it is the transparency the Panel provides that has a sizeable effect on Bank behaviour.

This finding suggests the Panel is performing as a true 'info-court'. As Hale (2008) explains, these institutions, 'while quasi-judicial in nature . . . do not issue legal decisions, but rather create non-binding reports that aim to clarify the facts of compliance or non-compliance in a particular case. The idea is to use transparency to create accountability.' That any policy changes emerged from Panel investigations (which do nothing more than bring the facts in a certain case to light – that is, they have no binding force) can be seen as a qualified success.

References

Bowles, I. A., and C. F. Kormos (1994–5). 'Environmental Reform at the World Bank: The Role of the U.S. Congress'. *Virginia Journal of International Law* 35: 777–839.

Bradlow, D. (1993–4). 'International Organizations and Private Complaints: The Case of the World Bank Inspection Panel'. *Virginia Journal of International Law* 34: 553–614.

Carmody, C. (1999–2000). 'Beyond the Proposals: Public Participation in International Economic Law'. *American University International Law Review* 15: 1321–46.

Clark, D., J. A. Fox et al. (2003). *Demanding Accountability: Civil-Society Claims and the World Bank Inspection Panel*. New York: Rowman & Littlefield Publishers.

Fox, J. A. (2000). 'The World Bank Inspection Panel: Lessons from the First Five Years'. *Global Governance* 6(3): 279–318.

Fox, J. A., and L. D. Brown (1998). *The Struggle for Accountability: The World Bank, NGOs, and Grassroots Movements*. Cambridge, MA: MIT Press.

Hale, T. N. (2008). '"Info-Courts" and the Accountability of International Organizations: Evidence from the World Bank Inspection Panel'. Paper presented at the Fourth Global Administrative Law Seminar, Viterbo, Italy, 13–14 June. Available at www.iilj.org/GAL/documents/Hale.pdf.

Hale , T. N., and A.-M. Slaughter (2006). 'Transparency: Possibilities and Limitations'. *Fletcher Forum* 30(1: Winter): 153–63.

Hunter, D. (2003). 'Using the World Bank Inspection Panel to Defend the Interests of Project-Affected People'. *Chicago Journal of International Law* 4(1): 201–12.

Shihata, I. F. I. (2004). *The World Bank Inspection Panel: In Practice*. New York: Oxford University Press.

World Bank (2000). 'China to Implement Qinghai Component of the China Western Poverty Reduction Project with Its Own Resources'. News release no. 2001/004/EAP 7 July, Washington, DC.

Part III
Multistakeholder Initiatives

Introduction

More and more actors participate in global politics today alongside nation states (Risse-Kappen 1995). These actors play a variety of roles, but one of the most crucial is to join with other actors to form hybrid governance mechanisms, the subject of this section. Most of these institutions involve at least one public (national or intergovernmental) actor, but some do not. They can serve a variety of functions, but service delivery (e.g. the Global Fund) and standard-setting (e.g. the World Commission on Dams) are the two most prominent.

Balancing different types of actors can lead to controversy. Some scholars have suggested that multistakeholder partnerships can provide public goods above and beyond what nation states can offer, particularly in a transnational context. For example, following the emergence of a series of public–private development partnerships that resulted from the 2002 World Summit on Sustainable Development, some observers favourably compared the 'jazzier dance' of the new initiatives to the 'stiff waltz' of traditional agreements (Witte, Streck et al. 2003). In this view, multistakeholder initiatives fill a key functional gap in the architecture of global governance by bringing a variety of resources and competencies to bear on common problems.

Other observers take a less sanguine view, arguing that outsourcing public goods to other actors represents a hollowing-out of public authority, or at best a malign neglect of public transnational responsibilities. They also question the legitimacy of allowing potentially self-interested private actors to perform governance functions that affect other individuals.

In all cases, some negotiation between the various actors must occur, and rarely are the normative issues perfectly clear. Sometimes the involvement of non-state actors seems to increase democratic legitimacy. For example, the World Commission on Dams allowed various interest groups, including the communities directly affected by dam projects, to discuss the policies governing dam construction around the world. In other cases, the participation of non-state actors raises questions. The contributions of private actors like the Rotary Club or the Gates Foundation to public health are certainly welcome to the millions of individuals whose suffering they alleviate. That these funds grant private donors influence over, for example, how developing countries structure their health systems (as in the International Health Partnership, chapter 23) does not diminish their generosity, though it does raise complicated questions over where the frontier between public and private authority should fall.

References

Risse-Kappen, T. (1995). *Bringing Transnational Relations Back In: Non-State Actors, Domestic Structures and International Institutions*. Cambridge: Cambridge University Press.

Witte, J. M., C. Streck et al. (2003). 'The Road from Johannesburg: What Future for Partnerships in Global Environmental Governance?' *Progress or Peril? Networks and Partnerships in Global Environmental* Governance, ed. T. Benner, C. Streck et al. Berlin: Global Public Policy Institute.

18

The Framework Convention Alliance
Ross MacKenzie

The Framework Convention Alliance (FCA) is a coalition of more than 350 nongovernmental organizations (NGOs) formed to coordinate NGO activity in support of the World Health Organization's (WHO) Framework Convention on Tobacco Control (FCTC), the first global public health treaty.

The FCA played a key supporting role during the FCTC process, and since the Convention entered into force in 2005 it has monitored its implementation, and has been involved in negotiations aimed at development of specific protocols. Founded in 1999 as a loose coalition of NGOs, the FCA is now a legal entity headquartered in Geneva, with a representative office in Washington DC and contacts in all WHO regions.

Development of the FCTC

Tobacco consumption is the leading preventable cause of global mortality. In 2005, an estimated 6.4 million deaths were attributed to tobacco use, a figure that will rise to between 7.4 and 9.7 million by 2030 (Mathers and Loncar 2006). The greatest burden of this pandemic will fall on low- and middle-income countries (LMICs), where some 6.8 million attributable deaths will occur by 2030, a doubling of the figure for 2002 (Mathers and Loncar 2006).

The growth of the tobacco pandemic and its shift to markets in Africa, Asia, Latin America and countries of the Former Soviet Union (FSU) have been largely the result of dramatic tobacco industry expansion facilitated by key components of globalization – liberalized trade and direct foreign investment; technological innovation that facilitates global advertising and promotion; and the international trade in contraband and counterfeit cigarettes.

In response to this looming public health crisis, the World Health Assembly (WHA), the global body comprising the member states of the WHO, proposed an international tobacco control instrument to the WHO Director General in May 1995. Four years later, the WHA convened an intergovernmental negotiating body (INB) to draft a framework convention. Following meetings by the FCTC working group, and six meetings of the INB in Geneva between October 2000 and February 2003, the treaty was adopted and opened for signature until 29 June 2004. The FCTC entered into force on 27 February 2005. As of 31 January 2010, 168 countries that account for more than 85 per cent of the world's population had ratified and accepted the Convention; notable exceptions include the United States and Indonesia.

Significance of the Convention

The FCTC is an evidence-based, legally binding agreement that, unlike previous drug control treaties, emphasizes the centrality of demand reduction strategies, as well as more typical initiatives aimed at supply issues. Demand-related treaty Articles cover price and taxation measures; regulation of content of tobacco products; packaging and labelling of tobacco products; public education; and restrictions on tobacco advertising, promotion and sponsorship. Provisions designed to regulate supply of tobacco products include controlling contraband trade and sales to and by minors, and support for establishing economically viable alternatives to tobacco production.

Subsequent to the FCTC's entry into force in February 2005, member states have turned to establishing protocols to the Convention via the Conference of the Parties (COP), the governing body of the FCTC comprising those countries that have signed and ratified it (WHO 2010a), and the formal process through which representatives gather to adopt guidelines and other regulatory aspects of the Convention.

Parties at the first COP session in Geneva in February 2006 addressed administrative and procedural matters related to implementation of the FCTC, and agreed to commence work on protocols on cross-border tobacco advertising, promotion and sponsorship, and illicit trade in tobacco products, as well as guidelines on protection against exposure to second-hand smoke and on tobacco product testing (WHO 2010a). Subsequent COPs in Bangkok in July 2007 (WHO 2010b), and in Durban, South Africa, in November 2008, have furthered this work, and set the agenda for the November 2010 meeting (WHO 2008).

The FCA: Civil Society and Tobacco Control

The FCA was formed in 1999 to improve communication amongst NGOs involved in the FCTC negotiation process, and to encourage other organizations to participate, particularly those in developing countries. As well as health-focused NGOs, the FCA includes environmental, human rights and women's organizations (Wipfli, Bettcher et al. 2001). The Alliance's self-described relationship to the FCTC is that of a 'watchdog' for the Convention (Framework Convention Alliance 2010), which entails development of tobacco control capabilities; support for development, ratification, accession and implementation of the FCTC; monitoring its implementation; and promotion and support of global tobacco control campaigns.

The FCA is particularly committed to assisting efforts by low- and middle-income countries (LMICs) to participate in the process. Among other initiatives, it has provided grants to tobacco control advocates from low-income countries, enabling them to be involved in the Convention process. This reflects not only the Alliance's commitment to equitable participation, but also the recognition that in many of the poorer countries which will benefit most from an effective treaty, NGOs are often at the forefront of tobacco control efforts (Hammond and Assunta 2003).

Involvement in Negotiations

Granting of provisional official relations status to member NGOs by the WHO allowed the FCA significant involvement in Convention negotiating sessions, most notably the right, at the invitation of the chair, 'to make a statement of an expository nature' (WHO 2000), which was generally restricted to a short statement at the end of a session.

As important as participation in formal negotiating sessions was, the FCA's role as the 'public health conscience during proceedings' (Collin, Lee et al. 2005), via its advocacy activities during negotiations, was arguably its most significant contribution. Prominent input to INBs included provision of meticulous policy advice to delegates via briefings, seminars and daily bulletins; lobbying of delegates and government representatives; and media communication through press conferences and publication of reports on a range of related themes. Throughout this process the Alliance, according to one observer, displayed 'remarkable political acuity and unwavering commitment' in its advocacy for the FCTC (Warner 2008).

Current Focus

Since the FCTC's entry into force in February 2005, Alliance activities have included the FCA FCTC Monitor project, a civil society-based approach to monitoring and evaluation of FCTC implementation that includes efforts to hold governments accountable to their legal obligations as Parties to the treaty (Jategaonkar 2007). It has also ana-lysed trade agreements and a range of tobacco industry activities.

The FCA is closely involved in protocol development, and supported initiatives at the second COP meeting to commence negotiations on a protocol to curb trade in contraband and counterfeit tobacco prod-ucts. Contraband poses a significant threat to progress on tobacco control, as suggested by the series of INB[1] meetings to formulate an Illicit Trade in Tobacco Products protocol. Work on other areas of urgency – including product regulation and disclosure, education, communication, training and public awareness, demand reduction measures, support for economically viable alternatives to tobacco production, and protection of the environment – were advanced in preparation for the fourth COP scheduled for November 2010 in Uruguay.

Despite the crucial impact of the FCA in the ongoing FCTC process, the organization faces considerable financial uncertainty, and contin-ues to work to resolve issues surrounding funding and mechanisms of assistance (Framework Convention Alliance 2008).

References

Framework Convention Alliance (2008). *FCA Bulletin* 85. Saturday 22 November. Available at www.fctc.org/dmdocuments/Issue%2085%20 saturday.pdf.

Framework Convention Alliance (2010). 'What is the Framework Convention Alliance?' Available at www.fctc.org/index.php?option =com_content&view=article&id=2&Itemid=9.

Hammond, R., and M. Assunta (2003). 'The Framework Convention on Tobacco Control: Promising Start, Uncertain Future'. *Tobacco Control* 12: 241–2.

Jategaonkar, N. (2007). *Civil Society Monitoring of the Framework Convention on Tobacco Control: 2007 Status Report of the Framework Convention Alliance.* Geneva: Framework Convention Alliance, 2007. Available at www.fctc. org/dmdocuments/fca-2007-mon-monitoring-report-en.pdf.

Mathers, C. D., and D. Loncar (2006). 'Projections of Global Mortality and Burden of Disease from 2002 to 2030'. *PLoS Medicine* 3(11). Available at http://medicine.plosjournals.decenturl.com/archive-1549-1676-3-11-pdf.

Warner, K. E. (2008). 'The Framework Convention on Tobacco Control: Opportunities and Issues'. *Salud Püblica Mexicana* 50(suppl. 3): S283–S291.

[1] The four INB sessions on a protocol on Illicit Trade in Tobacco Products were held in Geneva in February 2008, October 2008, June/July 2009 and March 2010.

Wipfli, H., D. Bettcher et al. (2001). 'Confronting the Global Tobacco Epidemic: Emerging Mechanisms of Global Governance'. *International Co-operation and Health*, ed. M. McKee, P. Garner et al. Oxford: Oxford University Press.

World Health Organization (2000). Intergovernmental Negotiating Body on the Framework Convention on Tobacco Control. First session. Provisional agenda item 7. A/FCTC/INB1/5. 29 August. 'Participation of nongovernmental organizations in the Intergovernmental Negotiating Body'. Available at www.who.int/gb/fctc/PDF/inb1/e1inb5.pdf.

World Health Organization (2008). Proceedings of the Third Session of the Conference of the Parties (COP3), Durban, South Africa, 17–22 November. Available at www.who.int/fctc/COP/COP3__in_brief_EN.pdf.

World Health Organization (2010a). Proceedings of the Conference of the Parties to the WHO Framework Convention on Tobacco Control, Geneva, 6–17 February. Available at www.who.int/fctc/cop/en/.

World Health Organization (2010b). Proceedings of the Second Session of the Conference of the Parties to the WHO Framework Convention on Tobacco Control, Bangkok, 30 June–6 July. Available at www.who.int/fctc/COP/second_session_COP/en/index.html.

19

Global Fund to Fight AIDS, Tuberculosis, and Malaria
Johanna Hanefeld

The Global Fund is a global public–private partnership dedicated to attracting and disbursing additional resources for fighting HIV, TB and malaria. It is a partnership between governments, civil society, the private sector and affected communities that represents a new approach to international health financing.

History

The Global Fund was created in 2002, following the UN General Assembly Special Session on HIV/AIDS (UNGASS), which underscored the need for dramatically increased funding for combatting HIV/AIDS. Since its creation in 2002, the Global Fund has become the main source of finance for programmes to fight AIDS, tuberculosis and malaria. By February 2010 the Fund had approved funding of more than $18.7 billion for more than 550 programmes in 140 countries.

It provides a quarter of all international financing for fighting AIDS globally, two-thirds for tuberculosis, and three-quarters for malaria (Global Fund 2010).

Approximately 60 per cent of Global Fund resources have been provided to countries in Sub-Saharan Africa, with the rest of funding evenly spread between South Asia, Latin America and the Caribbean, Eastern Europe and Central Asia; slightly more funding (13 per cent) was devoted to East Asia & the Pacific, and slightly less to the Middle East and North Africa region (Global Fund, 2010).

Structure and Operations

The Fund operates through a Secretariat in Geneva and awards grants on a competitive basis directly to countries. It is a financial mechanism, not an implementing agency, and the Fund has no presence in the countries it supports. Grants are made directly to principal recipients (PRs) in countries who then sub-grant to others. PRs include universities, government ministries and nongovernmental organizations. The Fund was one of the first international mechanisms to provide funding directly to civil society.

Grants are awarded on the basis of country proposals, and the Fund places a great emphasis on proposals reflecting country ownership (other funding principles include evidence-based, performance-based and inclusivity criteria). The primary mechanism at the country level for ensuring participation of all communities affected is the Country Coordinating Mechanism (CCM). The CCM develops Fund proposals, and representation from all sections of society is required, with 40 per cent of participants recommended to be from civil society (Global Fund 2008). The CCM process has been described by stakeholders at the country level as empowering, as it brings previously marginalized communities into the policy process, including providing them with greater access to government officials (Carceres et al. 2008).

In recipient countries the Global Fund appoints a Local Fund Agent (LFA). This is an independent organization, in most countries a local office of an international accounting firm, hired by the Global Fund Secretariat, that assesses the recipient's capacity to administer funds, and provides ongoing oversight and independent verification of financial and programmatic data provided (Starling, Walt et al. 2005).

Along with the CCM, the Fund's principal instrument to provide guidance to countries and implementers on specific aspects of policy is the guidelines it establishes for the application process. This kind of Global Fund policy guidance has in some countries led to change in government approaches to specific communities. For example,

China adopted harm reduction approaches as part of its HIV prevention strategy following Global Fund feedback on the country's proposal to the Fund, which had initially not included prevention efforts aimed at drug users (Hanefeld, Spicer et al. 2007).

Proposals made by countries to the Fund are evaluated by technical review panels (TRPs) comprising experts in HIV/AIDS, TB and malaria, which make recommendations to the Global Fund Board, which decides what grants will be awarded. The Board is comprised of representatives of all sectors, including the business sector, donor and recipient governments, affected communities and civil society. This inclusive decision-making process has been seen as a further innovative feature of the organization.

Challenges and Financing

The Global Fund relies on constant resources from donor governments, foundations, individuals and the private sector, and has in the past repeatedly faced challenges in securing continuous resources. This is an ongoing concern. By April 2010 the Global Fund had approved around $19 billion in total funding; 95 per cent of funds had been provided from countries' foreign aid budgets, with the remaining contributions from the private sector and foundations. At the same time it was estimated that, for the Fund to cover the expansion of programmes in line with the proposals submitted by countries which merit funding, it would have to expand its resources from $3 to $6 billion per year over the coming three years (Global Fund 2010).

A five-year evaluation of the Global Fund published in 2009 identified weak health systems as a key challenge to the Fund's programmes, requiring funding and strengthening to ensure the success of its programmes in the future. This has been taken up through increased funding for strengthening health systems, and in collaboration with other global health initiatives, such as the World Bank and the Global Alliance for Vaccines and Immunisation (GAVI) (England 2009). By early 2010 there was increasing discussion and debate to expand the Global Fund to Fight AIDS TB and Malaria into a Global Health Fund which would not only cover the sixth Millennium Development Goal (MDG) (AIDS, TB and Malaria) but also address maternal and child health (MDGs 5 and 4) (Sachs 2010).

Impact

The Global Fund has been subject to many evaluations focusing on a range of different aspects, from performance at country level to global-level funding policies. Most of these documents, including extensive documentation of the five-year evaluation of the Global Fund, are available at the Global Fund website. In March 2010 the Global Fund launched its 2010 Results report, which cited – amongst other achievements – that Global Fund-supported programmes saved at least 3,600 lives per day in 2009 and an estimated total of 4.9 million since its inception in 2002. The Global Fund supported the provision of antiretroviral treatment to 2.5 million people, with AIDS mortality declining in many high-burden countries. By December 2009, 6 million people who had active TB were treated through the Global Fund; 104 million insecticide-treated nets for preventing malaria were distributed.

The first country-level evaluation was a four-country study of programmes in Zambia, Uganda, Mozambique and Tanzania, led by R. Brugha and others. A summary of the study and its approach, as well as early findings, were published in the *Lancet* (Brugha, Donoghue et al. 2004). Findings at that stage focused mainly on initial problems with the Global Fund structures, including the CCMs. Outcomes of this research are summarized in a cross-country comparative report (Brugha, Donoghue et al. 2005).

Since 2006, the Global HIV Initiatives Network (GHIN) has conducted research on the Fund in eleven countries around the world. While this work continues to expand and be published, preliminary findings, including reports and presentations, are available on the GHIN website, which also has a database of all other publications on the Global Fund. These studies explore different aspects of the Global Fund at country level, including the participation of civil society in these processes, and the coordination between different actors at the country level. One of the challenges with Global Fund resources in Kyrgyzstan were the breaks in funding, which made continuity of services harder (Murzalieva, Aleshkina et al. 2009).

The Center for Global Development has conducted in-depth research since 2006 comparing performance of the Global Fund, US President's Emergency Plan for AIDS Relief (PEPFAR) and the World Bank Multi-Country AIDS Program (MAP) in Zambia, Uganda and Mozambique, examining not only programmes but specifically expenditure at country level (Omman, Bernstein et al. 2007). A series of reports focused on an analysis of expenditure (Bernstein and Sysaal 2007), the impact of Global Fund and other global health initiatives on aspects of health systems, including health information management systems and human resources for health (Omman and Bernstein 2008). Reports from Zambia, Mozambique and Uganda echoed findings from other regions which highlighted the initial delays in disbursements of funding but noted that these were mainly due to recipient organizations within countries and their management capacity. It also noted that variations in implementation between countries were as a result of the Global Fund's principle of country ownership and country-driven proposals.

Aspects of the Global Fund's impact at country level were also discussed in a review essay by the WHO Maximising Synergies Consortium published in the *Lancet* in June 2009, which examined the effect of global health initiatives, including the Fund's, on country health systems. Studies reviewed concurred that all initiatives reviewed had had both positive and some negative effects on country health systems. Greater need for better data at the national level was noted as a key limitation to fully assessing impact. The review confirmed the increase in civil society participation as a result of Global Fund processes, as well as the expansion and quality of services provided for treatment and care of focal diseases. It concluded that while global health initiatives, such as the Global Fund, had led to the rapid scale-up of services, their success had exposed the need for greater focus on strengthening health systems, as well as better coordination between the Global Fund and other global health initiatives (Maximising Positive Synergies 2009).

In addition there is an ongoing e-forum devoted to monitoring the Global Fund, called the Global Fund Observer. This provides on-going information, news and debate on all aspects of the Fund: www.aidspan.org/index.php?page=gfo.

References

Bernstein, M., and M. Sysaal (2007). 'A Trickle or a Flood: Commitments and Disbursement for HIV/AIDS from the Global Fund, PEPFAR, and the World Bank's Multi-Country AIDS Program (MAP)'. *HIV/AIDS Monitor*. Washington, DC: Center for Global Development.

Brugha, R., M. Donoghue et al. (2004). 'The Global Fund: Managing Great Expectations'. *Lancet* 364 (9428): 95–100.

Brugha, R., J. Cliff et al. (2005) 'Global Fund Tracking Study: A Cross-Country Comparative Analysis'. London School for Hygiene and Tropical Medicine'. Discussion Paper. Available at www.ghinet.org/summary.asp?Study_StudyID=59.

Carceres et al. (2008). 'Lessons Learnt from the Implementation of the GFATM Supported HIV/AIDS Projects in Peru'; Available at www.ghinet.org/countrystudies_americas_peru.asp.

England, R. (2009). 'The GAVI, Global Fund, and World Bank Joint Funding Platform. *Lancet* 374: 1595–6.

Global Fund (2008). 'A Strategy for the Global Fund'. Available at www.theglobalfund.org (accessed 10 February 2009).

Global Fund (2010). *The Global Fund 2010 Results Report: Innovation and Impact*. Geneva: Global Fund.

Hanefeld, J., N. Spicer et al. (2007). 'How have Global Health Initiatives Impacted on Health Equity? – A Literature Review'. WHO Commission on Social Determinants of Health, Health Systems Knowledge Network.

Maximising Positive Synergies (2009). 'An Assessment of Interactions between Global Health Initiatives and Country Health Systems'. *Lancet* 373(9681): 2137–69.

Murzalieva, G., J. Aleshkina et al. (2009) *Tracking Global HIV/AIDS Initiatives and their Impact on the Health System: The Experience of the Kyrgyz Republic, GHIN Final Report*. London: GHIN.

Omman, N., M. Bernstein et al. (2008). 'Seizing the Opportunity on AIDS and Health Systems'. *HIV/AIDS Monitor*. Washington, DC: Center for Global Development.

Omman, N., M. Bernstein et al. (2007). 'Following the Funding for HIV/AIDS: A Comparative Analysis of the Funding Practices of PEPFAR, the Global Fund and World Bank MAP in Mozambique, Uganda and Zambia'. *HIV/AIDS Monitor*. Washington, DC: Center for Global Development.

Sachs, J. (2010). 'Funding a Global Health Fund'. *The Guardian* 25 March 2010. Available at www.guardian.co.uk/commentisfree/2010/mar/25/global-health-fund-funding-tb-aids.

Starling, M., G. Walt et al. (2005). *Mozambique Country Study*. Global Fund Tracking Study, Progress report. London: Global Fund.

20

Global Polio Eradication Initiative
Mathias Koenig-Archibugi

The Global Polio Eradication Initiative (GPEI) has been described by the WHO as 'the largest public health initiative in history'. It was launched in 1988 with a goal to eradicate polio by the year 2000. At the time of writing, the goal has not been attained yet, although the global incidence of polio has been reduced by over 99 per cent. The main drivers of the partnership are the World Health Organization (WHO), UNICEF, the US Centers for Disease Control, and Rotary International, but the initiative depends on the cooperation of a range of state and non-state actors in virtually every country of the world. Health workers and volunteers have immunized over 2 billion children on National Immunization Days (NIDs), and international donors have contributed over $7 billion to the eradication effort.

History

Poliomyelitis is a viral infectious disease that can result in permanent paralysis and death. The development of polio vaccines in 1952 (by Jonas Salk) and 1962 (by Albert Sabin) resulted in the mass vaccination of children in developed countries and a drastic reduction of polio incidence in those countries. The successful eradication of smallpox, which was completed in 1977, stimulated discussions about which disease could be the next target for an internationally coordinated eradication programme. In the early 1980s there were significant differences of opinion among experts regarding the advisability of prioritizing polio for eradication.

Two events were decisive for the launch of the GPEI. First, in 1985 the member states of the *Pan American Health Organization* committed themselves to the goal of eliminating the indigenous transmission of polio in the Americas by the year 1990. This initiative was based on NIDs involving every child under five, and the surveillance of cases of acute flaccid paralysis (AFP) among children. The last case occurred in Peru in 1991 and the WHO certified the eradication of the diseases from the American region in 1994. Second, in 1985 Rotary International started a major fund-raising campaign to support worldwide polio immunization.

In 1988, the representatives of WHO member states convening in the 41st World Health Assembly committed themselves to the goal of eradicating polio by the year 2000, describing it as an 'appropriate gift, together with the eradication of smallpox, from the twentieth to the twenty-first century'. As Shiffman, Beer et al. (2002: 227) note, after that the goal of polio eradication 'swept across the developing world like a tidal wave'. They argue that the combination of three factors – scientists pointing out that polio was a burden in less developed areas, health leaders understanding that the disease was eradicable, and several international organizations pledging support to fight the disease – ensured that government after government mobilized for an eradication campaign. As had been the case in the Americas, the main strategy for eradication was the use of NIDs.

Structure

The governance of GPEI consists in primarily technical bodies staffed by public health experts – the Advisory Committee on Polio Eradication (ACPE) and the Global Commission for the Certification of the Eradication of Poliomyelitis – and the Interagency Coordinating Committee (ICC), whose objective is to bring transparency and

accountability to funding arrangements and requests from governments. The effort is coordinated by an informally structured 'global
polio management team'. The interaction between and within those
bodies is governed mainly by scientific–medical discourses about
appropriate priorities and methods of eradication.

An important feature of the GPEI is that the main organizations
that are involved stand in a relationship of horizontal accountability to each other, with reputation for sound scientific judgement
and managerial competence as a main mechanism of accountability. Furthermore, the substantial degree of autonomy of WHO
regional offices produces a multilayered network of reciprocal
influences, which is smoothly managed mainly through the informal
interaction of public health experts and managers, who often have
been involved in GPEI for many years. The fact that most concerns and disagreements are discussed and solved informally does
not mean that there are no open and formal forums for oversight
and control. Progress in polio eradication is discussed during the
meetings of the World Health Assembly (WHA), which offer also a
forum for interaction between representatives of donors and recipient countries. The GPEI provides information that facilitates public
accountability through the Strategic Plans, which establish 'milestones', and the Annual Reports, which assess whether these
'milestones' have been met and record the progress toward each
of them.

The GPEI as Solution to a Transnational Cooperation Problem

The eradication of a disease presents particular challenges for transnational cooperation. When the goal is merely to *control* a disease,
unilateral action by individual states may achieve significant results.
By contrast, *eradication* requires concurrent elimination of the disease
from *all* countries. Depending on the circumstances, eradication may
be preferable to control for a number of reasons, notably that the
higher cost of eradication may be amply compensated by the elimination of the need to vaccinate in the future. The necessity of international cooperation arises because policymakers may face two situations
(Barrett 2004). First, it may be in the interest of a state to eliminate a
disease from its territory *only if* all other states have eliminated the
disease in their own territories. In this 'coordination game' situation,
an efficient equilibrium can be reached if states could be reassured
that all other countries are also striving to eliminate the disease. Once
states receive such an assurance, they have no reason for not eliminat-

ing the disease themselves. What is required, then, is an institutional mechanism that can provide this assurance.

A different situation arises when it is not in a state's interest to eliminate a disease *even if* all others have done so. This scenario may correspond to a 'prisoner's dilemma'-type structure of incentives (Barrett 2004). This possibility is especially problematic since disease eradication is a clear example of a 'weakest-link' technology for producing a public good: if one single state fails to eliminate the disease, then the whole eradication effort fails (Barrett 2009). Solving prisoners' dilemmas requires institutions that are able to deter states from 'defecting' and sanction them if they fail to cooperate.

The GPEI performs the required functions to a significant extent. Several aspects of the initiative reassure states that other states are also investing resources in the elimination of polio and thus contributing to the eradication effort: the WHA resolution of 1988 and subsequent WHA resolutions on polio eradication express the commitment of all states toward this goal; regular reports by the GPEI provide a record of the activities performed in various countries; and the global system for certifying that countries, regions and the world are free from polio provides important information to states. Regular and credible reporting by an independent international agency does not only help to address the 'coordination problem' but also plays a role in mitigating the prisoner's dilemma that states may find themselves in. The commitment to polio eradication made through WHA resolutions is not legally binding on states. Partly for this reason, the enforcement powers of the GPEI are weak: they are essentially limited to 'naming and shaming' governments that appear not to act decisively. But this source of influence can be important in practice. An example is provided by the 2003–4 crisis concerning Nigeria, when polio vaccination was boycotted in Kano and two other northern Nigerian states. The GPEI team at the WHO was reportedly able to ensure the resumption of vaccination by persuading the Organization of the Islamic Conference (OIC) to put pressure on the leaders of those states, and by suggesting that travellers from Kano may have to be vaccinated at the airport before travelling abroad, including those involved in the annual pilgrimage to Mecca (Kaufmann and Feldbaum 2009).

The preceding analysis, which focuses on the incentives to provide public goods, can explain several features of the GPEI. But two further considerations need to be added. First, the GPEI is not just an institutional solution to cooperation problems stemming from given state preferences; it has also played an important role in shaping those preferences in the first place. It has provided a forum, or rather a complex and multilayered set of forums, where a large number of health actors and other officials were socialized into adopting a certain set of beliefs about health policy priorities. As Shiffman (2006: 412) notes:

> a state originally may not prioritize a health cause such as polio eradi-
> cation, but come to adopt the cause because domestic health officials
> learn at international gatherings that other countries are pursuing
> this goal and they are likely to be left behind. Thus, we may identify
> a global policy framework that presumes a cross-national diffusion of
> ideas and preferences as state and non-state actors learn from and
> influence one another.

The ideational functions of the GPEI are not limited to fostering and sustaining a worldwide commitment to eliminate polio, but also provide health authorities with a wide range of guidelines and standards on how to do it. One important example is the GPEI's promotion of the use of the OPV (oral polio vaccine) instead of the IPV (inactivated polio vaccine) in developing countries. Another example is the insistence that OPV vaccination needs to be terminated simultaneously in all countries once eradication is achieved, in order to mitigate the effects of outbreaks due to circulating vaccine-derived polioviruses. GPEI also promotes specific ways of implementing polio vaccination programmes, notably the involvement of large numbers of volunteers in National Immunization Days through 'a combination of high-level political advocacy and mass community mobilization' (Aylward and Linkins 2005: 270, emphasis removed).

The second consideration concerns the role of resource transfer. The GPEI does not affect the policies of states and other actors only by influencing their priority-setting, by reassuring them that other states are cooperating and by highlighting cases of insufficient action, but also by channelling material resources to poorer states. Over $7 billion have been contributed by donors and spent on vaccines and a wide range of support activities, and annual expenditures have increased almost every year since the programme's start in 1988 (figure 20.1). Funding comes from a variety of governmental and non-governmental sources, with the US government and Rotary International playing a major role (figure 20.2). Compared to other global public health efforts, the ability of the GPEI to mobilize resources is substantial (if compared to health spending in rich countries; however, the amount spent on global health programmes in general, and polio in particular, is negligible).

It should be noted that, while the amount of funding provided by governmental and nongovernmental donors for international eradication activities is significant, a substantial proportion of the cost of those activities was borne by the countries where they took place. Aylward, Acharya et al. (2003) note that, even in very poor countries

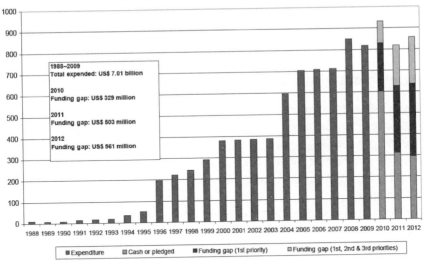

Figure 20.1   Global Polio Eradication Initiative annual expenditure, 1988–2009.

Source: www.polioeradication.org/fundingbackground.asp.

Contribution (US$ million)	Public Sector Partners	Development Banks	Private Sector Partners
> 1,000	United States of America		Rotary International
500–1,000	United Kingdom	World Bank	Bill & Melinda Gates Foundation
250–499	Japan, Canada, Germany		
100–249	European Commission, Netherlands, GAVI/IFFIm, WHO regular budget		
50–99	Norway, UNICEF regular resources		
25–49	Denmark, France, Italy, Sweden, Russian Federation		United Nations Foundation
5–24	Australia, Ireland, Luxembourg, Spain		Sanofi Pasteur, IFPMA. UNICEF National Committees, American Red Cross, Oil for Food Program
1–4	Austria, Belgium, Finland, Kuwait, Malaysia, New Zealand, Saudi Arabia, Switzerland, United Arab Emirates	Inter-American Development Bank, African Development Bank	Advantage Trust (HK), De Beers, International Federation of Red Cross and Red Crescent Societies, Pew Charitable Trust, Wyeth, Shinnyo-en, OPEC

Figure 20.2   Donor profile for 1988–2012.

As of February 2010.

Source: www.polioeradication.org/fundingbackground.asp.

such as Somalia and Afghanistan, between 25 and 50 per cent of the real cost of elimination activities were incurred locally. They also estimated that between 1988 and 2005 polio-endemic countries have contributed at least $1.8 billion in volunteer time alone, stressing that this is a very conservative estimate.

Assessment of the GPEI

There were an estimated 350,000 polio cases in 1988, while only 1,606 cases were reported globally in 2009. The reduction in incidence by over 99 per cent is a significant achievement of the initiative. However, eradication cannot be achieved as long as there are any cases of polio at all. It is still uncertain whether and when the eradication goal can be reached.

Over the years, the GPEI has been the subject of a number of criticisms, notably by observers who question whether the substantial amounts of funding and attention devoted to polio could have been directed more effectively toward other health goals. There is little doubt that polio has absorbed a share of global resources for health policies that is not in direct proportion to its impact on human health. Shiffman (2006) examined the money spent in 1996–2003 by forty-two donor organizations – governments, multilateral development banks, pharmaceutical companies and philanthropic foundations – in direct grants for the twenty diseases causing the most disease burden globally. Table 20.3 shows that there are very significant differences in the funding/DALY ratio among the diseases.[1] Polio is the disease that by far receives the most funds per DALY: it accounted for 0.04 per cent of the global disease burden, but received 14.61 per cent of all direct grants.

The priority accorded to polio is not necessarily problematic, if its eradication would be a relatively cost-effective way to use funds for public health goals.[2] However, several analysts have denied that this is the case. Taylor, Cutts et al. (1997) noted that most of the benefits of eradication will go to industrialized countries, whereas cost/benefit ratios suggest different priorities for poor countries. Sathyamala, Mittal et al. (2005) maintain that polio eradication should not have

---

[1] The WHO and other agencies measure and compare the impact of diseases by means of the disability-adjusted life-year (DALY), which is an indicator that integrates mortality and morbidity information.
[2] Or if the goal of polio eradication would allow health agencies to raise resources that otherwise would not be available for global health policies at all.

Table 20.3 Disease burden in the developing world versus share of donor funding, direct grants only*

Disease	Annual donor dollars per DALY, direct funding	Percentage of burden among 20 diseases	Percentage of direct funding among 20 diseases	Total direct funding 1996–2003 (thousands of dollars)
Polio	2,453.79	0.04	14.61	1,998,425
Onchocerciasis	146.96	0.35	8.17	1,117,553
Leprosy	138.07	0.04	0.90	122,858
Trachoma	54.79	0.22	1.93	263,851
Chagas disease	54.49	0.03	0.29	39,877
Japanese encephalitis	51.51	0.02	0.20	27,736
Hepatitis	21.27	0.64	2.18	297,667
Dengue fever	20.37	0.14	0.45	61,704
HIV/AIDS	9.25	31.13	46.21	6,320,599
Trypanosomiasis	7.94	0.58	0.74	100,594
Lymphatic filariasis	5.11	1.78	1.46	200,059
Tuberculosis	4.69	9.10	6.85	936,423
Meningitis	4.58	1.38	1.01	138,751
Malaria	3.92	14.30	9.00	1,230,574
Schistosomiasis	3.90	0.56	0.35	47,935
Leishmaniasis	3.33	0.63	0.34	46,148
Intestinal nematode infections	3.30	0.75	0.40	54,539
Tetanus	1.65	3.27	0.87	118,415
Measles	1.14	9.06	1.66	227,338
Acute respiratory infections	0.58	25.98	2.40	328,357

*Donor funding is considered for the years 1996–2003 in deflated dollars, with 2002 as the base year. Burdens are measured in DALYs for the year 2000 for developing countries. Percentages are of the total for the twenty diseases considered, not of all developing world diseases.
Source: Shiffman (2006).

been declared a priority for India and other developing countries. In recent years a number of experts have advocated an abandonment of the goal of eradication and a switch to control (Arita, Nakane et al. 2006; Roberts 2006). Other analysts insist that eradication is a cost-effective strategy. Thompson and Duintjer Tebbens (2007), for instance, estimated the cost difference between the post-eradication and control scenarios and concluded that 'we should be willing to invest more than $8,000 million to achieve eradication'.

One widely debated aspect of the GPEI is its impact on the regular health systems of poorer countries. Such debates are part of a wider controversy over the relative merits of, and the relationship between, 'vertical' and 'horizontal' approaches to healthcare support. Vertical approaches focus on one health problem or a small number of them, are guided by internationally defined targets and often managed internationally, and are time-limited. Horizontal approaches aim to improve the health systems of countries and are generally not time-bounded. Critics of vertical approaches allege that they do nothing to improve routine health services or even weaken them by deflecting human and material resources, while supporters of vertical approaches expect them to have positive 'indirect' effects on other healthcare provisions (the main arguments in the debate are reviewed by Atun, Bennett et al. 2008). The WHA resolution that started the GPEI in 1988 mandated that eradication activities be pursued in ways that strengthen the delivery of primary healthcare services, but whether this has actually occurred is still a matter of debate.

The WHO itself stresses the positive benefits of polio campaigns on other dimensions of healthcare systems. For instance, it noted that the GPEI 'has been the largest single source of funding for the refurbishment of the physical equipment required for routine immunization and surveillance in much of the developing world since the mid 1990s' (WHO 2002: 54). The spearheading agencies maintain that the laboratory networks created to support polio eradication have supported action against other diseases such as meningitis, diphtheria, rubella, dengue fever and yellow fever, and that the vast pool of health workers built up by GPEI will eventually become available for other immunization and disease control activities (WHO/UNICEF 2005: 20, 48).

Empirical studies seem to confirm the absence of major negative effects. Levin et al. (2002) examined sources and uses of funds for routine immunization programmes and polio eradication activities in Bangladesh, Côte d'Ivoire and Morocco for the years 1993–8 and found that all three governments and most bilateral and multilateral donors continued to fund routine immunization programmes at levels similar to those before the GPEI. Loevinsohn, Aylward et al. (2002) report the findings of three studies suggesting that the health system effects of polio eradication had mostly been positive or neutral, although NIDs caused some disruption to routine health service delivery. Bonu, Rani et al. (2004) examine the effect of the NIDs conducted under the GPEI on the vaccination coverage under the expanded programme on immunization (EPI) in fifteen countries of South Asia and Africa during 1990–2001. They found that NIDs were associated with an increase in the EPI in some countries (India, Nepal, Côte d'Ivoire and Ghana), a decrease in others (Nigeria and Zimbabwe), and no clear effect in the rest.

In sum, existing studies indicate that the net effect of the GPEI on healthcare systems has probably been positive or at least neutral in most countries. But this does not fully address the more fundamental criticism that the resources spent on polio elimination should have been used for the direct support of routine immunization and health-care activities. Such criticism hinges on the assumption that such resources could have been raised without linking them to polio eradication and its main implementation modality, the (politically attractive) NIDs. While the assessment of this counterfactual statement is exceedingly difficult, there are reasons to doubt that donors, political leaders and millions of health workers and volunteers would have shown similar levels of commitment in absence of the prospect that humankind could be ridded of another feared disease.

References

Arita, I., M. Nakane et al. (2006). 'Is Polio Eradication Realistic?' *Science* 312: 852–3.

Atun, R. A., S. Bennett et al. (2008). *When Do Vertical (Stand-alone) Programmes Have a Place in Health Systems?* Copenhagen: World Health Organization and European Observatory on Health Systems and Policies.

Aylward, R. B., A. Acharya et al. (2003). 'Polio Eradication'. *Global Public Goods for Health*, ed. R. Smith, R. Beaglehole et al. Oxford: Oxford University Press.

Aylward, R. B., and J. Linkins (2005). 'Polio Eradication: Mobilizing and Managing the Human Resources'. *Bulletin of the World Health Organization* 83(4): 268–73.

Barrett, S. (2004). 'Eradication versus Control: The Economics of Global Infectious Disease Policies'. *Bulletin of the World Health Organization* 82(9): 683–8.

Barrett, S. (2009) 'Polio Eradication: Strengthening the Weakest Links'. *Health Affairs* 28(4): 1079–90.

Bonu, S., M Rani et al. (2004). 'Global Public Health Mandates in a Diverse World: The Polio Eradication Initiative and the Expanded Programme on Immunization in Sub-Saharan Africa and South Asia'. *Health Policy* 70(3): 327–45.

Kaufmann, J., and H. Feldbaum (2009). 'Diplomacy and the Polio Immunization Boycott in Northern Nigeria'. *Health Affairs* 28(4): 1091–101.

Levin, A., S. Ram et al. (2002). 'The Impact of the Global Polio Eradication Initiative on the Financing of Routine Immunization: Case Studies in Bangladesh, Cote d'Ivoire, and Morocco'. *Bulletin of the World Health Organization* 80(10): 822–8.

Loevinsohn, B., B. Aylward et al. (2002). 'Impact of Targeted Programs on Health Systems: A Case Study of the Polio Eradication Initiative'. *American Journal of Public Health* 92(1): 19–23.

Roberts, L. (2006). 'Polio Eradication: Is It Time to Give Up?' *Science* 312: 832–4.

Sathyamala, C., O. Mittal et al. (2005). 'Polio Eradication Initiative in India: Deconstructing the GPEI'. *International Journal of Health Services* 35: 361–84.

Shiffman, J. (2006). 'Donor Funding Priorities for Communicable Disease Control in the Developing World'. *Health Policy and Planning*, 21: 411–20.

Shiffman, J., T. Beer et al. (2002). 'The Emergence of Global Disease Control Priorities'. *Health Policy and Planning* 17(3): 225–34.

Taylor, C. E., F. Cutts et al. (1997). 'Ethical Dilemmas in Current Planning for Polio Eradication'. *American Journal of Public Health* 87(6), 922–5.

Thompson, K. M., and R. J. Duintjer Tebbens (2007). 'Eradication versus Control for Poliomyelitis: An Economic Analysis. *Lancet* 369(9570): 1363–71.

WHO (2002). *Vaccines, Immunization and Biologicals: 2002–2005 Strategy.* Geneva: World Health Organization.

WHO/UNICEF (2005). *Global Immunization Vision and Strategy.* Available at www.who.int/immunization/givs/en/index.html (accessed 12 January 2011).

21

Internet Corporation for Assigned Names and Numbers
Jonathan Koppell

The Internet Coporation for Assigned Names and Numbers (ICANN) has been a controversial entity since its birth. It is not a government agency or an international organization per se. Rather ICANN is a unique non-profit corporation responsible for setting the rules of and overseeing the Internet's Domain Name System (DNS). Essentially this means ICANN is responsible for ensuring that when Internet users enter *www.theonion.com* in their web browser, they get the satirical news site and not a page devoted to onion aficionados. This involves selecting and overseeing the companies that register and manage domain names, establishing the rules for the settlement of disputes regarding domain names, and ensuring the physical maintenance of the DNS infrastructure. ICANN holds these responsibilities by virtue of a contractual agreement with the United States government, the force behind the development of the Internet and owner of the root servers which house its central directory. Since its creation in 1998, ICANN has experimented with different approaches to organization and representation, in response to evolving responsibilities and criticism, even as it carries out its substantive mandate. Most recently, ICANN announced that domain names will be available in non-Latin scripts (e.g., Cyrillic, Arabic) and that commercial entities will be allowed to register their names as top-level domains (i.e., .canon can be a domain alongside .com or .edu).

Development of ICANN

ICANN is an institutional descendant of a group of Internet pioneers who established the early working rules of the Internet. Under the banners of the Internet Society, Internet Engineering Task Force, Internet Architecture Board and Internet Assigned Numbers Authority (IANA), a relatively small number of engineers, mostly US government employees or researchers funded by government grants, set many of the early technical specifications of the Internet under a series of US government contracts and grants. Most directly related to ICANN's responsibilities was the IANA, an unincorporated entity that was essentially an organizational name for Jon Postel – considered by many the 'godfather' of the Internet – and his colleagues. IANA focused on the manner in which names were assigned to the many computers that were linked via computer networks; technically it still exists as an entity 'operated by ICANN' (IANA 2010). This became known as the Domain Name System and as the Internet became more widely used so too did conflicts related to it (Zittrain 1999; Mueller 2002).

Popular awareness of DNS issues first occurred in the late 1990s with 'cybersquatting' disputes arising when individuals registered trademarked brands as domain names (e.g., pepsi.com), but there were numerous other issues as well. There was little consensus, for example, as to the proper means of selecting new top-level domain names (e.g., .com and .edu). Postel and his colleagues moved to formalize IANA as the legitimate authority to resolve such disputes. He organized the Internet Ad Hoc Committee, a group that brought together some – but not all – interested parties to hammer out a memorandum of understanding, but the government contractor managing the root servers refused to add the domains suggested by the Ad Hoc Committee (Mueller 1999; Zittrain 1999). This impasse drew the US government into the conflict, specifically the National Telecommunications and Information Administration (NTIA), a unit of the Department of Commerce that had taken over management of Internet-related contracts from the National Science Foundation.

After a lengthy deliberation regarding the proper form of DNS governance, a call for proposals was issued and ICANN was selected to assume responsibility for the DNS (Froomkin 2000). The transfer of responsibility was intended to create some distance between the US government and the governance of the Internet. To facilitate this unprecedented shift of responsibilities to a nongovernmental organization, agreements were negotiated among the NTIA, Network Solutions (the contractor that had managed the DNS servers) and ICANN (Mueller 2002). ICANN's primary responsibilities – managing the DNS system (including addition of new domains), developing a dispute resolution system, overseeing registrar competition – seem largely technical but have far-reaching commercial and sometimes political implications. Domain name policies raise significant intellectual property issues, for example, and even the assignment of country-level domain names can be controversial (e.g., the creation of the .pa domain for the Palestinian territory). And so it was no small matter that the US government retained ultimate authority, reviewing the performance of ICANN and reaffirming the terms of a 'Joint Project Agreement' on a yearly basis.

Governance

Governance issues have been a constant source of debate in and around ICANN since its creation. Chartered as a non-profit corporation in Monterey, California, and answerable to the US government, the organization has strived to satisfy demands that it reflect the global reality of the Internet. It has self-consciously held its meetings around the globe and sought geographic diversity in its representation and staff. Still, critics object to the apparent US government dominance and have sought to diminish ICANN's authority if not to transfer its responsibilities elsewhere (Jones 2009). The World Summit on the Information Society (WSIS), held in 2003 and 2005 by the International Telecommunications Union, an intergovernmental body positioning itself as an alternative to ICANN, brought together organizational detractors and competitors. It spawned the United Nations Internet Governance Forum (IGF), a venue for discussing competing models for Internet governance that deemphasize ICANN and

American influence, but such efforts have generally petered out. On the other hand, defenders of ICANN's role have noted its technical performance and insulation from forces that might use influence over ICANN to create rules more conducive to censorship and centralized control (Reporters Without Borders 2009; Gjelten 2010).

ICANN is able to maintain its authoritative position because it has an advantage enjoyed by few global governance organizations. By virtue of its de facto control over the root servers of the Internet, ICANN exercises gatekeeper authority over a precious resource. Anyone wanting to register Internet domain names must go through ICANN-approved registrars and accept the rules that ICANN has laid out with respect to naming, dispute resolution and so on. Technically, this can be avoided by creating a different root – that is, a separate Internet with its own directory – but only computer-users with their browsers pointed to this alternative directory would find websites registered there. These are not meaningful alternatives to the ICANN-ordered Internet for anyone wishing to reach a mass audience. Thus the power dynamic around ICANN is different from that associated with most other organizations attempting to create and implement global rules. Most global rule-making bodies must maintain the support of key constituencies who could abandon the organization if it does not serve their interests. ICANN is not immune to pressure, as recent developments have suggested, but it has more leverage than most international organizations.

In September 2009, ICANN signed an 'Affirmation of Commitments' with the Department of Commerce that created a more formal set of mechanisms for review of ICANN activities by non-US governments through the already-existing Governmental Advisory Committee. This falls well short of the independence sought by critics but, by ending the annual renewal by the US government, it is a step in that direction. Over the years, ICANN has modified the process by which members of its governing Board of Directors are chosen. From a system that featured US-appointed directors, ICANN moved to one in which some directors were chosen by a global public vote of Internet users (since abandoned to the great disappointment of many who saw the opportunity to create a model of transnational democratic governance) (Crawford 2004). The current system, in which directors are chosen by 'Supporting Organizations' and advisory committees, emphasizes different constituent groups with an interest in ICANN policy. The intention is to facilitate a more bottom-up policy development process than the more closed approach that saw decisions emerge from a relatively opaque box. Nevertheless, the criticism that ICANN lacks transparency and remains too close to the original IANA template has persisted. Perhaps the most notable episode illustrating this matter involved an elected member of the ICANN Board suing the organization in a California court to gain access to internal records (Jesdanun 2002). This elected director, Karl Auerbach, prevailed in 2002, but is no longer a director; ICANN's experience with him may help explain the move away from popular elections.

Technical or Political?

The controversy regarding the structure and processes adopted by ICANN seemed to take some of its founders and early leaders by surprise. In their minds, ICANN was simply formalizing engineering functions that had been previously carried out in an ad hoc fashion. Those who saw ICANN as the emerging Internet government had it wrong, from this perspective. Esther Dyson, the first Chair of ICANN, noted in 1999 that the organization 'has a very limited mandate to administer certain (largely technical) aspects of the Internet infrastructure in general and the Domain Name System in particular' (Dyson 1999). It was therefore plausible to argue that ICANN's decisions represented the consensus of the Internet community, downplaying the idea that there would be conflicting viewpoints regarding policy decisions. This interpretation was never persuasive to segments of the Internet community who regarded ICANN's function as inherently political and possessing the power of law (Froomkin 2000). Although the issues changed over the years – from controversy regarding the extension of agreements with Verisign as the root manager to disputes regarding the process for selecting new top-level domain names – the difference in perspectives was a constant. To some ICANN is a technical body engaged in finding optimal engineering solutions; to others it is a political body, setting rules with commercial, social and political ramifications.

This is a critical issue not only for ICANN but also for many transnational governance organizations and so its experience is instructive. In situations of pure coordination (e.g., should we all drive on the left or the right?) our normative expectations regarding representation and due process are not terribly high because we are essentially indifferent regarding the end result. However, there are a great many situations where we have a collective interest in coordination but maintain distinctly different preferences. In game theory terms, this is often called 'battle-of-the-sexes' coordination, referring to the metaphor of a husband and wife eager to spend an evening together but divided on the activity of choice. Consistent with Dyson's characterization of ICANN's work as largely technical, the organization's leadership did not seem to emphasize issues of representativeness and participation in shaping the body and its processes. To ICANN's critics, both internal and external, the substance of the organization's work has always been far from pure coordination, notwithstanding its technical quality. The clashing perspectives were brought into vivid relief at the first ICANN public forum, held in Cairo 2000, and have persisted throughout the organization's history. To the surprise and frustration of ICANN's leaders, discussion turned repeatedly to procedural issues including the prohibitive costs of participation, availability of documents in multiple languages, and selection of Board members (Berkman Center for Internet & Society 2000).

ICANN is not alone among transnational governance organizations in confronting this tension because the notion that a technical rule-making body need not meet the same normative expectations as a policymaking body is intuitively appealing and instrumentally valuable. Global rule-making is even more challenging when the organization must meet standards imported from a domestic democratic governance context. Thus in a variety of policy areas, organizations frame their work as being highly technical – pure coordination rather than battle-of-the-sexes coordination – either pre-emptively or in response to criticism that their processes fall short of expectations. For example, many of the debates regarding the creation of international standards governing accounting or bank capital requirements sound similar to ICANN-related exchanges, even though they could not be more substantively different (see related chapters, this volume).

References

Berkman Center for Internet & Society (2000). 'Scribe's Notes'. Harvard Law School 2000. Available from http://cyber.law.harvard.edu/icann/cairo/archive/scribe-icann-030900.html (accessed 2010).

Crawford, S. P. (2004). 'The ICANN Experiment'. *Cardozo Journal of International and Comparative Law* 12: 409–48.

Dyson, E. (1999). 'Letter to Jamie Love and Ralph Nader'. Available from http://lists.essential.org/random-bits/msg00119.html (accessed 2010).

Froomkin, A. M. (2000). 'Wrong Turn in Cyberspace: Using ICANN to Route around the APA and the Constitution'. *Duke Law Journal* 50(17): 17–183.

Gjelten, T. (2010). 'Countries Try to Tame the Wild Territory of the Net'. National Public Radio. Available from www.npr.org/templates/story/story.php?storyId=125634056 (accessed 8 April 2010).

IANA (2010). 'IANA'. Available from www.iana.org/ (accessed 15 April 2010).

Jesdanun, A. (2002). 'Public Advocate on Key Internet Board Loses his Voice.' Associated Press Newswires.

Jones, H. (2009). 'EU Urges Internet Governance Revamp'. Reuters.

Mueller, M. (1999). 'ICANN and Internet Governance'. *Journal of Policy, Regulation and Strategy for Telecommunications Information and Media* 1(6): 497–520.

Mueller, M. S. (2002). *Ruling the Root: Internet Governance and the Taming of Cyberspace*. Cambridge, MA: MIT Press.

Reporters Without Borders (2009). 'Maintaining Status Quo is Lesser Evil'. Available from http://en.rsf.org/maintaining-status-quo-is-lesser -29–09–2009,34617 (accessed 8 April 2010).

Zittrain, J. (1999). *ICANN: Between the Public and the Private: Comments Before Congress Subcommittee on Investigations and Oversight of the House Commerce Committee Hearing Entitled 'Is ICANN out of Control?'* Washington, DC.

22

International Coral Reef Initiative[1]
Radoslav S. Dimitrov

Coral reefs, mong the most mesmerizing landscapes on the planet, are being degraded by land-based water pollution, mining, destructive fishing practices and climate change. According to one global assessment, 20 per cent of the world's coral reefs have been destroyed (Wilkinson 2004).[2] Concerns over the conditions of coral ecosystems have been expressed in various international fora, including the Convention on Biological Diversity, the Framework Convention on Climate Change, the Convention on International Trade of Endangered Species, and the Global Conference on Sustainable Development of Small Island Developing States (International Coral Reefs Initiative (ICRI) 1997). These discussions have not led to multilateral policy under a treaty, and problems with existing national policies persist. Hundreds of marine protected areas contain corals but most fail to achieve their objectives due to their small size and the low management capacity in local communities (Bryant, Burke et al. 1998: 44; Jameson, Tupper et al. 2002).

Today global coral reefs governance relies on loosely coordinated voluntary action without a formal international policy agreement. The principal governance mechanism is the ICRI, a multistakeholder part-

[1] Sections of this chapter appeared in Dimitrov (2006).
[2] The more recent 2008 assessment 'State of the Reefs' by the Global Coral Reef Monitoring Network (GCRMN) does not provide a global estimate of the extent of reef decline, only regional analysis.

nership that facilitates coral reef protection through awareness-raising and scientific research. Two distinct features of this arrangement are reliance on existing resources and the pronounced absence of efforts to create new formal governance structures. ICRI reflects scepticism regarding the effectiveness of intergovernmental policy programmes and relies on stakeholders to link local needs to existing national and international structures (Grigg 1994; Dight and Sherl 1997).

Several additional characteristics defining global coral reefs governance are notable. First, major countries have taken the political leadership in establishing the ICRI. Second, the small number of key players makes it potentially easy to create effective governance mechanisms. Nearly 100 countries have coral reefs, but over half of all coral reefs are under the jurisdiction of 6 states: Australia, Fiji, Indonesia, the Maldives, Papua New Guinea and the Philippines. Indonesia and Australia combined possess 35 per cent of reefs (Spalding, Ravilious et al. 2001). Third, policy options for reef preservation are often win–win solutions: measures to protect reefs bring additional benefits for tourism, reduced water pollution, and health benefits from improved sewage systems (Bryant, Burke et al. 1998: 5; Wilkinson 2004). Fourth, there are no interest groups opposing remedial policy action.[3] On the contrary, businesses such as pharmaceutical companies and tourist ventures have vested interests in reef preservation and should be active proponents of regulation. Finally, public support for reef preservation is relatively easy to generate because of the highly visual charisma of coral reefs.

Political leadership, the absence of opposition, the presence of supporting business interests, public appeal and the small number of actors involved are favourable factors that make puzzling the low level of collective state action. The coral policy realm is quiet and generally invisible at the international level, with few actors other than scientists and environmentalists becoming engaged. The tourist and pharmaceutical sectors have interests in coral reef preservation but have rarely mobilized to oppose destructive practices and have not been visible political forces in international coral reef fora (Barber and Platt 1998; Wilkinson and Salvat 1998).

ICRI History and Mandate

The most significant governance mechanism at the global level is the ICRI established in 1994. ICRI is a loose partnership of governments,

[3]P.c., R. Kenchington, head of the ICRI Secretariat; p.c., S. Colwell, Executive Director of Coral Reef Alliance; p.c., anonymous US Department of State official.

international development banks, nongovernmental organizations (NGOs), scientific associations and the private sector. The founding partners were the governments of Australia, France, Jamaica, Japan, the Philippines, Sweden, the United Kingdom and the United States (Mieremet 1995; private communication, Kenchington). It has involved representatives of eighty governments as well as international organizations such as the World Bank, United Nations Environment Programme (UNEP), United Nations Development Programme (UNDP), the United Nations Educational, Scientific and Cultural Organization (UNESCO) and the International Union for the Conservation of Nature (Kenchington 1998). The declared overarching goal of the initiative is to implement Chapter 17 of Agenda 21 that calls on states to identify marine ecosystems with high biodiversity and provide necessary limitations on their uses. Its stated objectives are: (1) strengthening government commitment and policy implementation; (2) incorporating coral management into existing policy plans; (3) capacity building; and (4) coordinating research and monitoring.[4]

ICRI's institutional profile was shaped at a four-day planning workshop in June 1995 in Dumaguete City, the Philippines, which involved participants from forty-four nations, intergovernmental organizations, NGOs, the science community and the private sector. The conference produced two documents. The first, *A Call for Action*, recognized that coral reefs are in serious decline due to various and complex causes, and urged actors to focus on coastal management, research and monitoring, and capacity building. The second document, *A Framework for Action*, outlined activities that governments could undertake to mitigate the plight of coral reefs. It embraced principles including that 'ICRI will facilitate the leveraging and channelling of existing resources among all sectors' (ICRI website). The *Framework for Action* encourages governments to: develop integrated coastal management plans; establish marine protected areas; improve coordination among international organizations, donors and NGOs; apply environmental assessment of development projects; control land-based marine pollution through economic incentives and voluntary programmes; establish networks of centres of expertise; support environmental education programmes; and encourage the private sector to manage coral reefs. These policy recommendations are suggestive and do not constitute a system of binding obligations.

The next phase comprised six regional workshops in the Caribbean, East African seas, South Asian seas, East Asian seas, the Western

---

[4]Information about ICRI and its Secretariat can be found at the official Internet site at www.icriforum.org (accessed 12 March 2010).

Indian Ocean, and the Pacific region. The purpose of these workshops was to translate the global *Framework for Action* into agendas for regional action.

ICRI Structure

ICRI has nineteen working groups, ad hoc committees and discussion groups. These informal bodies are dedicated to topics such as marine protected areas, the international coral trade, and fibre optic cables (laid on the ocean floor). As of March 2010, ICRI adopted twenty-eight decisions and resolutions on topics ranging from aquarium fish trade, to seagrass monitoring, to economic valuation of coral reefs, requesting partners to provide information, undertake case studies and report their results at ICRI meetings.[5] Early on, ICRI also established the International Coral Reef Action Network (ICRAN) whose mandate is to assist in capacity building for reef management in developing countries. To take one example of its activities, ICRAN was funded in March 2001 with $5 million by the UN Foundation to establish demonstration conservation sites.[6]

Partner countries take turns on a voluntary basis to host a small ICRI Secretariat for two-year periods. The Secretariat has no permanent staff and is funded by the hosting government. The staff performs ICRI functions in addition to their regular responsibilities in government. Past host countries include the United States, Australia, France, Sweden, the Philippines, the United Kingdom and the Seychelles (ICRI website).

ICRI is neither an international governance structure nor a policy-making body. Its expressly defined goal is to identify and promote needed action without directly engaging in policymaking and without developing or funding proposals. This loose institution is an informal network of interested parties, an open forum for like-minded political actors to discuss coral reef issues, share information, promote research, identify priorities and facilitate policy action. The initiative does not have a permanent bureaucratic structure or organization and does not engage in policy action. It only encourages stockholders to establish projects at the local community level, by generating and sharing information on the health of reefs, by increasing political support and through capacity building.

---

[5] ICRI decision texts available at www.icriforum.org/secretariat/ICRI_decision.html.
[6] P.c., C. Wilkinson, Coordinator of the GCRMN.

Scientific Cooperation

Much of the international collaboration on corals is related to scientific research. Concerted documentation of global coral decline began in earnest in the mid-1990s. Various review documents from that period indicated that comprehensive knowledge of the health and values of coral reefs was virtually absent (Bryant, Burke et al. 1998). Responding to the need for data, in 1996 the Intergovernmental Oceanographic Commission, the UNEP, the World Bank, and the International Union for Conservation of Nature formed a partnership to establish the GCRMN. Its goal is to collect, synthesize and disseminate information on coral reef health and to help communities and states build research capacity for coral assessment.

The GCRMN has been the main operational unit and key component of ICRI, intended to monitor reefs' conditions and provide the necessary data for effective reef management (Wilkinson and Salvat 1998: 17). The GCRMN employs hundreds of researchers and formed a partnership in 1998 with Reef Check, a network of 5,000 volunteers whom scientists train in monitoring and assessment techniques.[7] The results are then fed into ReefBase, the most comprehensive database on coral reefs' distribution, conditions and vulnerabilities.

For years, GCRMN provided only natural scientific information on the extent and causes of coral decline, and excluded altogether consideration of the social impacts on human communities (Dimitrov 2002). This information gap undermined governance processes as policymakers did not receive information on the negative consequences of reef degradation and had little incentive to protect the reefs. To address this omission, in 2002 the Global Socioeconomic Monitoring Initiative for Coastal Management (SocMon) was established to provide information relevant to policymakers.

Analytical Observations

Country officials involved in ICRI see it as 'an advocacy group', deliberately intended as an informal arrangement that serves as a temporary catalyst for action. Notably, most governments want to keep it that way. From time to time, there have been discussions on whether to formalize the initiative but members have unanimously preferred to stay with a flexible and informal mechanism rather than engage in the burdensome task of making institutional and financial arrange-

---

[7] P.c., C. Wilkinson.

ments.[8] The logic behind this is that ICRI would be more effective in influencing national governments and relevant international institutions as a flexible informal mechanism instead of a competing agency.[9] France is the only country that has expressed a preference for a more bureaucratized structure but they, too, want it to remain nonbinding.[10]

The lack of intergovernmental policy should not be equated to an absence of governance. Efforts to promote sustainable coral reef management are made through unilateral national policies, bilateral partnerships, and non-state initiatives (Dimitrov 2006). In December 2000, the US Coral Reef Conservation Act established a reserve in the Hawaii islands that contained nearly 70 per cent of coral reefs under US jurisdiction (Davidson 2002). On the other side of the world, 33 per cent of the Great Barrier Reef and associated ecosystems are declared protected areas or no-take zones (Wilkinson 2004). And some individual countries help protect coral reefs outside their jurisdiction. Sweden, in partnership with the World Bank and Finland, launched the CORDIO project to help investigate the impacts of coral bleaching in the Indian Ocean and seek ways to improve local management of affected reefs. In addition to national and bilateral governmental activities, a large number of NGOs are active in the field of coral reef preservation: the Coral Reef Alliance, REEF, Conservation International, The Nature Conservancy and the World Wildlife Fund, to name a few, have created training materials for developing and implementing marine protected areas in Southeast Asia and the Western Pacific.

Yet the absence of a formal policy agreement on coral reef preservation is peculiar in an age of proliferating environmental agreements. The unwillingness of states to consider a legally binding treaty is conditioned by shared knowledge about the problem. Available scientific information reveals few transboundary consequences of reef decline, and so deprives the issue of the elements of interdependence that provide incentives for binding collective action by states (Dimitrov 2006).

Indeed, analysis of international coral reef politics shows that the evolution of the international political process matches the local character of the issue. From the very beginning, participants defined a deliberate objective to turn the ICRI into a bottom-up process driven by local communities. In 1996, the management of ICRI changed from an executive committee to a coordinating and planning committee

[8] P.c., R. Kenchington.
[9] P.c., anon.; p.c., J. Reaser, former US State Department official; p.c., R. Kenchington
[10] P.c. C. Wilkinson; p.c., Colwell.

with a strong emphasis on regional capacity building, 'with the aspiration that sooner or later the international coordinating role can be phased down' (Kenchington 1998: 14). Even the GCRMN is intended to gradually devolve to lower levels, with support for it shifting to regions, countries and local organizations (Strategic Plan 1996).

References

Barber, C. V., and V. R. Platt (1998). 'Policy Reform and Community-based Programs to Combat Cyanide Fishing in the Asia-Pacific Region'. *Coral Reefs: Challenges and Opportunities for Sustainable Management*, ed. M. E. Hatziolos, A. J. Hooten et al. Washington, DC: World Bank.

Bryant, D., L. Burke et al. eds. (1998). *Reefs at Risk: A Map-Based Indicator of Threats to the World's Coral Reefs*. Washington, DC: World Resources Institute.

Davidson, M. G. (2002). 'Protecting Coral Reefs: The Principal National and International Legal Instruments'. *Harvard International Law Review* 26: 499–546.

Dight, I. J., and L. M. Sherl (1997). 'The International Coral Reef Initiative (ICRI): Global Priorities for the Conservation and Management of Coral Reefs and the Need for Partnerships'. *Coral Reefs* 16(suppl. S139–S147).

Dimitrov, R. S. (2002). 'Confronting Non-regimes: Science and International Coral Reef Policy'. *Journal of Environment and Development* 11(1: March): 53–78.

Dimitrov, R. S. (2006). *Science and International Environmental Policy: Regimes and Non-Regimes in Global Governance*. Lanham, MD: Rowman and Littlefield.

Grigg, R. W. (1994). 'The International Coral Reef Initiative: Conservation and Effective Management of Marine Resources'. *Coral Reefs* 13: 197–8.

ICRI (1997). 'ICRI report to the UN Commission on Sustainable Development'. Available at www.icriforum.org.

Jameson, S. C., M. H. Tupper et al. (2002). 'The Three Screen Doors: Can Marine "Protected" Areas Be Effective?' *Marine Pollution Bulletin* 44(11: November): 1177–83.

Kenchington, R. (1998). 'Status of the International Coral Reef Initiative'. *Coral Reefs: Challenges and Opportunities for Sustainable Management*, ed. M. E. Hatziolos, A. J. Hooten et al. Washington, DC: World Bank.

Mieremet, R. B. (1995). 'The International Coral Reefs Initiative: A Seed from the Earth Summit Which Now Bears Fruit'. *Ocean and Coastal Management* 21(1–3): 303–28.

Spalding, M., C. Ravilious et al. (2001). *World Atlas of Coral Reefs*. Berkeley: University of California Press.

Strategic Plan of the IOC/UNEP/IUC Global Coral Reef Monitoring Network (1996). Available at http://coral.aoml.Noaa.govgcrmn/gcrmn-strat.html (accessed 15 October 2000).

Wilkinson, C., ed. (2004). 'Status of Coral Reefs of the World: 2004', GCRMN. Available at http.www.gcrmn.org/status2004.aspx.

Wilkinson, C., and B. Salvat (1998). 'Global Coral Reef Monitoring Network: Reversing the Decline of the World's Reefs. *Coral Reefs: Challenges and Opportunities for Sustainable Management*, ed. M. E. Hatziolos, A. J. Hooten et al. Washington, DC: World Bank.

23

International Health Partnership and IHP+
Anna Holzscheiter

The International Health Partnership and Related Initiatives – commonly abbreviated as IHP+ – strives to improve health systems in developing countries by bringing together donor countries, bilateral and multilateral health initiatives and recipient countries in a 'single country-led national health strategy' (IHP+ 2010a). The IHP+ strongly builds on the core principles of the Paris Declaration on Aid Effectiveness as well as the Accra Agenda for Action, seeking to foster the essential principles of increased harmonization, alignment, country-ownership, mutual accountability and management for results in global and national health governance (High Level Forum 2005). As such, the IHP+ hopes to significantly improve cooperation between international institutions, donors and developing countries in the development and implementation of national health plans. IHP+ was launched in September 2007 and is open to all governments from developed and developing countries as well as other international governmental and nongovernmental agencies who agree to the commitments of the IHP+ Global Compact.

History of the International Health Partnership / IHP+

The International Health Partnership was launched in September 2007 at the initiative of the UK government as a concerted effort to accelerate progress on the health-related Millennium Development Goals (MDGs). In 2008, the IHP was expanded by including several 'related initiatives' such as the Harmonization for Health in Africa Initiative and the Global Campaign for the Health MDGs. The Partnership henceforth became known as the International Health Partnership and Related Initiatives (IHP+).

The IHP+ initially had twenty-six signatories – seven countries, eighteen multilateral and bilateral organizations, and the Bill and Melinda Gates Foundation. All of the eight major international organizations for health (often called the 'H8') are partners of IHP+. Rather than representing yet another of the numerous 'vertical' partnerships that tackle specific diseases or problems in the health arena, the IHP+ has set itself the goal of contributing to the overall improvement of health systems, strongly promoting and support-ing country ownership in health planning and implementation. Through its two main strategies – a Global Compact between development partners and developing countries' governments, and several Country Compacts agreed between a single partner country and its development partners – the IHP+ aspires to reduce the high transaction costs that occur wherever coordination between global agencies and local governments is poor. Douglas Alexander, UK Secretary of State for International Development, has described the IHP+ as follows: 'The IHP is not another funding mechanism to add to the myriad already available. Instead it aims to bring together the efforts of all, to produce more than the sum of its parts' (Alexander 2007: 804).

In 2009, the signatories of the Global Compact of IHP+ met in Geneva in response to the first independent evaluation of IHP+, in order to review the progress of the Partnership over the first two years of its existence. During those two years, Country Compacts had been agreed upon with three countries – Ethiopia, Mozambique and Nepal. The signatories of IHP+ acknowledged that little progress had been achieved so far and that the year 2009 should see more tangible success and change. As a consequence, IHP+ set the goal of completing ten Country Compacts by the end of 2009. However, by the end of 2009, only two more countries, Zambia and Mali, were preparing to sign compacts with IHP+.

Structure and Operation of International Health Partnership/IHP+

In line with its classification as a 'multistakeholder initiative', the IHP+ is not a formal institution. At the global level, an inter-agency steering group – the Scaling Up Reference Group (SuRG) – is respon-sible for overseeing the activities of IHP+ and agreeing on strategic directions (IHP+ 2010b). The SuRG is divided into a Business SuRG and a Steering SuRG. The World Health Organization (WHO) and the World Bank chair the former Group, in which the 'H8' and civil society organizations (CSOs) are represented. The Steering SuRG is composed exclusively of donor partners. Management of the IHP+ activities is carried out by an inter-agency Core Team that is based in Washington (World Bank), Geneva (WHO) and Brazzaville. This Core Team manages the routine interaction and communication with IHP+ partner countries.

The main operational bodies for developing country strategies and priorities, identifying core areas and challenges to coordination within countries, and evaluating progress are the various working groups of the IHP+. These non-permanent groups of experts convene to discuss specific policies and directions revolving around harmonization and alignment policies. The global structures of IHP+ are complemented by so-called 'Country Health sector teams' that are managed by national ministries of health and provide a collaborative framework within which country representatives of major global health agencies, civil society actors and other implementing agencies at country level come together (Conway, Harmer et al. 2008: 3).

The most significant component of the IHP+ is a Global Compact for the health-related MDGs, a mutually binding agreement between signatories at the global level. By signing the Compact, signatories confirm their commitment to greater accountability between development agencies and the governments of developing countries, to strengthen health systems, and to scale up health interventions. The Compact also includes commitments for both development partners and developing countries in terms of transparent, sustainable and equitable structures for health financing (Conway, Harmer et al. 2008).

At present, the IHP+ members include thirteen development partners (i.e. donor governments), twenty-one partner countries (i.e. developing countries' governments), thirteen international agencies (among them the WHO, UNDP, ILO, Gates Foundation, EU and the Global Fund) and two other organizations – OECD and the US President's Emergency Plan for AIDS Relief (PEPFAR) – that loosely support the work and philosophy of the IHP+ (IHP+ 2010c). CSOs are incorporated into some of the global structures of IHP+ – they send representatives to regular meetings of IHP+ groups such as the SuRG. However, the ministerial review of IHP+ in early 2009 concluded that civil society involvement at country level has proven more difficult, considering that 'there is limited coordination amongst CSOs working on health [and] limited capacity, experience and expertise amongst CSOs to participate in high level discussions that take place within Country Health Sector Teams' (International Health Partnership Ministerial Review Meeting 2009: 19).

Impact of International Health Partnership/IHP+ – Effectiveness and Legitimacy

In the few years of its existence, the IHP+ has shown its influence on global and local health policymaking. In particular, it has provided a framework of norms and principles on aid effectiveness, accountability and coordination that is increasingly referred to by development agencies and their developing country partners. Its principles and suggested mechanisms for increasing aid effectiveness and strengthening national health plans are being adopted by global and national policymakers alike and have begun 'to influence the scope and ambition of national health plans and budgets' (Conway, Harmer et al. 2008: 19).

However, regarding both its legitimacy (globally and locally) and effectiveness, the IHP+ has yet to fulfil the enormous aspirations and ambitious goals that the Partnership has promoted since it came into being in 2007. Even though the Partnership aims to fill a much debated and urgent 'gap' within the global health aid architecture – emphasizing the necessity for horizontal strengthening of health systems as a whole, rather than punctual, vertical interventions – the potential of IHP+ to live up to its promises is still met with great scepticism. This is, no doubt, partly due to the fact that the IHP+ is still in its infancy. The limited success of the Partnership, however, is also attributable to its unrealistically high policy goals and political commitments, and to the fact that the IHP+ has, so far, in many cases not succeeded in demonstrating the value it adds, particularly to developing countries. While developing countries' governments assume that the IHP+ will lead donors to increase the volume of aid for health, these partners still seem to be unsure 'whether the IHP+ is primarily about improving the effectiveness of existing aid, or about increasing the volumes of aid' (Conway, Harmer et al. 2008: 11). With regard to health financing and aid flows, therefore, the expectations of donor and recipient countries seem to diverge quite drastically. What is more, many of those involved in the IHP+ activities at global and national level point to the danger that it is 'becoming yet another institutionalized "big initiative" that will need to be managed and will add transaction costs over time' (Conway, Harmer et al. 2008: 20)

The first Country Compact signed (Ethiopia) is not a legally binding document. It has been described as 'well-crafted rhetoric that establishes high expectations for what the Government of Ethiopia would hope to achieve' (Conway, Harmer et al. 2008: 9). However, the extent to which external development partners will join this Country Compact is still being negotiated. A 2009 report on the health sector in Zambia, a country that has been preparing to sign a compact with the IHP+ for considerable time, states that the IHP+ Country Compact has little to add to an earlier Memorandum of Understanding (MoU) in which all major development partners in Zambia committed to support and align with the National Health Strategic Plan 2006–10 (Pereira 2009: 8). What is more, the country already has a Sector-Wide Approach (SWAp) for health in place, which most development partners prefer as a framework for strengthening the overall health system and harmonization and alignment efforts. The report acknowledges that, compared to the 2006 MoU, the IHP+ has introduced some significant new dimensions with regard to the inclusion of civil society in national harmonization, alignment and mutual accountability principles. However, the study reports that major national stakeholders such as the Zambian Ministry of Health doubt the added value of IHP+ and have described it as 'window dressing, because it does not offer anything new' (Pereira 2009: 16). It is a significant finding of this report that even the IHP+ national expert acknowledged that 'the IHP+ is not necessary in Zambia' (Pereira 2009: 16; see also Conway, Harmer et al. 2008: 9). Another significant finding of the study is that the two most important development partners in the health sector in Zambia – PEPFAR and the Global Fund – are not likely to join the IHP+ Country Compact in the foreseeable future (Pereira 2009: 17).

The first and only external review of IHP+ was carried out in 2008, a year after it began (Conway, Harmer et al. 2008). The review was commissioned by the IHP+ SuRG, focusing on the extent to which partners were keeping their commitments and on the progress achieved in signing and implementing the IHP+ Country Compacts. Even though the review, understandably, draws only tentative conclusions with regard to the effectiveness and legitimacy of IHP+, its findings are quite significant in terms of how quickly the IHP+ might achieve some observable progress in strengthening global and local commitments to National Health Plans. In particular, the evaluation comes to the conclusion that the IHP+ is an initiative whose efforts will probably only succeed after an 'evolutionary process that will continue to frustrate stakeholders because of the slow pace of change, rather than a revolutionary effort that will at least be adequate to achieve the high-level political commitments that have been made' (Conway, Harmer et al. 2008: iii).

As with the Zambia study, the IHP+ review concludes that the IHP+ has, so far, not been successful in showing the value it adds, particularly where it operates in national contexts in which comparable initiatives toward greater aid effectiveness are already in place. Whilst the authors of the review note that the IHP+ can potentially contribute significantly to scaling-up coordination among global development partners and within national health systems, it notes that the IHP+ has, to date, only had limited success in communicating its relevance to partner institutions and national stakeholders. Another significant finding of the first review is that, despite its strong emphasis on country ownership and country-led coordination processes, the IHP+ management is still a largely global affair, with the Core Teams in Geneva, Washington, and Brazzaville steering most of the preparations for and implementation of Country Compacts (Conway, Harmer et al. 2008: 18). Whilst the SuRG opposes the idea that the Core Team should be established as a permanent Secretariat, the present operating procedures of the IHP+ strongly suggest that the Core Team will remain the main managing body for considerable time.

The information that is publicly available on the IHP+ website confirms the finding of the slow progress the IHP+ has made in the first two years of its existence, inasmuch as comprehensive documents on progress – both in partners' commitments and in the IHP+ focus countries – are concerned. Most information given on critical components and potential achievements of the IHP+ appears to be rather provisional in nature and does not convey a transparent picture of accountable sharing of information. In particular, information on the progress of agreements with the IHP+ focus countries in terms of Country Compacts is either not up-to-date or simply lacking (IHP+ 2010d). Most of the information on how development partners and partner countries transform their commitments into tangible actions and results is vague, a finding that, following the conclusions of internal and external reviews mentioned above, confirms the large gap between rhetorical commitment on paper and tangible action 'on the ground'.

Apart from the various sources cited here, academic literature on and independent evaluations of the IHP+ is virtually nonexistent. What seems to be particularly needed are studies that seek to locate IHP+ within the broader global health aid architecture and to assess to what extent this Partnership offers a normative framework that is necessary or useful, or whether it has to be seen as yet another of the manifold initiatives that further contribute to the eternal problem of fragmentation and duplication of aid efforts in health.

References

Alexander, D. (2007). 'The International Health Partnership'. *Lancet* 370: 803–4.

Conway, S., A. Harmer et al. (2008). *2008 External Review of the International Health Partnership + Related Initiatives*. Johannesburg: Responsible Action.

High Level Forum (2005). 'Paris Declaration on Aid Effectiveness'. Paris, 28 February – 2 March 2005. Available at www.oecd.org/document/18/ 0,2340,en_2649_3236398_35401554_1_1_1_1,00.html   (accessed   26 February 2010).

IHP+ (2010a). 'Homepage'. www.internationalhealthpartnership.net/en/ home (accessed 26 February 2010).

IHP+ (2010b). 'How does the IHP function?' Available at www.internation-alhealthpartnership.net/CMS_files/userfiles/How%20does%20the%20 IHP+%20function.pdf (accessed 26 February 2010).

IHP+ (2010c). 'Partners'. Available at www.internationalhealthpartner-ship.net/en/partners (accessed 27 February 2010).

IHP+ (2010d). 'Country Profile: Zambia'. Available at www.international-healthpartnership.net/en/countries/zambia   (accessed   27   February 2010).

International Health Partnership Ministerial Review Meeting (2009). *International Health Partnership and Related Initiatives, 4th Progress Report*. Geneva: IHP+.

Pereira, J. (2009). *Zambia: Aid Effectiveness in the Health Sector*. Brussels: Action for Global Health.

24

Multistakeholder Involvement in UN Conferences
Kathrin Böhling

The United Nations frequently convenes global conferences and summits on issues of general concern, such as climate change, human rights or the 'digital divide', seeking consensus on practical solutions for inherent problems. Such conferences illustrate the dynamics of global governance beyond traditional nation state representation in international affairs. As the door of multilateral policymaking has opened to a broad range of issues and subjects, novel meeting formats were introduced in UN conferences that enlarge the scope of partici-pation to resolve common problems in new ways (Dodds 2002). More recently, the World Summit on the Information Society (WSIS), held in two phases (Geneva 2003 and Tunis 2005), has been a key site for the innovative multistakeholder approach to global governance (Raboy 2004; Kleinwächter 2005). It reflects a conception of stake-holder democracy in which those affected by a decision or with a stake in an issue should be involved in its resolution (Held 1997; Bäckstrand 2006).

UN conferences build institutional capacity to address global problems (e.g., the United Nations Development Program, the UN High Commissioner for Human Rights, or the UN Internet Governance Forum) and have become a means to legitimize global governance by making it more inclusive (Schechter 2005). Although they often do not produce treaties or binding law, UN conferences create norms around which actor expectations converge (Bernstein 2000). The agreement on the 'sustainable development' concept at the UN Conference on Environment and Development (UNCED) in Rio de Janeiro (1992) (the 'Earth Summit') and its evolution in subsequent international policymaking forums is a vivid example. Among these norms is also the 'pro-NGO international norm', which puts pressure on states and international organizations to include non-state actors in policymaking and implementation processes (Reimann 2006: 46).

This chapter shows that UN conferences have followed a long path to reach the point where the WSIS may be labelled a multistakeholder event. Since the early 1970s, non-state actors' presence in 'global conference diplomacy' (Rittberger 1983), seeking access to international deliberations and interest accommodations, changed the character of the conferences from predominantly functional events of multilateral policymaking into more public-oriented events of global norm setting (Brühl and Rosert 2008). Even if the participatory arrangements for non-state actors are not codified in conference rules of procedure, they have become an established tradition that is difficult to abandon (see, e.g., Weiss and Jordan 1976; Willets 1989; Clark, Friedman et al. 1998). The adoption of the multistakeholder approach at the WSIS is best seen as part of this evolution.

History of the Multistakeholder Approach in the United Nations

The basis for the evolving status of non-state actors in the UN is Article 71 of its Charter which states that the Economic and Social Council (ECOSOC) 'may make suitable arrangements for consultation with non-governmental organizations which are concerned with matters within its competence' (Willets 2000). Although not sufficient in its own right, Article 71 has led to a range of incentives and opportunity structures for pluralization of international dialogue and the proliferation of inclusive arrangements (Emmerij, Jolly et al. 2001). In retrospect it therefore seems safe to argue that the era of exclusive official diplomacy is over in some policy areas. Although the transformative effect of non-state actor involvement should not be over-emphasized, they 'have attained a legitimate and recognized role in the United Nations system' (Caldwell 1996: 106).

The situation was different in the early years of the UN's global conferences during the 1970s. At the first so-called 'mega conference' on the environment in Stockholm (1972) or the World Food Conference in Rome (1976), non-state actor involvement was the exception rather than the rule. With fewer than about 200 non-state actors as unofficial participants, involvement mainly took the form of lobbying. Increasingly, however, non-state actors met in unofficial side events, which, if organized effectively, may have affected intergovernmental negotiations in conference diplomacy (Weiss and Jordan 1976; Detter de Lupis 1989).

In the early years of global conference diplomacy, expansion of the event across the preparation, decision-making and implementation stages has become typical (Rittberger 1983; Willets 1989):

- In conference *preparation*, a series of regional and global meetings take place to develop a framework for negotiation, provide a draft agenda, approve the rules of procedure, and often prepare first drafts of the final conference documents. This stage is of utmost importance for the success or failure of global conference diplomacy, and it represents a major arena for non-state actor involvement.
- *Decision-making* is traditionally the exclusive province of governments. It takes shape in closed working groups with the plenary as the main formal element of conference decision-making. Governments lay out their views and negotiating postures in plenary sessions but cannot deliberate at this level.
- Historically, *implementation* of conference documents has been more of a formal target than practical reality. The early UN conferences in particular lacked the ability and the resources to prescribe policies and measures.

The early conferences became a breeding ground for stakeholder democracy. They produced 'a sense of alienation among concerned non-governmental actors which may indicate a legitimation problem of global conference diplomacy' (Rittberger 1983: 176). With informal participation of non-state actors in national delegations and the rise of parallel events solidifying, it became clear that the UN's problem-solving efforts 'were by no means always positive in the sense that they reflected states' determination to do something. Sometimes they were regarded as a way of avoiding action in the context of particular problems' (Taylor 1989: 9).

UN global conferences declined in the mid- to late 1980s, but then began again in earnest after the fall of the Berlin Wall as institutional responses to the need for governance in a globalized economy. A turning point in the history of non-state actor involvement at UN global conferences was the 'Earth Summit' in Rio de Janeiro, representing 178 national delegations. ECOSOC had relaxed the criteria for accreditation and 2,400 nongovernmental organization (NGO) representatives had official status as observers of the conference, while about 17,000 people took part in parallel forums. At the Earth Summit, any substantive claim on the environment and development made an NGO eligible for accreditation (Haas, Levy et al. 1992). This set a precedent for subsequent conferences: 30,000 individuals attended the parallel events at the fourth conference on women in Beijing (1995), and more than 5,000 were official participants of the conference itself; the second conference on human settlement in Istanbul (Habitat II, 1996) illustrates a similar pattern with 8,000 people attending the parallel forums and a large number of NGO representatives active in the conference itself (Emmerij, Jolly et al. 2001: 82–7).

> Not only did the numbers of NGO participation increase dramatically over two decades, but so did the variety of ways in which they were allowed to participate. Governments at the earlier conferences could virtually ignore the presence of NGOs ... By the 1990s, this was no longer possible, especially as NGOs were allowed to freely observe and lobby many governmental sessions. (Friedman et al. 2005: 159)

In the decade between the Earth Summit and the World Summit on Sustainable Development (WSSD) in Johannesburg (2002), it became a cornerstone of the UN's social and economic work to link stakeholding practices with formal intergovernmental decision-making and negotiation arenas (Bäckstrand 2006). Participation of non-state actors held the promise of linking global action with local problems (Hale and Mauzerall 2004). In Rio, non-state actors were strong promoters of the notion of sustainable development, and shaped to a large extent one of its final products, Agenda 21. At the Beijing women's conference, non-state actors successfully pushed to include gender mainstreaming in the action plans and played an important role in holding their governments accountable for promises made at the conference (Emmerij, Jolly et al. 2001). The WSSD generated 'type 2' partnerships. They are based on the idea that responsibility for implementing conference action plans rests not solely on governments but also on partners from NGOs and the private sector.

Institutionalization of the Multistakeholder Approach at the WSIS

WSIS and its follow-up is part of the dynamic trend that moved UN conferences toward endorsement of the multistakeholder approach (Selian 2004). When the UN General Assembly called for the Summit in 2002 (GA Resolution 56/183), it was the first time that non-state actors were officially invited to participate actively in the intergovernmental preparatory process and in the Summit itself. The multistakeholder approach implied for some that overall problem-solving capacity could be improved, and societal participation and control increased (Mueller, Kuerbis et al. 2007; Dany 2008). Deciding on this approach, however, was much easier said than done.

National delegations drew on codified experiences with non-state actor involvement in previous conferences to agree on rules of procedure for the WSIS, but discussions about non-state actor involvement continued throughout the overall Summit. At some stage, informal mechanisms were used to provide non-state actors with opportunities to affect the policy process. These included integration of non-state actors in national delegations in working groups – a practice that has become more common since the Rio conference – and the creation of a 'five-minute rule' that enabled non-state actors to make their arguments at the beginning of the working group sessions, after which they had to leave the room (Cammaerts and Carpentier 2005; Dany 2008). Simultaneously, civil society groups organized themselves into a 'Content and Themes Group' and an open 'Civil Society Plenary'. Doing so helped them to feed content into the drafting of Summit documents, to discuss subsequent steps, and to acquire authority vis-à-vis national delegations and international organizations (Mueller, Kuerbis et al. 2007).

Institutionalization of the multistakeholder approach in multilateral policymaking is also evident in the promising trajectory of the Internet Governance Forum (IGF) that emerged from the second phase of the WSIS in Tunis (2005). When the WSIS unexpectedly became the arena of contention about the most suitable form of governance for the Internet, governments in the end agreed to disagree and formed the Working Group on Internet Governance (WGIG) in 2003, which later transformed into the IGF. The IGF is a temporary UN body, in which representatives from governments, NGOs, the private sector, academia, and technical groups interact more or less equally to make recommendations on the future regulation of the Internet (Botzem and Hofmann 2008). This body was set up to hold the US model of private Internet governance – the Internet Corporation for Assigned

Names and Numbers (ICANN) – accountable to a broader public outside the US.

As an arena for deliberations on a 'regulative idea in flux' for Internet governance – which goes beyond domain names and Internet protocols to include also intellectual property rights, consumer and data protection, and cyber crime as core issues of Internet governance (Hofmann 2007) – the IGF shows that the multistakeholder process is deeply embedded in the administrative hierarchy and intergovernmental politics of the UN system (Mueller 2010). It is probably too demanding to expect these multistakeholder initiatives to cure the UN's 'democratic deficit'. Perhaps more interesting, however, is the unintended outcome of these initiatives – their potential to generate transnational institutions in a state-based system.

References

Bäckstrand, K. (2006). 'Democratizing Global Environmental Governance? Stakeholder Democracy after the World Summit on Sustainable Development'. *European Journal of International Relations* 12: 467–98.

Bernstein, S. (2000). 'Ideas, Social Structure and the Compromise of Liberal Environmentalism'. *European Journal of International Relations* 6: 464–512.

Botzem, S., and J. Hofmann (2008). 'Transnational Institution Building as Public-Private Interaction – The Case of Standard Setting on the Internet and in Corporate Financial Reporting'. Discussion Paper No. 51. Centre for Analysis of Risk and Regulation (CARR), London School of Economics.

Brühl, T., and E. Rosert (2008). 'Another Quiet Revolution? New Governance Forms in the United Nations System'. The Future of Civil Society Participation at the United Nations. Documentation of a workshop held at the ACUNS annual meeting, 6 June 2008, October 2008, pp. 5–20.

Cammaerts, B., and N. Carpentier (2005). 'The Unbearable Lightness of Full Participation in a Global Context: WSIS and Civil Society Participation'. *Towards a Sustainable Information Society: Beyond WSIS*, ed. J. Servaes and N. Carpentier. Bristol: Intellect.

Caldwell, L. K. (1996). *International Environmental Policy*. Durham and London: Duke University Press.

Clark, A. M., E. J. Friedman et al. (1998). 'The Sovereign Limits of Global Civil Society: A Comparison of NGO Participation in UN World Conferences on the Environment, Human Rights, and Women'. *World Politics* 51: 1–35.

Dany, C. (2008). 'Civil Society Participation under Most Favourable Conditions: Assessing the Deliberative Quality of the WSIS'. *Civil Society*

Participation in European and Global Governance: A Cure for the Democratic Deficit?, ed. J. Steffek, C. Kissing et al. Houndmills: Palgrave Macmillan.

Detter de Lupis, I. (1989). 'The Human Environment: Stockholm and its Follow-up'. *Global Issues in the United Nations' Framework*, ed. P. Taylor and A.J.R. Groom. Houndmills: Macmillan.

Dodds, F. (2002). 'The Context: Multi-Stakeholder Processes and Global Governance'. *Multi-Stakeholder Processes for Governance and Sustainability*, ed. M. Hemmati. London: Earthscan Publications Ltd.

Emmerij, L., R. Jolly et al. (2001). *Ahead of the Curve? UN Ideas and Global Challenges*. Bloomington and Indianapolis: Indiana University Press.

Friedman, E. J., K. Hochstetler et al. (2005). *Sovereignty, Democracy and Global Civil Society: State–Society Relations at UN World Conferences*. Albany: State University of New York Press.

Haas, P. M., M. A. Levy et al. (1992). 'Appraising the Earth Summit: How Should We Judge UNCED's Success?' *Environment* 34: 26–33.

Hale, T. N., and D. L. Mauzerall (2004). 'Thinking Globally and Acting Locally: Can the Johannesburg Partnership Coordinate Action on Sustainable Development?' *Journal of Environment & Development* 13: 220–39.

Held, D. (1997). 'Democracy and Globalization'. *Global Governance* 3: 1–28.

Hofmann, J. (2007). 'Internet Governance: A Regulative Idea in Flux'. *Internet Governance: An Introduction*, ed. R. K. J. Bandamutha. Hyderabad: The Icfai University Press.

Kleinwächter, W. (2005). 'A New Diplomacy for the 21st Century? Multi-Stakeholder Approach and Bottom-Up Policy Development in the Information Society'. *The World Summit on the Information Society: Moving from the Past into the Future*, ed. D. Stauffacher and W. Kleinwächter. New York: United Nations.

Mueller, M. L. (2010). 'A Funny Thing Happened on the way to the Forum: Multi-stakeholderism, International Institutions, and Global Governance of the Internet'. *Networks and States: The Global Politics of Internet Governance*, ed. M. Mueller. Cambridge, MA: MIT Press.

Mueller, M. L., B. N. Kuerbis et al. (2007). 'Democratizing Global Communication? Global Civil Society and the Campaign for Communication Rights in the Information Society'. *International Journal of Communication* 1: 267–96.

Raboy, M. (2004). 'The World Summit on the Information Society and Its Legacy for Global Governance'. *International Communication Gazette.* 66(3–4): 225–32.

Reimann, K. (2006). 'A View from the Top: International Politics, Norms and the Worldwide Growth of NGOs'. *International Studies Quarterly* 50: 45–67.

Rittberger, V. (1983). 'Global Conference Diplomacy and International Policy-Making: The Case of UN-Sponsored World Conferences'. *European Journal of Political Research* 11: 167–82.

Schechter, M. G. (2005). *United Nations Global Conferences*. London: Routledge.

Selian, A. N. (2004). 'The World Summit on the Information Society and Civil Society Participation'. *The Information Society* 20: 201–15.

Taylor, P. (1989). 'The Origins and Institutional Setting of the UN Special Conferences'. *Global Issues in the United Nations' Framework*, ed. P. Taylor and A. J. R. Groom. Houndmills: Palgrave Macmillan.

United Nations (2002). 'Resolution Adopted by the General Assembly: Resolution 56/183 World Summit on the Information Society'. Available at www.itu.int/wsis/docs/background/resolutions/56_183_unga_2002. pdf (accessed 12 March 2010).

Weiss, T. G., and R. S. Jordan (1976). *The World Food Conference and Global Problem Solving*. New York: Praeger Publishers

Willets, P. (1989). 'The Pattern of Conferences'. *Global Issues in the United Nations' Framework*, ed. P. Taylor and A. J. R. Groom. Houndmills: Palgrave Macmillan.

Willets, P. (2000). 'From "Consultative Arrangements" to "Partnership": The Changing Status of NGOs in Diplomacy at the UN'. *Global Governance* 6: 191–213.

25

World Commission on Dams
Navroz K. Dubash

The World Commission on Dams (WCD) emerged in 2000 from the globalization of what have historically been disconnected national debates. While dams have long aroused heated contestation in a variety of countries, the progressive globalization of dam financing and the emergence of a well-knit transnational advocacy network led to the emergence of dams as a subject of transnational governance. Once created, the WCD quickly acquired significance well beyond dams as an important moment in debates over development itself, and as a potential innovation in global governance. In the words of the WCD chair: 'we are much more than a "Dams Commission." We are a Commission to heal the deep and self-inflicted wounds torn open wherever and whenever far too few determine for far too many how best to develop or use water and energy resources . . . We do not endorse globalisation from above . . . we do endorse globalisation as led from below' (Asmal 2000). In this brief introduction to the WCD, I explain why, for many, the WCD represented the high-water mark of global 'multistakeholder initiatives'.

What Was the WCD and What Made It Unusual?

The WCD originated in a 1997 meeting between dam critics and proponents, convened by the World Bank and the World Conservation Union (IUCN). Participants in that meeting decided on the need for a much deeper understanding of the role of dams in the development process and also the need for a set of forward-looking recommendations. They recommended establishing an independent Commission that would:

- review the development effectiveness of large dams and assess alternatives;
- develop internationally acceptable criteria, guidelines, and standards . . . for . . . dams. (World Commission on Dams 2000)

Once established in May 1998, the WCD comprised twelve Commissioners who collectively spanned the full breadth of perspectives, from dam builders, to government officials, to committed anti-dam activists. In addition to a Secretariat, the WCD also established a 'Forum' of around seventy members to continue an ongoing consultation process with stakeholders. The Commission carried out an ambitious body of work to develop a 'knowledge base' around dams: 10 river basin and national studies; a survey of 125 dams; 17 thematic reviews on subjects such as social impacts and project finance; and a series of broad regional consultations (World Commission on Dams 2000; Dubash, Dupar et al. 2001). The Commission completed its work in 2000, producing a final report and establishing a five-year-long 'Dams and Development Project' (DDP) to carry forward its work through consultations.

This telegraphic description of structure conceals, however, what made the WCD truly interesting: the intense contention around every aspect of its creation and functioning. The WCD emerged from a decade of transnational civil society organizing and protest around large dams, punctuated by three collective declarations calling for an independent commission to examine the experience with dams – in San Francisco in 1988, Manibeli (India) in 1994, and Curitiba (Brazil) in 1997 (Khagram, 2004). For the World Bank, the WCD offered respite from Bank-focused criticism. For industry, it provided the prospect of a cease-fire – activist efforts were making dam construction financially unviable – and the possibility of predictable future rules (McCully 2000).

The WCD emerged, then, as an effort to bring warring factions to the table. From this followed many attributes of the process, notably efforts to bring into the fold the full spectrum of opinions on dams, and then to construct a transparent and open process that would maintain the confidence of all the participants.

How do Multistakeholder Initiatives have Impact? The Challenge of Evaluation

The WCD's final report did not lend itself to easy implementation. Instead, it laid out complex procedural recommendations organized around five values, seven strategic priorities and five decision points for decision makers (World Commission on Dams 2000). Neither governments nor international organizations could easily overlay this approach on national laws or operating procedures. However, the report did offer a substantially new way to think about the problem: managing rights and risks within a broader framework of human rights.

Stakeholders' reaction to the report was mixed and divided along partisan lines (Dubash, Dupar et al. 2001; Fujikura and Nakayama 2009). Nongovernmental organizations (NGOs) and social movements welcomed the report and sought implementation by the World Bank and governments. In contrast, trade and industry groups charged that transaction costs of doing business had increased rather than decreased. Indeed, the International Hydropower Association has since created an 'International Hydropower Sustainability Forum' aimed at creating a set of guidelines for hydropower, signalling significant differences from the WCD approach, which in turn has been criticized by NGOs.[1] The World Bank promised only to 'consider' the WCD recommendations (Dubash 2009).

National governments' engagement with the report was mediated by the five-year-long follow-up DDP, which organized national multistakeholder processes in at least twenty countries (United Nations Environment Programme (UNEP) 2007). For example, the widely commended South African process assessed domestic policy and institutional frameworks against the WCD recommendations, and called for changes to bring the two approaches into alignment (Hathaway 2004). More typical is the Indonesian approach, which called for the WCD report to be regarded as a reference in framing policies and regulations in relation to development (UNEP 2003).

[1] See www.hydropower.org/sustainable_hydropower/HSAF_About_the_Forum.html (accessed 24 February 2010). For a critique and an assessment of the differences from the WCD approach, see International Rivers (2009).

Financiers have typically also incorporated the WCD as guidance to be considered, rather than as a framework with which compliance is required. Following its initial non-committal stance, the World Bank endorsed the WCD's values and priorities, but did not translate the recommendations into its operational procedures (Dubash 2009). Export credit and guarantee agencies (ECAs) have explicitly incorporated WCD standards into their own guidelines, but most often as an influence to be considered or taken into account rather than rigidly followed (Knigge, Gorlach et al. 2003).

There are only a few instances of direct regulatory adoption of WCD guidelines. Among ECAs, exceptions to the general rule include the US Overseas Private Investment Corporation and the Swiss Exportrisikgarantie, which require explicit benchmarking against WCD standards (Asian Development Bank (ADB) n.d.). In an intriguing case of self-regulation, a private bank, HSBC, has tied itself to the WCD guidelines as a benchmark for its dam lending.[2] Finally, the European Union has directed that any hydropower projects seeking carbon credits must conform to the WCD guidelines (European Union (EU) 2004).

As these examples suggest, governments and financiers have reacted to the WCD largely through guidance or 'best-practice' formulations rather than compliance-oriented regulations.[3] Notably, much of the best-practice based reaction has emanated from financiers and industrialized countries rather than large developing countries at the forefront of dam construction today, which signals a broader shortcoming of the WCD in shaping regulative change.

However, beyond regulative change and guidance, there are several indications of the impact the WCD has had in the normative sphere. The WCD has been a significant discursive tool in global water debates, giving meaning to notions of participation and what Conca calls 'water democracy' (Conca 2005). Bradlow (2001) suggests that the WCD contributed to an ongoing shift in development decision-making that blurs the line between political and technical; rests on consultation, transparency and negotiation to resolve inconsistent objectives; and mandates consideration of alternative technologies and approaches. Consistent with this view, the WCD has also been read as an important contributor to winning acceptance for the idea of 'free, prior and informed consent' for indigenous peoples, as

---

[2] See HSBC, 'Freshwater Infrastructure Sector Guidelines', available at www.hsbc.com/1/PA_1_1_S5/content/assets/csr/freshwater_infrastructure_guideline.pdf (accessed 24 February 2010).
[3] These categories are taken from Bergkamp (2006), who has examined ECA reactions to the WCD guidelines.

enshrined in the United Nations Declaration on the Rights of Indigenous Peoples.[4]

The WCD suggests that evaluating the impact of a multistakeholder initiative is necessarily a multivalent effort, and also one that requires attention over a sufficiently long period.

Interpreting the WCD

In the last decade, a veritable 'cottage industry' of WCD assessments has emerged, much as predicted by one of the participants (McCully 2000: 1467). Early assessments interpreted the WCD as an exercise in problemsolving at the global scale. From this perspective, the absence of global democracy, combined with the growing role of private actors such as corporations and NGOs, requires global fora where all these actors can be brought together to problem solve (Dingwerth 2005; Dubash, Dupar et al. 2001). Thus, Reinicke and Deng (2000: 37) dub the WCD an 'almost archetypical trisectoral network', while Brinkerhoff (2002) sees the WCD as an exercise in constructing 'partnership' that allows 'mutuality' in interaction even while allowing all parties to maintain their separate identity.

While this literature on multistakeholder processes carries overtones of positive-sum oriented, somewhat genteel discussions, others view the same discussions as intensely political, with rather greater chances of zero-sum outcomes. Anti-dam activist McCully (2000: 1470) reflected that 'the WCD was a mere [instance] of anti-dam struggle by other means', while Khagram (2005: 210) notes that the WCD was 'as much a negotiating process' as a policymaking effort. Indeed, there was contestation around every decision, such as the selection of Secretariat members and consultants, choices of research topics, and even the location of hearings, as all sides sought even marginal gains in a discursive struggle (Dubash et al. 2001; Khagram 2005). From this perspective, the WCD was a potentially useful arena – in that it was focused and contained – for the unfolding of dam politics.

The politics of multistakeholder processes can, however, also be cosy and accommodating, suggests Ottaway (2001), who reads the WCD as an instance of 'corporatism gone global'. Ottaway sees real dangers in the direct representation of functional groups at the global scale; many such groups, such as NGOs or loose business coalitions, lack even minimal moorings of accountability relations. However,

---

[4]P.c., Joji Carino, Tebtebba Foundation, Former Commissioner of the WCD, 2 March 2010. For the UN Declaration, see www.un.org/esa/socdev/unpfii/en/drip.html (accessed 24 February 2010).

given what she sees as their weak legitimacy and therefore authority, they are 'less at risk of turning authoritarian than of remaining ineffectual'.

To answer Ottaway requires delving into the sources of legitimacy that a WCD-like process can offer. And the primary promise of such processes is enhanced democracy through a process that is transparent and inclusive, and provides a measure of accountability (Dubash, Dupar et al. 2001; Khagram 2004; Dingwerth 2005). In a variety of such ways, the WCD displayed a deep reflexivity about the links between its legitimacy and democratic process. For example, the Commissioners attempted to reach out to affected communities through public hearings. The Secretariat sourced its financing from governments and international organizations (half), the private sector (a quarter), and civil society and foundations (a quarter) with a cap on any single source. The Forum of stakeholders represented an effort to ensure inclusiveness.

Various assessments have disagreed on whether this was enough. Dubash, Dupar et al. (2001) conclude the process was essentially robust, given the constraints. Dingwerth (2005) argues that, despite these efforts, the WCD was found wanting in its democratic process, and argues that this case points to the need for more robust theorizing about democratic governance beyond the state. Fujikura and Nakayama (2009) also suggest that the implementation of the WCD was flawed, in particular because the process of formulating guidelines was relatively closed. Critics of the WCD's process, therefore argue that, while the conception was sound, flawed implementation undercut the WCD's democratic legitimacy.

By contrast, Dubash (2009) suggests that claims of procedural capture by losers in a discursive battle can always undercut democratic legitimacy. Consequently, it may be impossible to ensure democratic legitimacy solely on the basis of good process. Instead, the WCD rested its legitimacy at least as much on the basis of including the full spectrum of warring parties within the Commission as on the basis of democratic process. Consequently, it marked a departure from past models of global commissions based on eminence and technical detachment from contentious issues. However, legitimacy based on representation is itself no easy panacea and raises both conceptual challenges and practical difficulties.

Another response to challenges to the WCD's effectiveness and legitimacy lies in re-conceiving the WCD entirely, from a problem-solving body (whether with zero-sum or positive-sum overtones) to one that generates and amplifies norms at the global scale. If the WCD has been relatively ineffective as a rule-making body, perhaps it has been less so as a norm-changing process. If normative change requires winning discursive battles, then the test of the WCD's legitimacy lies, perhaps, in its ability to shape perceptions and norms through subsequent years of engagement with its output. This line of thinking particularly helps explain how multistakeholder processes relate to states. As Conca (2002) points out, the WCD was less a displacement of states and more a re-centring, since its conclusions had to eventually be re-worked through national democratic processes.

Elaborating on these themes, Dubash (2009) suggests the role of the WCD in global governance, and such processes more generally, is more usefully understood through the lens of norm-generation and propagation than as rule-making or problem-solving bodies. Even more expansively, Khagram and Ali (2008) conclude that global governance networks such as the WCD are sources of an 'organizational script for reconstruction of global governance' that allow for ways of contesting meanings of global problems.

Ten years later, the WCD remains a distinct example among global multistakeholder processes, notably for its attention to democratic process, and the broad representation of diverse views among its Commissioners. Its legacy to global governance debates, however, lies less in its design elements, and more in an understanding of whether and how the WCD brought about change. Few would argue that the WCD had much success in winning broad agreement on a solution to the problem of large dams. But the WCD has raised the intriguing possibility that multistakeholder processes are useful vehicles for generating norms and contesting meanings, and therefore an avenue for constitutive change in world politics.

References

ADB (Asian Development Bank) (n.d.). 'Initiatives of Some Export Credit Agencies Related to the WCD Report'. Available at www.adb.org/water/Topics/Dams/dams1025–10.asp (accessed 24 February 2010).

Asmal, K. (2000). 'Preface'. *Dams and Development: A New Framework for Decision-Making. An Overview*, ed. World Commission on Dams. London: Earthscan.

Bergkamp, G. (2006). 'OECD – Meeting of Export Credit Agencies: Recognising the Value of International Sources of Guidance: The World Commission on Dams (Presentation)'. Available at www.unepie.org/energy/activities/eca/pdf/WS5/WS5-Bergkamp.pdf (accessed 24 February 2010).

Bradlow, D. D. (2001). 'The World Commission on Dams: Contribution to the Broader Debate on Developmental Decision-Making'. *American University International Law Review* 16: 1531–72.

Brinkerhoff, J. M. (2002). 'Global Public Policy, Partnership, and the Case of the World Commission on Dams'. *Public Administration Review* 62: 324–36.

Conca, K. (2002). 'The World Commission on Dams and Trends in Global Environmental Governance'. *Politics and the Life Sciences* 21: 67–71.

Conca, K. (2005). *Governing Water: Contentious Transnational Politics and Global Institution Building*. Cambridge, MA: MIT Press.

Dingwerth, K. (2005). 'The Democratic Legitimacy of Public–Private Rule Making: What Can We Learn from the World Commission of Dams?' *Global Governance* 11: 65–83.

Dubash, N. K. (2009). 'Global Norms through Global Deliberation? Reflections on the World Commission on Dams'. *Global Governance* 15: 219–38.

Dubash, N. K., M. Dupar et al. (2001). *A Watershed in Global Governance? An Independent Assessment of the World Commission on Dams*. Lokayan and Washington, DC: World Resources Institute and LEAT.

EU (2004). 'Directive of the European Parliament and the Council'. Directive 2004/101/EC. Available at http://eur-lex.europa.eu/LexUriServ/site/en/oj/2004/l_338/l_33820041113en00180023.pdf (accessed 24 February 2010).

Fujikura, R., and M. Nakayama (2009). Lessons Learned from the World Commission on Dams'. *International Environmental Agreements: Politics, Law and Economics* 9: 173–90.

Hathaway, T. (2004). 'Turning the WCD into Action in South Africa'. International Rivers Network. Available at www.internationalrivers.org/files/050820turning_0.pdf (accessed 24 February 2010).

International Rivers (2009). 'A Critique of IHA's Draft Hydropower Sustainability Assessment Protocol'. Available at www.international-rivers.org/node/4764 (accessed 1 February 2010).

Khagram, S. (2004). *Dams and Development: Transnational Struggles for Water and Power*. Ithaca: Cornell University Press.

Khagram, S. (2005). 'Beyond Temples and Tombs: Towards Effective Governance of Sustainable Development through the World Commission on Dams.' *International Commissions and the Power of Ideas*, ed. R. Thakur, A. F. Cooper et al. Tokyo: United Nations Press.

Khagram, S., and H. Ali (2008). 'Transnational Transformations: From Government-Centric Interstate Regimes to Cross-Sectoral Multi-Level Networks of Global Governance'. *The Crisis of Global Environmental Governance*, ed. J. Park, K. Conca et al. London: Routledge.

Knigge, M., B. Gorlach, et al. (2003). *The Use of Environmental and Social Criteria in Export Credit Agencies' Practice*. Eschborn, Germany: GTZ and EcoLogic.

McCully, P. (2000). 'The Use of Trilateral Networks: An Activist Perspective on the World Commission on Dams'. *American University International Law Review* 16: 1453–75.

Ottaway, M. (2001). 'Corporatism Goes Global: International Organizations, NGO Networks and Transnational Business'. *Global Governance: A Review of Multilateralism and International Organizations* 7: 265–92

Reinicke, W., and F. Deng (2000). *Critical Choices: The United Nations, Networks and the Future of Global Governance*. Ottawa: International Development Research.

UNEP 2003, 'Summary of Conclusion of National Consultation on Dam Development'. Available at www.unep.org/dams/documents/Default. asp?DocumentID = 415 (accessed 24 February 2010).

UNEP (United Nations Environment Programme) (2007). 'UNEP Dams and Development Project: Final Report Phase 2'. Available at www.unep. org/dams/files/FinalReport_Phase2.pdf (accessed 19 February 2010).

World Commission on Dams (2000). *Dams and Development: A New Framework for Decision-Making*. London: Earthscan.

Part IV
Voluntary Regulations

Introduction

Voluntary regulations are perhaps the most common type of innovative transnational governance institution, influencing almost every sector of the global economy (Abbott and Snidal 2000; Vogel 2008; Green 2010). Under these arrangements an actor, typically a private company, agrees to abide by a certain social or environmental standard above and beyond those that bind it legally. These standards are sometimes little more than public relations tools, but they can also be sincere, substantive and ambitious. They can derive from formal laws or be completely self-generated. They can be adopted by a single firm, a group of firms, an entire industry or a broad swath of the economy. They can be created and operated by companies themselves, or in partnership with other private actors (typically nongovernmental organizations (NGOs)), with intergovernmental organizations, or with states. Additionally, these other actors can sometimes impose 'voluntary' regulation on companies through naming and shaming, market pressures, reputational benefits or other incentives.

As the following section demonstrates, voluntary regulations are remarkably diverse in the institutional arrangements they adopt to develop standards, monitor compliance with standards, and enforce them. For many, transparency and exposure are key to the process, the idea being that quantification and monitoring of targets (e.g. the Global Reporting Initiative) and exposure to public scrutiny (e.g. the Extractive Industries Transparency Initiative) will give companies incentives to improve their social and environmental performance. For labelling schemes, transparency is reinforced by market incentives (e.g. Rugmark, the Forest Stewardship Council), as the governance institutions seek to give consumers the ability to choose products with fewer environmental and social externalities. It is also important to note that not all voluntary regulations follow a logic of establishing a standard, monitoring compliance and enforcing behaviour. The UN Global Compact, for example, seeks to facilitate learning and capacity building around general environmental and social principles. This 'managerial' approach to regulation (Chayes and Chayes 1995) tracks similar developments in domestic regulatory policy (Orts 1995).

Whatever form it takes, voluntary regulation is rarely seen as a panacea. None of the institutions studied in this section manages to regulate more than a fraction of the economic activity it targets, raising doubts about the utility of this governance form. It is important to ask, however, what the alternative might be. Given the absence of a global regulator and the difficulties of bringing all sovereign states into agreement on regulatory policies, voluntary regulation can be understood as an innovative way to achieve what is politically possible. In some cases, this has led to real improvements for specific people and places, even if the larger transnational problems remain unresolved.

References

Abbott, K. W., and D. Snidal (2000). 'International "Standards" and International Governance'. Unpublished manuscript.

Chayes, A., and A. H. Chayes (1995). *The New Sovereignty: Compliance with International Regulatory Agreements*. Cambridge, MA: Harvard University Press.

Green, J. (2010). 'Private Authority, Public Goals: Non-state Actors in Global Environmental Politics'. Politics Department dissertation. Princeton University.

Orts, E. W. (1995). 'Reflexive Environmental Law'. Northwestern University Law Review 89: 779–94.

Vogel, D. (2008). 'Private Global Business Regulation'. *Annual Review of Political Science* 11: 261–82.

26

Carbon Disclosure Project
Eun-Hee Kim and Thomas P. Lyon

Investors constitute a relatively new but potentially important voice in global environmental governance. Investors have long voiced their concerns over corporate governance through shareholder resolutions. With increasing ownership shares held by institutional investors, activism targeting multiple companies at the same time has also arisen as a tool to address governance issues. For example, the California Public Employees' Retirement System (CalPERS) annually announces the so-called 'focus list', a list of poorly performing firms in terms of financial performance, aiming to improve their corporate governance and stock performance through active engagement with management. More recently, a large number of well-known institutional investors have taken coordinated action to combat climate change through the Carbon Disclosure Project (CDP). The CDP is noteworthy in that it is the first attempt by institutional investors to collectively address a global environmental problem that is less directly related to financial performance than to corporate governance issues. If successful, the CDP provides a valuable example of how investors, non-traditional actors, can promote global environmental governance.

Global environmental issues such as climate change present an ideal setting to explore the increasing role of non-traditional actors in governing the global common good. Traditional actors such as states and international institutions, although essential, have limitations in addressing global environmental issues. State actors, often focused on economic growth, pay little attention to mitigating global environmental problems; doing so inflicts net costs because the costs are borne by them whereas the benefits are shared around the globe. International institutions such as the United Nations play a necessary role in global environmental governance because they bring together state actors for a potential solution (Keohane, Hass et al. 1993). Whether international institutions are sufficient, however, is doubtful, as demonstrated by the difficulties in reaching even a weak collective agreement at the 2009 United Nations Climate Change Conference in Copenhagen.

The most prominent non-traditional actors are nongovernmental organizations (NGOs). NGOs not only pressure political actors such as states and international institutions to push environmental policy measures further, but also directly coerce private firms to take actions. Through negative campaigning, boycotting and public engagement, NGOs have achieved visible outcomes. The strategies of the CDP contrast with those of NGOs. Instead of actively engaging the public, the CDP simply encourages firms to disclose environmental performance and monitors them. A natural question is then exactly what the CDP accomplishes with its monitoring function. Does CDP affect firms' environmental performance? The remainder of this chapter discusses what the CDP is, how it works, and whether and to what extent it has been successful. The chapter concludes with an overall assessment of the CDP.

What Is It?

The CDP is a consortium of over 300 institutional investors with over $57 trillion in assets as of 2008, including Barclays Group, CalPERS, Goldman Sachs, Merrill Lynch, Morgan Stanley and UBS, among others. The CDP asks the world's largest companies each year to disclose their greenhouse gas (GHG) emissions and associated risks, opportunities and management strategies. Companies participate in the CDP on a voluntary basis. The CDP publicly discloses company responses on its website, in the hope that publicized information will ultimately change firm behaviour.

The CDP is an outcome of investors' concerns over the financial risks to which companies might be exposed due to their GHG emissions. Two types of potential financial risks are present. One is the direct effect of climate change via alterations in weather patterns and rising sea levels. The other is the effect of regulation, such as abatement and liability costs. With their large ownership stakes, institutional investors started to address these concerns collectively in 2002 via the CDP.

How Does It Work?

The CDP operates by collecting and disseminating climate-change-related information about companies to investors and other stakeholders. Thus, the proper functioning of the CDP depends critically on two factors: what kinds of information are collected, and which companies are asked to provide information. Since its inception in 2002, the CDP has evolved in both respects.

The first cycle of the project involved sending a letter and one-page questionnaire to the *Financial Times*'s 500 largest companies in the world. The letter was signed by thirty-five institutional investors who collectively held $4.5 trillion in assets. The CDP1 questions were targeted at broadly understanding emissions and emissions reductions throughout the product's manufacturing process and its life cycle. The questions, for example, asked for the quantity of annual GHG emissions produced by a company's operations, and whether the firm measured the quantity of emissions generated by the use and disposal of their products and by their supply chains.

By the fourth cycle of the project in 2006, the questions were considerably expanded. The CDP4 questionnaire asks companies not only what their emissions profile is but also who is responsible for emissions reductions, whether they are making necessary innovations, and what the impacts of existing and proposed regulations are. Specific CDP4 questions include the following: 'Who at board level has specific responsibility for climate-change-related issues and who manages your company's climate change strategies?'; 'What technologies, products, processes, or services has your company developed, or is developing, in response to climate change?'; 'What are the financial and strategic impacts on your company of existing regulation of GHG emissions, and what do you estimate to be the impact of proposed future regulation?' The questions about management responsibility, innovation and regulatory impacts are clearly designed to assess long-term performance of companies in a carbon-constrained world.

Furthermore, the number of invitees to CDP4 was vastly increased. Whereas the CDP1 invitation was sent out to the Global FT 500 companies, the CDP4 information request was sent out to about four times as many companies. The invitees were FT 500, S&P 500, 300 of the largest electric utilities globally, 300 of the largest emitters in Canada, 200 of the largest companies in Germany, 150 of the largest companies in Japan, 150 of the largest companies in Australia and New Zealand, 120 of the largest companies in France, 100 of the largest companies in the UK, 50 of the largest companies in Brazil, and 40 of the largest companies in Asia outside of Japan.

By the eighth, most recent, cycle of the project in 2010, the CDP sent out thirteen-page questionnaires to over 4,000 companies around the world. By then the CDP had been endorsed by 475 well-known institutional investors. Under the CDP8, companies in three GHG intensive industries – cars, electric utilities, and oil and gas – were asked to provide additional information tailored to their industry. For example, companies in the electric utility industry were asked to provide their fuel mix portfolio – i.e., coal, nuclear, oil, natural gas, solar, wind, etc. – and emissions allowances if they participate in the EU emissions trading scheme. These questions were intended to gauge industry-specific risks and opportunities, which are not captured in the general questionnaire.

In addition, the CDP8 questionnaire has become increasingly sophisticated as it has grown in length. For instance, questions about management responsibility go beyond asking where the highest level of responsibility for climate change lies within the company. The CDP8 asks if the highest responsibility is at the Board or other executive body level, and what the mechanism is by which they review the company's progress and status regarding climate change. If the responsibility lies at a lower level, CDP8 asks how overall responsibility for climate change is managed within the company. Questions about emissions and reductions are further refined so that details regarding sources, boundaries and locations of emissions, as well as baselines and methodology for calculating reductions, are clearly specified. In addition, the CDP8 includes questions integrating market and nonmarket strategy: how a firm's overall group business strategy links with actions taken on risks and opportunities, including any emissions reduction targets or achievements, public policy engagement and external communication; whether a firm engages with policymakers on possible responses to climate change, including taxation, regulation and carbon trading. The CDP8 questions, if properly answered, should provide a comprehensive picture of companies' future prospects in carbon-regulated economies.

Has It Been Successful?

From a global environmental governance perspective, the success of the CDP can be evaluated by two criteria: the extent to which companies respond to the CDP information request, and the extent to which companies that respond to the CDP request bring about significant environmental improvement as a result.

The CDP website provides information on the first measure for the FT Global 500 companies and for most non-FT Global 500 companies. Overall, the CDP response rates are high. Upon the CDP1 information request, 71 per cent of the FT Global 500 companies responded and 45 per cent answered the questionnaire in full; another 26 per cent provided some information but did not explicitly answer the questions. The response rate steadily increased until mid-2000. By the fourth cycle of the project (CDP4) in 2006, 91 per cent of the FT Global 500 responded and 72 per cent answered the questionnaire in full. Perhaps due to the economic downturn, however, the response rate fluctuated in the late 2000s. For CDP7 in 2009, it was 82 per cent. Of these 68 per cent disclosed their GHG emissions. Non-FT Global 500 companies showed lower or higher response rates depending on region. For example, S&P 500 firms generally show lower response rates than European firms; the highest response rate from the S&P 500 was 66 per cent in 2009. In Asia, companies in the information technology sector show a high response rate of 70 per cent, whereas companies in other sectors show low response rates of around 20 per cent. European companies overall show high response rates, equivalent to those of FT Global 500. It appears that in Europe, where the environmental movement is arguably the most advanced, the response rate is the highest. As pointed out in Kolk, Levy et al. (2008), response rates may also reflect the extent of institutional pressure faced by companies.

An important question from an environmental governance perspective is whether the CDP respondents change their environmental management behaviour due to participating in the CDP. Unfortunately, to our knowledge, no academic studies have systematically examined this question. Perhaps the difficulty lies in teasing out potential selection bias. We may find a positive relationship between CDP participation and good environmental performance. But it is hard to determine whether clean firms are simply more likely to respond to the CDP's information request or whether the CDP actually causes participating firms to improve their environmental performance. If the former, the CDP reduces the information asymmetry between companies and investors regarding companies' environmental performance, but the CDP does not directly bring additional environmental benefits. If the latter, pressure from the CDP to raise shareholder value drives firms to improve their environmental performance. One recent study finds that a firm is more likely to respond to the CDP request if it or other firms in the industry are being targeted by a shareholder resolution or government regulation on a related issue (Reid and Toffel, 2009). This result begins to provide concrete evidence on the circumstances in which the CDP information request is most effective.

Overall Assessment of the Carbon Disclosure Project

The CDP provides an unprecedented information collection and sharing system with regards to business strategies toward climate change. The 475 institutional investors that endorsed the most recent CDP information request exert significant pressure on thousands of companies to respond. The CDP questionnaire has been considerably expanded and polished since its inception. The latest questionnaire includes detailed questions about management responsibilities and innovations as well as emissions and regulations. If answered fully and properly, the CDP questionnaire should reveal firms' risks and opportunities with regards to climate change both in the short and the long run.

Despite its substantial potential as an instrument of global environmental governance, some weaknesses have been identified in the CDP. For example, Kolk, Levy et al. (2008) question the extent to which the CDP data provide an objective measure of firms' readiness to cope with climate change. They point out that the data have serious issues including consistency, completeness, reliability, and comparability across firms. Accordingly, Kolk, Levy et al. (2008) argue that the CDP data may not be as valuable to investors and other stakeholders as previously thought. Nevertheless, Kim and Lyon (2009) show that the CDP data are valuable to investors under certain circumstances. They find that CDP participants in countries without GHG regulations experienced a positive stock price shock when exogenous events caused the likelihood of climate change regulation to rise. Apparently, CDP participants were viewed as better prepared than non-participants to deal with climate shocks.

Perhaps the most important question from a global environmental governance perspective is whether the CDP induces changes in firm behaviour in terms of environmental management and environmental performance. So far, this remains still an open question.

References

Keohane, R., M. Hass et al. (1993). 'The Effectiveness of International Environmental Institutions'. *Institutions for the Earth*, ed. M. Hass, R. Keohane et al. Cambridge, MA, and London: MIT Press.

Kim, E., and T. Lyon (2009). 'When Does Institutional Investor Activism Increase Shareholder Value?: The Carbon Disclosure Project'. Working paper, University of Michigan.

Kolk, A., D. Levy et al. (2008). 'Corporate Responses in an Emerging Climate Regime: The Institutionalization and Commensuration of Carbon Disclosure'. *European Accounting Review* 17(4): 719–45.

Reid, E., and M. Toffel (2009). 'Responding to Public and Private Politics: Corporate Disclosure of Climate Change Strategies'. *Strategic Management Journal* 30(11): 1157–78.

27

Codex Alimentarius Commission
Tim Büthe and Nathaniel Harris

The Codex Alimentarius Commission (Codex) develops standards for hygienic handling, labelling and trade of food commodities, as well as the assessment of food-related safety risks. It is nominally a traditional international (governmental) organization with 182 member states, but plays an important role in *trans*national governance for two reasons. First, although national delegations are led by ministries/departments of agriculture or food regulatory agencies, they usually include many private actors, especially representatives from food industry multinationals and business associations. Second, standards set by the Codex play a crucial role in international trade, especially since Codex was officially sanctioned as an international standard-setter in the SPS-Agreement of the World Trade Organization (WTO). Codex standards therefore now govern the behaviour of agricultural producers and the choices available to consumers in many countries. As a consequence, material stakes and political conflicts over representation and participation are never far below the surface in Codex standard-setting, which is supposedly guided only by scientific methods and expertise.

History of Codex

The Codex Alimentarius Commission was established in 1963 to implement the agreement between the Food and Agriculture Organization (FAO) and the World Health Organization (WHO) to develop international standards that would facilitate trade in food products without endangering the health of consumers. It was motivated in part by European regional cooperation on food standards, launched in 1958, which prompted the United States to push for a broader international effort to safeguard against exclusion of US interests (Leive 1976; Randell 1995; Braithwaite and Drahos 2000: 400f.).

In the early years, Codex was very successful and gained prominence as an international food standard-setter. In annual meetings and specialized committees (which subsumed some private transnational standard-setting bodies, such as the standards committee of the International Dairy Federation), scientific and policy experts – from governments and industry – jointly developed standards for 'safe' levels of pesticide residues and other food-related issues (Kay 1976: 33f; Leive 1976). Correspondingly, membership of the Commission grew rapidly: from less than 25 per cent of the UN-recognized independent states in 1963 to about 70 per cent in the early to mid-1970s. With the onset of the global economic downturn, however, Codex ran out of steam: standardization slowed, the Commission switched to a biennial schedule, and membership stagnated. By the mid-1980s, Codex was characterized by 'apathy and inaction' (Victor 1997: 188) and considered 'largely moribund' (Büthe 2009: 99).

Codex then rose to new prominence after the Uruguay Round of trade negotiations (1986–94). Cross-national differences in food safety standards constitute a non-tariff barrier to trade. Agricultural exporters in the United States and the Cairns Group of countries therefore feared that importing countries might arbitrarily change food safety regulations to maintain a 'constant level of protection' (Bhagwati 1988) unless agricultural trade liberalization in the Uruguay Round was combined with enforceable provisions against such protectionist measures. This led to the Agreement on the Application of Sanitary and Phytosanitary Measures (SPS-Agreement), which is an integral part of the treaty establishing the WTO.

Binding on all WTO member states and enforceable via the Dispute Settlement Mechanism, the SPS-Agreement commits governments to using 'international standards' for domestic regulations whenever such standards can achieve the intended level of consumer protection. Negotiating international standards for food safety among diplomats and trade experts, however, required more specialized technical expertise than they generally had and would have proceeded too slowly to effectively address health issues that may arise in global trade in food products. The negotiators therefore agreed to delegate standard-setting to outside bodies (Büthe 2008). Specifically, for food safety, Annex A(3) defines international standards as the standards 'established by the Codex Alimentarius Commission'. Member states of the WTO retain the right to adopt divergent regulatory measures, but the SPS-Agreement made Codex standards the benchmark and thus raised the stakes in Codex standard-setting.[1]

---

[1]Under the SPS-Agreement, each WTO member state may determine maximum acceptable levels of health risks and may require all food products (without discrimination based on origin) to meet more stringent standards to achieve those levels. For regulatory measures not based on Codex standards, however, member states may be challenged to provide scientific evidence of their effectiveness based on risk assessments (Vogel 1995; Randall 2000; Epps 2008; Büthe 2009; Pollack and Shaffer 2009).

Institutional Structure and Standard-Setting Process

The Codex Alimentarius Commission is, strictly speaking, the assembly of the member states. It is the highest executive organ of the FAO–WHO Joint Food Standards Program. From 1974 through 2003, the Commission usually met biennially; it now holds one week-long 'session' each year.

Any member state can submit a proposal for Codex to develop a new standard or revise an existing one. The Executive Committee – elected by the Commission at large, subject to geographic diversity rules – conducts an initial 'critical review' of the relevance and timeliness of such proposals. It issues a recommendation to the full Commission, whose support is required for the official launch of the eight-step standards-development process (figure 27.1).[2] The Executive Committee also monitors the progress of standard-setting in the specialized subject or commodity committees, such as the committees for fresh fruits and vegetables, meat hygiene, food additives, pesticide residues, or methods for analysis and sampling.

Any standard agreed upon by the committee to which this task has been assigned, becomes a proposal to the Commission, which in the eighth and final step may formally adopt or reject it. Throughout the process, the organizational norms of Codex call for reaching consensus before moving from one step to the next and for the adoption of a standard. The notion remains, however, ill defined, and Codex's formal rules allow for adoption of a standard by simple majority vote, where each member state has one vote (Masson-Matthee 2007: 80–3).

Politics after Delegation: Codex under the WTO Regime

By delegating the task of setting standards for global trade to Codex, the WTO SPS-Agreement may have revived the organization, but it also politicized Codex. The WTO *Beef Hormones* case provides an illustration of the new risks countries face due to the linkage between Codex standard-setting and international trade law. In December 1985, the European Union (EU) banned the use of natural and synthetic hormones for growth promotion in livestock and prohibited the importation of meat from animals raised with such hormones. In 1987, the United States invoked the GATT Dispute Settlement Mechanism established under the Tokyo Round Agreement on

[2] For a critical discussion of the eight-step process, see Victor (1997) and Masson-Matthee (2007: 75ff.); for the formal rules governing the process, see Codex Alimentarius (2010: 25ff.).

Figure 27.1 Codex standard-setting process

Step		Major Actors and Procedure
1	Decision to develop/ revise standard	Codex member body or committee submits proposal to Executive Committee
2	Preparation of 1st draft	Secretariat arranges preparation of draft (usually by a member state); consultation of expert bodies
3	1st Review of draft standard by Codex Members	Secretariat submits draft to Codex member states and recognized observers for review
4	Revision by Codex Committee	The relevant subsidiary body (subject or commodity committee) discusses and amends the draft
5	Submission to Executive Committee and Codex Alimentarius Commission (CAC)	Draft is submitted to the Executive Committee, and subsequently to CAC for adoption of the draft standard
6	2nd review of draft standard	The adopted draft standard is sent back to members and INGOs for comments
7	2nd Revision by subsidiary body	Draft standard and submitted comments are discussed by the subsidiary body a second time
8	Final reading by CAC and adoption	The draft standard is submitted to the CAC for a second reading. The CAC can refer the draft back to any previous step, table the draft or adopt the standard.

Technical Barriers to Trade. However, the EU blocked an evaluation procedure (Kerr and Hobbs 2005). Both sides then sought to establish their respective views of the (non)risks of growth hormones as a Codex standard, which eventually resulted in the adoption (by a vote of 33 to 29 with 7 abstentions) of a Codex standard that essentially declared the use of growth hormones as practised by US cattle farmers safe for human consumption (Trebilcock and Howse 2005: 228). As soon as the WTO treaty entered into force, the United States used the new Dispute Settlement Mechanism to challenge the EU's continuing ban on hormone-treated beef. The WTO Appellate Body in the *Hormones* case clarified that the SPS-Agreement does not require countries to adopt international standards (Victor 2000; Roberts, Orden et al. 2004: 345). However, it ruled that the EU had not produced evidence to support its claim that the ban on hormone-treated beef achieved protection against any health risks for which there was a basis in scientific risk assessments, and thus had failed to adequately substantiate its deviation from the international (Codex) standard (Trebilcock and Howse 2005: 152; Pollack and Shaffer 2009: 151).[3]

Other countries also recognized the increasing importance of Codex. After stagnating until 1993 (when 75 per cent of all independent countries were Codex members), Codex membership again grew dramatically and now (May 2010) exceeds 92 per cent. More importantly, the number of countries that actually send representatives to the Codex meetings increased from an average of 57 in the 1980s to an average of 96 in 1995–9 and to about 120 in recent years. A corresponding development can be seen at the Committee level, where the average number of meetings increased from eleven a year during the eight years prior to the Uruguay Round to 17 per year during the eight years following the conclusion of the treaty, and to more than 19 per year recently, also with increasing attendance. All of these developments suggest that countries increasingly consider Codex rule-making as an activity in which they have a stake.

These changes have had real consequences. Veggeland and Borgen (2005) observe a change in member behaviour on several dimensions, reflecting the more binding nature of Codex standards. They find that political and economic interests are now more openly pursued in negotiations, and that countries are more likely, post-1995, to take positions in Codex that comport with their positions in international trade negotiations. Furthermore, our own analysis finds that, despite the move to electronic document distribution and various procedural changes introduced to accelerate the process, Codex standard-setting has only become marginally faster due to drawn-out conflicts of interest.

In sum, until 1995, Codex standards were only recommendations; governments were free to implement these or any other standards. This allowed anyone opposed to a given standard to abstain, and enabled adoption by 'consensus', but it also made the standards irrelevant for agricultural trade liberalization. When the SPS-Agreement raised the stakes, the balance between technical–scientific collaboration and political–strategic behaviour in standard-setting tilted

---

[3] Generally, EU efforts to have Codex standards reflect the principles underlying its approach to food safety have had 'mixed success' (Poli 2004), arguably reflecting the built-in bias in favour of US preferences due to the long-standing emphasis on trade liberalization in Codex (Drezner 2007: 162). This has prompted attempts to shift standard-setting for genetically modified organisms out of the Codex to other institutional settings that are more congenial to EU concerns (Pollack and Shaffer 2009).

toward the latter. Deliberative decision-making can still be seen within Codex, and standards-adoption by majority vote, which had been a purely hypothetical possibility until the SPS-Agreement, remains the exception (Codex 2008). However, when dealing with issues of risk management or standards clearly related to trade issues, bargaining behaviour has usurped the traditional consensus-based approach. The inclusion of trade negotiators in national delegations, the nature of food safety issues with attentive publics, and linkages to WTO law all have heightened the prominence of distributive concerns, as well as concerns about state autonomy and influence. This development may appear predictable in retrospect, though statements by governments and individual Uruguay Round negotiators suggest they did not anticipate these consequences of delegating standard-setting to Codex. International standardization often entails distributional conflicts even while it promises overall net gains, and the material stakes are generally high when dealing with standards that control market access (Büthe and Mattli 2011).[4]

Participation and Exclusion in Codex Rule-Making

Many conflicts of interest in Codex appear to be first and foremost conflicts between member states, in particular the United States – whose representatives have sought to promote the US approach to biotechnology regulation as a response to proven risks – and the EU, whose representatives have sought to secure recognition for the precautionary principle as a legitimate basis for its regulatory approach (Ansell and Vogel 2006; Pollack and Shaffer 2009: 136ff.; Vogel 2011). Closer examination, however, reveals two other prominent lines of contention. First, in developed countries, the key issue is the ability of *consumers* to have a voice in Codex standard-setting. Second, serious questions have been raised about the effectiveness of developing country participation.

Consumer representation

Individual consumers rarely think about international food standards. However, Codex standards for food safety, additives, pesticides and labelling tend to influence foods virtually everywhere, due to Codex's inclusion in the SPS-Agreement (McCrea 2000: 149). Consumer groups have therefore voiced concerns about industry domination of

[4] For a general discussion of the distributive implications of institutions, see Knight (1992).

the nominally intergovernmental Codex (Rosman 1993; Braithwaite and Drahos 2000: 401; Victor 2004; Post 2005). Industry representatives vastly outnumber consumer or general public interest non-governmental organization (NGO) representatives, both in plenary sessions and in committee meetings (Avery, Drake et al. 1993; Petts 2003). Consumer advocates argue that the proceedings favour trade interests at the cost of consumer concerns such as safety.

Codex claims to have recognized the importance of increasing consumer representation and allows international NGOs (INGOs) to participate as observers at Codex Committee and Commission meetings. NGOs can also participate as members of national delegations and through the political process by which domestic positions on standards are established. However, a 1997 study found that only 11 of the 111 INGOs recognized by Codex were not industry-funded, and a Consumers International survey of its member organizations indicated that only 46 per cent of them are regularly consulted by their domestic governments concerning food safety standards and related matters (McCrea 2000).

Developing countries and Codex

Developing countries have increasingly expressed concern that their membership – formally at no cost – amounts only to legitimation of global rule-making by advanced industrialized countries. Codex has grown from originally 30 to 183 members,[5] representing more than 98 per cent of the world population. However, examination of attendance shows that developing country members continue to be under-represented during the main sessions of the Commission and even more so in the committees that develop the standards. Moreover, since the size of national delegations is largely at the discretion of each government, attendees from Western Europe and North America often outnumber the delegates from the rest of the world combined.

Developing countries also often lack the institutions, expertise and resources to conduct risk assessments, to influence the standard-setting process, and to implement international standards in order to benefit from international harmonization (Marovatsanga 2000; Masson-Matthee 2007). This has left developing countries increasingly frustrated with their relative marginalization in Codex, as well as the costliness of the obligations incurred by committing to Codex standardization (Dubey 1996; Wilson and Abiola 2003; Singh 2006; Axelrod 2008).

[5] 182 member states and the EU.

Since the lack of financial resources necessary to participate in Codex is arguably the primary impediment, FAO and WHO established in 2003 the Codex Trust Fund for the Participation of Developing Countries and Countries in Transition. The fund has started to support developing country participation, though the contributions to the trust fund so far have fallen far short of the $40 million estimated as needed to fund at least minimal regular participation by the 116 countries considered eligible (Codex 2009).

Future of Codex

The legal status of Codex standards remains ambiguous. They are international standards for purposes of international trade, even when a standard is not adopted by consensus (as the Appellate Body clarified in the *Sardines* case), which imbues elements of Codex standards with de facto binding force (Masson-Matthee 2007). Yet, in *Beef Hormones*, the Appellate Body interpreted the SPS-Agreement's stipulation that national regulations shall be 'based on' as meaning less than 'conform to'. The extent to which deviations from international standards are permitted remains unresolved (Epps 2008: 122). The decision of the Appellate Body in this case further muddied the waters by adopting a broad notion of risk assessment, allowing for the necessary domestic political trade-offs within the risk regulation process.

A consensual approach may continue to play a prominent role in the Codex Alimentarius Commission. However, the relative influence of different stakeholders, public transparency, and democratic legitimacy will surely attract increasing scrutiny if international trade in food products continues to grow.

References

Ansell, C., and D. Vogel, eds. (2006). *What's the Beef? The Contested Governance of European Food Safety*. Cambridge, MA: MIT Press.

Avery, N., M. Drake et al. (1993). *Cracking the Codex: An Analysis of Who Sets World Food Standards*. London: National Food Alliance.

Axelrod, M. (2008). 'Saving Institutional Benefits: Path Dependence in International Law'. Ph.D. dissertation, Political Science Department, Duke University.

Bhagwati, J. (1988). *Protectionism*. Cambridge, MA: MIT Press.

Braithwaite, J., and P. Drahos (2000). *Global Business Regulation*. New York: Cambridge University Press.

Büthe, T. (2008). 'The Globalization of Health and Safety Standards: Delegation of Regulatory Authority in the SPS-Agreement of 1994 Agreement Establishing the World Trade Organization'. *Law and Contemporary Problems* 71(1: Winter): 219–55.

Büthe, T. (2009). 'The Politics of Food Safety in the Age of Global Trade: The Codex Alimentarius Commission in the SPS Agreement of the WTO'. *Import Safety: Regulatory Governance in the Global Economy*, ed. C. Coglianese, A. Finkel et al. Philadelphia: University of Pennsylvania Press.

Büthe, T., and W. Mattli (2011). *New Global Rulers: The Privatization of Regulation in the World Economy*. Princeton: Princeton University Press.

Codex Alimentarius (2008). 'Concept of Consensus and its Application within Codex'. FAO/WHO Document CL2008/34-GP (November 2008).

Codex Alimentarius (2009). 'FAO/WHO Project and Fund for Participation in Codex: Grouping of Eligible Countries'. Available at www.who.int/foodsafety/codex/trustfund/en/ (accessed 15 June 2010).

Codex Alimentarius (2010). *Procedural Manual*, 19th edn. Rome: FAO/WHO.

Drezner, D. W. (2007). *All Politics is Global: Explaining International Regulatory Regimes*. Princeton: Princeton University Press.

Dubey, M. (1996). *An Unequal Treaty: World Trading Order after GATT*. New Delhi: New Age International.

Epps, T. (2008). *International Trade and Health Protection*. Northhampton, MA: Edward Elgar Publishing.

Kay, D. A (1976). *The International Regulation of Pesticide Residues in Food*. St Paul: West Publishing.

Kerr, W., and J. Hobbs (2005). 'Consumers, Cows and Carousels: Why the Dispute over Beef Hormones is Far More Important than its Commercial Value'. *The WTO and the Regulation of International Trade*, ed. N. Perdikis and R. Read. Northhampton, MA: Edward Elgar.

Knight, J. (1992). *Institutions and Social Conflict*. New York: Cambridge University Press.

Leive, D. M (1976). *International Regulatory Regimes: Case Studies in Health, Meteorology, and Food*. 2 vols. Lexington, MA: Lexington Books.

Marovatsanga, L. (2000). 'The Need for Developing Countries to Improve National Infrastructure to Contribute to International Standards'. *International Standards for Food Safety*, ed. N. Rees and D. Watson. Gaithersburg, MD: Aspen.

Masson-Matthee, M. (2007). *The Codex Alimentarius and Its Standards*. The Hague: TMC Asher.

McCrea, D. (2000). 'A View from Consumers'. *International Standards for Food Safety*, ed. N. Rees and D. Watson. Gaithersburg, MD: Aspen.

Petts, J. (2003). *Feeding the Future: Policy Options for Local Foods*. London: Sustain.

Poli, S. (2004). 'The European Community and the Adoption of the International Food Standards within the Codex Alimentarius Commission'. *European Law Journal* 10 (5: September): 613–30.

Pollack, M., and G. Shaffer (2009). *When Cooperation Fails: The International Law and Politics of Genetically Modified Foods*. New York: Oxford University Press.

Post, D. (2005). 'Standards and Regulatory Capitalism: The Diffusion of Food Safety Standards in Developing Countries'. *The Annals of the American Academy of Political and Social Science* 598(1): 168–183.

Randall, A. (2000). 'The Work of the Codex Alimentarius Commission'. Paper presented at the OECD Conference on the Scientific and Health Aspects of GM Food. Edinburgh, Scotland. Available at www.oecd.org/subject/biotech/ed_prog_sum.htm.

Randell, A. (1995). 'Codex Alimentarius: How It All Began'. *Journal of Food, Nutrition and Agriculture* 13/14: 35–40.

Roberts, D., D. Orden et al. (2004). 'Sanitary and Phytosanitary Barriers to Agricultural Trade: Progress, Prospects, and Implications for Developing Countries'. *Agriculture and the New Trade Agenda*, ed. M. Ingco and L. A. Winters. Cambridge: Cambridge University Press.

Rosman, L. (1993). 'Public Participation in International Pesticide Regulation: When the Codex Commission Decides, Who Will Listen?' *Virginia Environmental Law Journal* 12(2: Winter): 329–65.

Singh, J. P. (2006). 'The Evolution of National Interest'. *Negotiating Trade: Developing Countries in the WTO and NAFTA*, ed. J. S. Odell. New York: Cambridge University Press.

Trebilcock, M., and R, Howse (2005). *The Regulation of International Trade*, 3rd edn. New York: Routledge.

Veggeland, F., and S. O. Borgen (2005). 'Negotiating International Food Standards: The World Trade Organization's Impact on the Codex Alimentarius Commission'. *Governance* 18 (4: October): 675–708.

Victor, D. (1997). 'The Operation and Effectiveness of the Codex Alimentarius Commission', in 'Effective Multilateral Regulation of Industrial Activity: Institutions for Policing and Adjusting Binding and Nonbinding Legal Commitments'. Ph.D. dissertation, Political Science Department, MIT, 175–215.

Victor, D. (2000). 'The Sanitary and Phytosanitary Agreement of the World Trade Organization: An Assessment After Five Years'. *NYU Journal of International Law and Politics* 32(4: Summer): 865–937.

Victor, D. (2004). 'WTO Efforts to Manage Differences in National Sanitary and Phytosanitary Policies'. In *Dynamics of Regulatory Change: How Globalization Affects National Regulatory Policies*, ed. D. Vogel and R. Kagan. Berkeley and Los Angeles: University of California Press.

Vogel, D. (1995). *Trading Up: Consumer and Environmental Regulation in a Global Economy*. Cambridge, MA: Harvard University Press.

Vogel, D. (2011). *The Politics of Precaution*. Princeton: Princeton University Press.

Wilson, J., and V. Abiola, eds. (2003). *Standards and Global Trade*. Washington, DC: World Bank.

28

The Equator Principles
Christopher Wright

Introduction

Large development projects can have a lasting, transformative impact on the environment and local communities. Open-pit mines may undermine the resource base of small-scale miners and contaminate ground water. Hydropower projects often fundamentally change river ways and force riverside communities to resettle elsewhere. And oil and gas pipelines in tropical forests may irreversibly harm biodiversity and the livelihoods of forest dwellers. In June 2003, ten commercial banks launched the Equator Principles, a set of operational principles and standards for managing the environmental and social impacts of loans to large development projects (Equator Principles 2003). The emergence of the voluntary framework was the culmination of a series of sustained public advocacy campaigns against a number of high-profile commercial banks in North America and Europe – including ABN AMRO (now Royal Bank of Scotland), Barclays Bank, Citigroup, and WestLB – for their involvement in development projects that generated significant adverse environmental and social impacts (Wright and Rwabizambuga 2006; Richardson 2008: 411–20; van Putten 2008: 178–216).

While only applicable to project financing – a specialized form of finance used to fund large development projects – the Equator Principles have nevertheless become the most influential voluntary initiative for corporate responsibility in the international banking sector. The emergence and evolution of the Equator Principles exemplify how civil society contestation of transnational investment flows can induce new forms of private cooperation that both enable and limit external accountability (for general discussions, see Newell 2001; Koenig-Archibugi 2004; Vogel 2008). By adopting the Equator Principles, commercial banks voluntarily committed to make the disbursement of project loans conditional on compliance with a set of environmental and social standards and procedures. Specifically, borrowers of project loans (known as project sponsors) would be required to identify, assess, and disclose the potential environmental and social impacts of projects, consult local communities, demonstrate compliance with a set of performance standards developed by the

World Bank Group's International Finance Corporation (IFC), and provide a grievance mechanism for project-affected communities. Since its inception, seventy-one commercial banks, export credit agencies and national development banks have become Equator Principles Financial Institutions (EPFIs) by virtue of publicly declaring a commitment to apply the Equator Principles to their project finance activities worldwide.[1]

Institutional Characteristics and Consequences

The Equator Principles have several notable features. First, they have embedded the lending policies of commercial banks (and other types of EPFIs as well) into a broader environmental and social policy framework that emerged and continues to evolve within the World Bank Group. The ten commercial banks that spearheaded the initiative chose to base the framework on the *Safeguard Policies*, a collection of well-recognized environmental and social policies and procedures routinely used by the World Bank and its private sector financing arm, the IFC (Wright 2009). The *Safeguard Policies* were originally developed by the World Bank and approved by its shareholder governments to ensure that its public sector loans would not harm the environment and local communities. In 1998, the IFC formally committed to requiring its private sector borrowers to comply with them, and by way of adopting the Equator Principles, a host of commercial and public financial institutions have done the same. In February 2006, the IFC replaced the *Safeguard Policies* with a new set of *Policy and Performance Standards on Social and Environmental Sustainability*, a policy framework it argued was better tailored to the operational context of private sector projects (IFC 2006).[2] Three months later, the EPFIs released a revised version of the Equator Principles (known as Equator Principles II) based on the new *Performance Standards*, thereby reconfirming their continued interests in harmonizing their own environmental and social lending standards with those of the IFC. As a result, a set of standards developed by an international organization to fulfil a public mandate defined by

---

[1] For a complete list of EPFIs, see www.equator-principles.com.
[2] As of March 2010, the Performance Standards are: Social and Environmental Assessment (PS1), Labour and Working Conditions (PS2), Pollution Prevention and Abatement (PS3), Community Health, Safety and Security (PS4), Land Acquisition and Involuntary Resettlement (PS5), Biodiversity Conservation and Sustainable Natural Resource Management (PS6), Indigenous Peoples (PS7) and Cultural Heritage (PS8).

its government shareholders was voluntarily adopted by a large group of commercial banks to maximize value for their commercial shareholders.

Second, unlike many other voluntary initiatives, the Equator Principles exhibit high levels of technical specificity and operational focus. EPFIs commit to classify all project proposals according to the magnitude of potential social and environmental impacts and risks – 'A', 'B' or 'C' – and according to the income level of the country in which the particular project is to be based. In turn, all projects likely to generate more than 'minimal' environmental and social impacts (e.g. all projects categorized as either 'A' or 'B') require an Action Plan that takes consultations with local communities into account and addresses risk mitigation, monitoring, and management of risk and schedules. The Action Plan for all category 'A' projects, and 'as appropriate' for all category 'B' projects, is subject to review by an independent expert not directly associated with the project sponsor. In addition, project sponsors need to have in place a Social and Environmental Management System that addresses the ongoing management of these impacts, risks, and corrective actions required. As part of this management system, they are required to establish a grievance mechanism, 'scaled to the risks and adverse impacts of the project', that allows them 'to receive and facilitate resolution of concerns and grievances about the project's social and environmental performance raised by individuals or groups from among project-affected communities' (Equator Principles 2006: 4).

Third, the Equator Principles have created a new transnational policy space for civil society groups to contest commercial project financing and engage in direct consultations with project finance executives at major commercial banks (van Putten 2008). In October 2003, a coalition of predominantly North American and European nongovernmental organizations (NGOs) formed Banktrack, a small secretariat which coordinates and disseminates public communications about campaigns against particular commercial banks and projects. It has become customary for Banktrack to release reports on the annual anniversaries of the Equator Principles that critically assess the effectiveness of implementation. For example, a survey in 2007 concluded that only twelve out of forty-five commercial banks with large project finance portfolios in 2006 had developed statements or guidelines for human rights practices or included general human rights statements in their principles of ethical business conduct (Banktrack 2007: 83). Members of the Banktrack network have also regularly been invited by EPFIs to partake in meetings with project finance executives to discuss the implementation and revision of the Equator Principles. Therefore, by inspiring the creation of Banktrack and facilitating regular NGO–EPFI consultations, the Equator Principles have given rise to a new transnational policy realm in which environmental and human rights NGOs have become vociferous and influential participants.

And fourth, the Equator Principles have provided a foundation for inter-bank policy coordination, innovation and diffusion. In April 2004, eleven commercial banks sent an open letter to World Bank President James Wolfensohn opposing the recommendations of the Extractive Industries Review that the World Bank phase out financing for coal and oil projects, and proposing that it adopt the principle of free, prior and informed consent (FPIC) in its relations with project-affected communities (EIR 2003; EPFI 2004a). Later that year, a group of sixteen commercial banks and the Danish export-credit agency sent an open letter to IFC calling for an extension to its ongoing public consultation period, arguing it was important that the revised framework be 'appropriate for use by private-sector financial institutions as well as for IFC as a development institution' (EPFI 2004b). In 2006, the release of Equator Principles II coincided with the establishment of a formal Equator Principles management structure led by a Steering Committee, and comprising numerous thematic and regional working groups of EPFIs mandated to promote adoption in non-OECD countries, engage with stakeholders, and discuss issues related to implementation.

Limits to Effective Implementation

Apart from these notable institutional characteristics and consequences, the actual effectiveness of the Equator Principles on the environmental and social impacts of projects is more disputed (Amalric 2005; Richardson 2008; van Putten 2008). Divergent assessments of effectiveness are more grounded in conflicting expectations about outcomes than in methodological differences. Banktrack considers the selection of projects as an important metric. While several EPFIs report that they have declined projects that are not in compliance with the Equator Principles, Banktrack frequently criticizes them for not disclosing which ones. Moreover, it laments the fact that adopting the Equator Principles has not prevented EPFIs from continuing to finance types of projects known to cause significant and irreversible damages to the environment and local communities, such as coal-fired power plants, palm oil plantations and open-pit mines (Missbach 2004; Banktrack 2007). Their disappointment lies in the fact that EPFIs principally view the Equator Principles as a process-oriented engagement tool that can reduce the risk of project disruptions and delays caused by a failure by the project sponsor to obtain environmental permits from regulatory agencies or a 'social license to operate' from local communities. The Equator Principles have prompted many EPFIs to invest in internal staff training programmes, develop new environmental and social lending policies, and embed the framework into internal credit risk processes (FBD 2005; Watchman, Delfino et al. 2006). Moreover, they frequently note in public communications that 80 per cent of project debt in developing countries is 'Equator compliant', by virtue of having been provided by loan syndicates including at least one EPFI (Caceres and Ellis 2006; EPFI 2008). An example of these diverging expectations is the Baku–Tblisi–Cayhan pipeline, dubbed the first 'test case' of the Equator Principles. While Banktrack heavily criticized the project for breaching the Equator Principles, banks disagreed, and claimed it was a milestone project that broke new ground in promoting sustainable development (ABN AMRO 2003; IFC 2003).

Apart from divergent expectations about outcomes, the effectiveness of self-regulation in this policy domain is also limited by institutional obstacles and conflicts of interest. Often, debt-financing is not organized until the planning of a project is at an advanced stage, leaving EPFIs with limited opportunities to push through environmentally and socially beneficial amendments to project design (Watchman, Delfino et al. 2006; Richardson 2008). EPFIs may also deem the political cost of effectively enforcing the Equator Principles to be too excessive, notably in cases where they are required to confront both project sponsors and host country governments on a sensitive political issue, such as indigenous peoples' rights. Assessing and monitoring compliance with the Equator Principles also requires technical knowledge and expertise that many EPFIs may not have. Outsourcing these responsibilities adds an administrative cost to project loans that EPFIs in an increasingly competitive marketplace may be reluctant to take on or pass on to project sponsors. Moreover, as EPFIs often have strong business relationships with project sponsors and depend on the continuation of individual projects to get their loans repaid, they are unlikely to address breaches of compliance solely with the public interest in mind. In addition, any corrective actions would necessarily require the consent of all syndicate members, and would therefore likely have to be justified within the commercial goals of the project.

Conclusion

The effectiveness of many new forms of voluntary business regulation often hinges on the sensitivity of transnational corporations to reputational risks (Vogel 2008). In the case of the Equator Principles, exposure to reputational risks varies greatly across EPFIs, and is therefore unlikely to induce consistent and uniform levels of compliance. While it is the most effectively organized network for staging civil society campaigns against projects, Banktrack is severely under-resourced to effectively monitor compliance with the Equator Principles. In any case, it is an advocacy coalition that seeks to maximize the impact of its scarce financial resources on particular environmental and social causes, with a mandate that is not particularly well suited to performing an independent oversight function on its own. Since neither the EPFI nor the project sponsor is required by the Equator Principles to publicly disclose loan agreements or compliance reports, third-party monitoring is in any case severely hampered by a lack of transparency. While the framework obliges each EPFI to 'report publicly at least annually about its Equator Principles implementation processes and experience, taking into account appropriate confidentiality considerations' (Principle 10), reporting to date has generally not enabled any kind of external accountability of specific project-level decisions that affect the environment and local communities. Therefore, while the Equator Principles have provided new political opportunities for civil society groups and facilitated a remarkable diffusion of environmental and social lending commitments across both commercial and national financial institutions, they have not yet produced an independent and credible mechanism for project-affected communities to hold EPFIs externally accountable for their lending decisions.

References

ABN AMRO (2003). 'ABN AMRO's Explanation of its Participation in the BTC Pipeline Project'. ABN AMRO press release, 10 December 2003.

Amalric, F. (2005). 'The Equator Principles – A Step Towards Sustainability?' Center for Corporate Responsibility and Sustainability, Working Paper Series No. 01/05, University of Zurich, January.

Banktrack (2007). *Mind the Gap – Benchmarking Credit Policies of International Banks*. Utrecht: Banktrack.

Caceres, V., and S. Ellis (2006), 'IJ First Half Review: Equator Principles Financing'. *Infrastructure Journal* 17 August.

EIR (2003). *Striking a Better Balance: The Final Report of the Extractive Industries Review*. Washington, DC: World Bank.

EPFI (2004a). 'Joint Letter to World Bank President James Wolfensohn', signed by ABN AMRO Bank NV, Citigroup, Credit Lyonnais/Calyon, Credit Suisse, Dexia, HVB Group, ING group NV, KBC Bank NV, MCC SpA, Mizuho Corporate Bank Ltd, and Westpac Banking Corporation. Available at www.equator-principles.com.

EPFI (2004b). 'Financial Institutions Call for Extension of Safeguard Review', joint letter signed by ABN AMRO Bank NV; Banco Itau SA; Bank of America, NA; Barclays plc; BBVA, SA; Calyon Corporate and Investment Bank; Citigroup Inc.; Credit Suisse First Boston; Dexia Group; Eksport Kredit Fonden; HSBC Group; HVB Group; KBC Bank NV; Mizuho Corporate Bank, Ltd; The Royal Bank of Scotland plc; Standard Chartered Bank' and WestLB AG. 13 December 2004. Available at www.equator-principles.com.

EPFI (2008). 'Equator Principles Celebrate Five Years of Positive Environmental Impact and Improved Business Practices'. The Equator Principles Financial Institutions (EPFIs), press release, 8 May 2008.

Equator Principles (2003). 'Equator Principles I', released 4 June 2003. Available at www.equator-principles.com.

Equator Principles (2006). 'Equator Principles II', released 6 July 2006. Available at www.equator-principles.com.

FBD (2005). 'Banking on Responsibility, Part One of Freshfields Bruckhaus Deringer Equator Principles Survey 2005: The Banks'. Freshfields Bruckhaus Deringer, July 2005.

IFC (2003). 'IFC Board Approves Investments in Caspian Oil and Pipeline Projects Expected High Development Impact with Environmental, Social, and Transparency Safeguards'. IFC press release, 4 November.

IFC (2006). *Policy and Performance Standards on Social and Environmental Sustainability*. Washington, DC: IFC.

Koenig-Archibugi, M. (2004), 'Transnational Corporations and Global Accountability'. *Government and Opposition* 39(2–3): 234–59.

Missbach, A. (2004). 'The Equator Principles: Drawing The Line for Socially Responsible Banks? An Interim Review from an NGO Perspective'. *Development* 47(3): 78–84.

Newell, P. (2001). 'Managing Multinationals: The Governance of Investment for the Environment'. *Journal of International Development* 13(7): 907–91.

Richardson, B. (2008). *Socially Responsible Investment Law – Regulating the Unseen Polluter*. New York: Oxford University Press.

van Putten, M. (2008). *Policing the Banks: Accountability Mechanisms for the Financial Sector*. Montreal: McGill/Queens University Press.

Vogel, D. (2008). 'Private Global Business Regulation'. *American Review of Political Science* 11: 261–82.

Watchman, P., A. Delfino et al. (2006). 'EP2: The Revised Principles: Why Hard-nosed Bankers are Embracing Soft Law Principles'. Report produced by Lebouf, Lamb, Greene and McRae LLP.

Wright, C. (2009), 'Setting Standards for Responsible Banking: Examining the Role of the International Finance Corporation in the Emergence of the Equator Principles'. *International Organizations and Global Environmental Governance*, ed. F. Biermann, B. Siebenhüner et al. London: Routledge.

Wright, C., and A. Rwabizambuga (2006) 'Institutional Pressures, Corporate Reputation and Voluntary Codes of Conduct: An Examination of the Equator Principles'. *Business and Society Review* 111(1): 89–117.

29

Extractive Industries Transparency Initiative
Helmut Weidner

The Extractive Industry Transparency Initiative (EITI) aims to increase the transparency of government revenues generated from the oil, gas and mining industry, and to strengthen accountability in the extractive industry sector through verification and publication of company payments to governments. EITI was established in September 2002 as a voluntary system initiated by a group of nongovernmental organizations (NGOs) and strongly supported by the British government. It represents an institutional innovation in the field of transnational collaboration toward a (voluntary) minimum standard for revenue transparency. Currently it comprises thirty EITI-implementing countries, most of them so-called 'candidate countries' that are expected to finish the validation process in 2010 in order to be deemed a 'compliant country'. However, only two countries have achieved this status so far, while other countries remain more or less inactive and almost all of them have requested deadline extensions.

History

EITI has its origins in the global movement to combat the 'resource curse', the idea that many developing countries rich in mineral and energy resources suffer from low living standards, corruption and undemocratic political structures because income from resource exports creates and sustains bad governance (Humphreys, Sachs et al. 2007). In response, Global Witness and other London-based civil society groups in June 2002 launched the Publish What You Pay campaign (PWYP) to promote transparency in the extractive industry sector, and so shine light on a major source of corruption and mismanagement among officials. With the help of prominent supporters (including the financier George Soros; Tony Blair, then British Prime

Minister; and Lord Brown, CEO of British Petrol) the PWYP campaign soon became a powerful movement which succeeded in creating the EITI shortly after it was announced at the World Summit on Sustainable Development in Johannesburg 2002.

Several factors favoured the rapid rise of the EITI and broad acceptance among developing countries. A worldwide social movement had placed mineral and oil companies under strong pressure, making it increasingly difficult for them to obtain a 'social licence' to operate. The movement also succeeded in politicizing the relevant international organizations (such as the World Bank Group and the International Monetary Fund (IMF)), which, due to their strong involvement in the extractive sector, were often seen as ignoring the social, ecological and also political consequences of their actions (see Babai 2001; Evans, Goodman et al. 2002). The World Bank reacted by launching the Extractive Industry Review, which resulted in a strong call for phasing out the Bank's support of the oil and coal mining industry (see Beattie 2003). At the same time, public criticism of British investments in socially and ecologically dubious projects increased, finding resonance within a British government with an enlightened self-interest in long-term energy security (cf. Oranje and Parham 2009: 6, 57ff.; Gillies 2010: 112ff., 119).

The diffusion of EITI was also facilitated by the rapid adoption by many companies and governments of transparency as an international norm. Concessions to NGO demands for transparency seemed to be an appropriate means to mitigate worldwide pressure on the extractive industry and its proponents. There also was good reason to assume that governments and companies adhering to the principles of transparency would find it easier to gain foreign direct investment or financial support from international organizations and would be able to borrow money at lower cost. Indeed, several donor institutions (e.g. the International Finance Corporation) began to require disclosure of payments, and rating agencies started to honour EITI endorsement (cf. Ölcer 2009: 15, 35; Gillies 2010: 108). EITI also received strong support from investment and pension management funds, including more than eighty signatories to the 'Investors Statement on Transparency in the Extractive Sector', which together represent some $18 trillion in funds (Oranje and Parham 2009).

Nigeria, ranked as one of the most corrupt countries, was the first to subscribe to EITI. It was followed by thirty-one countries – with one exception (Norway) all developing countries. In addition to implementing countries, EITI's participants include seventeen 'supporting' countries (which have formally endorsed EITI), forty-six of the world's largest extractive companies, and hundreds of civil society organizations (CSOs). All major Western oil companies are EITI supporters.

Furthermore, a broad variety of groups, organizations, companies and governments support the initiative by providing political, financial and technical support – among them the World Bank, IMF, the G-8 governments, the European Union (EU), International Council on Mining and Metals (ICMM) and over eighty global investment institutions.

Amongst developed countries, the UK government and its Department for International Development have championed and supported the EITI from the beginning. Among international organizations, the World Bank is the most important supporter. In 2005, for instance, the World Bank became administrator of the EITI Multi-Donor Trust Fund (MDTF) with a total budget of about $27 million for fiscal year 2010 – the UK being the founding and also the largest contributor. Since 2009 the MDTF has provided forty-seven countries with grants to implement EITI principles.

Additionally, in April 2008 the World Bank introduced a new approach based on amended EITI principles aimed at broadening the focus of EITI's revenue transparency agenda to include the entire natural resources value chain, from awarding concessions to the public spending of revenues. According to the World Bank, this initiative – ambitiously named EITI++ (EITI plus plus) – will complement EITI with additional World Bank funds and not replace it (World Bank 2010a). Since July 2005 the World Bank has provided technical assistance for CSOs working on EITI through its own Development Grant Facility. In the context of this three-year seed funding programme (2005–8) about $0.5 million was allocated per year (see World Bank 2010b) .

Within a short time the initiative has become the most influential and institutionalized transnational multistakeholder movement in the extractive industry sector. EITI receives funds from about forty institutions, totalling about $3 million per year for staff salaries and operational costs. It also receives 'a considerable number of EITI off-budget and in-kind support' (EITI 2010a).

How EITI Works

EITI is overseen by an International Board consisting of representatives from all stakeholder groups and administered by the Oslo-based International Secretariat. The highest governing body is the full Members' Meeting, held every two years.

EITI's basic approach is (theoretically, but not in reality) straightforward. Implementing countries have to ensure that all relevant companies – foreign and domestic – declare to the government their payments for extracting natural resources. This is usually done through persuasion and voluntary agreements, but in a few cases also via legal regulations. These figures are then compared against the host government's own declaration of revenues received. After the data have been checked and verified by independent bodies they must be made public. The final decision to do so lies with the EITI International Board.

The procedure involves various steps and actor groups. First, countries with significant extractive industries must take four basic actions to become 'candidates': make a public commitment to implementation, make a commitment to work with stakeholders, appoint a senior government official to work with stakeholders, and release a work plan (for principles, criteria and procedures, see EITI 2010b). After a period of two years at most (extension possible on special grounds), candidates have to start a validation process in order to achieve the status of 'EITI compliant'.

Achieving this goal has proven to be a rather complex and arduous process. Key requirements are the establishment of a (true) multi-stakeholder working group, the approval of an independent EITI administrator, and the disclosure and cross-checking of companies' payments and governments' revenues. After an (approved) EITI report has been made publicly available, a validation process may follow, in which an independent auditor assesses the programme based on criteria in the EITI Rules Book. The validator is selected by the multi-stakeholder group from a roster of, so far, thirteen companies accredited with EITI. After the multistakeholder group has agreed to both the draft and final reports submitted by the validator, it is the decision of the International Board to label a candidate country as EITI compliant or not. If both the validator and the International Board conclude that no 'meaningful progress' has been made, the country will be de-listed from EITI. This requirement is meant to encourage the participating countries not to protract the process, and to hinder countries from adorning themselves with the EITI label without seriously striving to meet its requirements. The deadlines were introduced in 2008, due largely to pressure from NGOs, especially the PWYP coalition.

The Struggle for Compliance

The IMF has defined more than fifty developing countries as 'resource rich', a group that is home to two-thirds of the world's poor. Currently, thirty countries are either EITI candidates or EITI compliant: Afghanistan, Albania, Azerbaijan, Burkina Faso, Cameroon, Central

African Republic, Chad, Democratic Republic of the Congo, Republic of Congo, Côte d'Ivoire, Gabon, Ghana, Iraq, Kazakhstan, Kyrgyzstan, Liberia, Madagascar, Mali, Mauritania, Mongolia, Mozambique, Niger, Nigeria, Norway, Peru, Sierra Leone, Tanzania, Timor-Leste, Yemen and Zambia (status February 2010). Twenty-two countries of this group became Candidates in 2008 and were required to complete validation by 9 March 2010. In 2010, seventeen countries requested an extension of their deadlines for completing validation, and for sixteen of these extensions were granted. Guinea has suspended its candidate status. Only two countries (Azerbaijan and Liberia) were recognized as compliant in 2009.

Obtaining compliance status does not necessarily mean that all requirements have been fulfilled. It is rather seen as the proper beginning of the implementation process on the road to full revenue transparency and accountability. Although almost all candidates failed to meet the deadlines, three quite problematic countries have just recently (February and April 2010) been accepted as candidates and were given the standard deadline for completing their validation processes: namely Afghanistan, Iraq and Chad. However, the decision on Ethiopia's application was deferred on grounds of the government's restrictive measures against civil society groups (see EITI 2010c).

The Impact of EITI

Since its inception almost eight years ago, EITI has become a broadly institutionalized movement to promote revenue transparency for sustainable development in resource-rich developing countries. EITI has achieved a rather impressive *output* in terms of governance structures, procedural rules, communication networks and the like. However, there is only scarce or vague information about its goal-related performance, that is, the *impact* of its activities on addressees (corporations, governments) and resulting *outcomes*, e.g. reduced corruption, improved governance, and strengthened sustainability of the whole system. Of course, outputs must come before outcomes can be measured. Since EITI is a fairly young initiative, no systematic and valid judgement on goal performance should be expected this early. However, outcome-oriented evaluations of EITI reveal some structural deficits aside from the shortcomings discussed in the (sparse) critical literature on EITI (Ocheje 2006; Ali and O'Faircheallaigh 2007; Hilson and Maconachie 2009; Ölcer 2009; Oranje and Parham 2009; Gillies 2010). The various studies call for, inter alia, stronger involvement at the sub-national level in reporting and participation; going beyond the basic criteria of EITI to address earlier and later stages of the extractive value chain; greater consistency in the quality of data provided by companies and governments, and more specificity regarding company payments; and developing an appropriate public audience for EITI reports.

NGOs often criticize the lack of a mandatory requirement for the disclosure of revenue payments. Global Witness, in one of its reports, asked, 'Disclosure of key financial data is required by law in every developed country, so why should it be different in Angola and other developing economies?' (Global Witness 2004: 7). NGOs also – in this case strongly supported by major international financial institutions – call for disclosure of contracts related to extractive industries.

For an analysis of possible structural deficits of the EITI, it is helpful to recapitulate the basic presumed political effects underlying the system. Disclosing payments and revenue from extractive industries is assumed to lead to less corruption and better governance, with positive effects for all groups of society. It is further assumed that a voluntary multistakeholder process based on negotiation, cooperation and soft law will suffice to reach such disclosure. The success of this approach deeply depends on the observance of rules mutually agreed upon not only by the various stakeholders but especially by those entrusted with the task of overseeing the implementation and verification of proper norm interpretation. In the case of EITI this means the EITI Secretariat and the Chair of the Board. If other stakeholders' trust in their commitment to the norms erodes, the entire legitimacy of the process may crumble, as has been observed in similar processes in other areas (Renn, Webler et al. 1995). Of course it is a general feature of voluntary multistakeholder cooperation that compromises have to be made, and a norm agreed upon in principle does not always provide a clear direction on how to proceed. However, one cannot escape the impression that the EITI management has stretched the rules in order to avoid sanctions (e.g. by 'delisting' them) against a large group of member countries that obviously do not meet the procedural requirements of the process. This would explain the fact that only two countries have been able to become EITI compliant thus far, while the majority of candidates have asked for extensions. The Secretariat and the Chair have stressed the obstacles these countries face in seeking to implement the measures, tacitly assuming that, in principle, these countries act in good faith. Leading EITI representatives have not yet publicly raised serious doubts concerning the true commitment of failing countries, as some NGOs have done (e.g. Human Rights Watch 2010). Instead of providing a critical, neutral analysis of the mismatches between rhetorical commitments and concrete actions, rather vague statements are made about a 'learning process for all' and that 'validation has taken longer than anticipated' (see EITI 2010c). A director of Human Rights Watch, and member of the EITI International Board, sees the situation as much more dramatic. 'EITI is at a crucial juncture', he warns, cautioning that it would be counterproductive to lower the standards for governments that actually are not interested in public scrutiny (Human Rights Watch 2010).

However, at its recent meeting in Berlin (15–16 April 2010) the EITI Board allowed sixteen of eighteen countries that missed the two-year deadline for validation to extend their candidacies. Only the two small West African countries, Equatorial Guinea and Sao Tome and Principe, were not granted extensions and 'delisted'. Under EITI rules extension can be granted when delays in completing the validation process are clearly due to 'exceptional and unforeseen circumstances outside the country's control'. Whether the Board's decision will be widely accepted by NGOs will depend on the detailed case-by-case rationale yet to be delivered (see the critical statements of Human Rights Watch and Revenue Watch on their websites: www.hrw.org and www.revenuewatch.org, respectively). It is to be expected that a broader discussion of the validation criteria and the rationale of the Board decision will take place when the grace period ends and a full review of the countries' achievements has been conducted.

References

Ali, S., and C. O'Faircheallaigh (2007). 'Extractive Industries, Environmental Policies and CSR'. *Greener Management International* 52: 5–17.

Babai, D. (2001). 'World Bank'. *The Oxford Companion to Politics of the World*, ed. J. Krieger, 2nd edn. Oxford: Oxford University Press.

Beattie, A. (2003). 'World Bank Advised to Pull out of Oil'. *Financial Times* 20 November 2003.

EITI (2010a). 'About Us'. Available at http://eitransparency.org/about/funding (accessed April 2010).

EITI (2010b). 'EITI Fact Sheet, 15 February 2010'. Available at http://eitransparency.org/files/2010-02-15%20EITI%20Fact%20Sheet.pdf (accessed 5 May 2010).

EITI (2010c). 'Minutes of the 11th EITI Board Meeting, Oslo, 9–10 February 2010'. Available at http://eitransparency.org/files/Final%20Minutes%20of%20the%2011th%20Board%20Meeting.pdf (accessed 5 May 2010).

Evans, G., J. Goodman et al., eds. (2002). *Moving Mountains: Communities Confront Mining and Globalisation*. London and New York: Zed Books.

Gillies, A. (2010). 'Reputational Concerns and the Emergence of Oil Sector Transparency as an International Norm'. *International Studies Quarterly* 54: 103–26.

Global Witness (2004). *Time for Transparency: Coming Clean on Oil, Mining and Gas Revenues*. London: Global Witness. Available at www.

globalwitness.org/media_library_detail.php/115/en/time_for_transparency (accessed 5 May 2010).

Hilson, G., and R. Maconachie (2009). 'The Extractive Industries Transparency Initiative: Panacea or White Elephant for Sub-Saharan Africa?' *Mining, Society, and a Sustainable World*, ed. J. P. Richards. Berlin and Heidelberg: Springer.

Human Rights Watch (2010). 'Decisive Moment for Global Transparency Effort', 9 March. Available at www.hrw.org/en/news/2010/03/08/decisive-moment-global-transparency-effort (accessed 5 May 2010).

Humphreys, M., J. Sachs et al., eds. (2007). *Escaping the Resource Curse*. New York: Columbia University Press.

Ocheje, P. D. (2006). 'The Extractive Industries Transparency Initiative (EITI): Voluntary Codes of Conduct, Poverty and Accountability in Africa'. *Journal of Sustainable Development in Africa* 8(3): 222–39.

Ölcer, D. (2009). 'Extracting the Maximum from the EITI'. OECD Development Centre, Working Paper No. 276. Paris: OECD.

Oranje, M. van, and H. Parham (2009). 'Publishing What We Learned. An Assessment of the Publish What You Pay Coalition'. Available at www.publishwhatyoupay.org/sites/pwypdev.gn.apc.org/files/Publishing%20What%20We%20Learned%20-%20EN.pdf (accessed 27 April 2010).

Renn, O., T. Webler et al., eds. (1995). *Fairness and Competence in Citizen Participation: Evaluating Models for Environmental Discourse*. Dordrecht, Boston and London: Kluwer.

World Bank (2010a). 'Fact Sheet: Extractive Industries Transparency Initiative Plus Plus'. Available at http://web.worldbank.org/WBSITE/EXTERNAL/NEWS/0,,contentMDK:21727813~pagePK:64257043~piPK:437376~theSitePK:4607,00.html (accessed 5 May 2010).

World Bank (2010b). 'Direct Grant Facility (DFG) Grants'. Available at http://web.worldbank.org/WBSITE/EXTERNAL/TOPICS/EXTOGMC/EXTEXTINDTRAINI/0,,contentMDK:21760854~menuPK:4974046~pagePK:64168445~piPK:64168309~theSitePK:3634715,00.html (accessed 5 May 2010).

30

Fair Labor Association
Kate MacDonald

The Fair Labor Association (FLA) is a US-based voluntary governance arrangement in which a number of high-profile apparel and sportswear companies work together with universities and nongovernmental organizations (NGOs) to promote compliance with core international labour standards within their supply chains. Since its establishment in the late 1990s, the Association has attracted significant attention and debate. Advocates of the Association regard it as a leader in developing innovative approaches to promoting compliance with international labour standards, pointing to its progress toward building independent auditing and complaints processes, and its efforts in recent years to strengthen the capacity building dimensions of its compliance programme. In contrast, critics question both the Association's accountability and its effectiveness, highlighting what they perceive to be its corporate-dominated governance structure, and its ongoing failure to achieve compliance with international labour standards within the supply chains of many FLA members.

The following discussion reviews the history of the Association's formation and evolution; outlines its composition and governance structure, functions and activities; and presents a brief evaluation of the major strengths and weaknesses of the Association in terms of its effectiveness, accountability and legitimacy.[1]

History

The FLA was established as a direct product of the 'anti-sweatshop' campaigns that emerged in the US during the 1990s. These campaigns were led by a small core of student, labour and human rights organizations, who demanded that major companies supplying US consumer markets take responsibility for labour conditions throughout their supply chains. In response to such ongoing activist pressures, the Clinton administration initiated and coordinated a series of meetings to bring major companies in the apparel and sportswear sectors together with some of the labour and human rights groups involved in the campaigns. According to key participants, government threats of regulation were explicitly deployed as means of pressuring corporate actors to engage with this negotiating process. The government's involvement during this initial period also provided an important source of credibility which helped to mobilize broader support for the initiative during its early stages.

In 1996 these companies and NGOs formed a loose organization known as the Apparel Industry Partnership (AIP). Three years later, the charter document set forth by this Partnership was amended to establish the FLA, although the two union organizations and one of the NGOs which had participated in the AIP refused to join the FLA,

---

[1] The discussion draws on a review of existing analysis of the FLA carried out by both scholars and practitioners, and on field research carried out by the author in Washington DC and Guatemala City, in May and June of 2005.

largely because of insurmountable differences regarding questions of 'living wages' and monitoring mechanisms (Bobrowsky 1999; Hemphill 2002).[2]

Structure and Activities

The FLA's multistakeholder character is reflected in the broad range of actors participating in the Association. There are three main categories of direct participants: *companies* involved in the design and marketing of branded apparel and sportswear products; *universities* who license many of their products; and Northern *NGOs* working on labour and human rights issues. Currently there is no direct government participation in the Association, though at various times the US government has provided funding for specific FLA projects.[3]

The FLA Board, which is responsible for setting the Association's strategic direction and overseeing its activities, is structured so that control is shared between the three core categories of participants (companies, universities and NGOs). The Board comprises six industry representatives, six labour/NGO representatives, six university representatives and a Chair,[4] and, according to the FLA charter, decision-making within the Board takes place via a combination of simple majority and super majority voting. The latter form of voting effectively gives veto power to any individual member category.[5] In

[2] The two union groups that refused to join the FLA were the Union of Needletrades, Industrial and Textile Employees (UNITE) and the Retail Wholesale Department Store Union, AFL-CIO (American Federation of Labor and Congress of Industrial Organizations). The human rights group that also refused to join was the Interfaith Center for Corporate Responsibility.

[3] For example, the US State Department contributed to funding of the FLA's Central America Project to tackle discrimination and violations of freedom of association in Honduras, Guatemala and El Salvador: www.fairlabor.org/what_we_do_special_projects_d3.html. The State Department and the United States Agency for International Development (USAID) also provided start-up grants when the FLA was first formed, as part of their 'strengthening human rights advocacy' programme.

[4] Originally there were only three University representatives, but the FLA Charter was later modified to provide for equal representation for universities. This change became effective from June 2007.

[5] A supermajority vote requires the approval of at least two-thirds of all of the industry Board Members and at least two-thirds of all of the labour/ NGO Board Members and at least two-thirds of the university Board Members, with the Chair having no vote on the matter.

practice, decision-making within the Board on almost all matters in recent years has been conducted on the basis of deliberation and consensus, with formal votes being extremely rare. The bargaining processes underpinning such dynamics achieve some degree of balance as a result of the *strategically* crucial source of bargaining power that each group wields over the others. Specifically, participating companies control the terms of their contracts with suppliers, while many regard the ongoing participation of NGOs to be necessary for the organization's credibility. University participation is required if the organization's financial viability is to be sustained without substantial increases in financial contributions by core participating companies, since each university brings to the Association all the licencees producing under its logo, thus significantly expanding the revenues from membership fees on which the FLA's budget largely depends.

Day-to-day management of FLA activities is undertaken by full-time professional staff, who are responsible for implementing Board decisions, initiating and formulating policy strategies and programmes, and liaising with the Association's members and stakeholders. Importantly, staff also have independent responsibility for a range of surveillance, monitoring and reporting functions. Some functions are delegated externally rather than being performed by the FLA's own employees. The most important of these functions are external performance audits; some service provision and capacity building programmes are also delegated externally.

In accordance with the FLA's overarching goal of promoting compliance with international labour standards, its core governance functions are largely 'regulatory' in both purpose and design. The FLA performs some *rule-making* or *standard-setting* functions: existing international labour standards are codified within the FLA Workplace Code of Conduct, and these are supported by some more informal guidelines relating to Code implementation. *Monitoring* of the Code within individual factories is carried out in part by individual participating companies, and in part via external monitoring visits managed by FLA staff (who plan and schedule these visits, and accredit and hire external monitors). The power to exclude non-compliant companies from the Association is the only significant *enforcement* mechanism at the disposal of the FLA. Beyond this, consequences of noncompliance ultimately depend on how a range of external actors (employees, consumers, shareholders, regulators, business partners, and so on) interpret and respond to the 'de-legitimizing' signal sent by such exclusion.

Promotion of 'remediation' processes in response to documented violations of the Workplace Code is another significant means by which the FLA attempts to achieve compliance with designated standards. Such remediation essentially consists of efforts to promote capacity building among suppliers by combining some degree of technical assistance with support for processes of ideational influence and learning. The FLA has placed increasing emphasis on such capacity building mechanisms in recent years, in response to the persistent failings of audit-based, 'policing' approaches. This shift is described in some of the FLA's materials as a shift from 'policing' to 'coaching' or 'partnership', and some observers have character-ized it as representing an important source of innovation in FLA compliance strategies (Locke, Qin et al. 2006; Locke, Amengual et al. 2009). Locke and colleagues refer to it as a 'commitment-oriented approach' based on a combination of 'root cause analysis', joint problem solving, information exchange and the diffusion of best practices. This is contrasted with a more traditional regulatory or 'compliance' approach. Capacity building approaches of this kind remain substantially underpinned by the ongoing use of monitor-ing and enforcement mechanisms, designed to pressure compan-ies to continue engaging with learning and capacity building processes.

Evaluation

Effectiveness

Operating via a combination of institutional mechanisms, the FLA has achieved some modest progress toward its overarching goal of pro-moting compliance with international labour standards within par-ticipating companies' supply chains. Evidence drawn from a wide range of observers suggests that some aspects of working conditions – particularly those relating to physical infrastructure within facto-ries – have undergone improvement which is at least partially due to FLA auditing and capacity building interventions.[6] Perhaps the most systematic research conducted to date in relation to factories supply-ing FLA member companies was carried out during 2006 and 2007 by

---

[6] Such evidence does, however, need to be interpreted with caution. It is very difficult to be precise regarding the extent of improvement to supply chain working conditions realized *as a result of FLA activities*, as opposed to those due to the interaction of FLA interventions with a wide range of other influences, such as the supply chain codes of conduct implemented by non-FLA companies with whom FLA-participating companies regularly share factories.

a team of researchers led by Richard Locke.[7] This work confirmed the widely noted structural weaknesses of a 'policing' approach to achieving FLA objectives, which reinforces the argument for increased investment in the FLA's 'sustainable compliance' approach. However, this research also confirmed that FLA members continue to fall far short of full *compliance* with core international labour standards throughout their supply chains. Many standards – particularly those relating to forced overtime and freedom of association – continue to be routinely violated in factories manufacturing products of participating companies.

Although it is difficult in many cases to causally link FLA activities with particular patterns of labour practices in specific factories, it is somewhat more straightforward to point to changes in institutional systems and processes to which the Association has directly contributed. Systems of rules governing supply chain business practices have been modified as a direct result of the extensive codification of supply chain labour standards implemented via the FLA's Workplace Code. Company auditing systems have also been strengthened, although these still have significant weaknesses as means of achieving sustainable change in factory working conditions. FLA activities have also increased the amount of capacity building and learning being undertaken by participating companies and licensees, and there has been some very modest increase in the scope of ad hoc 'distributive' or service-based programmes delivered by participating companies.[8]

From a longer-term, strategic perspective, many have expressed concern that the Association's existence and activities may generate negative externalities by providing camouflage for companies that are not seriously committed to improving working conditions, thereby diminishing the influence of future activist campaigns and/or 'crowding out' competing initiatives that might promote these goals more effectively (such as government regulation). In contrast, others regard

---

[7] The research conducted by Richard Locke and his team involved almost 300 interviews with factory owners, managers, workers, NGO representatives, government officials and union leaders in Bangladesh, China, the Dominican Republic, Honduras and India. Corporate compliance, operations and purchasing managers and senior executives were also interviewed. Researchers also observed audits by corporate compliance staff in each country, and conducted quantitative analyses of corporate factory audits conducted at approximately 1,000 suppliers located in over 30 countries.

[8] See www.fairlabor.org for details of some of these programmes.

the Association's long-term impact as likely to be positive, due to its promotion of broader processes of learning and norm diffusion among both industry participants and a wider public. While little evidence is available that could reliably substantiate either set of claims, the potential impact of FLA activities on longer-term political and regulatory dynamics continues to be a source of significant concern for many of the FLA's critics.

Accountability to stakeholders

FLA activities have significant effects on a range of stakeholders. Those whose interests are most substantially and directly affected by FLA decisions are factory workers in the facilities supplying FLA participating companies and licensees. Around 3.7 million workers in over 5,000 factories across more than 60 countries are affected in this way.[9] Factory managers, consumers (particularly students at participating universities), shareholders of FLA-participating companies, and potential workers are also widely acknowledged as relevant stakeholders.

The FLA's accountability to its stakeholders is constrained somewhat by the limited knowledge possessed by many regarding the substance of FLA decisions, the procedures through which these decisions are made, and in many cases regarding the very existence and purpose of the Association. Even managers in factories that directly supply participating companies typically have little knowledge of the FLA, tending not to distinguish its activities from those of their individual corporate clients.[10] In part such weaknesses result from limits to the *transparency* of FLA decision-making; although such transparency has improved significantly since the Association's establishment, there are still significant constraints on its release of information concerning important issues such as factory locations and the content of specific factories' audit reports. Poor stakeholder knowledge can also be attributed to the general failure to *actively disseminate* publicly available information to core stakeholders (particularly workers) in producing countries.

As well as having inadequate knowledge, core stakeholders have limited ability to *sanction* the FLA (and/or participating companies) for Code violations, or indeed for any of its other decisions that significantly affect them. Workers have little influence over the use

---

[9] www.fairlabor.org.
[10] Author interviews in Guatemala City, May–June 2005.

of internal enforcement mechanisms, such as the decertification of delinquent companies. Formally, workers have the capacity to initiate what the FLA refers to as third party complaints as a means of activating internal procedures of remediation and/or sanction. In a limited number of cases this mechanism has facilitated dispute resolution, but it has been widely criticized as operating effectively only in those few cases where worker demands have been backed by high-profile campaigns by Northern activists. The Central American Ombudsman initiative was designed to enable workers to directly initiate complaints against individual companies but it has so far contributed little to achieving this goal, in large part because it has operated on such a small scale and has not been underpinned by wider stakeholder engagement. In practice, the most effective mechanisms via which stakeholders are currently able to sanction the FLA are external to the FLA system – most notably by means of direct pressure exerted by Northern activists on companies and universities in response to worker complaints.

Structures of stakeholder *representation* within the FLA are also weak. While a very indirect form of 'interest representation' for workers is enabled to some extent by their participation in the FLA Board of US labour and human rights NGOs, there are no systems of direct representation through which individual stakeholders can select, sanction, or even routinely communicate directly with those Board members purporting to 'represent' their interests. Similarly, the concerns of factory managers remain largely unrepresented on the Board.

Direct involvement of FLA stakeholders in processes of *deliberation* is also limited. The FLA has organized several events referred to as 'stakeholder consultations', through which a broad range of stakeholder groups have been able to engage in two-way, deliberative discussions with FLA participants and staff. However, such events are not regular or institutionalized, and it is difficult to demonstrate their contribution to shaping either broad strategic priorities or specific policies of the Association. Rather, these events have typically been oriented toward identification and analysis of more specific compliance issues in particular locations. To the extent that stakeholder deliberation has significantly influenced FLA decision-making, this has tended to occur via much more diffuse and informal processes within the wider public domain, in which activist criticism of the Association's purpose, design and specific activities has influenced processes of internal FLA decision-making. For example, such dynamics were illustrated by the significant role of external activists in shaping the FLA's Charter reforms in 2001–2. However, such 'deliberative' processes have remained dominated by Northern activists;

worker input has been enabled only indirectly via links to transnational activist networks.

Legitimacy

Effectiveness and accountability appear to interact through strongly *complementary* processes in shaping the overall legitimacy of the FLA's existence and activities. This tendency can be attributed at least in part to the *dual functional role* of transparency and information flows in relation to core FLA activities: they serve not only as a basis for facilitating responsiveness to worker grievances and underpinning broader forms of stakeholder *accountability*, but also as a basis for the *effective* performance of monitoring and capacity building governance functions. Transparency of factory locations and audit results are particularly important as means of enabling actors external to the FLA to contribute meaningfully to continuous processes of monitoring and to the channelling of worker complaints. Strengthened accountability processes can also encourage factory managers and workers to engage more extensively with FLA activities, thereby promoting processes of learning, capacity building and ideational change that also tend to increase effectiveness. Strengthened legitimacy can in turn feed back into improved effectiveness, due to the importance of the FLA's reputation and credibility as a basis for securing the cooperation of a broad range of local stakeholders in supporting its activities and goals.

References

Bobrowsky, D. (1999). 'Creating a Global Public Policy Network in the Apparel Industry: The Apparel Industry Partnership', Case Study for the UN Vision Project on Global Public Policy Networks. Global Public Policy Institute.

Hemphill, T. (2002). 'The White House Apparel Industry Partnership Agreement: Will Self-Regulation Be Successful?' *Business and Society Review* 104(2): 121–37.

Locke, R., M. Amengualet al. (2009). 'Virtue out of Necessity? Compliance, Commitment, and the Improvement of Labor Conditions in Global Supply Chains'. *Politics & Society* 37: 319

Locke, R. M., F. Qin et al. (2006). 'Does Monitoring Improve Labor Standards?: Lessons from Nike', Corporate Social Responsibility Initiative, Working Paper No. 24. Cambridge, MA: John F. Kennedy School of Government.

31

The Fair Trade System
Kate MacDonald

The contemporary fair trade system has a distinctive, hybrid character as a production and trading network, a social governance arrangement, and a transnational social movement. From the perspective of global governance innovation, it can perhaps be best conceptualized as an 'alternative' normative and institutional system to both organize and govern production and trade. Its central purpose is to operate an alternative market through which commodities can be produced and traded on terms that promote sustainable social development among marginalized workers and producers, particularly those in the global South.

The institutional core of the fair trade system is built around its trading activities, which create alternative supply chain systems linking producers to participating fair trade buyers in countries where the products are consumed. This core institutional structure has loose links with a broad collection of organizations and networks with wider 'social movement' characteristics. An increasingly formalized governance system has been built to facilitate and regulate these core activities. Although the core activities of the system are market oriented, the principles orienting the governance system are overtly political, based on principles of economic justice and democratic governance.

The following discussion reviews the history of fair trade's emergence and evolution, outlines the system's key activities and organizational structures, and presents a brief evaluation of the system's strengths and weaknesses in terms of the democratic quality of its decision-making processes, the effectiveness of its efforts to promote goals of social development and trade justice, and the system's overall legitimacy.[1]

---

[1] Discussion draws on a review of a range of existing studies of the fair trade system by scholars and practitioners; on field research carried out by the author in Nicaragua in 2003–4 and in India in 2010; and on ongoing research and writing in this field by the author.

History

The fair trade system in its current form evolved from a range of secular and faith-based initiatives dating to the post-World War II period. It is linked historically to an even longer tradition of alternative approaches to social relations of production and consumption, in both the global North and South (Low and Davenport 2005; Raynolds, Murray et al. 2007). While the concept known as 'fair trade' is essentially a Northern development, indigenous attempts to empower producers and create alternatives to international trade have deep roots in the South. Southern fair trade organizations developed out of indigenous income generation initiatives in some cases, and with Northern nongovernmental organization (NGO) development assistance in others (Murray, Reynolds et al. 2003).

There is a great deal of diversity within the contemporary fair trade movement, in terms of both goals and organizational structures. Formal certification systems have operated since 1997, when alternative trading organizations operating within consuming countries in North America and Europe formed an overarching international body to coordinate their activities: the Fairtrade Labelling Organizations (FLO). Increasing volumes of fair trade coffee are now traded within the framework of this formal certification system, though more informal networks of fair trading continue. The contemporary fair trade movement encompasses a set of groups formally linked through participation in the FINE network, comprising the FLO, the World Fair Trade Organisation (WFTO; formerly the International Federation of Alternative Trade), the Network of European Worldshops (NEWS) and the European Fair Trade Association (EFTA).

Much of the discussion below focuses on the section of the fair trade system with the most visible and widely debated governance system: the Fairtrade product certification system organized by the FLO.

Activities

Regulatory modes of governance play a central role within the FLO system, taking the form of standard-setting, auditing, and certification functions. Fair trade standards regulate social, labour, environmental and democratic standards at the producer level, and also require buyers of fair trade products to comply with standards regulating issues such as payment of a 'fair' minimum price and social premium, pre-financing arrangements and the stability of trading arrangements. Certification and auditing aim to promote a developmental process through which designated standards (beyond specified minimums) can be progressively realized (United Students for Fair Trade 2004. Accordingly, FLO's producer standards are conceptualized as starting from 'minimum' requirements and developing through various 'progress' requirements. The former are required before certification is granted and the latter are requirements on which the producer groups must show ongoing improvement over time (Courville 2008).

The fair trade system also performs *redistributive* and *capacity building* functions intended to support the socioeconomic development and 'empowerment' of marginalized producers and workers. The required payment of a 'fair price' – calculated for specific products and regions or countries on the basis of the estimated cost of sustainable production – is the system's main instrument for mobilizing financial resources for social development. Producer participation in the fair trade system is also designed to generate more intangible resources in the form of enhanced knowledge and experience concerning production, trading, managerial and community-organizing activities. Many alternative trade organizations operating as fair trade buyers also provide direct training and capacity building opportunities for worker and producer organizations.

Some organizations in the fair trade system are also engaged in broader forms of *social mobilization and campaigning* around issues of trade justice. Such political activities have so far targeted mainly governments in the global North. Fair trade organizations have also attended international forums such as ministerial meetings of the WTO, the Summit of the Americas, the United Nations Conference on Trade and Development (UNCTAD) meetings, and the World Social Forum, and have prepared shared policy positions within these forums.

Organization

FLO's organizational structure mirrors the key activities the organization performs. Standards are developed by FLO's Standards and Policy Committee, in which representatives of national labelling initiatives, producer organizations, traders and other designated 'experts' participate (the Board then approve these standards). Auditing and certification of producers, traders and retailers is managed by FLO-Cert; this is a specialized certification agency that is owned by FLO International, but which has operated as a separate legal and managerial entity since 2004. Final certification decisions are made by a multistakeholder Certification Committee, and decisions can be appealed via a separate Appeals Committee. The Producer Business Unit plays a role in supporting producer capacity building, mainly by helping strengthen producers' access to fair trade markets and their understanding of certification requirements and processes. Its work is carried out by regional managers and coordinators, and in some locations also local liaison officers.

Decision-making authority within FLO is centred to a significant extent in the FLO Board of Directors, which is composed of: five representatives from the Labelling Initiatives; four representatives from Fairtrade Certified Producer Organizations (at least one each from Latin America, Africa and Asia); two representatives from Fairtrade Certified Traders; and two external Board Members. National labelling organizations elect their representatives to the Board every three years during their meeting of members. Producer and trader representatives are selected at the FLO Fairtrade Forum, held every three years. FLO's Director is answerable to the Board for the day-to-day running of the organization.

Evaluation

Democratic decision-making

Principles of democratic decision-making occupy a central role within normative accounts of 'fair trade'. In practice, the democratic credentials of the fair trade system have been widely questioned by critics who point to significant structural power imbalances between Northern and Southern participants. These power asymmetries influence day-to-day dynamics of operational decision-making, and the broader strategic governance of the system. FLO has instituted several reforms designed to strengthen the formal representation of Southern participants, though structural imbalances persist.

Critics have characterized the FLO-based system as having a 'pyramid decision-making structure, where the top often does not communicate with the base' (Franz VanderHoff Boersma, cited in Leigh Taylor 2005: 140). The majority of positions on the FLO Board are held by fair trade stakeholders from consuming countries rather than producers, and many key negotiations and meetings still take place in the North. Power asymmetries are also reflected in the dynamics of wider North–South interactions – both in the conduct of routine trading activities and within the deliberative processes through which agendas and priorities for the movement as a whole are debated and defined (Bacon 2010). These power imbalances partly result from asymmetries in financial and institutional resources between North and South. Other contributing factors include the conduct of much debate in consumer countries and in English, and associated information asymmetries stemming from the proximity of Northern participants to consumer markets and their consequent ability both to access market information and to engage directly with potential consumers and corporate buyers. Although consumers and major corporate buyers do not have any formal role within the FLO governance structure, their structural influence over managerial decision-making processes is significant.

While problematic asymmetries of power persist, FLO has undertaken a range of reforms and initiatives to strengthen the institutional position of producing country stakeholders within the fair trade system. Initial reforms to FLO governance included the opening-up of membership on the FLO Board and key committees to FLO certified producers (Nicholls and Opal 2005), creation of the Coordinadora Latinoamericana de Productores de Café FLO, the introduction of a FLO Fairtrade Forum (held every two years) to enable diverse stakeholders to meet and discuss key issues within the system, and the creation of Regional Producer Assemblies held regularly between Forums to strengthen producer involvement. Beyond the FLO system, both WFTO and the fair trade alliance NEWS have worked to create new global deliberative and communicative spaces involving fair trade groups, making use of transnational networks, newsletters, electronic updates and commercial contacts.

Effectiveness

The effectiveness of fair trade as a means of promoting the social development of marginalized workers and producers has been widely debated. Among advocates of the fair trade system, much emphasis has been placed on the redistributive functions of the minimum fair price and additional 'social premium' which must be paid to producers under Fair Trade rules. Fair trade co-operatives typically draw on these premiums – often supplemented by other sources – to contribute to provision of social services and infrastructure, for instance purchase of school equipment for children of participating farmers, improvements to housing, repair of community infrastructure such as roads, and in some cases the construction of community health and education facilities. The increased income stability associated with payment of a fair trade price floor has also been identified by various impact studies as being associated with strengthened security of land tenure, reduced pressure at the household level for individuals to migrate in search of wage income, and greater incentives for producers to invest in both increased farm productivity and more environmentally sustainable production methods (Murray, Raynolds et al. 2003; Macdonald 2007).

Another important mechanism through which the fair trade system has contributed positively to social development has been the strengthening of producers' and workers' organizations. In some cases, existing co-operatives or fair trade buyers play a direct role in facilitating and supporting the formation of new producer co-operatives or other organizational structures. In some cases buyers provide direct financial, technical or administrative assistance to fair trade co-operatives they work with. The fair trade system also promotes organizational strengthening more indirectly as a result of its provision of stable market access at sustainable prices. Over time, many producer organizations connected to fair trade markets have strengthened and expanded – incorporating new members, investing in productive and institutional capacity, and strengthening organizational skills in the performance of an increasing range of functions (Bacon 2005).

Fair trade's redistributive credentials have, however, been questioned from a number of perspectives. Some have highlighted the limited redistributive impact of the price floor and social premium in view of the very small percentage of total goods traded under the Fairtrade label in most product groups, and the small differences in income differentials between Fairtrade and conventional products during periods of high market prices. Others have criticized perceived inefficiencies in Fairtrade's redistributive mechanism resulting from both limited economies of scale and costly certification processes. Neoclassical economists have attacked what they perceive as price distortions inherent in the price floor mechanism, suggesting that these may contribute to persistent overinvestment in surplus capacity, compounding the structural causes of low commodity prices. Critics from within the fair trade system have questioned the potential for worker 'joint bodies' in certified plantations to facilitate the kinds of social mobilization and empowerment achieved by many smallholder associations participating in the fair trade system.

The impact of fair trade's social movement activities is difficult to evaluate, given the highly interactive and indirect channels through which such influence is exercised. There have been many claims in some countries of rising consumer awareness of ethical issues concerning traded commodities, and rising engagement with the agenda by some European governments, though the causal contribution of fair trade activities is difficult to document.

Legitimacy

From the perspective of both developmental impact and democratic governance, many still consider Fairtrade to be the 'gold standard' among social certification schemes. This widely perceived legitimacy is coming under increasing strain as the system expands. Pressures on the system's legitimacy result importantly from strategic tensions between the pursuit of different dimensions of effectiveness and between goals of effectiveness and democratic governance.

The desire to widen the system's impact by securing expanded fair trade markets for certified products has led to an increasing preoccupation with engaging large corporate buyers, a trend that some see as linked to a dilution of fair trade standards, particularly in relation to long-term trading relationships or pre-financing. Increasing influence of corporate buyers is also viewed by many as threatening both the integrity of the system's democratic processes and the critical edge of the system's political agenda. Moreover, the desire to supply large volumes of Fairtrade certified products in sectors such as tea and bananas has led to increasing participation by private or corporate-owned estates employing hired labour. Some see the widespread participation of estate producers as being in significant conflict with principles of worker and producer empowerment, in part because of concerns about smallholders being 'crowded out' of fair trade sectors dominated by estate production, but also because of the deeply entrenched inequalities of social power that typically characterize relationships between wage-labourers and landowners on estates. Negotiation between these competing conceptions of legitimate outcomes, democratic processes, and the trade-offs between them is likely to play a central role in the ongoing development of the fair trade system as it continues to work toward consolidation and expansion.

References

Bacon, C. (2005). 'Confronting the Coffee Crisis: Can Fair Trade, Organic and Speciality Coffees Reduce Small-scale Farmer Vulnerability in Northern Nicaragua?' *World Development* 33(3): 497–511.

Bacon, C. (2010). 'Who Decides What is Fair in Fair Trade? The Agri-environmental Governance of Standards, Access and Price'. *Journal of Peasant Studies* 37(1): 111–47.

Courville, S. (2008). 'Organic and Social Certifications: Recent Developments from the Global Regulators'. *Confronting the Coffee Crisis: Fair Trade, Sustainable Livelihoods and Ecosystems in Mexico and Central America*, ed. C. M. Bacon, C. M Mendez et al. Cambridge, MA: MIT Press.

Leigh Taylor, P. (2005). 'In the Market But Not of It: Fair Trade Coffee and Forest Stewardship Council Certification as Market-Based Social Change'. *World Development* 33(1): 129–47.

Low, W., and E. Davenport (2005). 'Postcards from the Edge: Maintaining the "Alternative" Character of Fair Trade'. *Sustainable Development* 13: 148–53.

Macdonald, K. (2007). 'Globalising Justice within Coffee Supply Chains? Fair Trade, Starbucks and the Transformation of Supply Chain Governance'. *Third World Quarterly: Special Issue on 'Beyond CSR? Business, Poverty and Social Justice'* 25(7): 793–818.

Murray, D., L. Raynolds et al. (2003). 'One Cup at a Time: Poverty Alleviation and Fair Trade Coffee in Latin America'. Colorado State University. Available at www.colostate.edu/Depts/Sociology/FairTradeResearchGroup.

Nicholls, A., and C. Opal (2004). *Fair Trade: Market-driven Ethical Consumption.* London: Sage Publications.

Raynolds, L., D. Murray et al. (2007). *Fair Trade: The Challenges of Transforming Globalization.* London: Routledge.

32

Clean Clothes Campaign
Niklas Egels-Zandén

Introduction

In the late 1980s in the Netherlands, the Clean Clothes Campaign emerged as one of Europe's most influential multistakeholder initiatives for pressuring companies to assume responsibilities for workers' rights at their suppliers' factories. The Clean Clothes Campaign has since then spread to 13 European countries and comprises over 200 partner organizations (including both nongovernmental organizations (NGOs) and labour unions). This chapter focuses on formation of the Swedish branch of the Clean Clothes Campaign and its struggle to influence the Swedish garment industry.

The Swedish Clean Clothes Campaign (SCCC), like similar workers' rights initiatives, represents an important innovation in governance. In the twentieth century, workers' rights issues have been largely addressed through collective bargaining and industrial agreements between firms and unions, with various degrees of government intervention across different countries (e.g. Emery and Thorsrud 1969; Bamber and Lansbury 1998). This industrial relations landscape is currently undergoing two fundamental changes. First, the arenas in which industrial relations are being enacted are becoming increasingly transnational, and second, NGOs are emerging as worker representatives alongside labour unions. As Thomas Kochan (2006: 12 – italics in original) puts it: 'I would cite the entry of the range of NGOs that have sprung up to promote worker rights and publicize violations of core labour standards in developing nations of Asia as one if not *the* most important institutional innovations of our time.'

This chapter shows how the emerging transnational governance system of workers' rights encompasses a conflict between global rules and a local bargaining logic. On the one hand, NGOs attempt to establish a system based on unilateral corporate codes of conduct with legitimacy stemming from compliance with pre-defined minimum requirements. On the other hand, labour unions attempt to establish a system based on negotiated International Framework Agreements (IFAs) with legitimacy stemming from the process of collective bargaining. This conflict and its consequences are illustrated through the example of the SCCC and the Swedish garment industry between 1996 and 2006 (Egels-Zandén and Hyllman 2006; Ählström and Egels-Zandén 2008).

Transnational Governance and the SCCC

Prologue: the international scene (prior to 1996)

As multinational corporations shifted production to mainly Asian countries in the late 1980s and early 1990s, they became targets of Western unions and NGOs' critiques. In the aftermath of numerous international media 'scandals' in the early 1990s, firms such as Levi's, GAP, Nike and Reebok started to acknowledge an extended sense of responsibility for workers' rights at their suppliers' factories (e.g., van Tulder and Kolk 2001; Braun and Gearhart 2004). Despite this international controversy, few voices regarding supplier responsibilities were raised in Sweden before 1996.

The initiation of a transnational governance system (1996–2001)

In 1996, the recently founded Swedish NGO, Fair Trade Center (FTC), came in contact with the Dutch Clean Clothes Campaign and decided to initiate an SCCC, to pressure Swedish garment retailers to extend their responsibility for workers' rights at their suppliers' factories. The purpose was to improve workers' rights, mainly in Asia, and, rather than pressuring suppliers or national governments, FTC envi-

sioned that pressuring Swedish garment retailers was the most effective strategy for achieving improvements.

By enrolling seven other NGOs – such as Red Cross Sweden Youth
and the SAC (Central Organization of the Workers of Sweden)
Syndicalists – in the campaign, as well as two Swedish labour unions
involved in the garment industry, the SCCC gained strength. The
NGOs saw the inclusion of unions as critical, as Swedish unions traditionally have negotiated workers' rights issues with Swedish
garment retailers. At this time, the unions claimed not to have developed a position regarding workers' rights outside Sweden. They,
however, sympathized with the aims of SCCC and, inspired by FTC's
enthusiasm, they decided to join.

Campaign activities quickly started with a postcard campaign targeting the shoppers at four of Sweden's largest garment retailers:
Hennes & Mauritz (H&M), Lindex, KappAhl and Indiska.[1] At the same
time, FTC, through SCCC, made contact with the four retailers, with
the aim of persuading them to adopt codes of conduct regarding
workers' rights at their suppliers. Throughout this stage of the process
the unions attended SCCC meetings and were part of the core SCCC
working group, but remained passive in terms of offering suggestions
as to how the campaign should proceed.

After several media 'scandals', the Swedish garment retailers in
1997 assumed responsibility for workers' rights at their suppliers by
adopting codes of conduct. To harmonize the retailers' codes and to
create an independent monitoring system, the four retailers in 1998
joined and financed an SCCC project – called 'DressCode' – initiated
by FTC. The DressCode project comprised representatives from retailers, NGOs and unions.

Reasonably quickly, a harmonized code was developed in the
DressCode project. The code was based on FTC's suggestions with
exception of the 'living wage' criterion, which was – based on corporate demands – replaced with 'minimum wage'. Over a two-year
period the DressCode project then explored different monitoring
options, mainly NGO-led. This led to the proposal to create an independent foundation that would own a non-profit organization that
in turn would sell independent monitoring to all interested Swedish
garment retailers. The foundation would be founded and co-owned
by Swedish NGOs and unions. Most of these ideas were suggested by

[1] In total, H&M, Lindex, KappAhl and Indiska had a turnover of SEK 64,000
million in 2004 (approximately $9,000 million) and directly employed
over 35,000 people worldwide, plus many thousands indirectly in their
supply chains.

FTC and the firms. The unions remained fairly passive, accepting and supporting FTC's suggestions.

The governance collapse (2002)

In 2002, the unions decided to reject the suggested code of conduct and monitoring system, the first time during the six-year process that the unions expressed a clear disagreement. The unions presented two main reasons for their withdrawal.

First, they claimed that codes of conduct were an unsatisfactory way to operationalize retailers' responsibilities for workers' rights at suppliers. The unions instead preferred to enter into negotiated International Framework Agreements (IFAs) with the firms. The unions, at this stage, claimed to have initially been too positive toward codes of conduct, and argued that codes were a convenient way for firms to legitimize their supplier relationships without union involvement.

Second, the unions claimed not to have the mandate to negotiate on behalf of workers at suppliers' factories in developing countries. The unions said that they had initially wanted to improve the workers' situation without giving the issue of mandate any thought; later, however, the unions argued that local and national unions should negotiate with the firms regarding the terms of the IFAs. In this way, the unions discarded codes of conduct and even framed them as inhibiting progress toward workers' rights improvements.

Additionally, it is worth mentioning that at a global level the union movement had, at the beginning of the twenty-first century, started to promote IFAs and criticize codes of conduct, realizing that the latter were not solely about solidarity and philanthropy but also about the emergence of a transnational governance system of workers' rights based on unilateral corporate policies (Egels-Zandén and Hyllman 2006). Codes of conduct thus threatened the unions' position as a key actor in governing workers' rights.

Since FTC and the other NGOs did not want to endorse a code of conduct and monitoring system lacking union support, the unions' withdrawal led to the collapse of the DressCode project, the harmonized code of conduct, and the suggested independent monitoring system. The collapse was criticized by both NGOs and retailers, which argued that the unions had previously supported all the aspects that they later came to criticize.

Competing ways of creating governance (2002–2006)

Since the collapse of DressCode, the Swedish garment industry has lacked a unified workers' rights policy and monitoring system. The unions tried to persuade retailers to adopt IFAs that are monitored by local unions. However, the retailers were reluctant to accept IFAs, arguing that such contracts are unrealistic due to the low membership density and organizational characteristics of unions in the countries in which they operate. Instead, the retailers continue to work with codes of conduct and monitoring, each firm developing its own system.

Additionally, H&M initiated discussions with the Fair Labor Association (FLA) and the Fair Wear Foundation – two initiatives with similarities to the cross-sectoral DressCode project. KappAhl began collaborating with the Norwegian Ethical Trading Initiative (IEH) and made SA8000 inspections at some of its suppliers' factories, and KappAhl and Lindex joined the corporate-dominated Business Social Compliance Initiative (BSCI).

After the collapse of DressCode, FTC and the other NGOs in SCCC initially continued to argue in favour of harmonized codes of conduct and independent monitoring. However, as time has passed, the NGOs have become more receptive to the unions' argument, with many NGOs in principle supporting IFAs (although being sceptical of the potential to successfully make retailers sign IFAs). NGOs have also started to recognize the role of local unions in Asian countries, and have begun to aid in their formation. Nevertheless, the Swedish NGOs view codes of conduct as their main approach to workers' rights, and spend most of their time trying to enforce this approach.

Rules vs Bargaining in Transnational Governance

The SCCC case and the collapse of the DressCode project illustrate the tension between two competing logics of how to govern workers' rights. First, the logic that legitimacy stems from *outcomes* in the form of compliance with pre-defined minimum requirements. This logic is materialized in codes of conduct and promoted in the SCCC by the NGOs – particularly FTC – and the retailers. Workers' rights are here generally defined and universally determined, and legitimacy is thus shifted from negotiated bargains to codified global rules such as the United Nations (UN) Universal Declaration of Human Rights and the International Labor Organization (ILO) Declaration on Fundamental Principles and Rights at Work. This underlying 'rules' logic of transnational governance gains support from much of the Corporate Social Responsibility (CSR) movement, with, for example, the UN Global Compact being based on a similar logic of codified global rules (cf. Kuper 2004). More generally, the rules logic also gains support from the move toward an 'audit society' (Power 1997), with a growing number of rules and standards governing organizations (e.g., Brunsson and Jacobsson 2000; Jutterström 2006).

One effect of creating transnational governance based on a rules logic is that procedural aspects are downplayed. This is clearly illustrated in the SCCC case, with the proposed code of conduct and monitoring not including any procedural aspects of workers' rights negotiations. The rules logic is also evident in that no local Asian unions or NGOs were involved in the DressCode project. Since legitimacy is envisioned to stem from the codified rules defined by global actors, there is little need to include local organizations in the process of developing codes of conduct.

In sharp contrast, the labour unions in the SCCC promoted a type of logic in which legitimacy stems from the collective bargaining process. This logic, embodied in IFAs, attempts to transfer the bargaining processes of traditional, national tripartite industrial relations systems to the transnational level (cf. Bamber and Lansbury 1998). Through negotiations, legitimacy is produced via interpersonal relationships rather than through the application of codified rules (Granovetter 1985). The bargaining logic underpins most, if not all, union-based industrial relations systems, but is particularly strong in Scandinavia (e.g., Nielsen and Pedersen 1988). The bargaining logic comes across strongly in the SCCC case when, for example, the unions dismissed codes of conduct and opted for IFAs, and when they claimed not to have the mandate to negotiate on behalf of workers in Asia.

To conclude, the SCCC case illustrates how conflicts between the underlying rules and bargaining logics were materialized and enacted in micro-level conflicts between codes of conduct and IFAs, and conflicts between NGOs and unions. In the Swedish setting, these conflicts led to collapse of the cross-sectoral DressCode project that in turn allowed Swedish garment retailers largely to dictate themselves how to govern workers' rights transnationally via corporate-specific codes of conduct and monitoring systems. In other settings, the consequences might differ. The underlying conflict between the rules and bargaining logics is, though, likely to persist, since they comprise two distinctly different ideas of how to create transnational governance of workers' rights issues.

References

Ählström, J., and N. Egels-Zandén (2008). 'The Processes of Defining Corporate Responsibility: A Study of Swedish Garment Retailers' Responsibility.' *Business Strategy and the Environment* 17(4): 230–44.

Bamber, G. J., and R. D. Lansbury, eds. (1998). *International and Comparative Employment Relations*. St Leonards, Australia: Allen & Unwin.

Braun, R., and J. Gearhart (2004). 'Who Should Code Your Conduct? Trade Union and NGO Differences in the Fight for Workers' Rights.' *Development in Practice* 14(1–2): 183–96.

Brunsson, N., and B. Jacobsson, eds. (2000). *A World of Standards*. Oxford: Oxford University Press.

Egels-Zandén, N., and P. Hyllman (2006). 'Exploring the Effects of Union–NGO Relationships on Corporate Responsibility: The Case of the Swedish Clean Clothes Campaign'. *Journal of Business Ethics* 64(3): 303–16.

Emery, F. E., and E. Thorsrud (1969). *Form and Content in Industrial Democracy*. London: Tavistock.

Granovetter, M. (1985). 'Economic Action and Social Structure: The Problem of Embeddedness'. *American Journal of Sociology* 91(3): 481–510.

Jutterström, M. (2006). *Corporate Social Responsibility: The Supply Side of CSR-Standards*. Stockholm: Score.

Kochan, T. A. (2006). 'Adapting Industrial Relations to Serve Knowledge-based Economies'. *Journal of Industrial Relations* 48(1): 7–20.

Kuper, A. (2004). 'Harnessing Corporate Power: Lessons from the UN Global Compact'. *Development* 47(3): 9–19.

Nielsen, K., and O. K. Pedersen (1988). 'The Negotiated Economy: Ideal and History'. *Scandinavian Political Studies* 2: 79–101.

Power, M (1997). *The Audit Society: Rituals of Verification*. Oxford: Oxford University Press.

van Tulder, R., and A. Kolk (2001). 'Multinationality and Corporate Ethics: Codes of Conduct in the Sporting Goods Industry'. *Journal of International Business Studies* 32(2): 267–83.

33

Forest Stewardship Council
Philipp Pattberg

Introduction

Voluntary regulation – i.e. codes of conduct, industry standards and monitoring and certification systems created by a mix of public and private actors – presents a viable alternative to public and state-based forms of environmental and social governance. One issue area in particular that has received enormous attention in recent years is global forest governance (e.g. Pattberg 2007; Auld, Gulbrandsen et al. 2008). On this account, forest governance has been a prime site for experimenting with novel instruments for and approaches toward halting environmental degradation. In particular, the instrument of certification has been frequently invoked as an example of non-state market-driven governance (Cashore 2002). This chapter will provide a more detailed account of the formation process as well as the measurable impacts of the Forest Stewardship Council (FSC), which is regarded as the global 'gold standard' in sustainable forest management and certification.

The FSC is a private non-profit organization with a heterogeneous membership consisting of environmental and social nongovernmental organizations (NGOs), corporations in the forestry sector, scientific institutions, and individuals from more than sixty countries. The FSC administers a self-elaborated third-party certification system on wood and timber products that serves to verify whether products originate from sustainable forestry. The basis of the certification scheme is the FSC's international standard Principles and Criteria for Forest Stewardship, which are transformed into national standards that serve as a basis for the on-ground certification of forest management units by independent, FSC-accredited auditing firms. The FSC's day-to-day operations are managed by a Board of Directors and an international secretariat, situated in Bonn, Germany, while the highest decision-making power rests with the General Assembly. Constituting a novelty in the field of voluntary regulation, the General Assembly represents environmental, social and economic stakeholders in three chambers with equal voting power and an additional North/South quota. As a consequence of this 'democratic' decision-making structure, observers have called the FSC 'perhaps the best current model of a civil regulation organization' (Murphy and Bendell 1999: 58).

To date more than 325 million hectares of forest have been certified by various certification programmes, approximating roughly 8 per cent of the global forest cover. Whereas Africa, Latin America, Asia and Oceania together have only 6 per cent of their total forest area under certification, North America has certified 38 per cent of its forests, while Western European countries reached a remarkable 53 per cent in 2009. The estimated potential global industrial roundwood supply from certified forests amounts to 411 million cubic metres annually, which equals 26 per cent of total industrial roundwood supply.[1] The FSC's contribution to these figures is substantial. As of early 2010, more than 123 million hectares of forests had been certified in accordance with the FSC standard, approximating 5 per cent of the world's productive forests. The geographic spread of

---

[1] Annual figures are for the period May 2008 until May 2009. See UNECE/FAO (2010).

FSC-certified forests is the following: 46.6 per cent of FSC-certified forests are located in Europe, 36.5 per cent in North America, and roughly 16 per cent are located in Latin America, Africa, Asia and Oceania (FSC 2010).

The Emergence of Voluntary Regulation in the Global Forest Sector

In March 1991, a group of dedicated individuals and representatives from a wide range of organizations, including environmental NGOs, retailers, trade unions and indigenous interest groups, convened in California to discuss the need for a credible system for identifying well-managed forests as a trustworthy source for sustainable timber products. After an intensive eighteen-month consultation and testing period in ten countries – including the US, Canada, Sweden, and Peru – in October 1993, the FSC held its first General Assembly in Toronto, Canada. Although consultations among the different stakeholders had been going on since the early 1990s, it was not until 1994 that the founding members of FSC agreed upon the first version of the 'FSC Standards and Principles', the substantive basis of FSC's work. The emergence of 'the most important example of increasingly successful certification systems that are transforming major industries around the world' (Conroy 2007: 95) has to be placed within the context of four distinct developments within the issue area of forestry at that time.

(1) By the late 1980s, buying tropical timber had become a contentious issue among Northern consumers. Extensive media-coverage on tropical deforestation and related social issues, such as the Amazonian rubber tappers' protest against illegal logging and the subsequent investment in cattle, had quickly turned the term 'tropical timber' into a negative synonym for environmental degradation and human exploitation.

(2) Faced with environmental NGOs organizing boycotts against timber retailers, and some governments discussing the possibility of banning timber imports, companies were looking for ways to protect their business. Leading corporations realized that in fact they could not account for the origin (and thus social/environmental quality) of their raw materials, which in turn made them vulnerable to civil society protests and, as a result, created a need for transparent product labels (which were nonexistent at that time). In addition, some NGOs were unhappy with a timber boycott as the main campaigning tool, which especially the moderate World Wide Fund for Nature saw as counter-productive.

(3) The conflicting interests of the major stakeholders became evident at that point in time. An increasingly competitive global market for timber products put large multinational corporations under pressure while at the same time brand reputation became a major topic of concern. Small forest owners demanded their share of the market, but at the same time were eager to maintain their independence; communities relied on forests to finance community infrastructure; indigenous people demanded the recognition of fundamental rights while workers sought to secure employment and the application of fundamental labour standards. Environmental organizations, in turn, focused on protecting and preserving the integrity of the forest ecosystems within the discursive context of biodiversity conservation and sustainability.

(4) By 1992, the ongoing negotiations over an international agreement on the world's forests had raised expectations among NGOs, corporations and the wider public of a credible solution to the global forest crisis. In the end, it was the failure of the intergovernmental process that gave an additional boost to the idea of establishing voluntary regulation in the global forestry area. Remarking on the disappointing results of the United Nations Conference on Environment and Development (UNCED), FSC's first Executive Director Timothy Synnott concludes that '[a] clear impulse for the formation of FSC in 1993 came out of the failure of the Rio conference in 1992 and its failure to produce a legally binding forestry element' (quoted in FSC and WWF-Germany 2002: 8).

In sum, while the 1992 UNCED was unable to deliver a binding agreement on the world's forests, it nevertheless provided important input to the FSC's formation process. The Rio conference was the place where the concept of sustainability took centre-stage. Based on the 1987 Brundtland Report, UNCED agreed on the Agenda 21 as the blueprint for sustainability in the twenty-first century, calling on governments to identify appropriate national strategies for the sustainable use of forest resources, acknowledging the crucial contribution of nongovernmental actors and business interests. Observers called the FSC the 'archetype of the participatory process envisioned by Agenda 21' (FSC and WWF-Germany 2002: 3).

Evaluation of Voluntary Regulation in the Global Forest Sector

Although the FSC is widely acknowledged to be the most rigorous, transparent and participatory certification scheme in global forest governance, a number of sustained criticisms have been raised against it (Councell and Loraas 2002; Schepers 2010). When evaluating the FSC's performance, I will therefore focus on two contested issues: first, the concrete and measurable impacts on environmental indicators such as biodiversity, reduced-impact logging, and pesticide use; and second, the North/South dimension of forest certification, including questions of market access, price premiums and management costs. However, any evaluation that attempts to capture the true extent of the FSC's impacts will have to consider additional effects beyond the amount of hectares certified or certificates issued (cf. Dingwerth and Pattberg 2007). Consequently, I will also briefly discuss the FSC's impact on government and corporate policies.

Environmental impacts

The FSC's environmental impact can be assessed in relation to four key areas: biodiversity conservation, reduced-impact logging, fire management and pesticide use. With regard to biodiversity conservation, research has found – based on an analysis of 129 certification reports from 21 countries – a number of positive environmental impacts in the key areas, including aquatic and riparian zones, sensitive sites and high conservation value forests, as well as threatened and endangered species (Newsom and Hewitt 2005). Other studies are more cautious when it comes to the measurable effects on biodiversity conservation, but nevertheless conclude that 'FSC certification of timber production forests can potentially contribute to biodiversity conservation' (Gullison 2003: 162). With regard to reduced-impact logging, a case study analysis from Malaysia found that FSC-certified forests (in comparison to conventionally logged forests) perform better with regard to the composition and richness of tree species, macro fauna, insects and mammals (Mannan, Kitayama et al. 2008). Case study research from Guatemala found that FSC certification significantly reduced deforestation and the incidence of wildfire (Hughell and Butterfield 2008), while a case study from Germany demonstrated that FSC certification has encouraged a reduction in the use of pesticides when compared to business-as-usual scenarios (Hirschberger 2005).

North/South dimension

One of the most contentious issues within the forest certification debate is the North/South dimension. Stakeholders in the developing countries expressed the concern that the FSC standards mainly reflect the interests of campaigners from the North, and that the effects of the FSC could be harmful from a development perspective. On this account, FSC certification is compared by some authors to the tropical timber boycotts of the 1980s (Smouts 2002):

> So far, the main result has been to boost the comparative advantages of temperate forests on the timber marketplace. . . . Over 90 per cent of the FSC certified forests are temperate and boreal forests. Conclusion: if you feel you must have FSC certified timber, buy Scandinavian, Eastern European and North American wood, not tropical wood. If that is not a boycott, it bears a close resemblance.

This criticism is underscored by the fact that over four-fifths of the FSC-certificated wood still originates from Europe and North America. In this way certification gives advantage to producers from countries whose legal requirements are already in-line with the FSC standards. In contrast, the situation for developing countries is different as timber-producing countries from the South and the North are hardly alike. Whereas industrialized countries have to make relatively few changes to their existing forestry practices as a result of already high standards in most Northern producer countries, developing nations have to make substantial investments in order to meet the certification requirements, often resulting in a comparative disadvantage vis-à-vis their competitors.

On the whole, Canadian, Swedish or Polish producers benefit from the success of the FSC much more than producers in, for example, Malaysia and Indonesia. Currently, wood imports to industrial countries increasingly originate from other industrial countries. The causes for that are naturally manifold, but they include the demand for certified wood in industrial countries, which has been strongly increasing in the same period. In short, timber producers from developing countries have difficulty gaining significant access to premium markets in the OECD region (Gullison 2003: 158). In addition, looking at the roundwood production from certified sources per region, the neglect of certain geographic areas becomes painstakingly visible: zero per cent of global certified roundwood supply came from Africa in the period 2007–9 (UNECE/FAO 2010).

Additional effects on government policies and global timber corporations

One concrete example of how the effects of voluntary regulation can go beyond their initial aims is the uptake of private standards by governments. A number of countries have adopted national legislation that resembles FSC rules, requires FSC certification in exchange for long-term concessions of state-owned forests, or exempts holders of FSC certificates from particular forms of public control (Domask

2003: 176). For instance, Bolivian forest legislation introduced in 1996 stipulates that independent certification can replace public monitoring of national forest management standards (Conroy 2007: 81). The South African government ties the privatization of state-owned forests to FSC certification, and legislation in Mexico and Guatemala is also partially linked or adapted to FSC standards (Segura 2004; Pattberg 2006: 591). In addition, a number of governments have enacted timber procurement policies that acknowledge FSC certification as the appropriate benchmark (Lopez-Casero 2008).

Further to influencing public policies, the FSC has induced a substantial unintended side-effect: the creation of numerous alternative and competing certification schemes in the forestry sector. In the words of Auld, Gulbrandsen and colleagues (2008: 200): '[P]robably the most significant unintended outcome of the creation of the FSC was how producers around the world responded by creating their own national certification schemes.' Evaluations of this outcome are mixed. While additional certification programmes have increased the overall coverage of sustainable forest management around the globe, competing claims and alternative standards have allowed companies to benefit from the general positive connotation of forest certification without making substantive changes to their operations. Given the various competing labels in the marketplace, it becomes increasingly difficult for consumers to assess the claims made on behalf of the various certification programmes.

In recent years, the arena of forest governance has proven to be a prime laboratory for innovative instruments and institutions of voluntary regulation. On this account, the Forest Stewardship Council comes close to the 'gold standard' in forest governance. However, while the FSC's democratic quality is widely acknowledged, conclusions about its concrete and measurable effects are less straightforward. Next to imposing a severe market barrier on Southern producers and giving mixed signals to consumers as a result of the many alternative certification schemes that have sprung up as a response to the FSC's initial success, a number of positive effects are noticeable. In particular the steady growth of certified timber in the market as well as the rather positive support from governments justifies calling the FSC the most promising voluntary regulation scheme in forest governance today.

References

Auld, G., L. Gulbrandsen et al. (2008). 'Certification Schemes and the Impacts on Forests and Forestry'. *Annual Review of Environment and Resources* 33: 187–211.

Cashore, B. (2002). 'Legitimacy and the Privatization of Environmental Governance: How Non State Market-Driven (NSMD) Governance Systems Gain Rule Making Authority'. *Governance* 15(4): 503–29.

Conroy, M. E. (2007). *Branded: How the Certification Revolution Is Transforming Global Corporations*. Gabriola Island: New Society Publishers.

Councell, S., and K. T. Loraas (2002). *Trading In Credibility: The Myth and Reality of the Forest Stewardship Council*. London: Rainforest Foundation.

Dingwerth, K., and P. Pattberg (2007). 'Wirkungen Transnationaler Umweltregime'. *Politische Vierteljahresschrift (PVS)* 39: 133–56.

Domask, J. (2003). 'From Boycotts to Global Partnership: NGOs, the Private Sector, and the Struggle to Protect the World's Forests'. *Globalization and NGOs: Transforming Business, Government, and Society*, ed. J. P. Doh and H. Teegen. Westport and London: Praeger.

Forest Stewardship Council (2010). 'Global FSC Certificates: Type and Distribution, January 2010'. Available at www.fsc.org/fileadmin/web-data/public/document_center/powerpoints_graphs/facts_figures/Global-FSC-Certificates-2010-01-15-EN.pdf (accessed 23 February 2010).

Forest Stewardship Council, and WWF-Germany (2002). *Forest Stewardship Council: Political Instrument, Implementation and Concrete Results for Sustainability since 1993*. Frankfurt: FSC/WWF-Germany.

Gullison, R. E. (2003). 'Does Forest Certification Conserve Biodiversity?' *Oryx* 37(2): 153–65.

Hirschberger, P. (2005). 'The Effects of FSC-certification in Estonia, Germany, Latvia, Russia, Sweden & the United Kingdom: An analysis of Corrective Action Requests'. Summary report, WWF European Forest Programme.

Hughell, D., and R. Butterfield (2008). 'Impact of FSC Certification on Deforestation and the Incidence of Wildfires in the Maya Biosphere Reserve'. Rainforest Alliance, USA.

Lopez-Casero, F. (2008). 'Public Procurement Policies for Legal and Sustainable Timber: Trends and Essential Elements'. Powerpoint Presentation to the Forum on China and the Global Forest Products Trade, Beijing, 18–19 June 2008, Institute for Global Environmental Strategies (IGES) Forest Conservation, Livelihoods and Rights Project.

Mannan, S., K. Kitayama et al. (2008). 'Deramakot Forest Shows Positive Conservation Impacts of RIL'. *ITTO Tropical Forest Update* 18(2): 7–9.

Murphy, D. F., and J. Bendell (1999). 'Partners in Time? Business, NGOs and Sustainable Development'. UNRISD Discussion Paper No. 109. Geneva: UNRISD.

Newsom, D., and D. Hewitt (2005). 'The Global Impacts of SmartWood Certification, Final Report of the TREES Program for the Rainforest Alliance'. Available at www.rainforest-alliance.org/forestry/documents/sw_impacts.pdf.

Pattberg, P. (2006). 'Private Governance and the South: Lessons from Global Forest Politics'. *Third World Quarterly* 27(4): 579–93.

Pattberg, P. (2007). *Private Institutions and Global Governance: The New Politics of Environmental Sustainability*. Cheltenham, and Northampton, MA: Edward Elgar.

Schepers, D. H. (2010). 'Challenges to Legitimacy at the Forest Stewardship Council'. *Journal of Business Ethics* 92: 279–90.

Segura, G. (2004). *Forest Certification and Governments: The Real and Potential Influence on Regulatory Frameworks and Forest Policy.* Washington, DC: Forest Trends.

Smouts, M.-C. (2002). 'Forest Certification and Timber Labelling: The Hidden Agenda'. Paper presented at 43rd Meeting of the International Studies Association, New Orleans, 24–27 March.

UNECE/FAO (2010). 'Forest Products Annual Market Review, 2008–2009'. Available at http://timber.unece.org/fileadmin/DAM/publications/Final_FPAMR2009.pdf (accessed 22 February 2010.

34

Global Corporate Governance Principles
Andrew Baker

Introduction

Corporate governance is the set of institutional arrangements and procedures that allocate decision-making authority between managers, shareholders and employees. It refers to the authority system within the firm, defined by a legal structure of company law, securities regulation, accounting/auditing standards and labour relations law (Cioffi 2003; Gourevitch and Shinn 2005). It has profound consequences for important issues such as job security, workers' rights, and wealth distribution in society. The formation of international corporate governance principles formulated and edited by the Organisation for Economic Co-operation and Development (OECD), and assessed by the World Bank, is often associated with efforts to promote convergence on an Anglo-American model of corporate governance oriented toward the promotion of shareholder value. However, in terms of content, the principles are relatively generic, eclectic and ambiguous. Moreover, they were formulated through an inclusive consultative multistakeholder process, while the means by which they are assessed has involved a reciprocal mutually dependent process involving a form of pragmatic ongoing policy dialogue that is designed to facilitate mutual learning, by both assessed and assessor. Consequently, the principles are a tool for structuring an inclusive policy dialogue rather than disciplinary enforcement.

Corporate Governance

In the early years of the twenty-first century, the question of how firms are governed rose to prominence on the political agenda following a spate of scandals involving companies such as Enron, WorldCom, Ahold, Vivendi, Hollinger and Parmalat. Corporate governance refers to long-standing questions of how large private enterprises should be governed and structured, how they should distribute and use their financial surpluses, to whom they should be responsible and accountable, and even what function they should fulfil in society. As giant global corporations operating across several continents have emerged over the course of the twentieth century, the impact of such decisions on the livelihood and welfare of billions of people around the globe has intensified. The future savings, investment and pensions of ordinary citizens are bound up with the performance of these corporations as measured by share prices. Such developments have had the effect of widening the constituencies concerned with corporate governance and pushing the issue up the public policy agenda. Several studies have successfully demonstrated how corporate governance is inherently political – reflecting political choices and contestation, with profound distributional implications (Gourevitch and Shinn 2005; Overbeek, Van Apeldoorn et al. 2007).

One of the key debates in the corporate governance literature concerns the issue of convergence, particularly toward an Anglo-American or outsider model characterized by the following features: a high reliance on equity finance; dispersed ownership; strong legal protection of shareholders (including minority holdings); little role for other stakeholders such as employees and creditors in company management; strong disclosure requirements; and a liberal approach to mergers and acquisitions. Forces for convergence highlighted by the literature include global investment flows and activist shareholders (Coffee 2002), political pressure from the dominant state, which may suffer negative externalities from divergence (Simmons 2001); international accounting standards (Perry and Nölke 2006),; and pressure and support from Anglo-American financial forces involving the construction of specific international principles for corporate governance (Soederberg 2003). It is the latter of these that is the concern of this chapter.

OECD Principles

As corporations have become more global in their operations, they have been subjected to competing regulations, norms and practices

(Overbeek, Van Apeldoorn et al. 2007). In response, efforts to build a global corporate governance regime have intensified and a variety of global standards and principles have emerged. The centrepiece of these standards is the OECD's corporate governance principles.

In 1999 the OECD formulated principles for corporate governance at the insistence of its member governments, and later revised them in 2004 (OECD 2004). The process was distinctive for its wide-ranging outreach. These principles have come to be regarded as 'the international benchmark for corporate governance, forming the basis for a number of reform initiatives, both by governments and the private sector' (Jesover and Kirkpatrick 2005: 127–8). They also became one of the twelve standards and codes for international financial stability introduced after the Asian financial crisis.

The OECD principles themselves and the process through which they were formulated have four distinctive characteristics worth reflecting on. The first of these is that the principles represent a compromise between institutional investors from the Anglo-American world and elites in emerging markets, with a few concessions thrown in for Western labour along the way (Rosser, 2008). The nature of the political compromises in the principles have reflected certain power differentials, for example international investor associations such as the Institute for International Finance (IIF) and the International Corporate Governance Network (ICGN) have had their views represented in the actual principles to a greater extent than groups such as organized labour. The political compromise represented by the principles is therefore more heavily tilted in the direction of investor associations pushing shareholder activism and shareholder rights, but political compromise is nevertheless a key defining feature of the principles.

Second, the principles were put together through a process based on dialogue, inclusion, social partnership and compromise. An Ad Hoc Task Force on Corporate Governance, consisting of representatives from OECD member countries, and from the World Bank, the IMF, the International Organization of Securities Commissions, and the Basel Committee, and involving occasional appearances from private sector experts, was established to take the process of formulating international corporate principles forward. Views were also sought from the Trade Union Advisory Committee (TUAC) representing Western organized labour, and the Business and Industry Advisory Committee (BIAC) representing Western business associations. Consultations were also held with non-OECD governments, and submissions were obtained from the public via an OECD website. The 2004 revisions to the principles involved a yet more extensive series of consultations, including three major consultative meetings with broad participation; two informal meetings with representatives from international organizations, labour and business; and an opportunity for all interested parties to submit comments on an early draft of the revised principles through an Internet site, with submissions received from the Institute of International Finance, International Federation of Human Rights, the International Metalworkers Federation and the International Federation of Trade Unions, amongst others (OECD 2004). Furthermore, much of the revision of the principles in 2004 was driven by consultations with non-OECD members through the regional corporate governance roundtables, particularly the Latin American roundtable (Jesover and Kirkpatrick 2005).

Third, the principles involve a process of continuous critical reflection, involving a dialogue amongst a range of stakeholders discussing the use and practicalities of the principles, which is overseen by OECD staff in their role as 'editor' of the principles. OECD staff treat the principles as a 'living document'. Principles on state-owned enterprises now exist, along with a boardroom guide to using the principles, while work on applying the principles to hedge funds and private equity has been ongoing. Currently, extensive work and consultations on corporate governance and the financial crisis are underway. A final report was due to be published in November 2009, with the OECD seeking to re-examine the adequacy of its corporate governance principles in relation to risk management systems, executive salaries, accounting standards and the remuneration of boards (Kirkpatrick 2009). The focus of this latest review was not to indicate that the principles and their inadequacies were culpable and responsible for the 2008–9 financial crisis, but to identify how they can be improved or amplified, and to provide more detailed guidance on the issues listed above. OECD staff have sought to make the dialogue surrounding the principles as inclusive as possible. In short the principles have involved a continuous 'learning by monitoring', or a 'learning by consulting', process amongst OECD staff and a range of stakeholders. This process has a resemblance to Charles Sabel's notion of 'experimental governance' that encourages deliberation, reasoning and the active incorporation of very localized information into broader governance processes, as decision makers learn from and correct one another (Sabel 2004). Benchmarks, such as the principles, provide common goals, assembled from existing information, but are continuously being rebuilt as new information is found and efforts are made to identify the root causes of errors, with inclusive reason and dialogue used to solve problems (Sabel 2004).

Fourth, the content of the principles reflects the multistakeholder nature of the process surrounding them and the political compromises alluded to earlier. Key areas of concern for the principles are shareholder rights, transparency, accountability and the responsibilities of company boards, all of which resonate with the Anglo-American model (Rosser 2008). A stakeholder chapter was first included by the OECD secretariat, then withdrawn on the insistence of the Ad Hoc Task Force, before a watered-down stakeholder chapter was inserted, following threats from the Austrian government to veto the principles. Part of the cost for securing a stakeholder chapter was that two chapters were dedicated to shareholder interests – the rights of shareholders and the equitable treatment of shareholders. Those forces connected to the outsider model and the institutional investor community were therefore more influential in determining the content of the principles than the union movement, which suffered a notable defeat in not having a chapter included on the behaviour and conduct of CEOs, although general guidelines on remuneration were included. Ultimately, while shareholder interests and the outside investor model have had the biggest single influence on the form the principles have taken, the inclusion of a stakeholder chapter and the acknowledgement of blockholder rights have meant that concessions are made to insider models. For example, an active participatory role for stakeholders and workers on supervisory boards cannot be automatically condemned as bad practice through the application of the principles in assessment exercises. In this sense, the principles remain eclectic, generic and ambiguous. They endorse and legitimate stakeholder practices, without actually promoting them, or obligating Anglo-American governments to adopt. The way in which the principles are written also makes it very difficult for them to be used to promote the Anglo-American model in places where this model does not already exist. The principles are intended and designed to be sufficiently broad, or ambiguous, to avoid suffocating national cultures, traditions and preferences. As Jacqueline Best has pointed out (Best 2005), 'ambiguity' can provide political space for domestic actors to manoeuvre and interpret commonly agreed standards, resulting in a degree of intersubjective flexibility as to how international principles are interpreted.

The World Bank and the Reports on the Observance of Standards and Codes Process

The extent to which the OECD principles are reflected in practice in particular national jurisdictions is assessed by a World Bank team, which publishes reports known as ROSCs (Reports on the

Observance of Standards and Codes). The World Bank began publishing individual country reports on the extent to which the OECD's corporate governance principles were embodied in different jurisdictions, from 2000 onwards, at a rate of about ten a year (IMF / World Bank 2005). For Susanne Soederberg, the OECD's principles place greater emphasis on shareholder value than other types of corporate governance, with the assessment of the principles through the ROSC process potentially acting as a catalyst for capital flight and investment strikes if the principles are not complied with (Soederberg 2003: 13). However, there is little evidence that private investors or financial markets have been using the ROSC reports in any systematic fashion to inform their investment decisions (IMF / World Bank 2005).

World Bank officials have enjoyed some degree of autonomy in interpreting the task of producing ROSCs, in the form of a 'learning by doing' exercise. There has been a shift away from trying to use ROSCs to inform investors and to facilitate 'market discipline', as envisaged by G-7 finance ministries and central banks after the Asian financial crisis. Instead, the reports are seen as catalysts for reform in assessed countries through an iterative and reciprocal policy dialogue. In interpreting how the ROSC should operate, World Bank officials decided that reports should act as a development tool to develop institutions, capital markets, and growth in accordance with the overall macro mission of the organization. As a consequence, development has come to trump financial stability considerations as a rationale for corporate governance ROSCs.

The ROSCs themselves have become progressively longer and now contain more qualitative policy recommendations and advice, as countries with less expertise and technical capacity have entered into the process. Originally, it was envisaged that ROSCs would be short and pithy, written with potential investors in mind, but they now adopt a more qualitative tone, having evolved from an evaluative diagnostic tool that documented existing practice to a prescriptive remedial tool that also suggests possible reforms. Market participants have actively voiced a preference for shorter reports, including a scorecard-style rating, because this could more easily be factored into risk management models (IMF / World Bank 2005). Quantitative measures of compliance and annual updates as demanded by market participants have not been embraced by World Bank staff. Bank staff have come to recognize the merits of the iterative process used to compile qualitative reports, as the starting point for a longer policy dialogue (IMF / World Bank, 2005). Consequently, World Bank staff have largely resisted pressure from market actors and institutional investors, while developing a rather different purpose for the corporate governance ROSC than that envisaged by transparency advocates following the Asian financial crisis.

The ROSCs have come to operate as a mutual learning device, for both assessed countries and assessors, rather than a disciplinary tool of enforcement. The procedures and power relations represented by the ROSC process are more consensual and reciprocal than many expected. For example ROSCs are voluntary, host authorities retain a power of veto over the publication of the final report, and they are not part of formal World Bank conditionality. Prior to formal publication of their assessment reports, Bank staff need to attain the approval of the host authority and a round of negotiation or exchange of views usually precedes the publication of a ROSC. The publication of corporate governance ROSCs remains constant at around 80 per cent (IMF / World Bank 2005; Nenova 2005) and most published ROSCs retain a critical edge, even if their production is a great deal more consensual than most critics would allege.

In effect, the ROSC process takes the form of a voluntary health check, based on dialogue and mutual exchanges, in which both the assessed and the assessors seek to obtain information and other gains, while using the contents of the detailed report for their own distinct purposes. Certain national regulators will attempt to use the ROSC reports to empower themselves *vis-à-vis* recalcitrant firms that may be attempting to evade regulation, or legislators who may be seeking to water down corporate governance provision or restrict budgets. In this respect, the World Bank's ROSC team can become the champion for the local securities commission in particular jurisdictions; such commissions are sometimes under-resourced, but they are also often sympathetic to the objective of enhancing the corporate governance and regulatory framework.

Conclusion

The argument that the OECD's principles of corporate governance promote convergence toward an Anglo-American model of corporate governance is overstated. The OECD and the World Bank have treated the principles as a tool for mutual, reciprocal and pragmatic policy dialogue between multiple stakeholders to facilitate progressive learning, rather than as a tool of disciplinary enforcement. The principles actually preserve some degree of domestic policy space. The consequence of this is that the principles are most likely to result in the introduction of some very selective and limited features of Anglo-American corporate governance, creating hybrid systems, rather than a process of outright convergence.

References

Best, J. (2005). *The Limits of Transparency: Ambiguity and the History of International Finance*. Ithaca: Cornell University Press.

Cioffi, J. (2003). 'Expansive Retrenchment: The Regulatory Politics of Corporate Governance Reform and the Foundations of Finance Capitalism'. Paper presented at the annual meeting of the American Political Science Association, Philadelphia, PA, 27 August.

Coffee, J. (2002). 'Racing towards the Top? The Impact of Cross Listings and Stock Market Competition on International Corporate Governance'. *Columbia Law Review* 102(7): 1757.

Gourevitch, P., and J. Shinn (2005). *Political Power and Corporate Control: The New Global Politics of Corporate Governance*. Princeton: Princeton University Press.

IMF / World Bank (2005). *The Standards and Codes Initiative – Is it Effective? And How Can It Be Improved?* Washington, DC: IMF / World Bank.

Jesover, F., and G. Kirkpatrick (2005). 'The Revised OECD Principles of Corporate Governance and their Relevance to non-OECD Countries'. *Corporate Governance* 13(2): 127–36.

Kirkpatrick, G. (2009). 'The Corporate Governance Lessons from the Financial Crisis'. *Financial Market Trends*, Vol. I. Paris: OECD.

Nenova, T. (2005). 'A Corporate Governance Agenda for Developing Countries'. *Contaduría y Administración* 217.

OECD (2004). 'OECD Principles of Corporate Governance'. Paris: OECD.

Overbeek, H., B. van Apeldoorn et al., eds. (2007). *The Transnational Political Economy of Corporate Governance Regulation*. London and New York: Routledge.

Perry, J., and A. Nölke (2006). 'The Political Economy of International Accounting Standards'. *Review of International Political Economy* 13(4): 559–86.

Rosser, A. (2008). 'The Political Economy of Financial Reform since the Asian Financial Crisis: The Case of Corporate Governance'. *Power and Politics after Financial Crises: Rethinking Foreign Opportunism in Emerging Markets*, ed. J. Robertson. London: Palgrave.

Sabel, C. F. (2004). 'Beyond Principal–Agent Governance: Experimentalist Organizations, Learning and Accountability'. *De staat van de democratie: democratie voorbij de staat*, ed. E. Engelen and M. S. D. Ho. Amsterdam: Amsterdam University Press.

Simmons, B. (2001). 'The International Politics of Harmonization: The Case of Capital Market Regulation'. *International Organization* 55(3): 589–620.

Soederberg, S. (2003). 'The Promotion of "Anglo-American" Corporate Governance in the Global South: Who Benefits from the New International Standard?' *Third World Quarterly* 24(1): 7–27.

35

Global Reporting Initiative
Halina Szejnwald Brown

Introduction

The Global Reporting Initiative (GRI) is the best-known set of guidelines for producing voluntary sustainability reports worldwide. GRI was created in 1999 by two institutional entrepreneurs connected to two nongovernmental organizations (NGOs) in Boston through an alliance of multinational companies, the financial sector, civil society organizations, organized labour, international consultancies, academics, environmental organizations and others (but not governments).

Despite the limited resources, visibility and political power of its founders, GRI has been remarkably successful, judging by the *rate of uptake* (by 2007 over 1,000 companies and other organizations in sixty-five countries structured their sustainability reports along the GRI guidelines), *comprehensiveness* (three categories of impacts are reported: environmental, social and economic), *productivity* (by 2009 three successive versions of the Guidelines and fifteen sector-specific supplements), *visibility* (its annual meetings feature royalty, heads of international governmental and non-governmental organizations and global business), *prestige* (for example, the formal partnership with the United Nations Environment Programme (UNEP)) and *reputation* (Brown, de Jong and Lessidrenska 2009; Brown, de Jong and Levy 2009).

Despite these successes, GRI has not reached its goal of becoming a standard and effective source of information about firms' social and environmental performance. Competing standards abound, and key stakeholders like institutional investors and NGOs have largely not relied upon GRI reports to push firms for better performance. These shortcomings demonstrate the limitations of information-based multistakeholder governance.

History and Goals

GRI emerged on the crest of the debate during the 1990s over corporate social responsibility (CSR), the appropriate roles for the business, government and civil society in the sustainability transition, and private forms of governance (John 1994; White 1999; Zadek 2001; Waddock 2004). GRI was until 2002 part of Ceres, a CSR network, whose member companies voluntarily adopted codes of conduct (Ceres Principles) and committed to voluntary performance reporting. Ceres, in turn, emerged in 1989 from the Social Investment Forum, which was founded in 1982. Through these historical ties, and the individuals and organizations who initially built it, GRI was also a descendant of social movements of the 1970s and 1980s.

GRI's explicit goal was to harmonize the numerous environmental and sustainability reporting systems used at the time, and to create free access to standardized, comparable and consistent information about corporate performance. Working within existing institutions and power relations, GRI's template was the US Financial Accounting Standards Board (FASB), which GRI expanded in reach (global), scope (social, economic and environmental performance indicators), flexibility (descriptive and quantitative indicators) and stakeholder base (highly diverse and international). The case for enlisting the support and participation of diverse actors was framed as 'win–win'. Specifically, it sought to benefit each stakeholder by producing efficiency gains (one set of guidelines, one report, information in the form that could be benchmarked and cross-compared), by empowering the users of reports to hold companies accountable for their performance and claims, and by creating an opportunity to influence an emerging influential set of rules. Modelling GRI on the familiar financial reporting system reduced uncertainty, increased legitimacy, and appealed to the accounting and consulting sectors as a potential new business opportunity (Brown, de Jong and Lessidrenska 2009).

In addition to these instrumental goals, the GRI institutional entrepreneurs (Maguire, Hardy et al. 2004; Levy and Scully 2007) also envisioned creating an influential global platform for broadly based discussion on sustainability performance and expected behavioural norms. This vision grew out of two widely shared, but largely untested, assumptions: (1) information and discourse mobilize civil society and the financial sector to demand corporate accountability, and as such are an instrument of private regulation; and (2) multistakeholder partnerships are an effective new form of collaborative governance for sustainability. The information-based approach to regulation offered a much sought-after supplement to the 'command-and-control' and market-based environmental policies of the 1970s, 1980s, and 1990s (Florini 1998; Tietenberg and Wheeler 1998; Graham 2002). The idea of partnership-based governance was increasingly promoted during the 1990s by the policy, academic and global business communities alike. (e.g. UN Global Compact; Ceres Principles; Forest

Stewardship Council) (Reinicke 1998; Reinicke and Deng 2000; Glasbergen and Groenenberg 2001; Ottaway 2001; Biermann 2007).

In short, working within existing structures and power relations the GRI founders aspired to build a new global institution for promoting sustainable behaviours by companies and other organizations worldwide (Brown, de Jong, and Lessidrenska 2009).

Structure and Activities of GRI as an Institution

The GRI Secretariat is a lean organization located in Amsterdam. Together with the Board of Directors and the 'legislative' Stakeholder Council, it develops policies and oversees various working groups, including the Technical Advisory Council. There is also a group of Organizational Stakeholders, with an unlimited membership, that is the platform for multistakeholder participation. Funding has been one of the GRI's persistent problems. Its strategic exclusion of governments precluded access to public funding, and after initial foundation support, GRI has become dependent on users' fees and its own fund-raising efforts among the best-resourced supporters.

Figure 35.1 depicts the lifecycle of reporting under GRI (Brown, de Jong and Levy 2009). It highlights the feedback loops between the three stages as well as links with other CSR activities; the activities

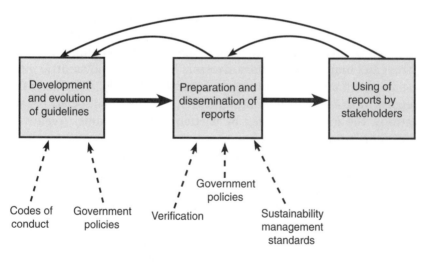

Figure 35.1   GRI reporting lifecycle.

and actors in this 'organizational field' comprise *the institution of GRI* (Powell and DiMaggio 1991; Scott 1991, 1995). Development of the Guidelines has been a very successful participatory process (over 4,000 individuals and organizations representing 60 countries have participated during the first decade), though it never attracted more than a handful of small to medium-size companies (SMEs). Participation by organized labour and NGOs has been steadily declining since the mid-2000s. Since the first 2001 version of the Guidelines, numerous innovations have been introduced, such as sector-specific Supplements and country-specific Annexes, emphasizing 'materiality' (addressing the stakeholders' principal concerns) and others. The number of reporters who follow the Guidelines precisely ('in accordance') and more loosely (mostly large multinational organizations from Europe, the US and Japan) levelled off around 2007 as that market became saturated. Since then, GRI's slower growth occurred mostly in Brazil, South Africa, Australia and new EU member states. After 2007 the Secretariat has also invigorated its outreach to SMEs.

GRI has created a lively market for international CSR consultancies and accounting firms who prepare and independently verify the reports (e.g. SustainAbility, AccountAbility, KPMG, PwC, Ernst &Young and Deloitte&Touche, members of the CSR Network, and others). Some leading international consultancies have also sought to stabilize this market by developing standards for verification and stakeholder engagement (e.g. AA 1000, AA 1010 or ISEA 3000).

The use of GRI reports by their intended audiences has been, however, very low. The shareholder activist organizations and socially responsible investors (SRI) treat GRI reports as a supplemental rather than a principal source of their research and strategizing, while Wall Street and major institutional investors have so far shown little interest in non-financial performance criteria. Similarly, the use of GRI reports by NGOs, consumer organizations, labour, civil society organizations, the media and even by participating companies (regarding the competition) has been low.

The key problem is that the information in GRI reports does not meet the very specific but diverse needs of its potential audiences (from issue-specific social activists to risk assessors among the investment community, and so on). Despite the efforts at standardization, GRI data – partly numerical and partly descriptive – have limited usefulness for benchmarking and cross-comparing performance on most criteria (Kolk 2004; O'Dwyer and Owen 2005; Daub 2007). Additionally, the uneven quality of reports and their visible selectivity as to what issues they address deter many potential users.

In short, GRI has not delivered on the promises of harmonization, standardization, efficiency gains and empowerment. Most companies claim to issue GRI reports as a form of reputation management, brand protection and sustainability management, the latter including various formal standards and accreditation procedures (e.g. EMAS, SA 8000, ISO 14,001 and many others, national and international) (Palenberg, Reinicke et al. 2006).

Table 35.1 summarizes GRI's organizational field: its activities and key actors. Three observations emerge. First, there is a strong overlap of actors participating in various areas. Second, the heaviest activity occurs at the supply end of the GRI reporting lifecycle, with very little at the user-end. Third, the most active and influential actors (not counting the GRI Secretariat) are large multinationals, leading accountancies and international consultancies, followed by UNEP and idea entrepreneurs. The latter term denotes individuals who identify and frame problems and propose solutions. Idea entrepreneurs – who mostly represent international CSR consultancies and accounting firms, large multinational corporations and banks, and UNEP – are highly influential in setting the agenda, building legitimacy for ideas, and influencing policy debates.

Collectively, these leading actors fill the ranks of GRI Organizational Stakeholders and multistakeholder working groups, form coalitions, enter into partnerships with each other and with national governments and UNEP, publish influential joint reports, and influence policy debates relative to CSR and accountability. Through engagement in multiple activities in the organizational field, they frame the debate over what matters most and what should therefore be reported, and influence the outcome of any emerging consensus.

Impacts

GRI has been a successful institutionalization process by several measures. It has greatly contributed to the popularization of the concept of social impact indicators and materiality. It helped solidify sustainability reporting as a taken-for-granted standard business practice, and led to the emergence of a thriving industry around it. GRI has institutionalized sustainability reporting as an expected behavioural norm, created a language in which it should be conducted (in particular, the category of social impacts), and criteria by which such reports and the underlying process should be judged. It has also inspired a heated policy debate over whether such reporting should be mandated through regulations. GRI's signature inclusive multistakeholder process for designing the Guidelines, and for obtaining external input in preparing sustainability reports, has become a template for organizations and partnerships worldwide for creating a

Table 35.1 Actors and their activities in the GRI organizational field

ACTIVITIES

Actors	Guidelines development	Reporting	Sustainability management	Report verification	Standards for verification	Use of reports
GRI Secretariat	**	**	*	**	**	
Large MNCs	**	**	**	*		
Accountancies & international consultancies	**	**	**	**	**	
Idea entrepreneurs	**				**	
Multilateral org: UNEP	**				**	
International business associations	*					
Investors & capital markets	*					*
International activist organizations	*?					*?
National/local activist organizations	*?					
Governments						
Organized labour						
SMEs						

** Signifies high involvement of an actor in an activity;
* Signifies one of the following: moderate/low involvement of the entire group or high/moderate involvement by only some members of the group;
*? Signifies moderate/low activity that seems to be declining.

discussion platform on 'what issues really matter' and for reaching out to stakeholders.

But so far, instead of unification of the social reporting field around a single set of standards, GRI has added to the fierce competition among the existing reporting frameworks; it has not resulted in the generation of data that are of high and consistent quality and that can be easily compared across companies; and has not delivered the promised efficiency gains to the many potential users of reports. Nor has it stimulated the emergence of a single community of financial, labour, civil rights, environmental or consumer activists around these reports.

Conclusions

GRI's contribution to strengthening new approaches to governance is open to question. Its emergent institutional logic is primarily that of a *tool for sustainability, reputation and brand management by companies.* This logic leaves out the central element of its founding vision: empowering users of GRI reports to become a nascent movement toward collaborative multistakeholder global governance. The new institution instead reflects GRI's current dominant constituency: large global companies and financial institutions and international business management consultancies.

The GRI case highlights the importance of economic structures and resources in shaping emerging institutions, and illustrates how the process of institutionalization tends to reproduce the existing power relations (Brown, de Jong and Levy 2009; Levy, Brown et al. 2010). GRI demonstrates the need for, and usefulness of, providing an independent platform to publicly debate the issues central to a wide range of stakeholders. But it also exposes the inherent paradox of maintaining such an independent platform: its independence derives from inclusiveness, broad participation and the absence of government mandates, but without public financing the platform becomes dominated by its most influential constituents.

The GRI shows the limits of standardized information disclosure as an instrument for mobilizing action through markets and political channels. It therefore reveals the limitations of voluntary transparency and multistakeholder collaboration as an instrument for effective institutionalized forms of governance.

References

Biermann, F. (2007). 'Earth Systems Governance as a Cross-cutting Theme of Global Change Research'. *Global Environmental Change* 17(3–4: August–October): 326–37.

Brown, H., M. de Jong, and D. Levy (2009). 'Building Institutions Based on Information Disclosure: Lessons from GRI's Sustainability Reporting'. *Journal of Cleaner Production* 17(4): 571–80.

Brown, H. S., M. de Jong, and T. Lessidrenska (2009). 'The Rise of Global Reporting Initiative (GRI) as a Case of Institutional Entrepreneurship'. *Environmental Politics* 18(2): 182–200.

Daub, C.-H. (2007). 'Assessing the Quality of Sustainability Reporting: An Alternative Methodological Approach'. *Journal of Cleaner Production* 15(1): 75–85.

Florini, A. M. (1998). 'End of Secrecy'. *Foreign Policy* 111(Summer): 50–63.

Glasbergen, P., and R. Groenenberg (2001). 'Environmental Partnerships in Sustainable Energy'. *European Environment* 11(1): 1–13.

Graham, M. (2002). *Democracy by Disclosure: The Rise of Technopopulism.* Washington, DC: Brookings/Governance Institute.

John, D. (1994). *Civic Environmentalism: Alternatives to Regulation in States and Communities.* Washington, DC: Congressional Quarterly Press.

Kolk, A. (2004). More than Words? An Analysis of Sustainability Reports. *New Academy Review* 3(3): 59–75.

Levy, D., H. S. Brown et al. (2010). 'The Contested Politics of Corporate Governance: The Case of the Global Reporting Initiative'. *Business and Society* 49(1: March): 88–115.

Levy, D., and M. Scully (2007). 'The Institutional Entrepreneur as Modern Prince: The Strategic Face of Power in Contested Fields'. *Organization Studies* 28: 971–91.

Maguire, S., C. Hardy et al. (2004). 'Institutional Entrepreneurship in Emerging Fields: HIV/AIDS Treatment Advocacy in Canada'. *Academy of Management Journal* 47(5): 657–79.

O'Dwyer, B., and D. L. Owen (2005). 'Assurance Statement Practice in Environmental, Social and Sustainability Reporting: A Critical Evaluation'. *The British Accounting Review* 37(2): 205–29.

Ottaway, M. (2001). 'Corporatism Goes Global: International Organizations, Nongovernmental Organizations Networks, and Transnational Business. *Global Governance* 7(3): 265–92.

Palenberg, M., W. Reinicke et al. (2006). 'Trends in Non-Financial Reporting'. Paper Prepared for the United Nations Environment Programmes, Division of Technology, Industry and Economics (DTIE), November 2006. Berlin, Germany: Global Public Policy Institute. Available at www.gppi.net.

Powell, W. W., and P. J. DiMaggio (1991). *The New Institutionalism in Organizational Analysis.* Chicago: University of Chicago Press.

Reinicke, W. H. (1998). *Global Public Policy: Governing without Government?* Washington, DC: Brooking Institution Press.

Reinicke, W. H., and F. Deng (2000). *Critical Choices: The United Nations, Networks, and the Future of Global Governance.* Ottawa: International Development Research Centre.

Scott, W. R. (1991). 'Unpacking Institutional Arguments'. *The New Institutionalism in Organizational Analysis,* ed. W. W. Powell and P. J. DiMaggio. Chicago: University of Chicago Press.

Scott, W. R. (1995). *Institutions and Organizations*. London: Sage.

Tietenberg, T., and D. Wheeler (1998). 'Empowering the Community: Information Strategies for Pollution Control'. Paper presented at the Frontiers of Environmental Economics Conference, Arlie House, Virginia, 23–25 October.

White, A. L. (1999). 'Sustainability and the Accountable Corporation'. *Environment* 41(8): 3–43.

Zadek, S. (2001). *The Civil Corporation: The New Economy of Corporate Citizenship*. London: Earthscan Publications.

36

International Organization for Standardization
Jonathan Koppell

The International Organization for Standardization (typically referred to as ISO) is the most widely recognized standard-setting body in the world. Its standards are employed by a wide variety of industries and are commonly incorporated into domestic law and international agreements. In recent years, ISO has expanded the range of issues covered by its standards from more technical matters – product specifications, engineering requirements, terminology, etc. – to process concerns. These include the ISO 9000 series of standards that deals with 'quality management systems', a broad category covering everything from record-keeping to production-monitoring. The ISO 14000 series of standards concerns 'environmental management systems', codifying the procedures to be employed by firms to monitor and calculate the environmental impact of operations. Such developments have raised the profile of the organization considerably.

Created in 1947, ISO is a membership organization based in Geneva, Switzerland, composed of the standards bodies from 161 countries. ISO itself is a nongovernmental, non-profit entity but most of the member bodies are either government agencies or have some formal connection with national governments. The United States representative, for example, is the American National Standards Institute (ANSI), a nongovernmental organization (NGO) designated to represent the US in ISO by the National Institute for Standards and Technology (NIST), a government agency; there are strong connections between ANSI and NIST. All of the ISO member bodies draw upon manufacturers, professional societies, government agencies, consumer groups and other interested parties (Murphy and Yates 2009). There is an ISO General Assembly made up of member representatives that meets annually to deal with overarching issues. It elects an intermediary Council that oversees the Secretariat and handles major issues, and also selects committees devoted to specific policy matters such as the implications of standards for developing countries and consumers.

The Standard-making Process

The permanent staff of ISO is only about 150 people, much smaller than most international organizations. This is possible because the Secretariat plays a largely supporting role in a standard-setting process that emphasizes member participation. Like other standard-setting bodies, ISO has adopted a process that brings together representatives of concerned industries to develop standards that will facilitate trade and make production more efficient. The work is done primarily through permanent 'technical committees' devoted to particular industries or technologies that develop new standards or revise existing standards. Any new standard must be approved by organization-wide bodies including the 'Technical Management Board'.

Like other standard-setting organizations, ISO has rules governing the interaction among participants and the steps required to move a proposed standard to completion (Brunsson and Jacobsson 2000). These procedures attempt to balance considerations of efficiency, representation and technical quality (Tamm Hallstrom 2000, 2004). ISO and the International Electrotechnical Commission (IEC), a similar but more focused standard-setting body, jointly issued *ISO/IEC Directives, part 1*, a document defining the appropriate procedures and expectations for participants in standard-setting. Participatory standard-setting processes are designed to allow for ongoing collaboration among interested parties (Brunsson and Jacobsson 2000). A good portion of the rule-making deliberation takes place outside the confines of working group meetings in the direct exchanges between members that occur, as a long-time IEC staff member says, 'outside the room'. The formality only governs part of the process – and some say it is the less important part (Koppell 2010).

ISO 'technical officers' ensure the consistency of work by offering advice to the leaders of each technical committee and monitoring their processes to maintain some level of consistency. The focus is on 'due process' rather than substance, although the permanent staff serves as a liaison between ISO and the working group and may communicate concerns regarding the output of the working group.

Implementation

Completed standards are sold by ISO, through its member bodies, for use by individual firms, trade associations and governmental bodies. Combined with dues paid by member bodies, the revenue generated from this operation makes ISO self-sustaining (like other standard-setting organizations). ISO does not have the power to compel adoption of its standards, even among its members. Nevertheless, the pressure to implement ISO standards can be multifaceted and intense (Murphy and Yates 2009). Trading partners will expect that these standards are followed, and any firm or nation that does not will face considerable obstacles in exporting and importing goods. Even ISO, which points out clearly that it does not 'regulate or legislate', acknowledges that 'although ISO standards are voluntary, they may become a market requirement' (ISO 2007). This reflects the value industry places on standardization and the reality that standards often *are* given force of domestic law by virtue of their incorporation into domestic and international legal frameworks.

Market pressure

All standard-setting organizations rely upon the demands of market participants to make standard adoption and implementation worthwhile (Coglianese 2000; Nye and Donahue 2000). Complying with the international standards makes your firm and the products you offer more attractive to customers and investors. Perhaps more importantly, failure to comply with ISO rules puts your firm at a disadvantage relative to your competitors. For example, standards laid out in ISO 9635–2:2006 specify construction and performance requirements and test methods for isolating valves, intended for operation in irrigation systems. Valves that do not meet this standard are not likely to sell, and irrigation systems that do not accept such valves will similarly have limited appeal. This dynamic renders all market participants *de facto* enforcement agents because the costs associated with buying a non-compliant product are significant (Ahrne and Brunsson 2006). If a manufacturer uses a component that does not meet an ISO standard, the end product could be worthless. Thus consumers of components and associations of producers are motivated to ensure that the standards are adopted and met by their members of their association. Socially oriented market-based strategies (e.g., Forest Stewardship Council) that are receiving more attention of late are essentially taking ISO's long-standing approach, harnessing market forces to compel adherence with standards related to environmental protection, labour standards, food production, etc. (Cashore, Auld et al. 2004).

Legal pressure

The market-driven 'soft law' aspect of ISO standards implementation is often emphasized, but the degree to which ISO standards are also integrated into 'hard law', both domestic and international statutes, should not be overlooked. ISO standards are adopted in jurisdictions around the world to fill out building codes, environmental regulations, safety requirements and a host of other legal and regulatory regimes. In such cases, compliance with ISO standards is no more voluntary than any other legal requirement.

More interesting is the way ISO and other international standards are integrated into formal international agreements. International rule-making bodies essentially leverage existing treaties, particularly those that are backed by meaningful sanctioning authority, to put more force behind a set of rules. Most prominently, this approach is centred on the World Trade Organization (WTO), a centralized body created to oversee the negotiation and implementation of multilateral and bilateral trade agreements. A nation found to have violated an existing bilateral or multilateral trade agreement exposes itself to WTO-approved sanctions by the aggrieved nation (Shaffer 2005; Zweifel 2006). This arrangement provides real bite and makes the presumptive legitimacy of standards very important. The Agreement on Technical Barriers to Trade, for example, makes reference to international standards in its rules for adjudicating conflicts. Standards produced in line with the WTO's requirements (including those promulgated by ISO, IEC and others) are presumed to be legitimate national requirements and thus not violations of free-trade agreements.

Cooperation and Competition

The 'piggybacking' approach to implementation links ISO to organizations like the WTO, but stops short of joint action. However, ISO often collaborates with other standard-setting bodies, in particular the IEC and the International Telecommunications Union (ITU). In several areas, these organizations have avoided duplicative efforts by forming joint committees that work on standards for simultaneous adoption by two or three international organizations. The IEC is focused on electrical and mechanical devices and technology. Founded in 1906 by private electrical societies from industrial nations around the world, the IEC continues to be relevant and successful in preparing international standards and assessing the extent to which its members conform to these norms. In its organizational structure and approach to rule-making, IEC closely resembles ISO; its standard-setting process is designed to allow participants to work toward a mutually acceptable solution that can, in turn, be approved by the Standardization Management Board. This makes cooperation in areas of obvious overlap relatively easy from a procedural point of view.

The Joint Technical Committee (JTC) brings ISO and the IEC (and, in some cases, the ITU) together to tackle information technology issues. Within the single JTC, there are about twenty working groups organized around more specific areas such as 'documents description and processing languages', 'software and systems engineering' and 'biometrics' (JTC 1 2008). This collaboration is far preferable to competitive independent rule-making, which representatives of all organizations regard in negative terms (Koppell 2010). In some cases, ISO will simply designate another body's rule-making group an ISO technical committee. For example, the Unicode Consortium, another standard-setting body that is focused on representation of characters in computer code, integrates its work in a collaborative effort that brings it together with ISO and IEC under the umbrella of the JTC (UC 2007).

These cooperative efforts underscore a distinctive feature of the international standards arena. The very organizations that cooperate on some projects remain competitors in other spaces. All the standard-setting bodies deny they are competitors, and yet in conversation they will invariably stress the advantages they offer over their rivals (Koppell 2010). The IEC and ITU, for example, have emphasized initiatives to reduce the average production time for standards to better meet market needs. The IEC established an electronic working environment to help experts around the world collaborate more quickly and efficiently in the development of standards. As noted earlier, the business model of these organizations requires the production and adoption of standards that are useful to industry. Without sales of standards, the organization will lose its revenue stream.

Issues

The increased attention ISO has received in the last few years has introduced a significant issue: public participation in the standard-making process. The initiation of the ISO 26000 process to create a standard regarding the social responsibility of corporations and other organizations shone a spotlight on ISO and the way in which it makes rules. This amplified concerns over public participation raised following the widespread adoption of ISO 14000 standards (Murphy and Yates 2009).

Critics argue that the standard-making process gives inordinate influence to companies and industries rather than the general public. As the standards produced by ISO technical committees are often integrated into law and international agreements, this raises a red flag. Although technical committees are open to a wide variety of participants, the practical demands of participation create barriers even in the face of formal opportunities. For one thing, many people do not understand the importance of ISO and other standard-setting bodies, let alone the mechanisms for participation (Ahrne and Brunsson 2006; Jacobsson and Sahlin-Anderson 2006). Moreover, participating requires significant resources to remain informed, travel to relevant meetings and carry out research that is persuasive to other members. Only one non-commercial group is a regular participant in ISO technical committees: Consumers International (CI). Focusing on issues related to consumer safety and health, CI devotes resources in order to participate on an even playing field with corporate representatives but the organization must carefully choose which areas to prioritize.

The ISO 26000 initiative inflamed the issue because social responsibility is an accessible topic of broad interest. Ultimately, ISO created a far more accessible process to develop this standard – with more translations, more meetings, more documentation – in response to the high level of interest. As people become more aware of the importance of ISO standards in other arenas, however, calls for similar adjustments will likely proliferate.

References

Ahrne, G., and N. Brunsson (2006). 'Organizing the World.' *Transnational Governance: Institutional Dynamics of Regulation*, ed. M.-L. Djelic and K. Sahlin-Andersson. New York: Cambridge University Press.

Brunsson, N., and B. Jacobsson (2000). *A World of Standards*. Oxford and New York: Oxford University Press.

Cashore, B. W., G. Auld et al. (2004). *Governing through Markets: Forest Certification and the Emergence of Non-State Authority*. New Haven: Yale University Press.

Coglianese, C. (2000). 'Globalization and the Design of International Institutions'. *Governance in a Globalizing World*, ed. J. N. J. Donahue. Washington, DC: Brooking Institution Press.

ISO (2007). 'Overview of the ISO System'. Available from www.iso.ch/iso/en/aboutiso/introduction/index.html#one (accessed 19 July 2007).

Jacobsson, B., and K. Sahlin-Andersson (2006). 'Dynamics of Soft Regulation'. *Transnational Governance: Institutional Dynamics of Regulation*, ed. M.-L. Djelic and K. Sahlin-Andersson. New York: Cambridge University Press.

JTC 1 (2008). *ISO/IEC JTC 001: Information Technology*. IEC/ISO Joint Technical Committee.

Koppell, J. G. S. (2010). *World Rule: Accountability, Legitimacy and the Design of Global Governance*. Chicago: University of Chicago Press.

Murphy, C., and J. Yates (2009). *The International Organization for Standardization (ISO): Global Governance through Voluntary Consensus*. London and New York: Routledge.

Nye, J. S., and J. D. Donahue (2000). *Governance in a Globalizing World, Visions of Governance for the 21st Century*. Cambridge, MA and Washington, DC: Brookings Institution Press.

Shaffer, G. (2005). 'Power, Governance and the WTO: A Comparative Institutional Approach'. *Power in Global Governance*, ed. M. N. Barnett and R. Duvall. Cambridge and New York: Cambridge University Press.

Tamm Hallstrom, K. (2000). 'Organizing the Process of Standardization'. *A World of Standards*, ed. N. Brunsson and B. Jacobsson. Oxford and New York: Oxford University Press.

Tamm Hallstrom, K. (2004). *Organizing International Standardization: ISO and the IASC in Quest of Authority*: Cheltenham: Edward Elgar.

UC (2007). *The Unicode Standard 3.0*. Unicode Consortium 2005. Available from http://unicode.org/book/uc20ch1.html (accessed 21 February 2007).

Zweifel, T. D. (2006). *International Organizations & Democracy: Accountability, Politics, and Power*. Boulder: Lynne Rienner Publishers.

37

International Organization for Standardization 14001

Matthew Potoski and Elizabeth Elwakeil

The International Organization for Standardization (ISO) 14001 is a voluntary environmental programme that requires participating facilities to adopt an environmental management system and have it certified by third-party external auditors. In return, participating facilities can use their ISO 14001 certification to signal to their stakeholders that their environmental management practices are stringent, information that stakeholders would otherwise have difficulty obtaining credibly. Preliminary lessons on why facilities join ISO 14001 and whether it improves their environmental performance are starting to emerge from research in a variety of academic fields. ISO 14001 does help signal facilities' environmental activities and joining the programme appears to induce some environmental performance above what would otherwise have occurred, though both these effects have not been consistently found in the literature. The broad contours of the literature suggest that ISO 14001 is more likely to be effective where facilities are most in need of a credible signal – such as developing country facilities looking to export to environmentally demanding countries – where government regulations are more lax, and where third-party auditors are effective.

Background

ISO supplies product and process standards to commercial actors engaged in international trade and commerce (see chapter 36 in this volume for more details). Since its inception in the early twentieth century, the ISO has developed over 16,000 international standards in response to demands for standardized standards and processes. Its acronym, ISO, is no accident: 'Iso' is a Greek word meaning 'equal'. Starting in the 1990s, this governor has expanded its product menu to include management process standards, including quality management (ISO 9000), environmental management (ISO 14001) and, more recently, corporate social responsibility (ISO 26000). Our discussion will focus on ISO 14001, a voluntary programme that requires participating industrial facilities to adopt an environmental management system for their internal operations.

Voluntary programmes such as ISO 14001 are a fast-growing and important policy tool across countries, industries, and issue areas. Firms, governments, businesses and nongovernmental organizations (NGOs) have all created and participated in a diverse array of programmes. Voluntary programmes seek to create institutional incentives for participating actors (typically firms but also NGOs, or even governments) to adopt specific codes of conduct and practices beyond what is legally required of them. The expectation is that these codes and practices create positive social externalities, which are particularly needed in the developing world where governance deficits are all too often quite severe. The challenge is to motivate firms to incur private costs in the pursuit of a broader social good. Why would firms or any instrumental actor voluntarily join a programme that requires members to assume the costs of internalizing their negative externalities?

The benefit of affiliating with a voluntary programme's brand image is the primary payoff for firms to join the programme and produce the positive social externalities required by membership. Stakeholders may be willing to reward companies that produce positive externalities – consumers may pay a price premium for 'green' products or regulators may offer flexible regulatory enforcement for environmentally conscious production – but because so much of firms' activities is not observable to stakeholders, the latter need a credible signal to identify which firms deserve the awards. Membership in an effective voluntary programme identifies which firms are producing positive externalities, thereby allowing stakeholders the means to accordingly reward and punish them. Unfortunately, not all voluntary programmes are successful in this way; in some cases, firms that joined a particular voluntary programme produced no more positive externalities than those that did not join. Perhaps the most famous example of an unsuccessful programme is Responsible Care, the Chemical Manufacturers Association's voluntary programme from the early 1990s (King and Lenox 2000; see also chapter 42, 'Responsible Care', this volume).

How ISO 14001 Works

Successful voluntary programmes, those that induce members to produce positive social externalities, have two key features. First, they have a set of programme standards that clearly specify how members will produce positive externalities. Second, they have a monitoring and enforcement mechanism to ensure that participating firms are living up to their obligations as programme members. ISO 14001 has been a successful voluntary programme in the developed and developing world. Like Responsible Care, it requires participating firms to adopt an environmental management system, but where Responsible Care has a weak peer audit monitoring and enforcement mechanism, ISO 14001 requires more stringent third-party audit and verification to ensure participants are living up to their programme obligations.

ISO 14001's environmental management system (EMS) is quite extensive and expensive (Delmas 2002). An ISO 14001 calibre EMS is an organizational structure that enables facilities to manage their processes by identifying their environmental impacts, developing goals for environmental improvement and regulatory compliance, and establishing procedures and management responsibility for meeting them. Implementing such an EMS requires specialized training for staff, policy statements, articulation of goals and documentation of procedures, and allocation of resources (Coglianese and Nash 2001). An ISO 14001 EMS can cost up to $100,000 to set up, in addition to ongoing maintenance costs (Prakash and Potoski 2006). Rather than being based on outcomes or production technologies, the purpose of a systems-based standard is to ensure smooth and effective operation of processes and management within the firm. Therefore, while ISO 14001 requires firms to initiate an EMS system before certification can be granted, subsequent demonstration of improvement in compliance is not required; it is only the commitment to regulatory compliance that is needed for membership with ISO 14001. In this way, desirable outcomes are expected to follow from the implementation of appropriate internal mechanisms such as planning and reorganization that will help firms meet the environmental standards endorsed by ISO 14001 (Prakash and Potoski 2006). EMS programmes are also designed to enforce compliance with existing governmental regulations while encouraging firms to take steps above and beyond what is required of them by such laws. Firms' EMS programmes are subjected to periodic audits, which constitute the second institutional feature of ISO 14001: the monitoring and enforcement component.

Enforcement of firms' compliance is necessary to maintain the integrity of the ISO 14001 programme. Periodic external audits are the means by which ISO issues and renews certification to facilities. Audits are carried out by a panel of certified third-party auditors. Certification of auditors is obtained through specific accreditation boards which exist separately in each country and are recognized by ISO as proper authorities to certify auditors. Examples of auditor accreditation authorities include the American National Standards Institute and the United Kingdom Accreditation Service. Facilities of ISO 14001 members must undergo complete audits every three years as well as annual surveillance audits. To maintain certification, firms must successfully implement and maintain their EMS.

Impact

Judging by the number of participants, ISO 14001 has been an incredibly successful programme. Following years of exponential growth since its launch in 1994, as of December 2004 there were 188,815 certified facilities worldwide, including 7,682 in Africa and the Near East, 4,654 in Central and South America, 78,118 in Europe, 89,894 in Asia and 7,194 in North America (International Standards Organization 2008). Cross-national differences in ISO 14001 adoption rates stem from a number of factors, for example firms adopt ISO 14001 to signal their environmental activities in export markets and when their domestic markets have more experience with management-based standards, and firms are less likely to adopt ISO 14001 when their domestic regulatory environment is less flexible and more adversarial (Potoski and Prakash 2004a; Prakash and Potoski 2006).

ISO 14001 has been submitted to extensive scrutiny to determine whether firms in the programme produce positive externalities in the form of a cleaner environment or better compliance with government regulations. In the developed world, the results are somewhat mixed, but on balance suggest that ISO 14001 certification does lead to better pollution and regulatory compliance outcomes. The ISO 14001 literature is too vast to fully cover in a short chapter such as this, but some highlights are worth noting. For examples, Prakash and Potoski (2006) study around 3,000 facilities in the US and find that certification reduces air pollution emissions and improves compliance with government regulations. Other studies showing environmental improvement from ISO 14001 certification in the developed world include Chapple, Cooke et al. (2001) in the United Kingdom; Delmas (2002) in Japan and the European Union; Mori and Welch (2008) in Japan; and Hamschmidt and Dyllick (2001) in Switzerland. Conversely, Barta (2007) finds that ISO 14001 certification did not reduce pollution emissions among Canadian pulp and paper mills, and Boiral (2007) charges that ISO 14001 certification creates 'rational myths' within Canadian firms, which lead to empty organizational behaviours that have little impact on environmental outcomes. One explanation for these disparate findings is that the effect of ISO 14001 on environmental performance may depend on how firms manage their EMS (King, Lenox et al. 2005).

There has been less research on ISO 14001's effects in the developing world, perhaps due to the challenges of acquiring systematic data. Raines (2002) finds that, in developing countries, ISO 14001 certification leads to reductions in operating costs, and compliance is driven by genuine concern rather than profits. Dasgupta, Hettige et al. (2000) find that ISO 14001 improves Mexican facilities' compliance with government regulations. ISO 14001 certification has been shown to improve environmental performance in developing countries as diverse as Turkey (Turk 2009) and China (Fryxell, Lo et al. 2004). While the research on ISO 14001's performance in the developing world is thinner and less methodologically rigorous, there does appear to be some grounds for a cautiously optimistic assertion that ISO 14001 certification improves facilities' environmental performance and compliance with government regulations. These findings are encouraging because the developing world countries will play the key roles in solving many environmental problems, from global warming to fishery depletion, yet their regulatory governance institutions are all too often weak.

There is stronger and more consistent evidence for why facilities join ISO 14001. While not all studies explicitly frame the issue in stakeholder signalling terms, it is clear that external pressures are important in both the developed and developing world (e.g., Bansal and Hunter 2003; Christmann and Taylor 2006). Stakeholders in this sense can include government regulatory enforcement officials (Coglianese and Nash 2001; Kollman and Prakash 2002; Potoski and Prakash 2004a, 2004b), as well as trade partners, both domestic (King, Lenox et al. 2005; Delmas and Montiel 2009) and international (Prakash and Potoski 2006; Nishitani 2010). Overall, the research suggests that facilities are more likely to join ISO 14001 when their stakeholders have higher demand for positive environmental outcomes, are able to exert some influence or pressure on the facilities (such as through regulatory enforcement actions or purchasing decisions), and otherwise have difficulty accessing information about facilities' environmental impact.

Conclusion

ISO 14001 can play a positive role in national and transnational governance. By facilitating communication between facilities and their stakeholders, it can allow stakeholders that demand stronger environmental performance to reward facilities that adopt stringent environmental management processes. While research suggests its potential is not always fully realized, ISO 14001 can help improve environmental conditions in the developing world by improving the management practices and environmental outcomes of certified firms. ISO 14001 can also improve domestic and international trade by helping environmentally conscious purchasers identify which facilities have higher-standard environmental management practices.

References

Bansal, P., and T. Hunter (2003). 'Strategic Explanations for the Early Adoption of ISO 14001'. *Journal of Business Ethics* 46(3): 289–99.

Barta, P. (2007). 'ISO 14001 Certification and Environmental Performance in Quebec's Pulp and Paper Industry'. *Journal of Environmental Economics and Management* 53(3): 291–306.

Boiral, O. (2007). 'Corporate Greening through ISO 14001: A Rational Myth?' *Organization Science* 18(1): 127–46.

Chapple, W., A. Cooke et al. (2001). 'The Characteristics and Attributes of UK Firms Obtaining Accreditation to ISO 14001'. *Business Strategy and the Environment* 10(4): 238–44.

Christmann, P., and G. Taylor (2006). 'Firm Self-Regulation through International Certifiable Standards: Determinants of Symbolic versus Substantive Implementation'. *Journal of International Business Studies* 37: 863–78.

Coglianese, C., and J. Nash, eds. (2001). *Regulating from the Inside: Can Environmental Management Systems Achieve Policy Goals?* Washington, DC: Resources for the Future.

Dasgupta, S., H Hettige et al. (2000). 'What Improves Environmental Compliance? Evidence from Mexican Industry'. *Journal of Environmental Economics and Management* 39(1): 39–66.

Delmas, M. (2002). 'The Diffusion of Environmental Management Standards in Europe and in the United States: An Institutional Perspective'. *Policy Sciences* 35(1): 91–119.

Delmas, M., and I. Montiel (2009). 'Greening the Supply Chain: When is Customer Pressure Effective?' *Journal of Economics & Management Strategy* 18(1): 171–201.

Fryxell, G., C. W. H. Lo et al. (2004). 'Influence of Motivations for Seeking ISO 14001 Certification on Perceptions of EMS Effectiveness in China'. *Environmental Management* 33(2): 239–51.

Hamschmidt, J., and T. Dyllick (2001). 'ISO 14001: Profitable? Yes! But Is It Eco-Effective?' *Greener Management International* 34: 43–54.

International Organization for Standardization (2008). 'The ISO Survey – 2008'. Available at www.iso.org/iso/survey2008.pdf (accessed 26 April 2010).

King, A., and M. Lenox (2000). 'Industry Self-Regulation without Sanctions: The Chemical Industry's Responsible Care Program'. *Academy of Management Journal* 43(4): 698–716.

King, A., M. Lenox et al. (2005). 'The Strategic Use of Decentralized Institutions: Exploring Certification with the ISO 14001 Management Standard'. *Academy of Management Journal* 48(6): 1091–105.

Kollman, K., and A. Prakash (2002). 'EMS-based Regimes as Club Goods: Examining Variations in Firm-Level Responses to ISO 14001 and EMAS in U.K., U.S., and Germany'. *Policy Sciences* 35(1): 43–67.

Mori, Y., and E. W. Welch (2008). 'The ISO 14001 Environmental Management Standard in Japan: Results from a National Survey of Facilities in Four Industries'. *Journal of Environmental Planning and Management* 51(3): 421–45.

Nishitani, K. (2010). 'Demand for ISO 14001 Adoption in the Global Supply Chain: An Empirical Analysis Focusing on Environmentally Conscious Markets'. *Resource and Energy Economics* 32(3).

Potoski, M., and A. Prakash (2004a). 'Regulatory Convergence in Nongovernmental Regimes? Cross-National Variation in ISO 14001 Adoption'. *Journal of Politics* 24(3): 885–905.

Potoski, M., and A. Prakash (2004b). 'The Regulation Dilemma and US Environmental Governance'. *Public Administration Review* 64(2): 137–48.

Prakash, A., and M. Potoski (2006). *The Voluntary Environmentalists.* Cambridge: Cambridge University Press.

Raines, S. S. (2002). 'Implementing ISO 14001 – An International Survey Assessing the Benefits of Certification'. *Corporate Environmental Strategy* 9(4): 418–26.

Turk, A. M. (2009). 'The Benefits Associated with ISO 14001 Certification for Construction Firms: Turkish Case'. *Journal of Cleaner Production* 17(5): 559–69.

38

Kimberley Process
Carola Kantz

The Kimberley Process Certification Scheme (KPCS) is an international trade agreement created to curb trade in conflict diamonds. It is the first attempt to seriously address the issue of trafficking of natural commodities which also holds the private sector to account. It is an example of successful transnational governance, as it was negotiated in a multistakeholder initiative and now combines an intergovernmental regime with industry self-regulation. Despite some criticism, the Kimberley Process is considered by many to be a successful institution with strong compliance and enforcement mechanisms that serves as a role model for new regimes in the field.

History

The KPCS was created in 2002 to curb trade in conflict diamonds. Conflict diamonds are rough diamonds that combatants in civil wars sell in order to finance their military activities. Such diamonds have fuelled the civil wars in Angola, Sierra Leone and the Democratic Republic of Congo (DRC) (see e.g. Berdal and Malone 2000; Collier 2000). With the escalating atrocities in the civil wars of Angola and Sierra Leone, the international community took the first steps to curb the trade in conflict diamonds at the end of the 1990s. The United Nations Security Council imposed an embargo on all exports of rough diamonds which were not certified by the governments of Angola and Sierra Leone. As the UN sanctions proved inefficient, an international nongovernmental organization (NGO) campaign against conflict diamonds evolved (see Smillie 2004). The NGOs and the United Nations Security Council's Sanctions Committee on Angola, chaired by the Canadian Ambassador Robert Fowler, blamed the diamond industry and African government officials for facilitating the trade of conflict diamonds. The diamond industry, in particular, had earned notoriety for its secretive business operations (see Bernstein 1992; Kantz 2007). The lack of transparent and accountable standards in the industry facilitated the entry of conflict diamonds into the legal trade (Global Witness 1998).

The campaign against conflict diamonds put both the industry and African producer countries – especially those that produce 'conflict-free' diamonds such as Botswana, Namibia and South Africa – under pressure. In early 2000, South Africa invited interested governments, civil society groups, and representatives of the diamond industry to Kimberley, South Africa, to discuss the issue (Grant and Taylor 2004). In the following thirteen meetings, the participants devised an international certification scheme for rough diamonds. The negotiations of the KPCS took place as a multistakeholder initiative. Industry representatives and NGOs had the same participation rights as government officials. The original agreement of the KPCS was launched in January 2003. Its provisions, however, have been significantly strengthened since then.

Governance

The KPCS was designed to take into account both the distinct position of the diamond industry and the peculiarity of the diamond trade. The KPCS is an intergovernmental regime, but is complemented by industry self-regulation, the System of Warranties (SoW).

The intergovernmental regime consists of a set of politically binding common standards, enacted by each state through its own national legislation (Wright 2004). The standards determine how member states handle the trade in rough diamonds and establish cooperation, transparency, and monitoring processes among members. The diamond industry is represented through the World Diamond Council, an industry body specifically created for this purpose. Civil society is represented by Global Witness and Partnership Africa Canada.

The SoW was established by the diamond industry to address one significant loophole of the KPCS, as the intergovernmental regime is only concerned with trade in rough diamonds (Kantz 2007). The industry self-regulation addresses the issue by regulating trade in cut and polished stones as well.

The KPCS has acquired a global reach. As of January 2010, forty-eight countries and the European Community participate. Unlike many voluntary regimes, the monitoring, enforcement and sanctions mechanisms are very developed in the KPCS. Initially, countries like Russia, China and Israel succeeded in resisting efforts to introduce independent monitoring (Smillie 2005). A coalition of governments, NGOs and representatives of the World Diamond Council were able to push for a voluntary monitoring process shortly after the KPCS was officially launched. In contrast to other voluntary regimes, such as the Forest Stewardship Council, compliance is not monitored by an independent body, but by a peer-review mechanism. Although the review is not mandatory, the participants exert considerable peer-pressure so that no government can avoid it in practice. The monitoring capacity of the scheme is significantly strengthened by the inclusion of NGOs and the industry as 'watchdogs'. The KPCS also has tough provisions on enforcement. The participants are only allowed to trade rough diamonds with each other (Schefer 2005). Since the participants account for approximately 99.8 per cent of the global production of rough diamonds, this creates a very strong incentive to become and remain a participant. Being expelled from the Kimberley Process means being cut off from the legal global diamond market. The compliance and enforcement mechanisms do not apply for the SoW, which is audited differently across the participating countries. Within the European Community, for instance, complying with the SoW is mandatory as the industry has to audit its compliance. Many other countries, however, consider the SoW as a voluntary addition to the KPCS with no special auditing requirements. Here, the NGOs fulfil a crucial watchdog role (Kantz 2008).

The KPCS also requires the governments to provide reliable production statistics so as to be able to detect smuggling and laundering. Enacting more transparency in the trade was one of the thorniest issues during the negotiations as many countries considered their statistics a state secret, and the diamond industry was initially very reluctant to provide data on their commercial secrets. The secretive approach was partly considered necessary due to the value of the commodity. During the negotiations to the KPCS, Russia, in particular, had blocked more ambitious disclosure requirements referring to its domestic legislation on diamond trade statistics as a state secret. Since 2005, however, KPCS participants have been able to make more and more of their trade statistics available. A window of opportunity opened in 2005 when Russia wanted to become chair of the KPCS. A coalition of NGOs and like-minded KPCS governments exerted pressure on Russia to commit the country to further disclosure (Kantz 2008). Considering that secrecy used to be a major component of the workings of the industry, the disclosure of trade statistics is a major breakthrough.

Impact

The civil wars in Angola, Sierra Leone and the DRC came to an end not through the Kimberley Process but by military operations. Nevertheless, the certification scheme has contributed to render peace more sustainable by depriving rebels of a vital revenue source. Due to the clandestine nature of the issue, it is as yet difficult to measure whether the Kimberley Process succeeded in keeping conflict diamonds out of the legal trade. According to official sources, 4 per cent of the world's diamond output stemmed from illegal sources in 2000. NGOs, however maintain that an estimated 15 per cent of the global output were conflict diamonds in the 1990s (Partnership Africa Canada 2006). The Kimberley Process can certainly take credit for having the percentage reduced to an estimated 1 per cent today. By restoring consumer confidence, the Kimberley Process has also helped to restore the legal diamond industry in Angola, the DRC and Sierra Leone, and, thus, contributed to the economic development of these countries.

Equally, the Kimberley Process has had a great impact on the diamond industry. As an industry that had been notorious for its opaque trading traditions, the Kimberley Process has been a huge leap toward more transparent business operations. Both the diamond industry and producer countries are now obliged to lay open their trade statistics and stockpiling. In 2007, for the first time, those statistics were published on the Kimberley Process website. Moreover, the culture of the diamond industry has changed significantly. Cooperating in the Kimberley Process introduced the notion of corporate social responsibility to the sector. The certification scheme has often been criticized for ignoring social and environmental issues in the upstream diamond industry. Hence a new initiative was created recently, the Diamond Development Initiative (DDI), in which the industry and NGOs have started to address these issues.

Moreover, considering that the Kimberley Process is not a legally binding regime, it has exerted significant pressure on non-compliant members. Early on, diamond experts had the suspicion that conflict diamonds from the DRC and Angola were being laundered in the neighbouring Republic of Congo. A review mission sent to Brazzaville in 2004 confirmed the suspicion and only one month later the country was suspended from the KPCS. Since this incident, several other countries, such as Venezuela and Côte d'Ivoire, have also been suspended.

Controversies

Despite its successes, the KPCS has generated some controversy. One of the greatest criticisms – the Kimberley Process being too weak and therefore not being able live up to its expectations – proved largely unfounded as the scheme was strengthened in the first years of operation. While the Kimberley Process has demonstrated that it can reduce the flow of conflict diamonds, it still suffers from a significant loophole. In order to regulate the commodity chain of diamonds effectively, three main sectors need to be addressed: mining, rough diamond trading, and cutting and polishing. The KPCS addresses international rough diamond trading and the SoW focuses on regulating cut and polished stones. One major issue, however, remains the domestic regulation of diamond producer countries. Given that it is an international trade scheme and given that it is voluntary, the Kimberley Process can only recommend best practices on the regulation of the domestic mining industry. However, internal controls for alluvial diamonds are not required. Thus, the Process is not able to effectively address domestic smuggling and laundering as recent examples in Brazil and Guyana have shown (Partnership Africa Canada 2006; Even-Zohar 2009).

Linked to the issue of patchy internal controls is the question of industry self-regulation. The auditing and sanctions mechanism of the SoW remains very controversial, as the requirements are up to the discretion of each participating government. As mentioned above, the European Community decided to adopt the most rigorous requirements for self-regulation, requiring regular audits by independent auditors of members of each self-regulating body. But many other countries lack rigorous guidelines for auditing. As for the sanctions mechanism, in theory, non-compliant companies are expelled from the leading industry bodies, the World Federation of Diamond Bourses and the International Diamond Manufacturers' Association. However, in practice, those rules have never been enforced.

The Kimberly Process is further criticized for ignoring social and environmental issues in the context of alluvial diamond mining (Even-Zohar 2009). In countries such as Sierra Leone, Angola, Guinea and the DRC, diamond mining is carried out by artisanal miners. Working outside the formal economy, they are often exposed to criminal predation, human rights abuses, environmental degradation and diseases such as HIV/Aids. While they produce as much as a billion dollars' worth of diamonds a year, most of the miners earn less than a dollar a day, thus living in absolute poverty. The Kimberley Process, however, being designed as an international trade regime, has little capacity to improve the livelihoods and working conditions of artisanal miners. Other initiatives, such as the DDI, were created for addressing these issues. What the Kimberley Process achieved was to raise global awareness.

Finally, as mentioned before, the Kimberley Process is a voluntary regime. Hence, the success of the KPCS is dependent on political will as – at the international level – it is not legally enforceable. The recent success of the certification scheme is due to great public attention, voluntary leadership of committed countries, and peer pressure among the participants to comply with the regulation. NGOs are vital for ensuring that the Kimberley Process lives up to its expectations. With public attention being diverted to other international crises, the Kimberley Process still needs to demonstrate its long-term effectiveness.

Conclusion

The Kimberley Process is an example of how transnational issues can be addressed by involving public and private actors in multistakeholder initiatives. Despite some criticism, the KPCS is now widely considered as a success. One of the reasons for its success has been its flexibility. As a politically binding regime, it started off with very soft requirements. Adopting a 'learning by doing' approach, the Process had the ability to make incremental enhancements whenever participants could achieve a new consensus on a specific issue. It now serves as a role model for other transnational governance initiatives regulating trade with natural commodities. For instance, the Extractive Industries Transparency Initiative (EITI) and the EU's Forest Law Enforcement, Governance and Trade Initiative (FLEGT) have reproduced some of the properties of the Kimberly Process.

References

Berdal, M., and D. M. Malone (2000). *Greed and Grievance: Economic Agendas in Civil Wars*. Boulder, CO: Lynne Rienner.

Bernstein, L. (1992). 'Opting Out of the Legal System: Extralegal Contractual Relations in the Diamond Industry'. *Journal of Legal Studies* 115: 21.

Collier, P. (2000). *Economic Causes of Civil Conflict and Their Implications for Policy*. Washington, DC: World Bank.

Even-Zohar, C. (2009). 'Ian Smillie quits Kimberley Process'. *Diamond Intelligence* 28 May 2009.

Global Witness (1998). *A Rough Trade: The Role of Companies and Government in the Angolan Conflict*. London: Global Witness.

Grant, A. J., and I. Taylor (2004). 'Global Governance and Conflict Diamonds: The Kimberley Process and the Quest for Clean Gems'. *The Round Table* 93 (375: July): 385–401.

Kantz, C. (2007). 'The Power of Socialization: Engaging the Diamond Industry in the Kimberley Process'. *Business and Politics* 9(3): Article 2.

Kantz, C. (2008). 'Precious Stones, Black Gold and the Extractive Industries: Accounting for the Institutional Design of Multi-Stakeholder Initiatives'. International Relations Department dissertation, London School of Economics.

Partnership Africa Canada (2006). *Killing Kimberley? Conflict Diamonds and Paper Tigers*. Ottawa: Partnership Africa Canada.

Schefer, K. N. (2005). 'Stopping Trade in Conflict Diamonds: Exploring the Trade and Human Rights Interface with the WTO Waiver for the Kimberley Process'. *Human Rights and International Trade*, ed. T. Cottier, J. Pauwelyn et al. Oxford: Oxford University Press.

Smillie, I. (2004). 'Climb Every Mountain: Civil Society and the Conflict Diamonds Campaign. *Fighting for Human Rights*, ed. P. Gready. London: Routledge.

Smillie, I. (2005). 'Lessons from the Kimberley Process'. *Profiting from Peace: Managing the Resource Dimensions of Civil War*, ed. K. Ballentine and H. Nitzschke. London: Lynne Rienner.

Wright, C. (2004). 'Tackling Conflict Diamonds: The Kimberley Process Certification Scheme'. *International Peacekeeping* 11(4): 697–708.

39

Marine Stewardship Council
Thomas Hale

Recent studies predict that overfishing will lead to the global collapse of fish species on which humans depend for food and livelihoods by 2048 (Worm, Barbier et al. 2007). This bleak outlook poses a serious concern for consumers, companies, and fishermen. The Marine Stewardship Council (MSC) is a private certification body that sets environmental sustainability standards for commercially harvested fish. Fisheries that meet the MSC criteria may sell their products under the MSC label, allowing customers to distinguish between sustainable and non-sustainable fish. In this way the MSC serves as a voluntary, market-based transnational regulatory mechanism. As of 2009, some 7 per cent of the world's edible fish sold commercially was certified under the programme, with a retail value of approximately $1.5 billion (MSC 2009).

Origin

The MSC enjoys a somewhat improbable parentage. It was founded, in 1997, by the multinational food giant Unilever and the global environmental organization World Wide Fund for Nature (WWF). The MSC has operated as an independent organization since 1999. WWF drew from its experience in creating the Forest Stewardship Council (FSC), a similar programme in the forest sector, to generate the basic structure and mission of the organization.

WWF pushed for the creation of the MSC largely due to the failure of the multilateral fishing governance regime. International regulation of fisheries dates at least to Ancient Rome (Allison 2001). Modern efforts, however, have centred around the UN Convention on the Law of the Sea (UNCLOS) and its related components, the FAO, and regional agreements. These latter bodies have perhaps the greatest impact on fisheries management; some are linked to the FAO and some are independent. UNCLOS, agreed in 1982 and in force after 1994, covers an enormous range of marine issues. Perhaps most importantly, it assigns nations a 200-mile exclusive economic zone (EEZ) in which they enjoy sovereignty to exploit marine resources, including fish. The FAO is the primary forum for fisheries policy within the UN system.

Under the FAO, governments have agreed two legally binding treaties regulating member states' fisheries, the Agreement to Promote Compliance with International Conservation and Management Measures by Fishing Vessels on the High Seas (1993) and the United Nations Agreement for the Implementation of the Provisions of the United Nations Convention on the Law of the Sea of 10 December 1982 relating to the Conservation and Management of Straddling Fish Stocks and Highly Migratory Fish Stocks (1995). The FAO has also created an extensive and detailed Code of Conduct for Responsible Fisheries (CCRF) which is meant to provide governments with a model for fisheries management but not to bind them to specific practices. Adoption and implementation of the CCRF have been promoted via four Plans of Action on issues ranging from seabird conservation to shark conservation. Other major multilateral environmental agreements also bear on fisheries, most notably the Convention on Biological Diversity (CBD; through the 1995 Jakarta Mandate on Marine and Coastal Biodiversity), and the Convention on the International Trade of Endangered Species.

These regulations did not go far enough for private groups like WWF and Unilever. Green groups like WWF had long been concerned with the consequences of overfishing and were frustrated with efforts to push fisheries in a sustainable direction. Unilever, which boasts about 20 per cent of the American and European frozen fish markets, was also concerned about the impact of overfishing on its business model, which relied heavily on frozen whitefish. In the late 1990s many whitefish populations, such as cod, were in serious decline, threatening the continuance of Unilever's low-cost frozen fish business (p.c., Scott Burns, former director of MSC, 8 July 2007).

Despite successful lobbying attempts to, for example, create the FAO Code of Conduct, nongovernmental organizations (NGOs) largely concluded that 'effective management of fisheries is the exception rather than the rule' (p.c., Burns). The problem for NGOs was less their inability to convince governments to take steps to protect fisheries, and more the ineffectiveness of the measures that could likely be achieved through a state-focused strategy. Even with cooperation from governments, implementation and enforcement of fisheries standards has proven difficult.

Moreover, WWF's experience with the FSC gave it a clear model and base of knowledge on which to build the MSC. However, from the outset WWF believed it needed to partner with a major corporation in order to create trust with industry, a lesson learned from the FSC experience. Unilever, though already engaged in corporate responsibility programmes, found WWF's independence an attractive enhancement to its credibility.

WWF's experience seeing competitor schemes spring up to compete with the FSC made it concerned that the MSC would also face competition. Indeed, the initiative has faced criticism from both environmental groups (recently abated following management changes at the MSC) and some fisheries that complained the certification procedures were too costly. However, the MSC seems to have been able to prevent this discontent from splintering its coalition, in part due to the initiative's growing market penetration in Northern Europe and the 2006 commitment from the massive retailer Walmart to source all its US seafood from MSC fisheries within five years.

How the MSC Works

The MSC is a kind of 'eco-label' – that is, a branding tool that is designed to give consumers reliable information about the environmental quality of a product. The MSC sets standards tha fisheries must meet to be considered sustainable, and then requires independent certifiers to confirm that a fishery meets those standards before it may use the MSC logo. Consumers provide the 'enforcement' component behind the standards, by favouring MSC products over non-certified alternatives.

Standards

The MSC Principles and Criteria – i.e. the standards against which it judges fisheries – draw from the FAO Code of Conduct for Responsible Fisheries and were formulated in consultation with various stakeholders from 1996 to 1999. The three core principles are:

1. A fishery must be conducted in a manner that does not lead to over-fishing or depletion of the exploited populations and, for those populations that are depleted the fishery must be conducted in a manner that demonstrably leads to their recovery.
2. Fishing operations should allow for the maintenance of the structure, productivity, function and diversity of the ecosystem (including habitat and associated dependent and ecologically related species) on which the fishery depends.
3. The fishery is subject to an effective management system that respects local, national and international laws and standards and incorporates institutional and operational frameworks that require use of the resource to be responsible and sustainable.

(MSC 2010)

Certification

Fisheries that wish to sell their products under the MSC label must be accredited by a certified accreditation agency. It is important to note that the MSC does not itself certify fisheries, outsourcing this task to other organizations that must meet certain criteria for independence. The cost of accreditation varies widely (depending on the size and complexity of the fishery being certified), but has ranged from $35,000 to $500,000. Fisheries may be accepted, rejected or asked to take specific steps to come into compliance with MSC standards. Certified fisheries must ensure that their products are fully traceable throughout the entire chain of custody in order to use the MSC label, guaranteeing sustainability 'from ocean to plate'. Certification is valid for a five-year period, and then must be renewed.

Individuals who take issue with the certification of a particular fishery have a fifteen-day period in which they may file an official objection with the MSC. Objections are assessed by an independent adjudicator and, if deemed by the adjudicator to warrant investigation, lead to independent re-evaluations of the certification decision and, potentially, arbitration proceedings.

Governance and Participation

The MSC is governed by a fifteen-member Board of Trustees, supported by a group of technical advisors and a Stakeholder Council. The

Technical Advisory Board is appointed by the Board of Trustees and advises on issues relating to standard-setting, licensing and certification. The Stakeholder Council consists of thirty to fifty representatives of social, economic and environmental interests. It was added in 2000 after criticisms that the MSC was disconnected from those it affected. Although it lacks decision-making authority, the Stakeholder Council may offer the governing board its opinions on all matters.

Beyond the Stakeholder Council, the MSC attempts to engage individuals affected by its projects directly in the certification process. The MSC defines its stakeholders broadly as any affected by a decision about a fishery's assessment for MSC certification, including those who have an interest in the resources affected by certification or those with information relevant to the certification process. The certification process is meant to gather information from these individuals, and to allow them to comment on draft reports, as well as file formal objections to certification decisions.

Effectiveness of the MSC

The MSC has achieved some notable successes in its first decade. It now labels or is currently assessing about 7 per cent of the world's commercially caught fish (MSC 2009), covering more fish than most countries' regulations. Some of the world's largest fish retailers have become lead partners. Unilver set itself the goal of sourcing all of its fish from MSC sources by 2005, though managed to certify only 46 per cent of its European products by this date (Jacquet and Pauly 2007). In 2006 Walmart announced its ambition to source all of its wild-caught fish from MSC-certified sources by 2011, though it has yet to achieve this ambitious goal. A private organization has become arguably the most important global regulator of the ocean's fisheries.

Two significant questions remain, however. Does MSC certification actually lead to concrete improvements in environmental quality, or does it merely reinforce existing good practices? And can the MSC expand to the point where it can have a substantial impact on the global fishery crisis?

On the issue of impact, Jacquet and Pauly (2007) criticize the MSC for not rigorously measuring its ecological effects, though the MSC did conduct one study of its environmental impact in 2006 and another in 2009 (MSC 2009). The 2006 study was not particularly encouraging. Though it identified several improvements in the fishing process that might lead to better ecological outcomes, the only specific gain directly attributable to the MSC was a reduction in the number of seabirds inadvertently caught in the South Georgia Patagonian toothfish (i.e. Chilean seabass) fishery (Gulbrandsen 2009).

The 2009 study cited several more concrete improvements, including the recovery of the controversial New Zealand hoki fishery (see below) and a sharp reduction in the number of birds inadvertently killed by hake fishermen in South Africa. The study also identified economic and social benefits for fishermen in the form of new markets for North Sea saithe (pollock), price premiums for MSC-certified fish in the United States, United Kingdom and Australia, and increased governmental recognition and support for lobstermen in Mexico.

A larger question remains, however, regarding how much these successes mean. Gulbrandsen (2009) distinguishes between narrow and broad effectiveness. The MSC may be succeeding in the fisheries in which it works, but can it or similar methods make a real difference to the larger picture?

While the MSC has achieved significant coverage of the global market in a short period of time, most of this comes from Western Europe and North America. A major barrier to effectiveness is the MSC's lack of penetration in the developing world, and especially Asia, which consumes two-thirds of the world's seafood but lags in green consumerism (Jacquet and Pauly 2007). As of 2010, only three developing country fisheries have been certified – Argentine scallops, South African hake and Vietnamese clams. As Asian and other developing countries grow and increase their fish consumption, the environmental impact of the MSC may remain limited to niche markets.

Controversies

Beyond questions of coverage and effectiveness, some disputes have emerged over MSC certification. Some fisheries certified as MSC-compliant have been criticized by environmentalists as ecologically problematic. For example, the New Zealand hoki (a large-eyed, deep-water fish) fishery was certified as MSC-compliant against the misgivings of the local branch of WWF and other New Zealand environmental groups. One such group, the Royal Forest and Bird Protection Society, lodged a formal complaint, but MSC accreditation went forward nonetheless. When the New Zealand hoki fishery's certification was up for renewal, environmental groups – including the local chapter of the WWF – filed objections, which led to remedial measures but did not prevent certification.

Drawing on the case of the South African hake industry, Ponte (2006) criticizes the MSC and similar standards for remaining inaccessible to fishermen in developing countries. The costs of certification can be quite large for artisanal fisheries in developing countries, and it may be far more difficult to gather the required scientific data (Gulbrandsen 2009). Because Southern fisheries find it more difficult to comply with MSC standards, they may face *de facto* protectionism when trying to sell their goods in environmentally conscious markets. But, as Jacquet and Pauly (2007) ask, 'if eco-labelling cannot serve the needs of small-scale fishers, i.e. the vast majority of fishers worldwide, how can it be considered in the global improvement of fisheries management?'

References

Allison, E. H. (2001). 'Big Laws, Small Catches: Global Ocean Governance and the Fisheries Crisis'. *Journal of International Development* 13(7: October): 933–50.

Gulbrandsen, L. H. (2009). 'The Emergence and Effectiveness of the Marine Stewardship Council'. *Marine Policy* 33: 654–60.

Jacquet, J. L., and D. Pauly (2007). 'The Rise of Seafood Awareness Campaigns in an Era of Collapsing Fisheries'. *Marine Policy* 31: 208–313.

Marine Stewardship Council (2009). 'Annual Report 2008–2009', London. Available at www.msc.org/documents/msc-brochures/annual-report-archive/MSC-annual-report-2008–09.pdf.

Marine Stewardship Council (2010). 'MSC Fishery Standard, Version 1.1', May 2010, London. Available at www.msc.org/documents/scheme-documents/msc-standards/MSC_environmental_standard_for_sustainable_fishing.pdf.

Ponte, S. (2006). 'Ecolabels and Fish Trade: Marine Stewardship Council Certification and the South African Hake Industry'. Trade Law Center for Southern Africa, Working Paper No. 9/2006, August.

Worm, B., E. B. Barbier et al. (2007). 'Impacts of Biodiversity Loss on Ocean Ecosystem Services'. *Science* 314(5800).

40

OECD Guidelines for Multinational Enterprises
Elisa Morgera

In looking at the transnational governance features of the OECD Guidelines for Multinational Enterprises (hereinafter, the Guidelines), two vantage points may be used: transnational governance in standard-setting, and transnational governance in implementation. After a short introduction to the Guidelines, these two aspects will be analysed in turn.

Background

The Organisation for Economic Co-operation and Development (OECD)[1] was created in 1961 as an organization of countries sharing a commitment to a market economy and a pluralistic democracy (OECD 2008: 8). The OECD first approved the Guidelines for Multinational Enterprises (MNEs) in 1976, as part of the Declaration on International Investment and Multinational Enterprises, designed to improve the international investment climate and to strengthen the basis for mutual confidence between enterprises and the society in which they operate.

The Guidelines are non-binding recommendations agreed upon by governments of OECD and non-OECD member countries (adhering countries), formulated to directly address MNEs operating in or from adhering countries. Although limited to forty-two states,[2] the Guidelines' importance is linked to the fact that adhering countries represent the source of the large majority of the world's foreign direct investment and the headquarters of a majority of the world's largest MNEs (Ward 2004: 2). The Guidelines cover employment and industrial relations, human rights, environmental protection, information disclosure, combating bribery, consumer interests, science and technology, competition and taxation.

A significant turning point for the Guidelines since their adoption was their review in 2000, when they were amended to expressly state their applicability to the operations of MNEs and all their entities (Guidelines, chapter 2, para. 10) in adhering countries and abroad (Guidelines, chapter 1, para. 2). They also stress that all business entities, not just MNEs, are subject to the same expectations of good corporate conduct (Guidelines, chapter 1, para. 3).

Although the OECD Guidelines are a voluntary initiative, they contain an implementation mechanism (Huner 2000: 200). To this end, the Guidelines embody one formal obligation for adhering countries – to set up national contact points (NCPs) charged with promoting the Guidelines at the national level, encouraging their observance

---

[1] Currently, there are thirty member states: Australia, Austria, Belgium, Canada, the Czech Republic, Denmark, Finland, France, Germany, Greece, Hungary, Iceland, Ireland, Italy, Japan, Korea, Luxembourg, Mexico, the Netherlands, New Zealand, Norway, Poland, Portugal, the Slovak Republic, Spain, Sweden, Switzerland, Turkey, the United Kingdom, and the United States.

[2] Besides the OECD member states, these states also include Argentina, Brazil, Chile, Egypt, Estonia, Israel, Latvia, Lithuania, Morocco, Peru, Romania and Slovenia.

in the national context, gathering information on national experience, and reporting annually to the Committee on Investment and Multinational Enterprises (CIME). Governments are free to decide how to organize their NCPs, but most tend to set up government offices, which are expected to operate in accordance with 'core criteria of visibility, accessibility, transparency and accountability', according to the Guidelines' Procedural Guidance.

Significantly, NCPs handle 'specific instances', which are means for any 'interested party' to draw the NCP's attention to a company's alleged non-observance of the Guidelines. NCPs make an initial assessment of the issue and then offer their services as mediators. If the conflict is not resolved, it can be referred to CIME, where non-binding decisions are taken by consensus (Morgera 2006: 763–4).

The CIME comprises all OECD members and observers. It responds to requests from adhering countries on specific or general aspects of the Guidelines, organizes exchange of views on related matters, issues clarifications (providing additional information about whether and how the Guidelines apply to a particular business situation, without assessing the appropriateness of that enterprise's conduct), reviews the Guidelines and related procedural decisions to ensure their relevance and effectiveness, reports to the OECD Council, and is ultimately responsible for the interpretation of the Guidelines (Acconci 2001: 140–1).

Transnational Governance and Standard-setting

Transnational governance characterizes both the wording of the Guidelines, and the process through which they were drafted and are reviewed. As mentioned above, the Guidelines are drafted as recommendations directly addressed to enterprises, while at the same time they are a typical international soft law instrument: a text negotiated and agreed upon by national governments with the understanding that it is not legally binding. As such, the OECD Guidelines are considered 'a common frame of reference [in] assisting MNEs to ensure that their operations are compatible with expectations by host countries' (Karl 1999: 90) and for legitimizing the social sanctions performed by non-state actors against irresponsible companies, such as boycotts and general advocacy campaigns (Tru 1992: 54). The Guidelines can also be seen as a tool for interpreting the meaning, and guiding the application, of other international instruments and domestic laws (International Council on Human Rights Policy 2010: 68). They are accompanied by a Commentary, which, however, is not officially annexed to them, and cannot therefore be considered a formal means of interpretation of the Guidelines (Van der Gaag 2004: 2).

In terms of process, it should be noted that the Guidelines were originally drafted with extensive involvement of business and labour organizations through the Advisory Committees of Business and of Labor Federations (Huner 2000: 201). This participatory process was considered to have helped 'prevent misunderstandings and build an atmosphere of confidence and predictability between business, labour and governments' within the OECD (Karl 1999: 89–90). The Business and Industry Advisory Committee (BIAC) was founded in 1968 and is still active as an independent international business association that is officially recognized as representing the 'OECD business community' (www.biac.org). The Trade Union Advisory Committee (TUAC) was founded in 1948 and has acquired consultative status with the OECD and its various committees (www.tuac.org).

Nongovernmental organization (NGO) engagement with the OECD began more recently, with the 2000 review process, when for the first time the CIME proposed the establishment of an NGOs' representative committee, like those of business and labour unions (Smith 2003: 12). Instead, NGOs opted for the establishment in 2003 of an independent network of civil society organizations, OECDWatch, which aims to 'inform the wider NGO community about policies and activities of the OECD's Investment Committee and to test the effectiveness of the OECD Guidelines' (OECDWatch 2011). Environmental NGOs, such as Friends of the Earth and Greenpeace, seem particularly active within OECDWatch and generally interested in increasing the use of the Guidelines implementation procedure, coordinating such efforts, and challenging disappointing decisions by NCPs (Morgera 2006: 764–71). The special role played by environmental NGOs is likely to expand thanks to the Aarhus Convention on Access to Information, Public Participation in Decision-making and Access to Justice in Environmental Matters, to which most of the OECD states are parties or signatories.[3] Based on Article 3(7), parties have the obligation to promote the application of the principles of the Aarhus Convention in international environmental decision-making processes and within the framework of international organizations in matters pertaining to the environment (United Nations Economic Commission for Europe (UNECE) 2005). Arguably, the review and implementation of the OECD

---

[3] The OECD states that are parties to the Aarhus Convention are: Austria, Belgium, Czech Republic, Denmark, Finland, France, Germany, Greece, Hungary, Italy, the Netherlands, Norway, Poland, Portugal and Spain. Signatories to the Convention are: Germany, Greece, Iceland, Ireland, Luxembourg, Sweden, Slovakia, Switzerland and the United Kingdom.

Guidelines, at least partly, fall within the scope of this provision (Morgera 2006: 775).

An OECD Forum was also established in 2000 as a multistakeholder consultation process open to representatives from business, labour, civil society and the general public (OECD 2010) to discuss with government ministers the key issues on the agenda of the annual meeting of the OECD Council, which is the highest decision-making body within the OECD. The Forum and the Council often discuss questions related to the Guidelines. It is the OECD Council that adopted the 2000 review of the Guidelines and that in June 2009 welcomed 'further consultation on the updating of the OECD Guidelines to increase their relevance and clarify private sector responsibilities' (OECD 2009).

In addition, a certain degree of cooperation has been established between the OECD and the United Nations (UN). In particular, the Special Representative of the Secretary-General on the Issue of Human Rights and Transnational Corporations and other Business Enterprises took into account experience accrued in the context of the Guidelines in the elaboration of the corporate responsibility to respect human rights as part of the 'Protect, Respect and Remedy' Framework on Business and Human Rights (UN Special Representative 2009a: para. 47), and also expressed willingness to participate in the proposed 2010 review of the Guidelines (Special Representative 2009b: 1).

Overall, the process for the development and review of the Guidelines has increasingly been characterized by dialogue between the OECD and the Guidelines adhering country governments on the one side, and stakeholders such as representatives of the labour, business and NGO communities, as well as relevant UN bodies, on the other, through a variety of permanent and periodic arrangements.

Transnational Governance and Implementation

As anticipated, the implementation procedure of the Guidelines is also significantly characterized by transnational governance. The OECD defines the institutional set-up for the Guidelines implementation as comprising NCPs, CIME, BIAC, TUAC and OECDWatch. As provided for in the Procedural Guidance, the NCPs meet in June each year to share their experiences and to report to the OECD Investment Committee. In addition to submitting their annual reports and discussing activities associated with the Guidelines at a national level, the NCPs hold consultations with BIAC, TUAC and NGOs, notably OECDWatch. In addition, a back-to-back roundtable with practitioners is organized to assist NCPs to better understand emerging issues and policy developments relevant to the Guidelines.

The report by the chair of the NCP annual meetings reviews activities to promote and implement the Guidelines undertaken by adhering governments. It also provides an annual overview of NCPs' action on specific instances. As this information may be considered insufficient (Morgera 2006: 774), OECDWatch produces an independent quarterly update on the filing, conclusion or rejections of instances and keeps an independent database (OECDWatch 2011).

At the national level, NGOs have increasingly made use of the Guidelines implementation procedure, notwithstanding the mixed results achieved so far. NCPs have followed quite heterogeneous procedures and timelines in reacting to the submission of instances by NGOs and have been exercising a varying degree of pressure on MNEs (Morgera 2006: 763–70). Thus, during the 2000 review, NGOs expressed their disappointment with the weak implementation mechanism of the Guidelines, largely depending on the willingness and capacities of NCPs (FOE 2002: 6). Nonetheless, NGOs continue to file complaints before an NCP as a means of getting access to discussions with the company concerned and to publicize the results of complaint procedures as part of a broader strategy for putting pressure on MNEs (FOE 2002: 10). The risk that instances of non-compliant corporate behaviour will be highlighted by the NCP special instances processes is considered by NGOs as an incentive for MNEs to comply with the Guidelines (Calder and Culverwell 2005: 28).

UN bodies have also participated in the annual NCP meetings. The UN Conference on Trade and Development (UNCTAD), for instance, used this opportunity to state that the Guidelines implementation mechanism was ineffective (UNCTAD 2003: 6). The UN Special Representative on business and human rights also participated in annual meetings, noting that certain NCPs make direct reference to the 'Protect, Respect and Remedy' Framework on Business and Human Rights (UN Special Representative 2009a, paras. 39).

Furthermore, UN bodies have also relied on and directly participated in the implementation procedure of the Guidelines. One of the most interesting cases concerns the UN Security Council action on the illegal exploitation of natural resources in the Democratic Republic of Congo (DRC), in the context of which both the standards embodied in the Guidelines and their implementation procedure were involved. The Security Council established an international, independent fact-finding body ('experts group') to conduct field visits and investigate directly the irresponsible conduct of MNEs in DRC. Annexes to the experts group's report listed individuals, states and companies whose international violations had been documented by the experts group, using the OECD Guidelines as a benchmark in assessing the conduct of companies (UN Security Council 2002). Listed companies had either been involved in natural resources exploitation in a way directly linked to the funding of the conflict (Annex I) or failed to ensure that their commercial links did not contribute to funding and perpetuating the conflict (Annex III) by breaching the OECD Guidelines. The report indicated that eighty-five companies, including fifty-seven companies headquartered in ten adhering countries, had not observed the Guidelines. In terms of institutional interactions, during the investigations the experts group communicated with the CIME, thus developing a *modus operandi* according to which the experts group would pass over to NCPs information on companies incorporated in their jurisdiction (UN Security Council, 2003). Overall, however, NGOs noted that only a few NCPs initiated any inquiries in response to the UN Security Council Report (OECD 2004: 4–5; Morgera 2006: 771–3).

Overall, the Guidelines implementation procedure mirrors the increasing transnational governance characteristics of standard-setting in the context of the Guidelines. Interactions between the OECD bodies, national governments, civil society and UN bodies occur both at the OECD level through the NCPs' annual meetings, and at the national level in the context of the specific instances submitted to individual NCPs. These interactions have provided significant opportunities for peer pressure and mutual learning among NCPs, as well as for increased stakeholder participation in the implementation procedure.

References

Acconci, P. (2001). 'The Promotion of Responsible Business Conduct and the New Text of the OECD Guidelines for Multinational Enterprises'. *Journal of World Investment* 2: 123.

Calder, F., and M. Culverwell (2005). 'Following up the WSSD Commitments on Corporate Responsibility and Accountability: Options for Action by Government'. Available at www.chathamhouse.org.uk/files/3212_csr-wssdf.pdf (accessed 20 March 2010).

Friends of the Earth (FOE) (2002). 'Using the OECD Guidelines for Multinational Enterprises: A Critical Starterkit for NGOs'. Available at www.corporate-accountability.org/eng/documents/2002/using_the_oecd_guidelines.pdf (accessed 20 March 2010).

Huner, J. (2000). 'The Multilateral Agreement on Investment and the Review of the OECD Guidelines for Multinational Enterprises'. *Liability of Multinational Corporations under International Law*, ed. M. T. Kamminga and S. Zia-Zafiri. The Hague: Springer.

Karl, J. (1999). 'The OECD Guidelines for Multinational Enterprises'. *Human Rights Standards and the Responsibility of Transnational Corporations*, ed. M. K. Addo. The Hague: Springer.

Morgera, E. (2006). 'An Environmental Outlook on the OECD Guidelines for Multinational Enterprises: Comparative Advantage, Legitimacy, and Outstanding Questions in the Lead-up to the 2006 Review'. *Georgetown International Environmental Law Review* 18: 751.

OECD (2004). 'Report by the Chair: OECD Guidelines for Multinational Enterprises: 2004 Annual Meeting of the National Contact Points'. Available at www.oecd.org/dataoecd/5/36/33734844.pdf (accessed 20 March 2010).

OECD (2008). 'The OECD'. Available at www.oecd.org/dataoecd/15/33/34011915.pdf (accessed 20 March 2010).

OECD (2009). 'Consultation on an Update of the OECD Guidelines for Multinational Enterprises: Consultation Note'. Available at www.oecd.org/dataoecd/32/62/44168690.pdf (accessed 20 March 2010).

OECD (2010). 'Evolution of the OECD Forum'. Available at www.oecd.org/document/63/0,2340,en_21571361_22024020_22374783_1_1_1_1,00.html (accessed 20 March 2010).

OECDWatch (2010). https://oecdwatch.org (accessed January 2011).

Smith, J. (2003) 'A Tool to Combat Violations of Environmental and Workers' Rights?' Paper presented at the International NGO Training and Strategy Seminar on the OECD Guidelines for Multinationals, 20–22 March. Available at www.irene-network.nl/download/NCP-OECD.pdf (accessed 20 March 2010).

Tru, N. H. (1992), 'Les Codes de Conduite: Un Bilan', *Revue Générale de Droit International Public* 96: 45.

UN Conference on Trade and Development (UNCTAD) (2003). 'Disclosure of the Impact of Corporations on Society: Current Trends and Issues'. UN Doc. TD/B/COM.2/ISAR/20. Available at www.unctad.org/en/docs/c2isar20_en.pdf (accessed 20 March 2010).

UN Economic Commission for Europe (UNECE) (2005). 'Report of the Second Meeting of the Parties, Addendum, Decision II/4, Promoting the Application of the Principles of the Aarhus Convention in International Forums'. UN Doc. ECE/MP.PP/2005/ 2/Add.5. Available at www.unece.org/env/documents/2005/pp/ece/ece.mp.pp.2005.2.add.5.e.pdf (accessed 20 March 2010).

UN Security Council (2002). 'Final Report of the Panel of Experts on the Illegal Exploitation of Natural Resources and Other Forms of Wealth of the Democratic Republic of the Congo'. Annexes I–III, UN Doc. S/2002/1146.

UN Security Council (2003). 'Letter from the Chairman of the Panel of Experts to the Secretary-General'. UN Doc. S/2003/1027.

UN Special Representative of the Secretary-General on the Issue of Human Rights and Transnational Corporations and other Business Enterprises (UN Special Representative) (2009a). 'Report to the Human Rights Council on Business and Human Rights: Towards Operationalizing the "Protect, Respect and Remedy" Framework'. UN Doc. A/HRC/11/13.

UN Special Representative (2009b). 'Keynote Presentation' EU Presidency Conference on the 'Protect, Respect and Remedy' Framework, Stockholm, 10–11 November. Available at www.reports-and-materials.

org/Ruggie-presentation-Stockholm-10-Nov-2009.pdf   (accessed   20 March 2010).

van der Gaag, P. (2004). 'OECD Guidelines for Multinational Enterprises: Corporate Accountability in a Liberalised Economy?' Available at www.oecdwatch.org/docs/paper%20NC%20IUCN.pdf (accessed 20 March 2010).

Ward, H. (2004). 'The OECD Guidelines for Multinational Enterprises and Non-Adhering Countries: Opportunities and Challenges of Engagement'. Paper Presented at the OECD Global Forum on International Investment: Investment for Development, New Delhi, 19–21 October. Available at www.oecd.org/dataoecd/6/62/33807204.pdf (accessed 20 March 2010).

41

Partnering against Corruption Initiative and the Business Principles for Countering Bribery
David Hess

Approximately $1 trillion in bribes change hands in the world each year (Eigen 2008). This corruption causes significant harm, especially in developing countries, through waste and misallocation of limited government resources, stifled economic development, exacerbation of poverty conditions, and other harms. To combat corruption, regulation and governance initiatives must focus on both the demand side of corruption (e.g., government officials requesting bribes) and the supply side of corruption (e.g., multinational corporations paying bribes). This chapter's focus is limited to voluntary governance initiatives aimed at reducing the supply side of corruption in international business.

There are a variety of voluntary initiatives to assist businesses in countering corruption. The primary initiatives, discussed in this chapter, are:

- Transparency International's Business Principles for Countering Bribery (BPCB)
- World Economic Forum's Partnering Against Corruption Initiative (PACI)
- United Nations Global Compact's Tenth Principle.

Before describing each initiative, it is useful to note a few general features. These initiatives are all multistakeholder initiatives, but they are strongly connected to their sponsoring organization. For example, the BPCB is a nongovernmental organization (NGO) led initiative and the PACI is a business-led initiative. Although separate initiatives, they are not in competition but instead often work together in attempting to achieve their goals. A common fourth member on projects is the International Chamber of Commerce's Anti-Corruption Commission, which published the first version of its *Rules of Conduct and Recommendations for Combating Extortion and Bribery* in 1977.

Transparency International's Business Principles for Countering Bribery

Transparency International and Social Accountability International started the BPCB in 2002.[1] Transparency International is the leading NGO working on anti-corruption issues and Social Accountability International is one of the leading NGOs working on human rights for workers. The BPCB is overseen by a steering committee consisting of corporate members, NGOs and trade unions, and principles are updated periodically based on consultation with the committee.

The BPCB consists of two basic principles – that the company shall prohibit bribery and that the company shall implement a programme to counter bribery – and then additional principles on setting the scope of the company's anti-corruption programme (e.g., what types of payments to work toward eliminating) and the requirements of an effective programme (e.g., training of employees, establishment of internal controls). There is also a second version of the BPCB for small and medium-size enterprises.

These principles are not presented for corporations to publicly 'adopt'. Instead, the project is primarily focused on providing tools to assist companies in implementing an effective anti-corruption compliance programme. To this end, Transparency International has produced several other documents. The *Guidance Document* is essentially an elaboration of the principles and provides more detailed information on the background behind the various principles and how to implement specific principles. There is also the *TI Six Step Process: A Practical Guide for Companies Implementing Anti-Bribery Policies and Programmes*. This tool provides a framework for companies to work through the entire process from deciding to adopt a programme, setting the scope of the programme and implementing it, and then

[1] The full text of the principles and all documents discussed in the section are available online at: www.transparency.org/global_priorities/private_sector/business_principles.

monitoring and evaluating the programme. The *Self-Evaluation Tool* is a very practical, hands-on tool that provides a series of checklists under each principle to allow a company to easily determine how well it has implemented its programme. At the time of this writing, Transparency International – in connection with others – is working on developing standards for independent assurance professionals to assess the implementation effectiveness of a company's anti-corruption programme. External verification or assurance of a compliance programme is a practice that the BPCB recommends that companies consider.

Transparency International also takes on additional activities outside the BPCB and its steering committee. In these activities, Transparency International has moved beyond just awareness-raising and support for sharing best practices, and toward accountability for some aspects of an anti-corruption programme. In 2009, the organization published *Transparency in Reporting on Anti-Corruption: A Report on Corporate Practices*. The report reviews how well 500 of the largest publicly traded corporations in the world are providing public disclosure on their anti-corruption practices. Although the corporations are not named and ranked based on their performance, the report is the first in a planned series of reports on the topic and it states that future reports may include such named rankings.

World Economic Forum's Partnering against Corruption Initiative

PACI was started in January 2004 as an initiative of the World Economic Forum. Transparency International is also a partner in this initiative, which results in the PACI being very similar to the BPCB. For example, PACI's description of a compliance programme closely tracks the BPCB's guidelines. The initiative has three basic goals (Frei and Weinzierl, 2006). First, PACI seeks to create a common language on bribery – that is, to have companies in all industries focus on the appropriate issues and work toward developing better compliance programmes. Second, the initiative focuses on obtaining anti-corruption commitments from the top management of companies through public adoption of the principles. The signatories to the principles are listed on the PACI website. This is a key difference from the BPCB, where the initiative does not seek public adoption. Third, PACI works to spread best practices and provide support for the development of effective compliance programmes. One way it does this is through regular meetings of signatory companies' officials for sharing experiences. In addition, and typically in conjunction with the other initiatives discussed here, PACI produces various publications to support the development of effective compliance programmes. For example, these initiatives published the RESIST (Resisting Extortion and Solicitation in International Transactions) programme, which consists of cases for use in training employees on how to avoid making corrupt payments.

UN Global Compact's Tenth Principle

In 2000, the UN Global Compact was initiated. As initially formulated, the Global Compact was a voluntary initiative designed to encourage corporations to align their operations with nine basic principles on human rights, labour and the environment. In 2004, a tenth principle was added, which states: 'Businesses should work against corruption in all its forms, including extortion and bribery.' To implement this principle, the Global Compact suggests three actions. First, internally, businesses should develop an effective compliance programme. Second, externally, businesses should report on progress and share best practices with other members of the Global Compact. Third, they should work with other companies in their industry and with other stakeholders to collectively combat corruption.

The primary criticism against the Global Compact is that it lacks an effective mechanism for ensuring accountability (see Cavanagh 2004; Williams 2004). Although corporations are required to produce an annual report (termed a Communication on Progress) on the company's actions and outcomes with respect to the principles, many view this as an ineffective accountability mechanism. To that end, and working with Transparency International, the Global Compact published a detailed framework for how corporations should produce an annual report on their compliance with the Tenth Principle.[2] As already mentioned, the Global Compact has also worked on some of the projects above with the other initiatives discussed here. As another example, the Global Compact has also produced an inventory of anti-corruption tools.[3]

[2] The framework is available online at www.unglobalcompact.org/docs/issues_doc/Anti-Corruption/UNGC_AntiCorruptionReporting.pdf (accessed January 2011).
[3] The inventory is available at www.business-anti-corruption.com/anti-corruption-tools-inventory/.

Discussion

Before these initiatives existed, there were multiple problems in the fight against corruption's supply side. First, there were problems with companies' anti-corruption policies and procedures (see Hess and Dunfee 2003). Many corporations did not specifically deal with matters of corruption in their codes of conduct, and those that did defined the issues in a wide variety of ways and with varying levels of depth. Similarly, programmes and procedures designed to ensure compliance with the code of conduct and relevant laws also varied greatly in their sophistication and effectiveness. These initiatives seek to solve these problems by raising awareness of these issues and providing practical guidance to companies on how to design and implement appropriate policies and procedures. This guidance is based on the experiences and best practices of companies operating throughout the world. The initiatives collect this information and then disseminate it in a usable form, as demonstrated by the various tools and frameworks described above.

Second, there were problems with accountability, such as with companies that publicly stated a commitment to prohibiting the use of bribes but then did not follow through with that commitment in any meaningful way. This problem is due in part to the fact that corruption is a collective action problem. Companies that are opposed to bribes may still make wrongful payments out of fear that a competitor will pay bribes to win business. The initiatives described here work to solve this problem by building coherence and credibility (see Hess and Dunfee 2000). Coherence refers to assurance that all companies are working toward ending corruption in a similar, thorough manner (e.g., not sidestepping their responsibilities by using corrupt agents). Credibility refers to accountability mechanisms that ensure corporations live up to their commitments. The examples of work in this area described above include efforts to provide companies with guidance on public disclosure and then monitoring the quality of those disclosures.

In addition to attempting to directly affect companies' behaviour, these initiatives also provide a catalyst for other stakeholders to push corporations to improve their anti-corruption efforts. For example, when the FTSE created its FTSE4Good investment index series, it relied on the BPCB to determine its standards for corporations' anti-corruption policies and management (Wilkinson, 2006). Thus, shareholders are using these initiatives to seek to hold corporations accountable. International development banks may also use the BPCB as a pre-qualification requirement for bidders (Eigen 2008).

Overall, it is difficult to assess the effectiveness of these approaches and currently there are no empirical studies directly on this issue. Because bribery is typically secret, and few criminal bribery cases are brought against companies, the analyst's ability to compare the behaviour of adopters of these approaches against non-adopters is limited. Instead of measures of outcome effectiveness, the effectiveness of these initiatives could be measured on such issues as the quality and comprehensiveness of anti-corruption policies and practices.

However, one partial measure of effectiveness is the number of companies that participate in these programmes. The BPCB does not require corporations to publicly endorse the principles, making it difficult to know the extent to which a corporation has adopted the principles. The other two initiatives differ significantly in the number of adopters; PACI has 145 signatories while the UN Global Compact has over 5,000. However, among Global Compact adopters, the issue of corruption is apparently secondary to some of the other principles as it is under-represented in company progress reports (Barkemeyer 2009).

References

Barkemeyer, R. (2009). 'Beyond Compliance – Below Expectations? CSR in the Context of International Development'. *Business Ethics: A European Review* 18(3): 273–89.

Cavanagh, G. F. (2004). 'Global Business Ethics: Regulation, Code, or Self-Restraint'. *Business Ethics Quarterly* 14(4): 625–41.

Eigen, P. (2008). 'Removing a Roadblock to Development: Transparency International Mobilizes Coalitions against Corruption'. *Innovations* 3(2): 19–33.

Frei, C., and V. Weinzierl (2006). 'Case Story: World Economic Forum Partnering Against Corruption Initiative'. *Business against Corruption: Case Stories and Examples*, ed. B. Errath. New York: United Nations Global Compact Office.

Hess, D., and T. W. Dunfee (2000). 'Fighting Corruption: A Principled Approach'. *Cornell International Law Journal* 33(3): 593–626.

Hess, D., and T. W. Dunfee (2003). 'Taking Responsibility for Bribery: The Multinational Corporation's Role in Combating Corruption'. *Business and Human Rights: Dilemmas and Solutions*, ed. R. Sullivan. Sheffield: Greanleaf Publishing.

Wilkinson, P. (2006). 'Reporting on Countering Corruption'. *Business against Corruption: Case Stories and Examples*, ed. B. Errath. New York: United Nations Global Compact Office.

Williams, O. F. (2004). 'The UN Global Compact: The Challenge and the Promise'. *Business Ethics Quarterly* 14(4): 755–73.

42

Responsible Care
Ivan Montiel

The Responsible Care programme is an international voluntary certification programme for environmental protection, health, and safety (EHS) within the chemical industry. It is developed, enforced and monitored by national chemical associations who mandate or advise companies to adopt Responsible Care. Member companies conduct self-evaluations annually and rate themselves on a scale, and report their evaluation to the chemical association of their respective country.

History

Responsible Care's roots have been attributed to a response by the chemical industry after the world's worst industrial accident. On 3 December 1984, a Union Carbide plant leaked 32 tons of toxic methyl isocyanacite gas in Bhopal, India, killing thousands of people (Givel 2007). The following year, the Responsible Care programme was developed in Canada.

The Canadian Chemical Producers' Association (CCPA) designed the Responsible Care programme, building on a set of guiding principles first developed during the 1970s.

In 1988 the programme was adopted by the Chemical Manufacturers Association, renamed the American Chemistry Council since 2000, in the United States. Most European chemical associations adopted the programme during the 1990s. Chemical associations in Asia and Central and South American also recently adopted the programme.

Throughout the 1980s and 1990s, Responsible Care was largely based on codes of management practices. A total of six codes identified best practices that members were expected to assess themselves against, reporting findings and progress to the chemical association. The codes included: (i) employee health and safety, (ii) process safety, (iii) product stewardship, (iv) distribution, (v) community awareness and emergency response, and (vi) pollution prevention (Phillips 2006). The goal of the employee health and safety code was to protect and promote the health and safety of people working at or visiting chemical facilities. The process safety code was designed to prevent fires, explosions and accidental chemical releases. The product stewardship code's purpose was to integrate health, safety and environmental protection as an integral part of designing, manufacturing, marketing, distributing, using, recycling and disposing of the products. The distribution code aimed to reduce the risk of harm posed by the distribution of chemicals to the general public, to chemical industry employees and to the environment. The goal of the community awareness and emergency response code was to ensure emergency preparedness and to foster community right-to-know. Finally, the pollution prevention code aimed to achieve ongoing reductions in the amount of pollutants released into the air, water and land.

Structure

Responsible Care is an EHS voluntary code of conduct within the chemical industry (Howard, Nash et al. 2000). It is developed, enforced and monitored by national chemical associations. The objective of the programme is to regain public trust by demonstrating that chemical firms can be responsible corporate citizens who self-regulate (King and Lenox 2000). A related objective is to limit the significant negative publicity imposed on the whole chemical industry by accidents occurring in any firm (Prakash 2000). The public concern raised by industrial accidents has reinforced the image of chemicals as dangerous for both the environment and human health and safety (Hoffman 2001). Chemical companies have been the focus of more public scrutiny from pressure groups than other types of manufacturing companies (Ramus and Montiel 2005). Responsible Care aimed to send the signal to these pressure groups that the industry was taking EHS issues seriously.

The Programme Revisited: Responsible Care Global Charter

Twenty years after the inception of Responsible Care in 1985, the International Council of Chemical Associations (ICCA) Group in charge of managing Responsible Care, the Responsible Care Leadership Group, established the Responsible Care Global Charter (RCGC). This Group includes representatives of all associations that implement Responsible Care at the national and regional levels, as well as participants from companies. They publicly launched the RCGC at the first International Conference of Chemicals Management (ICCM) in Dubai in 2006 (ICCA 2009). The goal of the Global Charter is to harmonize, govern and expand the Responsible Care ethic globally. The Charter contains nine key elements: (1) adopt global Responsible Care

Core Principles, (2) implement fundamental features of national Responsible Care programmes, (3) commit to advancing sustainable development, (4) continuously improve and report performance, (5) enhance the management of chemical products worldwide, (6) champion and facilitate the extension of Responsible Care along the chemical industry's value chain, (7) actively support national and global Responsible Care governance processes, (8) address stakeholder expectations about chemical industry activities and products, and (9) provide appropriate resources to effectively implement Responsible Care (ICCA 2008).

Recent Activity

The most recent addition to the ICCA's RCLG was the Russian Chemists Union in 2007. Also in 2007 the China Petroleum and Chemical Industry Association (CPCIA) established a Responsible Care pilot programme involving thirteen companies and four chemical industry parks in China (ICCA 2009). According to ICCA, there are currently forty state-owned Chinese chemical manufacturers implementing Responsible Care.

Today, fifty-three national chemical associations in different countries have joined the programme (ICCA 2008). National chemical trade associations can mandate or advise members to adopt Responsible Care. For example, countries such as Australia or Germany require Responsible Care if chemical firms want to be part of the national chemical association.

Responsible Care and Other Industry Self-regulation Programmes

Some studies have compared Responsible Care with similar voluntary self-regulation initiatives such as the international environmental management standard ISO 14001.[1] Prakash (1999) questioned whether the release of ISO 14001, a less stringent international standard, in 1996 could undermine more stringent standards such as the Canadian Responsible Care. In an empirical study, Delmas and Montiel (2008) analysed the international diffusion of several management standards and found that the longer the experience with the Responsible Care programme within a country, the more it was likely that chemical firms would also adopt the ISO 14001 programme. Also, the

---

[1] See ch. 37, this volume.

requirement to adopt Responsible Care in order to become members of the country's chemical association had a positive impact on the diffusion of ISO 14001 within the chemical industry. Therefore, international voluntary environmental standards should not be treated as alternatives to one another but rather as complementary to each other.

The US Case: The Third-party Certification of Responsible Care

In 2002, the American Chemistry Council (ACC) adopted ambitious changes to Responsible Care in the United States after realizing that US legal regulation had caught up with Responsible Care requirements (Phillips 2006). That year, only 25 per cent of Responsible Care requirements were beyond regulatory requirements, while in 1988 87 per cent were. The ACC decided to establish mandatory third-party certification at the headquarters and facility levels to demonstrate conformance to the Responsible Care or the RC14001 technical specification.

The RC14001 technical specification

Because of the worldwide recognition of ISO 14001 and its resulting popularity with stakeholders, companies sought an approach that would avoid duplicating the Responsible Care and ISO 14001 audit processes. The RC14001 technical specification was designed to integrate elements of both the Responsible Care requirement for third-party certification and ISO 14001, allowing a single certification process to fulfil both programme requirements (Phillips 2006). In the RC14001, the scope of ISO 14001 is extended to include 'Responsible Care and health, safety and security' at each reference to 'environment' within the ISO 14001 standard. To obtain RC14001 certification, organizations must conform to the ISO 14001 standard as well as the other health, safety and security requirements.

The Responsible Care Management System

The Responsible Care Management System (RCMS) is a formal structure to help companies manage their Responsible Care activities and codes of management practices (DNV 2010). The RCMS is intended for implementation throughout ACC member and partner companies' organizations (that part of US operations corresponding to their ACC dues). The RCMS must be certified through an approved, independent, third-party audit.

Impact of Responsible Care

Scholars and practitioners have evaluated both the strengths and weaknesses of voluntary programmes such as Responsible Care. On one hand, Responsible Care has been found to help chemical firms to reduce their releases into the air, water and land. It has also improved workplace and community safety, expanded programmes to research and test chemicals for potential health and environmental impacts, and improved community relationships (Yosie 2003). According to the ACC, not only does Responsible Care help improve EHS performance but also it provides bottom-line benefits such as financial marketplace recognition, increased efficiency, improved community relations, competitive advantage and insurance to adopting firms (ACC 2010).

On the other hand, the effectiveness of Responsible Care in improving the EHS of chemical firms has been questioned. In their empirical analysis of the US chemical industry, King and Lenox (2000) did not find better environmental performance among Responsible Care adopting firms. They highlighted the potential for opportunistic behaviour due to the lack of explicit sanctions in industry self-regulation programmes.

A research study examining the intent and motivation of the chemical industry's social implementation of Responsible Care found that one of the primary goals was opposing stricter and more expensive governmental regulations (Givel 2007). Rather than being a proactive initiative, Responsible Care has been seen by some parties as an initiative to oppose support for stronger and more expensive public health and environmental legislation and regulation of chemical products.

A US study analysing data compiled by the National Response Center found that, since 1990, two years after the Responsible Care programme was adopted in the United States, accidents had not declined at member companies' facilities (Purvis and Bauler 2004). The study reported that the number of accidents increased in 2002, the year the chemical industry claimed to have increased security and safety measures in the wake of 11 September 2001.

References

ACC (2010). *Responsible Care Toolkit: Bottom-Line Benefits*. Arlington County, VA: American Chemistry Council.

Delmas, M., and I. Montiel (2008). 'The Diffusion of Voluntary International Management Standards: Responsible Care, ISO 9000, and ISO 14001 in the Chemical Industry'. *Policy Studies Journal* 36(1): 65–93.

DNV (2010). RC14001 & Responsible Care Management System'. Norway: Der Norske Veritas.

Givel, M. (2007). 'Motivation of Chemical Industry Social Responsibility through Responsible Care'. *Health Policy* 81(1): 85–92.

Hoffman, A. (2001). *From Heresy to Dogma*. Stanford, CA: Stanford University Press.

Howard, J., J. Nash et al. (2000). 'Standard and Smokescreen? Implementation of a Voluntary Environmental Code'. *California Management Review* 42(2): 63–82.

ICCA (2008). *Responsible Care Status Report 2008*. Brussels: International Council of Chemical Associations.

ICCA (2009). *Annual Review 2008–09: Worldwide Voice of the Chemical Industry*. Brussels: International Council of Chemical Associations.

King, A., and M. Lenox (2000). 'Industry Self-Regulation without Sanctions: The Chemical Industry's Responsible Care Program'. *Academy of Management Journal* 43(4): 698–716.

Phillips, D. (2006). 'RC 14001: An Integrated Management Systems Approach'. *Quality Digest* May.

Prakash, A. (1999). 'A New-Institutionalist Perspective on ISO 14000 and Responsible Care'. *Business Strategy and the Environment* 8(6): 322.

Prakash, A. (2000). 'Responsible Care: An Assessment'. *Business & Society* 39(2): 183–209.

Purvis, M., and J. Bauler (2004). *Irresponsible Care: The Failure of the Chemical Industry to Protect the Public from Chemical Accidents*. Washington, DC: United States Interest Research Group Education Fund.

Ramus, C., and I. Montiel (2005). 'When Are Corporate Environmental Policies a Form of Greenwashing?' *Business & Society* 44(4): 377–414.

Yosie, T. (2003). 'Responsible Care at 15 Years'. *Environmental Science & Technology* 37(21): 400–6.

43

Rugmark
Mathias Koenig-Archibugi

Rugmark[1] is a market-based certification mechanism for hand-made carpets produced in India, Nepal and Pakistan, which is supported by a private governance structure that spans developing and developed countries. Probably the most precise description is a transnational federation of certification organizations. Rugmark inspectors monitor production sites and provide assurances that no illegal child labour has been employed in making Rugmark-labelled carpets. Part of the

---

[1] This chapter covers Rugmark's structures and activities from its origins to 2007.

fees paid by exporters and importers is used for education and social welfare activities in the carpet-producing districts.

History

Rugmark's roots can be found in the activities of a number of Indian activists who, in the early 1980s, campaigned against bonded child labour in a number of economic sectors, targeting specifically the carpet industry. By the early 1990s the head of the South Asian Coalition on Child Servitude (SACCS), Kailash Satyarthi, had established links with several German religious human rights and development organizations and with them he launched a consumer awareness campaign on child labour. Initiatives in Germany were flanked by organizations in other Western countries, notably the National Consumers League and the International Labor Rights Fund in the United States, Anti-Slavery International in the United Kingdom, and the India Committee of the Netherlands. Activists believe that the international consumer campaign had a significant impact on sales of hand-knotted carpets: David Harvey (1996) reported that 'India's export of hand-knotted carpets grew significantly in recent years, from $65 million in 1979 to $229 million in 1983, and then, following exposure of abusive child labour involved in their production, declined to $152 million in 1993.' These developments were, however, undesirable from the point of view of many campaigners, because they were severely hitting the industry and deprived adult carpet weavers of an essential source of income. The idea of a labelling scheme emerged from discussions that involved a range of actors: the main players were a group of Indian carpet manufacturers and exporters who were concerned about developments in their export markets and formed a Carpet Manufacturers Association Without Child Labor (CMAWCL), the Indo-German Export Promotion Program (IGEP, a programme of the German Development Agency, GTZ) and SACCS. After initial discussions, a number of important producers and exporters and, more generally, India's official Carpet Export Promotion Council abandoned negotiations with CMAWCL, IGEP and SACCS, which continued discussions and created the labelling system called Rugmark. It was granted foundation status by the Indian government in September 1994. Following parallel negotiations, Rugmark Nepal was created in December 1995 and Rugmark Pakistan in August 1997.

Structure and Activities

Rugmark consists of six distinct organizations that work under a common umbrella, Rugmark International. Three organizations are located in carpet-exporting countries – India, Nepal and Pakistan – and three are located in importing countries – Germany, USA and the United Kingdom. Each of these organizations has a separate governing board, management and budget. Because of Rugmark's confederal nature, each national office defines its mandate in a somewhat different way. Offices in importing countries are, above all, marketing and fund-raising organizations. The Rugmark Foundation India has two main functions: to run a monitoring and certification system for carpets manufactured without child labour and to provide social welfare and education facilities in carpet-producing communities. There is some ambiguity regarding the guarantee provided by the Rugmark label. Rugmark publicity in India stresses the guarantee of no child labour supposedly provided by the label. Rugmark Foundation India states that '[b]uyers of RUGMARK carpets can take pride in knowing that a child's fingers did not make their carpet' (www.rugmarkindia.org/assurance/label.htm, accessed 27 July 2006) and SACCS states that 'This label called the RUGMARK guarantees the buyer/consumer that the carpet is manufactured without child labour' (www.bba.org.in/campaigns/rugmark.php3, accessed 27 July 2006). These are misleading statements since children are allowed to work on family looms under Indian law and thus by Rugmark rules. Rugmark organizations in consumer countries tend to be more cautious in their description of the message conveyed by the label. Rugmark Foundation USA and Rugmark UK now more modestly claim that 'the RUGMARK label is your best assurance that no illegal child labour was employed in the manufacture of a carpet or rug'.

Impact of Rugmark

The effectiveness of Rugmark is disputed, not least because a range of criteria can be used to assess it. Rugmark has been able to achieve a number of 'internal' objectives, notably to increase the public recognition and visibility of Rugmark and to increase the number of Rugmark licensees, the number of imported carpets bearing the Rugmark logo, and the budget of Rugmark organizations. Most observers, however, would define effectiveness as solving the problems that prompted Rugmark's creation. To the extent that many importers and exporters involved in the Rugmark initiative hoped that it would protect them from adverse consumer reaction to publicity about child labour in their industry, there are indications that it may have had some success, since sales figures of Rugmark exporters appear to be stronger than the overall trend in the industry (Rugmark Germany Annual Report 2003). It is more uncertain whether the Rugmark inspection and labelling system in India has been able to ensure that labelled carpets are not produced with illegal child labour. Rugmark-registered looms are dispersed widely across a myriad of villages in the carpet belt, and inspectors face various logistical difficulties (bad roads, lack of street and house numbers in remote villages, etc.) that limit the number of looms they are able to inspect in a day. Rugmark India claims to have inspected 176,881 looms between 1995 and March 2006 (www.rugmarkindia.org/about/facts. htm, accessed July 2006). This amounts to an average of about 16,000 per year. If the looms were selected randomly, each of the registered 32,000 looms is likely to be inspected at most once every two years. Even assuming that the inspectors can rely on precisely updated lists of the looms that are active at any given time (which is doubtful), and that they account for half of all registered looms, each active loom is only likely to be inspected approximately once a year. The rarity of inspections and the difficulty of performing 'surprise' visits in the rural villages where most carpet looms are located have led many commentators to dismiss the claim that inspections can be performed effectively (e.g. Panagariya 1996; Betz 2001). This scepticism is shared by several prominent child rights activists operating in the carpet belt, such as Shamshad Khan and Swami Agnivesh. Moreover, a substantial number of Rugmark-certified looms are located outside the core carpet belt in eastern Uttar Pradesh, and their likelihood of ever being inspected is even lower. In addition, the ability of Rugmark inspectors to verify whether children working on family looms (work that is allowed by Indian laws and Rugmark rules) actually attend school, and to ascertain whether minimum wages are paid to adults, is limited. However, a study conducted by the Institute for Human Development in 1999 and based on a sample of 5,545 workers showed there is a substantial difference between Rugmark looms and non-registered looms in the extent to which they are operated by hired child labour: only 1 per cent of workers in Rugmark looms are hired (and thus illegally working) children, while their number in unregistered looms is 7 per cent (Sharma, Sharma et al. 2000). This could suggest that the deterrent effect persists despite the low likelihood that hired child labourers will actually be discovered on looms. On the other hand, the proportion of the total workforce consisting of children working with their families is about the same on Rugmark looms and on non-registered looms (16 per cent).

However, these data do not necessarily show that Rugmark has contributed to reducing the number of children employed in the carpet industry (as implied by Rugmark's promotional material – for instance, the 2004 Report of Rugmark USA states that 'RUGMARK's system of monitoring has been remarkably successful, with the numbers of children found on the looms steadily decreasing. Experts estimate that child labour on South Asia's carpet looms has dropped from 1 million to 300,000 since the launch of RUGMARK nine years ago'). Economists modelling the effects of product labelling find that children may simply switch from labelled to unlabelled looms. For instance, Panagariya (1996) warned that:

> The separation of carpets by the label need not move children out of the carpet industry in significant numbers. It could simply create dual markets: a low-price market for carpets made by children and a high-price market for carpets made by adults. Thus, the production and marketing of carpets made with child labour could continue, only the wages paid to children would decline due to the decrease in the price of carpets made by them.

Finally, initiatives aimed at removing children from hazardous work are arguably based on a concern for the children's quality of life rather than simply on the consumers' distaste for goods produced with their work. Even if a labelling scheme were to succeed in its aim of removing children from carpet production, by itself this does not guarantee an improvement in the lives of the children. It is therefore necessary to consider the effects of the certification and welfare programmes of Rugmark on the well-being of children previously employed in the carpet industry. Rugmark does not have a tracking system for children formerly working on the looms it certifies, and moreover its impact may extend to non-certified looms, and thus there are no systematic data to assess this aspect of Rugmark's effectiveness. An evaluation of the welfare effect of Rugmark would require a tracking of the living conditions of a representative sample of children whose working and schooling status may have changed as a result of the existence of Rugmark. Until more systematic evidence is collected, researchers must rely at least to some extent on theoretical reasoning. For instance, Drusilla Brown (1999) builds an economic model of child labour labelling and concludes that: 'from an analytical point of view, product labelling is unlikely to materially improve the standard of living for working children and from a practical perspective it is virtually impossible to design a workable labelling program'. Recent data collected in Nepal, however, may justify a more optimistic assessment. A team of researchers collected and analysed data obtained from interviews with 410 households in Kathmandu Valley in Nepal, with the aim of assessing the impact of two labelling initiatives, Rugmark and Care & Fair (Chakrabarty, Grote et al. 2006). Their econometric results show that the likelihood of a child working is affected by the income of the adults in the household (as well as by the education and age of the head of the household and the number of children), but that the most important factor in determining child labour is whether the household members work in industries registered by labelling nongovernmental organizations (NGOs) or not. The results show also that labelling NGOs have a significant positive influence on the likelihood that ex-child labourers are sent to school, and that children work more hours in non-labelling industries than in labelling industries. It should be considered, however, that environmental conditions and the design of Rugmark operations in Nepal are so different from those in India that it may be difficult to generalize those results across countries.

References

Betz, J. (2001). 'Internationale Siegelungskampagnen im Teppichsektor: kein wirksames Instrument gegen Kinderarbeit. *Internationale Politik und Gesellschaft Online* (3). Available at www.fes.de/ipg/ipg3_2001/artbetz.htm.

Brown, D. K. (1999). 'Can Consumer Product Labels Deter Foreign Child Labor Exploitation?' Discussion Paper 99–19: Department of Economics, Tufts University.

Chakrabarty, S., U. Grote et al. (2006). 'The Trade-Off between Child Labor and Schooling: Influence of Social Labeling NGOs in Nepal'. ZEF – Discussion Papers on Development Policy No. 102. Bonn: Center for Development Research.

Harvey, P. (1996). *Rugmark After One Year*. Washington, DC: International Labour Rights Fund.

Panagariya, A. (1996). 'Curbing Child Labor: Rugmark Label on the Mat'. *Times of India* 14 November.

Sharma, A. N., R. Sharma et al. (2000). 'The Impact of Social Labelling on Child Labour in India's Carpet Industry'. ILO/IPEC Working Paper. New Delhi: Institute for Human Development.

44

Social Accountability International
Rainer Braun

Social Accountability International (SAI) is a multistakeholder human rights nongovernmental organization (NGO) and a leading voluntary initiative for labour rights (Hassel 2008). It is best known for developing SA8000, a certification standard that acts as a private governance element in the international labour rights regime. As of December

2009, more than 2,100 facilities in 63 countries have received SA8000 certification, covering 1.2 million workers (SAAS 2009).

Institutional Background

SAI was founded in 1997 in New York as the offspring of a long-established corporate social responsibility NGO, the Council on Economic Priorities. During the mid-1990s, a multitude of brands were implicated in labour rights violations in low-skill manufacturing industries, particularly in apparel production. The predominant corporate response was to adopt codes of conduct that held suppliers responsible for social standards. These early codes often did not include established labour rights such as freedom of association and collective bargaining, and did not provide adequate mechanisms for code implementation and verification (Varley 1998: 11). SAI developed SA8000 as a response to these challenges.

SAI is an attempt to merge the idea of corporate social responsibility, which is generally characterized as voluntary and charitable business activities, with human rights, which are built on the concepts of obligations and entitlements. In contrast to 'traditional' human rights NGOs, which act as watchdogs, SAI functions as its own governance mechanism. It seeks to bring an element of transparency to the field of international labour rights, which has been characterized by strong norms and weak enforcement. The degree to which consumers and investors reward this kind of transparency is still unclear, but SAI's institutional growth indicates sustained demand for this kind of service.

The result is a decentralized private certification system that uses mainstream business auditing techniques to verify that workers' rights are being respected. For businesses, the programme serves as a management tool for improved supply-chain management (Henkle 2009), while for civil society organizations certification is a way to commit companies publicly to international labour standards (Kearney and Gearhart 2004).

Governance Structure

In contrast to some of its peers in the field of voluntary regulation, SAI was not launched by a government, an industry or an issue group. Instead, it represents the diverse interests of corporations, trade unions and NGOs through a multistakeholder advisory board. This body takes responsibility both for developing the standards and for the mechanism through which they are implemented. SAI seeks legitimacy through this multistakeholder process and by employing a technical approach toward improving working conditions that is strictly based on United Nations (UN) and International Labour Organization (ILO) norms.

The corporate members of SAI's advisory board are a heterogeneous group. SAI does not hold these corporations directly accountable for labour conditions in their operations, but offers audits and capacity building to improve their supply chain management. SAI has not shied away from engaging with controversial companies. Notably, both Chiquita and Dole, who have a long and ongoing track record of labour rights violations (Frundt 2007), serve on its advisory board.

Corporate participants on SAI's advisory board serve in an advisory function in the same way as representatives of trade unions and civil society organizations. SAI also runs a separate corporate membership programme. This programme mostly involves capacity building for labour and supply chain management, but not all corporations on the advisory board participate. The corporate membership programme is a minor funding source for SAI. The two major income sources are training and capacity building programmes that are paid for by fees and subsidized through development grants and fees from accreditation activities.

In 2007, prompted by a peer review through the International Social and Environmental Accreditation and Labelling (ISEAL) Alliance, SAI separated the technical accreditation process from its work on the review of the standard and its training programmes by creating a new organization, Social Accountability Accreditation Services (SAAS). This is intended to avoid conflicts of interest. Due to substantial overlap in the make-up of their respective boards, this institutional division is not yet entirely convincing.

In addition to its work on labour rights, SAI has also cooperated with Transparency International on standards for countering bribery, and with InterAction Alliance on standards for the accountability of charities.

The SA8000 Model

SA8000 certification provides a multistakeholder seal of approval for decent working conditions at a specific farm or factory. In order to obtain certification, individual companies invite third-party auditors to inspect their facilities. SAI trains these auditors to carry out inspections while SAAS supervises the auditing companies. SAI does not itself certify facilities.

In contrast to industry-specific initiatives that developed around the same time, SA8000 is a general standard, applicable to workplaces of any size in any sector: agricultural and manufacturing, as well as services. Since the standard is built on UN and ILO human rights norms, it allows for certification anywhere. In deference to the normative framework created by the United Nations and its agencies, certification is not possible in countries that they deem to be in persistent violation of fundamental labour rights (e.g. Myanmar) as certifications cannot 'outrank' the ILO's expertise in this area.

Most voluntary compliance initiatives agree on the basic normative framework for labour standards, which addresses the prohibition of child and forced labour, non-discrimination, basic health and safety standards, and an acknowledgement of the rights to freedom of association and collective bargaining. SA8000 additionally demands a self-defined living wage (Vogel 2005) and it includes a 'strong provision on freedom of association' (Elliott and Freeman 2003: 61). This is particularly relevant and challenging in China, where SAI faced criticism early on for not adequately implementing this provision (Elliott and Freeman 2003).

Certification with SA8000 is a supply-chain management tool, intended to (a) reduce reputational risk for transnational corporations that might be adversely affected by stories about abusive working conditions, and (b) stabilize the supply-chain itself by improving efficiency and reliability. Certification does not lead to the social labelling of products for consumers, as in the case of fair-trade initiatives, and the effects of certification on product marketing are debated (Miles and Munilla 2004).

The strength of this model is the decentralized approach of distinguishing between good and bad factories. The management of local factories has an ownership role in assuring that labour conditions are acceptable. The factory, not their brand clients, pays for the certification, selects the auditing company, and bears full responsibility for the conditions at hand. As long as a brand acknowledges SA8000 as an acceptable standard, it can source from a facility without having to carry out its own inspections. The incentive for a supplier to get certified is to distinguish itself from its competitors; SA8000 is thus intended to be a carrot, rather than a stick, of voluntary regulation.

Critics of this approach, including fellow voluntary regulators the Ethical Trading Initiative (ETI) and the Fair Labor Association (FLA) (Utting n.d.), see this shift of responsibility from brands to mostly developing country producers as a problem, because it does not force brands to own up to their role in setting social standards. Global competition for low-skill jobs leaves suppliers with little negotiating power, whereas brands and retailers set prices and product specifications without having to consider the effects of their policies on workers. The fundamental question for the feasibility of a certification scheme such as SA8000 is whether socially responsible production is possible and profitable without a regulatory framework for the transnational corporations that determine global sourcing structures. If the demands of the brands as price makers on their suppliers make production in accordance with labour standards impossible (as implied in the 'race to the bottom' argument), then factories will be forced to cheat in order to attain certification.

SAI's approach is to offer a 'bottom-up' administrative tool that complements the more structural 'top-down' attempts to regulate global supply chains. SA8000 is an instrument to reduce uncertainty in complex production networks and is thus intended to facilitate international trade. The SA8000 model emphasizes the role of inefficient production processes and lack of management expertise as important reasons for the persistence of sweatshops. Accordingly, management training programmes and joint worker–management workshops are a substantial part of SAI's approach.

In order to allow for a technical, non-politicized approach to inspections, in the tradition of financial auditing or quality control monitoring, SA8000 is built on the International Organization for Standardization's quality and environmental auditing systems ISO 9000 and 14000. The actual workplace inspectors are officers of a certification body, accredited by SAI (since 2007 by SAAS), but otherwise independent of it. Any organization can obtain accreditation from SAAS as long as it meets the requirements of ISO 17021, a set of general auditing procedures. The key criteria for ISO standards certification are the existence of management systems demonstrating ongoing compliance, rather than the observance of immediate practices.

SA8000 audits, which are scheduled twice a year, do include worker interviews, but not continuous observation of workplace practices. The system is designed to leave the ongoing monitoring to the workers themselves. SA8000 requires that workers be able to elect a worker representative from among their peers. The function of the audit is to verify the monitoring by ascertaining that management systems are in place and that the books are in order (workers are of legal age, wages are paid, worker–management communications and grievance mechanisms are established, etc.). Audits and certifications are explicitly not meant to replace the workers' right to represent themselves, as this would violate ILO principles.

One challenge to this model is that monitoring is most necessary where human rights and labour organizing are repressed. Management systems auditors often have a background in financial and quality auditing and are not versed in the complexities of how human rights can be undermined. SAI therefore requires them to consult with local stakeholders, i.e. third parties familiar with prevailing local practices and problems. Human rights, social justice, and development NGOs that have precisely this kind of expertise could theoretically become auditors themselves, but the ISO requirements are a costly hurdle to their certification. So far, no NGOs with this kind of expertise have pursued accreditation. Civil society organizations do play a role, however, in challenging certifications through a complaints process that may be initiated by any party.

A second challenge is to assess the effectiveness of SA8000 as a human rights tool. The number of certified facilities shows that the model is attractive to suppliers, despite the fact that certification is costly and not a guarantee for increased orders. The effect of certifications on workers is difficult to estimate, however. This is due to a methodological challenge. Factories that seek certification tend to already offer better conditions than their competitors, and there is no reliable way of establishing how much labour standards improved from the time before the auditing process began. Without clearly defined baselines, the question of whether certifications such as SA8000 passively identify or actively improve norm compliance remains open. Yet, in comparison to the state-centric human rights regime that relies on self-reporting and intentions rather than inspections, identification alone is a step toward greater corporate accountability in global production processes.

References

Elliott, K. A., and R, B. Freeman (2003). *Can Labor Standards Improve under Globalization?* Washington, DC: Institute for International Economics.

Frundt, H. (2007). 'Organizing in the Banana Sector.' *Global Unions: Challenging Transnational Capital through Cross-Border Campaigns*, ed. K. Bronfenbrenner. Ithaca: Cornell University Press.

Hassel, A. (2008). 'The Evolution of a Global Labor Governance Regime'. *Governance: An International Journal of Policy, Administration, and Institutions* 21(2): 231–51.

Henkle, D. (2009). 'Gap Inc.'s Journey toward Corporate Social Responsibility'. *SA8000: The First Decade*, ed. D. Leipziger. Sheffield: Greenleaf Publishing.

Kearney, N., and J. Gearhart (2004). 'Workplace Codes as Tools for Workers'. *Development in Practice* 14(February): 216–23.

Miles, M. P., and L. S. Munilla (2004). 'The Potential Impact of Social Accountability Certification on Marketing: A Short Note'. *Journal of Business Ethics* 50(March): 1–11.

Social Accountability Accreditation Services (SAAS) (2009). *Certified Facilities List*. Available at www.saasaccreditation.org/certfacilitieslist.htm (accessed February 2010).

Utting, P. (n.d.). Fair Trade, Corporate Accountability and Beyond: Experiments in 'Globalising Justice'. Available at www.celrl.law.unimelb.edu.au/download.cfm?DownloadFile = C65361DE-1422–207C-BA514B6088B18D86 (accessed February 2010).

Varley, P. (1998). *The Sweatshop Quandary: Corporate Responsibility on the Global Frontier*. Washington, DC: Investor Responsibility Research Center.

Vogel, D. (2005). *The Market for Virtue: The Potential and Limits of Corporate Social Responsibility*. Washington, DC: Brookings Institution Press.

45

International Council of Toy Industries Code of Conduct
Reinhard Biedermann

Introduction

The toy industry's code of conduct (ICTI CARE Foundation 2004) aims to govern the working and health conditions of workers in toy factories, mainly in China, where up to 80 per cent of the world's toys are manufactured. Notwithstanding growing stakeholder support in other industries toward sector standards (Krueger 2008), the toy industry can be regarded as avant-garde in adopting a sector strategy, in which the whole industry actively assumes responsibility for suppliers' production conditions (Biedermann 2009).

The International Council of Toy Industries (ICTI), a global association of twenty-one national toy industry associations, is committed to promoting ethical manufacturing, in the form of fair labour treatment as well as employee health and safety, in the toy industry supply chain. In 2001, ICTI began to draw up a monitoring and certification programme for factories, following several revisions of the initial industry code from 1995. The code is based on International Labour Organization (ILO) core principles on workers' rights and the specific situation in the toy industries.

To implement these standards, ICTI has also founded the ICTI CARE Foundation, a non-profit organization incorporated in the State of New York which is responsible for the ICTI CARE (Caring, Awareness,

Responsible, Ethical) process. This programme aims to provide a 'single, fair, thorough and consistent programme to monitor toy factories' compliance with ICTI's code of Business Practices' (see www. icti-care.org/, accessed January 2011). The basic provision is that factories must be accredited by an independent auditor company to obtain a certificate, confirming that the factory produces toys according to the standards. The buyers, namely the Western brands, retailers and trade associations, are urged or convinced by ICTI to demand the supplier's certification.

One of the main tasks of the ICTI CARE Foundation, alongside continuous improvement of its implementation, is to convince retailers and brand names to join the programme. Much success has been made in this area in recent years. According to ICTI figures, as of 2010 the certified factories represent about 75 per cent of world toy business. This means that 2,148 factories are registered in the process (representing around 1.7 million workers), while 1,048 factories hold the ICTI Seal of Compliance, which is the certificate. The certificate has to be renewed on a yearly basis. Around 700 Western companies have committed to 'Date Certain', which means the buyers or brands have signed a statement declaring they will only buy from certified factories going forward.

Why a Sector Standard?

Theoretically, cooperation in an anarchic environment is assumed to be established through hegemony of one or more powerful actors (Kindleberger 1973) or through institutionalization, whereby mutual gains prevail and no end to cooperation is envisaged (Axelrod and Keohane 1985). How can a sector code in an industry with few market leaders and thousands of actors with diverging interests succeed in an anarchic, highly competitive business environment? From a management theory perspective, there is no incentive for cooperation through sector approaches for market leaders, since brands compete not only with their products, but also with their images. CSR has to be managed in a pro-active manner (Koplin, Seuring et al. 2007), and market leaders strive for the highest reputation effects or for first-mover advantages (Tiemann 1999). With their huge purchasing power, they might implement their codes unilaterally. Therefore, a common sector approach appears unattractive, because it allows the slowest actor and lowest common denominator to define standards (Sethi 2003). The question thus arises of why market leaders have in recent years supported sector approaches and sometimes even give up their unilateral approach.

Group theory (Olson 1992), cooperation theory (Axelrod and Keohane 1985) and game theory (see e.g. Stein 1982) provide useful theoretical explanation for how sector-wide cooperation might evolve. A group of market leaders can act as a collective hegemony to force suppliers to follow. A sector code can act as a private trade barrier, an ethical cartel from which non-compliers are excluded. If many major actors in a sector are involved, they have more leverage to impose codes of conduct on factories.

These interdependences create incentives for cooperation. In recent years, the codes in several sectors have become more and more similar (Rivoli 2003), including the toy industry (Biedermann 2007). When, to use game theory terminology, the problem resembles a simple coordination game, harmonizing standards into a single code becomes an attractive way to achieve cooperation (Stein 1982). Actors have incentives for coordination, since gains are quite easy to achieve, and divergent rules can lead to bad results, like civil protests by NGOs. To make sector codes attractive for business leaders, they have to be approximately as high as market leaders' codes. When market leaders move first to coordinate their standards on a high sector standard, they can then institutionalize cooperation in a second step with the many thousand suppliers with training measures, independent monitoring, certification, and sanctioning of misbehaviour if needed. To secure the legitimacy of the sector approach, it is important that the standards are developed through discourse and contain commonly accepted principles identified by all stakeholders (Müller, dos Santos et al. 2009).

Development of the Programme

In the 1990s, Hong Kong NGOs with a strong understanding of the power dynamics of the toy market set out to change the way toys are produced. They sought to shift responsibility for toy workers to the large brands, since local factories were hard to attack. After two devastating fires in toy factories in China and Thailand, the formerly sheltered production system of the toy industries cracked open. In 1995, the Hong Kong Toy Coalition launched a campaign to urge toy-making enterprises to adopt a safety code of conduct (Asia Monitor Resource Center 1998). The Hong Kong groups revealed humiliating working and living conditions in factories and dormitories, also demonstrating that Chinese producers manufactured a large share of toys for famous world brands. Between 2 and 3 million mostly female workers from rural provinces produced toys for these brands in roughly 5,000 factories in China's southern province of Guangdong (following product scandals in 2007, hundreds of factories went bankrupt). Only a small number of factories were joint ventures, and the largest share of producers were formally independent manufacturers. Answering to the campaign's demands, the first toy association to adopt a code of conduct to regulate workers' rights was the British Toy and Hobby Association (BTHA) in January 1996. Later that year, ICTI invented a code of conduct following the British example with a set of basic labour standards and health provisions. But for many years, the ICTI code existed mainly on paper. The largest brands developed their own codes of conduct to handle NGO pressure. In-house monitoring (businesses conducting their own inspections) became the preferred procedure in the toy industries, although NGOs demanded independent monitoring (Biedermann 2007).

Mattel, the producer of the Barbie doll, provides an illuminating example of how the ICTI progressed between 2001–3, when the ICTI code became operational (after revision and accreditation of independent auditing companies), and 2004, when the leading brands Mattel and Hasbro together declared their support for the ICTI code in the future. Mattel is a large employer with 9 production facilities and around 30,000 employees worldwide, who produce half of Mattel's total output. The other half comes from independent suppliers. The corporation is said to be a leading actor in CSR activities, with high positions in CSR rankings in business magazines. But even the market leader had to learn that it is almost impossible to implement standards in factories which produce also for other toy brands. According to NGOs, Mattel successfully transformed its own facilities into showplaces for CSR activities, while at the same time overlooking its independent suppliers. Mattel therefore remained a target of NGOs, and more negative reports about factories that produced for Mattel were issued (Biedermann 2007).

Mattel and other companies had to learn that they are interdependent on other brands that use the same suppliers and have their own codes of conduct. The many codes were often contradictory, making it still harder to implement even basic security standards. Business statements revealed that some suppliers underwent fifty or more auditing and certification procedures a year, contributing to a growing certification industry with dubious success and at a significant cost to the industry. Moreover, NGO criticisms were not allayed, but turned even more sceptical given the many inefficient codes of conduct. Crucially, the industry as a whole failed to give coherence to the range of unilateral approaches, which remained a piecemeal of restrictions on working hours and guarantees of payments and better working conditions.

Mattel and Hasbro (a company that already claimed to follow the ICTI code before 2004) worked together within the US association Toys Industries of America (TIA) to make the ICTI sector code operational. After Mattel and Hasbro declared their support for the ICTI code, more and more brand name corporations followed their example. The ICTI CARE Foundation developed into a real actor that negotiated with leading retailers like Walmart and Toys 'R' Us in the USA, and major European retailers, to get them to accept the ICTI standards as their own. The strategy to include retailers further increased the pressure on brand name companies to participate in the Date Certain Campaign, since they feared losing their largest customers. The processes of inclusion have taken time, since many businesses have a 'wait-and-see' attitude, according to Christian Ewert, the President of ICTI CARE Foundation (Biedermann 2007). In 2009, Mattel even transitioned its own social responsibility independent audit programme to the toy industry's ICTI CARE Process, ending almost completely its unilateral approach to conditions. Mattel justified that decision by declaring that the ICTI CARE Process was 'the product of an approach that Mattel has long supported' (http://corporate.mattel.com, accessed January 2011).

The Legitimacy of the ICTI Programme

The ICTI shows how global harmonization of regulations can become important for businesses. But the sector approach of the ICTI also depends on civil society actors for legitimacy and thus success. According to Müller, dos Santos et al. (2009), legitimacy criteria include a well-conducted management of *inclusivity* and *discourse* with all stakeholders, including NGOs. Also important are the *control* by certification and accreditation, the integration of all participants along the *supply chain*, and finally *transparency* of the results. NGOs in general support the ICTI code and pressure brands to participate in the programme. They have been and are still today indispensable in the process of implementing CSR.

One example is the German 'Aktion fair spielt' under the leadership of the large development organization Misereor. Misereor has played a considerable role, financing the research of partner organizations in Hong Kong, holding press conferences at the world's largest toy fair in Nuremburg, publishing reports, and networking with businesses, the German government and ICTI. 'Aktion fair spielt' continues to push for better results, especially after the ICTI code was recently criticized by Hong Kong NGOs alleging that certified corporations had in fact failed to meet its requirements (Kleinert and Strohscheidt 2009).

Under similar pressure from NGOs, the ICTI programme has also adopted a stronger focus on sub-suppliers to certified corporations. In 2010, ICTI will begin issuing an Annual Report, and there will be more stakeholder communication with factories, toy brands, retailers, licensors, NGOs and other interested partners. Still, NGOs have also demanded the transformation of the Governance Board of the ICTI CARE Foundation into a real multistakeholder initiative, with NGOs acting on equal footing with business representatives.

References

Asia Monitor Resource Center (1998). *The Working Conditions of the Toy Industry in China, 1998*. Hong Kong: AMRC.

Axelrod, R., and R. Keohane (1985). 'Achieving Cooperation under Anarchy: Strategies and Institutions'. *World Politics* 38(1): 226–54.

Biedermann, R. (2007). *Sozialstandards durch Private Governance: Zwei-Stufen-Kooperation in der globalen Spielzeugbranche*. Baden-Baden: Nomos.

Biedermann, R. (2009). 'Private Governance in der Spielzeugindustrie – Voraussetzungen und Strategien zur Durchsetzung einer Branch envereinbarung'. *Zeitschrift für Wirtschafts- und Unternehmensethik* 10(1): 18–36.

ICTI CARE Foundation (2004). 'International Council of Toy Industries' Code of Business Practices. The CARE Process'. Hong Kong Toys Council under the Auspices of the Federation of Hong Kong Industries, Hong Kong.

Kindleberger, C. (1973). *The World in Depression 1929–1939*. Berkeley and Los Angeles. University of California Press.

Kleinert, U., and E. Strohscheidt (2009). *A Long Run-up – Yet Only a Short Leap Forward*. Discussion paper of the German toy campaign Aktion fair spielt on the ICTI CARE Process. Heidelberg: Aktion fair spielt. Available at www.fair-spielt.de/.

Koplin, J., S. Seuring et al. (2007). 'Incorporating Sustainability into Supply Policies and Supply Processes in the Automotive Industry – The Case of Volkswagen'. *Journal of Cleaner Production* 15(11): 1053–62.

Krueger, D. A. (2008). 'The Ethics of Global Supply Chains in China – Convergences of East and West'. *Journal of Business Ethics* 79(1–2): 113–20.

Müller, M., V. G. dos Santos et al. (2009). 'The Contribution of Environmental and Social Standards towards Ensuring Legitimacy in Supply Chain Governance'. *Journal of Business Ethics* 89(4): 509–23.

Olson, M. (1992). *Die Logik kollektiven Handelns. Kollektivgüter und die Theorie der Gruppen*, 3rd edn. Tübingen. Mohr-Siebeck.

Rivoli, P. (2003). 'Labor Standards in the Global Economy: Issues for Investors'. *Journal of Business Ethics* 43(3): 223–32.

Sethi, P. (2003). *Setting Global Standards: Guidelines for Creating Codes of Conduct in Multinational Corporations*. New Jersey: John Wiley and Sons.

Stein, A. (1982). 'Coordination and Collaboration: Regimes in an Anarchic World'. *International Organization* 36(2): 299–324.

Tiemann, R. (1999). *Ethische Branchenstandards: Ein Lösungsweg für Unternehmen aus moralischen Dilemmata*. Munich/Mering: Hampp.

46

United Nations Global Compact
Thomas Hale

The Global Compact is a multistakeholder initiative through which transnational corporations pledge to uphold ten principles relating to the environment, labour standards, human rights and corruption. Sponsored by the United Nations (UN) and including a range of business, non-governmental, labour, and governmental representatives, the Compact aims to facilitate the adoption of social and environmental norms into global business practices through learning and dialogue. The Global Compact is the largest corporate social responsibility initiative in the world, though critics have questioned its effectiveness and accused it of aligning the UN too closely with business interests.

History and Purpose

The Global Compact was announced by UN Secretary-General Kofi Annan on 31 December 1999 at the World Economic Forum in Davos. Annan called upon the assembled business leaders to uphold social and environmental principles as a way to underpin the global economy with shared social values. The UN, he pledged, would work collaboratively with transnational corporations and other stakeholders – namely nongovernmental groups, organized labour and governments – to make responsible social and environmental practices part of global business standards.

The Compact represents a new phase of the UN's engagement with business. During the 1970s and 1980s developing countries made efforts to regulate transnational businesses through the UN. While opposition from the developed world stymied these efforts, many elements within the UN continued to regarded transnational corporations with suspicion due to their perceived impacts on human rights, the environment, labour standards and development. Many businesses, for their part, were equally suspicious of UN efforts to regulate them.

The stated goal of the Global Compact is to recast this competitive relationship as a cooperative one (Kell and Ruggie 1999) through which business becomes a responsible partner in promoting UN principles and goals. In this view, turning from a 'command and control' regulatory mentality – for which the UN had neither the political mandate nor the implementation capacity – to a cooperative framework leverages the UN's greatest strengths: normative authority and convening power (Kell, Slaughter et al. 2007).

How the Global Compact Works

In order to join the Global Compact the highest-ranking executive of a business must send a letter to the UN Secretary-General stating the company's commitment to the principles. The company then is expected to set 'in motion changes to business operations so that the Global Compact and its principles become part of strategy, culture and day-to-day operations'. Such changes should aim to ensure that the company is not violating any of the principles and also making positive contributions to the goals of the UN.

Businesses must report their progress to the Global Compact secretariat annually. These 'communications on progress' are published on the Compact website. Companies that fail to report are labelled 'inactive' and may be de-listed from the Compact.

The Global Compact is distinct from most corporate codes of conduct, certification schemes or other corporate social responsibility initiatives. Instead of binding companies to specific practices, the Compact is a vehicle through which companies declare their commitment to ten universal values derived from UN treaties. The idea is that the Compact can serve as both a catalyst to encourage companies to consider their social and environmental responsibilities and a learning forum to build their capacity to fulfil those responsibilities.

Beyond the ten principles, the Compact has occasionally promoted optional, more specific mandates in areas like climate change and water. It has also encouraged companies to negotiate with labour groups on a global basis.

The Global Compact aims to promote learning in three ways. First, the 'communications on progress' posted on the website are meant to serve as case studies businesses can use to learn from each other's experiences. Second, the Global Compact hosts regular meetings in

Human rights

Principle 1: businesses should support and respect the protection of internationally proclaimed human rights; and

Principle 2: make sure that they are not complicit in human rights abuses.

Labour standards

Principle 3: businesses should uphold the freedom of association and the effective recognition of the right to collective bargaining;

Principle 4: the elimination of all forms of forced and compulsory labour;

Principle 5: the effective abolition of child labour; and

Principle 6: the elimination of discrimination in respect of employment and occupation.

Environment

Principle 7: businesses should support a precautionary approach to environmental challenges;

Principle 8: undertake initiatives to promote greater environmental responsibility; and

Principle 9: encourage the development and diffusion of environmentally friendly technologies.

Anti-corruption

Principle 10: businesses should work against corruption in all its forms, including extortion and bribery.

Figure 46.1 The Global Compact principles.

which participants can share experiences more directly. Third, the Global Compact Office has also produced a number of materials explaining how corporations can realize the Compact's principles.

Governance

Since 2005 the Global Compact has operated under a pluralist governance structure involving six main components.

- Global Compact Leaders Summit: held every three years, this summit convenes the heads of all Global Compact stakeholders to reaffirm and deepen their commitment to the principles.
- Local networks: a variety of Compact participants have organized into local, self-governing networks.
- Annual Local Networks Forum: representatives from local networks meet yearly to discuss issues that cut across their respective regions.
- Global Compact Board: consisting of twenty members from the private sector, civil society, labour and the UN, the Global Compact board is meant to serve as an advisory and advocacy body for the Compact.
- Global Compact Office: this office is the official UN entity charged with managing the Global Compact. Its current Director is Georg Kell.
- Inter-Agency Team: six UN entities are involved with the Global Compact's work: the Office of the UN High Commissioner for Human Rights (OHCHR), the International Labour Organization (ILO), the United Nations Environment Programme (UNEP), the United Nations Office on Drugs and Crime (UNODC), the United Nations Development Programme (UNDP) and the United Nations Industrial Development Organization (UNIDO).

While the Compact does not have a mandate to 'discipline' participants for violating its principles, it has adopted a set of 'integrity measures' that aim to prevent abuse of the program. The Global Compact Office will entertain 'credible complaints of systematic or egregious abuse of the GC's overall aims and principles' and respond, if it deems necessary, by attempting to engage the relevant stakeholders on the substantive nature of the complaint. Should the participant prove unwilling to engage with the Global Compact or other relevant bodies (e.g., local networks or other UN agencies), it may be categorized as 'inactive' or de-listed.

Scope of the Global Compact

The Global Compact is the largest corporate social responsibility initiative in the world. As of mid-2010, it claimed 7,700 participants, 5,300 of them corporations, in over 130 countries. As of 2007 this number included 108 of the *Financial Times* Global 500 firms, employing some 10 million workers and possessing a market capitalization of approximately $5 trillion. The Global Compact also includes around 50 country-level networks which serve as smaller groupings specifically attuned to local contexts.

These numbers, though impressive, must be weighed against the reality that an estimated 70,000 transnational corporations do not participate in the initiative. Moreover, only around 4 per cent of members are North American firms, representing a sizeable gap in one of the world's most important markets (Kell, Slaughter et al. 2007).

Evaluating the Global Compact's Effectiveness

The effectiveness of the Global Compact is inherently difficult to assess. Because it promotes adherence to general principles and an ethos of corporate citizenship rather than specific policies, it is difficult to measure the precise impact of joining the Global Compact on firms' behaviour. The causal direction between joining the Compact and improving business practices is also open to debate: does participation make firms better corporate citizens, or do companies that already exhibit or plan to exhibit high standards join the Compact to showcase their responsibility? The vast number of firms participating and the relatively small amount of information they produce regarding their engagement with the Compact complicate empirical research efforts.

These difficulties have, understandably, resulted in diverging evaluations of the Compact's effectiveness. Ultimately, how successful one deems the Compact depends on the criteria used to evaluate it.

Arguably the most important criterion, and the one most commonly referred to by the Compact's critics, is the extent to which the Compact changes firms' behaviour. Can the Compact actually improve business practices through learning and dialogue? While some corporations have published case-study testimonies of how participation in the Compact has changed their business practices (see McIntosh, Waddock et al. 2004), independent, aggregate studies are lacking. Without such research, critics of the Compact (see below) are unlikely to be mollified.

While determining the precise impact of the Compact on firms' behaviour is a central question, it is hardly the only determinant of effectiveness. Indeed, a case can be made that the abstract nature of the Compact means it should be evaluated on more general grounds, for example its ability to engage with large swaths of the international business community and its contribution to the discourse on global corporate responsibility. It is not unreasonable, the Compact's advocates argue, to expect these more abstract measures of success to generate changes in firms' behaviour, though the exact paths of causality would be impossible to trace. In this view, we may deem the Compact a success to the extent it reaches large numbers of the business community and to the extent its principles enter the discourse of corporate responsibility.

By these measures the Compact has performed quite well. Its growth, noted above, has been prodigious over the first years of its existence. If the Compact continues to add members at a rapid pace, it may be concluded that it is effectively promulgating its principles into the business world. However, should uptake lag, a possible explanation may be that the Compact's early growth was mostly a product of socially minded corporations joining an initiative with which they already agreed. The Compact's ability to reach beyond the 'low-hanging fruit' – for example, its ability to penetrate the recalcitrant North American market – will be a critical test of its effectiveness.

With regard to discourse, evaluations of the Compact should seek to assess the impact of the Compact's particular brand of global corporate citizenship on the general corporate social responsibility discourse. To the extent the Compact has shifted the debate to conceptions of *global* corporate responsibility, as opposed to local or national commitments, and to the extent such responsibility refers to the treaty-based principles the Compact advances, it may be considered a success. However, detailed discourse analyses have not been undertaken.

Critical Views of the Global Compact

Critics have accused the Global Compact of 'blue-washing' transnational corporations – that is, conferring the legitimacy of the UN on companies that, through pollution, human rights abuses or violations of labour standards, in fact work against the principles the UN seeks to promote (Karliner and Bruno 2000).

Such critiques tend to emphasize the 'soft' nature of the Compact. Dialogue and learning are weak tools with which to hold corporations accountable, critics contend. Stronger regulation of corporations at the global level, including binding minimum standards, is needed to make real progress toward correcting the imbalances of the global market. Indeed, by providing a veneer of action on this issue, the Global Compact may in fact be diluting political pressure for effective regulation of corporations, and thus working against its stated goals.

Against the charge of blue-washing the Compact's supporters note that the Global Compact is not a certification scheme; participation does not represent the UN's endorsement of a business, but rather a company's commitment to hold itself to a higher standard. Participation should thus strengthen, not dilute, the scrutiny a company faces from civil society or other stakeholders. Determining how the Global Compact 'brand' is actually interpreted by concerned stakeholders – as a mark of approval or an invitation to greater scrutiny, or some combination of the two – is thus important to assessing the charge of blue-washing.

Critics also contend that opening the UN to private companies may lead the organization to compromise its principles. For these observers, the Compact represents a way for business to increase its influence over UN policymaking, with adverse implications for social protections and development (Zammit 2003).

References

The Global Compact Office maintains an extensive bibliography of academic work on the initiative on its website, which complements the resources presented here: www.unglobalcompact.org/NewsAndEvents/academic_articles_and_books.html.

Karliner J., and K. Bruno (2000). 'The United Nations Sits in Suspicious Company'. *International Herald Tribune* 10 August 2000.

Kell, G., and J. G. Ruggie (1999). 'Global Markets and Social Legitimacy: The Case for the "Global Compact"'. *Transnational Corporations* 8(3: December): 101–20.

Kell, G., A.-M. Slaughter et al. (2007). 'Silent Reform through the Global Compact', *UN Chronicle* 1.

McIntosh, M., S. Waddock et al. (2004). *Learning to Talk: Corporate Citizenship and the Development of the UN Global Compact*. Sheffield: Greenleaf Publishing).

Zammit, A. (2003). 'Development at Risk: Reconsidering UN–Business Relations'. United Nations Research Institute for Social Development, Geneva. Available at www.globalpolicy.org/reform/business/2003/risk.pdf.

47

Voluntary Principles on Security and Human Rights
Chip Pitts

The Voluntary Principles on Security and Human Rights (VPs) aim to address one of the most persistent patterns of human rights abuse and violations of corporate social responsibility standards: the deaths, kidnappings, torture and physical harm historically caused by oil, gas, mining and extractive companies attempting to protect their assets in host countries.

Iconic cases such as Shell's complicity in the mid-1990s execution of Ken Saro-Wiwa and the other Ogoni activists in the Niger Delta, Chevron's ongoing involvement in repression of protesters there, and BP's historic involvement with paramilitaries in Colombia all represented egregious corporate conduct harking back to colonialism and the exploitation pioneered by chartered companies such as the British and Dutch East Indies companies, Cecil Rhodes's British South African Company, and Belgian King Leopold's atrocities while extracting rubber from the Congo. Such techniques are not sustainable in the contemporary environment of transparency and scrutiny accompanying globalization.

In order to stave off more mandatory regulation, shore up company reputations and brands, manage risk, preserve both company assets and 'social licence to operate', and respond to pressure from governments and other stakeholders, the VPs were proposed by the US and UK governments and launched in 2000 in partnership with major human rights and development nongovernmental organizations (NGOs) and certain major extractive and energy industry companies, namely Freeport McMoRan, Shell, BP, Rio Tinto, Chevron and Texaco (prior to their merger into ChevronTexaco). New companies and governments have joined by invitation of the existing participants.[1] At the time of writing, no state-owned enterprises from developing

---

[1] These include Anglo American, AngloGold Ashanti, BG Group, BHP Billiton, ConocoPhillips, ExxonMobil, Hess Corporation, Marathon Oil, Newmont Mining Corporation, Occidental Petroleum Corporation, Statoil, Talisman Energy and the governments of the Netherlands, Norway, Canada, Colombia and Switzerland.

countries participate. Also notably absent are governments from priority countries in Africa, Latin America and Asia where the Principles have most current relevance, namely countries like Nigeria, the Democratic Republic of the Congo, Ghana, Gabon, Peru, Ecuador, Bolivia and Papua New Guinea. The participants meet in plenary every six months, deciding amongst themselves whether to invite other participants.

Content of the Principles

After a brief introduction, the Principles address risk assessment, public security, then private security. Since 2004, Business for Social Responsibility (BSR) and the International Business Leaders Forum (IBLF) have acted as a Secretariat – although with uncertain role and resources.

The VPs aim to facilitate stakeholder dialogue and guide companies on how to promote human rights and the rule of law while achieving operational security. The VPs thus embrace the attention to stakeholders and the transparency and precautionary risk management that are so fundamental to corporate social responsibility (although the commitment to transparency is subject to 'confidentiality constraints'). Taking the Universal Declaration of Human Rights (UDHR) and international humanitarian law as touchstones, the VPs commit the companies to act consistently with local law, and to 'be mindful of the highest applicable international standards' – including applicable international law enforcement principles (e.g., the United Nations Code of Conduct for Law Enforcement Officials and the UN Basic Principles on the Use of Force and Firearms by Law Enforcement).

The risk management section aims to prevent abuses before they occur. Risks are thus understood to be not only risks to company assets and interests, but also to communities and human rights. The VPs emphasize obtaining and sharing the widest variety of information and perspectives. Effective risk assessment requires identifying the potential for violence, performing due diligence regarding the human rights records of public security forces and the reputation of private security, recognizing the presence or absence of the rule of law (including prospects for accountability for violations while respecting the rights of the accused), considering the risks associated with equipment transfers (including the need for adequate controls against potential misuse and abuse) and understanding the root causes of conflict.

The second section, on interactions with public security forces, recognizes the reality that companies are often expected or required to contribute to the public security costs of protecting their facilities and personnel – but fails to clarify how these payments are to be distinguished from illicit bribes that risk fuelling conflict. The Principles call for regular consultation regarding the impact on communities, communication of company policies and expectations regarding human rights and ethical conduct, trained personnel, and transparency consistent with safety concerns. Equipment provided should be accompanied by measures to 'mitigate any foreseeable negative consequences', including abuses and illegality. The Principles rely on the humanitarian law concept of proportionality to the threat. Instead of the 'political neutrality' which companies historically invoked to essentially turn a blind eye to significant human rights abuses, the Principles clearly call for companies to affirmatively 'use their influence' to avoid abuses and rights violations, including by promoting observance of applicable legal principles, avoiding engaging those credibly implicated in human rights abuses, prohibiting unnecessary or disproportionate force, and avoiding repression against those merely exercising peaceful assembly and related UDHR or workers' rights. Incidents involving physical force are to be reported to public authorities, and medical aid provided to the injured, including offenders. Significantly, companies are urged to consider collective action when they have common concerns about security in a region. Companies are also encouraged to support human rights training, record and report to host government authorities credible allegations of abuse, protect sources, and urge and follow up on investigations. The Principles are in fact used in training by participating companies, some private security companies, and some authorities.

The third section, on interactions with and standards of conduct regarding private security forces, limits these to 'preventative and defensive services' and not activities in the exclusive province of the state military or law enforcement. Standards expected to be complied with – and contractually documented 'where appropriate' – include company policies concerning ethics and human rights, law, professional standards, best practices, applicable international guidelines on the use of force (and 'rules of engagement'), and promoting observance of international humanitarian law. Private security, like public security, should not involve people credibly implicated in human rights abuses, and should not use unnecessary or disproportionate force or violate associational or related rights. Also, like public security forces, private security should be monitored, and allegations of abuse or illegality should be investigated. Private security should report incidents of physical force to the company (and, 'where appropriate', to public authorities), provide medical care in such situations (including to offenders) and impose disciplinary action if warranted. The confidentiality obligation of private security forces may be trumped by jeopardy to the VPs themselves.

Impact of the VPs

The VPs have clearly had a positive – if slow – impact in terms of raising awareness of these issues among companies, changing practices to some extent, increasing dialogue among stakeholders, and in several cases leading to clear improvements in certain concrete country situations (Freeman, Pica et al. 2001; Williams 2004). The growing popularity of human rights impact assessments – as used, for example, in BP's LNG project in Tangguh, Indonesia – and approaches like Chevron's more recent Global Memoranda of Understanding with local communities thus build in part on the insights from the VPs about the value of stakeholder engagement. The 'due diligence and risk assessment' approach also informs the UN's new tripartite 'protect, respect, remedy' framework for business and human rights proposed by the UN Special Representative of the Secretary-General on the subject. Increased attention to good practice in risk assessment by the UN Global Compact and other organizations should result in further improvements. And companies authentically committed to protecting human rights have excellent operational starting points to follow within the VPs. A number of companies have now incorporated references to them in contracts with security forces, thus reducing their 'voluntary' nature and giving them the force of (at least) mandatory private law.

Nevertheless, the crucial test for the VPs is whether conditions have actually improved on the ground. While the data remain incomplete, reports continue of security overreaction and human rights abuses even in the Niger Delta and in other areas originally targeted for reform, as even a casual search of the leading human rights organization's websites or www.business-humanrights.org will attest. Medical assistance is often absent after incidents, and few investigations by the companies or the governments involved occur – all in blatant violation of the VPs. Even strong friends of the VPs, 'present at the inception', have acknowledged drift, lassitude and failure to meet the goals of the process over the last few years. A number of NGO and even company representatives have in confidential interviews with the author been even more biting, considering the Principles 'worthless' in their current incarnation.

Criticisms of the VPs and Required Reforms

In addition to questions about their net impact, the Principles may be criticized for the distinction they try to make between 'voluntary' and 'mandatory' action. The distinction is increasingly outdated, as revealed by the references in the Principles themselves to international human rights and humanitarian law (which binds both states and, increasingly in myriad ways, companies). There must be a greater recognition on the part of companies that, their historic efforts to the contrary notwithstanding, compliance with basic human rights and humanitarian legal standards is not a matter of 'voluntary discretion' but a basic requirement of doing business. This suggests that the Principles should be strengthened accordingly, so that their form comes closer to this reality.

Increasingly, 'soft law' standards such as the VPs – while formally 'non-binding' – are rightly taking on harder law significance. This can occur for several reasons: such initiatives are often sponsored by governments; they can become the basis for rewards and punishment by governments and other stakeholders; they define industry standards and fiduciary and other duties in the eyes of courts, administrative agencies and other stakeholders; and in the event of non-compliance they can result in both legal and non-legal sanctions (in forms including boycotts, protests, adverse media publicity and divestment).

A related criticism is that the attempt in the Principles to distinguish between the need to comply with local law (reflected in a 'commitment' to comply) and to meet 'the highest applicable international standards' (reflected in merely a weak willingness to 'be mindful') is unsupportable as a practical matter in light of the legal content in those high global standards, the expectations of society, and the legal as well as non-legal (market) penalties for non-compliance. For this reason, many leading companies, including many of those participating in the VPs, recognize the practical need to act consistently with the highest global standards in order to avoid the liability and other risk that can come from double standards, especially given the *über*-transparency characterizing global business today.[2] The distinction embodied in the VPs, still disturbingly dominant in a number of companies, derives from the myopic failure of some company lawyers, in particular, to recognize that risk is best managed by proactively avoiding double standards. Instead, many corporations fight a reactive rear-guard action by arguing post hoc that, after all, the higher standards were not binding 'hard law'.

[2] See Pitts (2009: ch. 8 on 'Consistent Best Practices').

Although the VPs laudably recognized that companies sometimes have duties to affirmatively influence government conduct, the Principles may be criticized for not going further in requiring companies and governments to safeguard the environment and human rights. Companies have not used their influence positively as contemplated. The weakly urged 'collective action' has not happened, powerful though it would be. The idea that political engagement is beyond the proper role of companies is at odds with the enthusiasm of companies in lobbying for tax concessions, subsidies and other benefits, and disregards the myriad ways – ranging from private diplomacy to public advocacy – in which businesses could usefully intervene. Businesses should not be so reluctant to lobby for the rule of law and human rights that are so indispensable to development, on which businesses, no less than individuals, depend for long-term success.

The current language of the VPs allows for too much flexibility in meeting the obligations, such as having to contractually document requirements and exchange information only 'when appropriate'. Especially as the BRIC countries (Brazil, Russia, India, China) continue to develop, maintaining clear and strong global standards will be important in addressing transnational problems. The VPs themselves could benefit from greater incorporation of this systemic view, recognizing more explicitly how, for example, lack of transparency, corruption and environmental harms integrally affect security abuses. Garnering the public relations benefits of involvement with initiatives like the VPs, while continuing hypocritical inaction (or action) that tolerates or leads to environmental or human rights harm, is inconsistent with an authentic commitment to CSR and the goals of initiatives such as the VPs.

The main Achilles' heel of the VPs, however, remains the lack of rigorous reporting and enforcement mechanisms to ensure that companies 'walk the talk'. The limited (two-page) voluntary reporting requested at the 2006 plenary is clearly inadequate, and the tentative criteria for reporting agreed to in 2009 are only a first step. The current reporting criteria for the Principles continue to neglect the need for attention to quality (of training, etc.) as opposed to more superficial indicators. Reports should not relate merely to procedural matters (e.g. the number of trainings or stakeholder consultations held), but to the substance of what happens on the ground (including incidents, investigations, and behavioural change or lack thereof). This lawyerly reluctance to meaningful reporting puts the VPs at odds with most leading multistakeholder initiatives today, and again fails to recognize that transparency can help substantive risk mitigation while secrecy can increase risk.

In terms of enforcement, deeper and more continual engagement with NGOs beyond the current plenary meeting schedule could help, including with external monitoring and verification and perhaps even in rating degrees of compliance (e.g. minimum versus best practice). So could broadening participation to include more companies and governments – especially from emerging markets. Governments could do a better job of enforcing the human rights norms referenced in the VPs and of strengthening both reporting and accountability for their violation. In the inaugural decade, the US Bush administration instead intervened several times to oppose accountability, and hopes are high that the Obama administration will weigh in more productively. Even the broad-based Global Compact now 'de-lists' companies (nearly 2,000) that have failed to communicate on progress as required; laggards failing to implement the VPs should also be kicked out, and yet the complaints/expulsion process agreed on in 2007 has yet to prove up to the task. By the same token, a stronger governance structure (e.g. a board composed of leaders) and better-resourced and empowered Secretariat are also clearly needed for the Principles to fulfil their potential in their second decade.

Conclusion

The positive content and concepts in the VPs could and should undergo continuous improvement in much the same manner as the Global Reporting Initiative, becoming the basis for a stronger and more comprehensive global standard and custom in this area. The VPs at their inception were an excellent attempt at the multistakeholder, rights-based 'new governance' so needed to begin making more progress on intractable global issues threatening people and the planet. To continue to be relevant the VPs need to incorporate more meaningful and obligatory commitments and qualitative, uniform reporting to ensure compliance and credibility.

References

Pitts, C., ed. (2009). *Corporate Social Responsibility: A Legal Analysis*. Markham, Ontario: LexisNexis.

Freeman, B., M. B. Pica et al. (2001). 'A New Approach To Corporate Responsibility: The Voluntary Principles on Security and Human Rights'. *Hastings International and Comparative Law Review* 423: 24.

Williams, C. A. (2004). 'Civil Society Initiatives and "Soft Law" in the Oil and Gas Industry'. *NYU Journal of International Law and Politics* 457: 36.

48

Worker Rights Consortium
Robert J. S. Ross

The Worker Rights Consortium (WRC) describes itself as 'an independent labour rights monitoring organization, conducting investigations of working conditions in factories around the globe' whose 'purpose is to combat sweatshops and protect the rights of workers who sew apparel and make other products sold in the United States' (WRC 2009a). The WRC was formally launched in April 2000 at a meeting in New York City.

Created by the 'sweatfree campus' movement organized by United Students Against Sweatshops (USAS) in the mid-1990s, the WRC had, as of March 2010, 185 university and college and 4 high-school affiliates. University affiliations to the WRC have, in part, been voluntary, but some affiliations came only after student sit-ins and/or hunger strikes (see Featherstone and USAS 2002).

Governance and Approach

The WRC is governed by a Board composed of five representatives of university affiliates, five members of USAS and five members selected from its Advisory Committee composed of labour rights experts. (Full disclosure: the current author is an Advisory Committee member.) The Board excludes corporate members; this is in response to the founding impulse for the WRC, which was based on a rejection by USAS of what it understood as the overly business-influenced structure of the competing Fair Labor Association (FLA).

The WRC and the sweatfree campus movement led by USAS are based on consumers as agents for ethical change. They are strategically different from other consumption-based movements in that they are examples of a social movement using *collective* rather than *individual* consumption as the lever of change. They are also different from previous consumer-based anti-sweatshop movements in the priority they place upon labour rights – i.e., the importance of empowering workers as the movement's goal. One contrast would be to the National Consumers League (NCL) of the beginning of the twentieth century and its 'White Label' certifying no child or tenement sweatshop labour was involved in producing women's underwear (Ross

2006a). The White Label did not guarantee a certain wage or grant unions status, and the NCL withdrew it when a White Label factory was struck by a union in 1916.

Another contrasting approach to raising or enforcing labour stand-ards is through corporate self-monitoring of a code of conduct. In common with individual consumer-oriented certifications, this Corporate Social Responsibility (CSR) approach locates agency apart from the workers affected by the standards, in the hands of the cor-porations that operate factories (Esbenshade 2001, 2004).

The WRC-suggested Codes of Conduct include 'protective rights' such as health and safety, overtime, minimum wages, and also women's rights such as protection from obligatory pregnancy tests, which are used to screen out workers who might qualify for benefits (WRC 2007). However, WRC action has been most frequently spurred by violations of 'enabling rights' – that is, freedom of association and the right to collective bargaining, which it strongly supports.

Labour-oriented scholars are somewhat divided about the impor-tance of substantive – i.e., protective – rights v. process – i.e., enabling – rights. Elliott and Freeman (2003) and Esbenshade (2004) argue that enabling or process rights put workers' self-activity at the forefront of the effort to abolish sweatshop (hyper-exploitative) conditions. Chan (2001: 236), on the other hand, thinks a substantive 'right' to a living wage should be part of the more process-oriented 'core' labour rights of the International Labour Organization (1998).

How the WRC Works

University 'logo' clothing is a source of royalty revenue for the largest schools ('licensors'), and the industry has approximately $3 billion in sales. WRC member schools adopt codes of conduct which are imposed on the brands ('licensees') as part of the contractual conditions that give them the right to make and sell the apparel. The WRC conducts investigations of allegations about working conditions which may violate licensor codes of conduct and labour rights violations among the factories that produce clothing for the brand name apparel makers under licence from its affiliates. In turn, the brands take on the nominal responsibility to enforce these codes on the contractor fac-tories that they engage for actual production.

Affiliates of the WRC develop their own codes of conduct for licen-sees based on the WRC model code. These variations all provide at least 'basic protection for workers in each of the following areas – wages, hours of work and overtime compensation, freedom of associa-tion, workplace safety and health, women's rights, child labour and forced labour, harassment and abuse in the workplace, non-discrim-ination and compliance with local law' (WRC 2009b). WRC affiliates also require of their licensees that they make a public disclosure of the locations of contractor production. This produces a widely used online database that, among other things, allows groups of workers and their allies to discover whether the factories in which they may have an interest are party to WRC codes of conduct. Many worker-initiated campaigns for union recognition and improved working conditions have begun before workers were aware of the WRC, but upon discovery of this resource they obtain allies otherwise unavail-able. This is an example of what Keck and Sikkink (1998) call the 'boomerang pattern' of transnational network alliances.

The WRC works in partnership with labour rights nongovernmen-tal organizations (NGOs) and is in contact with labour unions in the countries that export clothing to the US. It has had collaborative rela-tions with the US labour federation's Mexican and Latin American offices – the AFL-CIO Solidarity Center. When local groups bring viola-tions to the attention of the WRC, and one of their affiliates is involved, the WRC conducts an investigation. Violations are reported to licen-sors who may apply pressure on the brands to rectify the situations. The WRC is widely respected for the professionalism of its reports.

Impact and Challenges

Between six and ten times annually, the WRC publishes reports on allegations of labour rights violations in licensee factories. An example of this process occurred in Honduras during 2007–9. Russell Athletic Company, which has numerous licence agreements with universities, closed a plant and dismissed 1,200 workers in a long-running union dispute. Upon request, the WRC repeatedly investigated allegations of labour rights violations (see WRC 2009c). Its reports documented the violations extensively. USAS then embarked on a campaign to influence university licensors to stop contracting with Russell. This campaign met with considerable success (Zagier 2009). Russell eventu-ally agreed to reopen a factory, rehire the dismissed workers and recognize the union (WRC 2010).

The footloose nature of the global apparel industry (Ross 2004) creates difficulties for the WRC model (Ross 2006b). Past 'victories' of the WRC and USAS have been subverted by plant closings and the movement of apparel production toward Asia in an apparent 'race to the bottom' in labour standards (Chan and Ross 2003). The most recent strategic initiative of the WRC and USAS, the Designated Supplier Program (DSP), aims to overcome the tendency of contractors to close or move their plants in response to union campaigns by steering licensees to suppliers who promise to respect labour rights and give evidence of having done so.

Under the DSP, university licensees would be required to source university logo apparel from supplier factories that verifiably respect the right to organize and to collective bargaining. DSP factories would be required to pay an objectively determined living wage. The incentive for factories to achieve and maintain compliance with these standards would be licensees' obligations to pay suppliers prices commensurate with the cost of producing under higher standards. In addition, the brands – the licensees – would be required to maintain long-term relationships with suppliers and to ensure that each supplier factory participating in the programme receives sufficient orders for the majority of the factory's production to be for the collegiate market. The WRC has fashioned an agreement with Knights Apparel, which sells logo gear in bookstores, to support such a factory in the Dominican Republic. Committed to paying three times the prevailing wage and respecting the right to organize, the new brand – Alta Gracia – will constitute a new chapter in consumer-initiated labour rights advocacy.

References

Chan, A. (2001). *China's Workers under Assault: The Exploitation of Labor in a Globalizing Economy*. Armonk, NY: M.E. Sharpe.

Chan, A., and R. J. S. Ross (2003). 'Racing to the Bottom: International Trade without a Social Clause'. *Third World Quarterly* 24(6): 1011–28.

Elliott, K. A., and R. B. Freeman (2003). *Can Labor Standards Improve under Globalization?* Washington, DC: Institute for International Economics.

Esbenshade, J. (2001). 'The Social Accountability Contract: Private Monitoring from Los Angeles to the Global Apparel Industry'. *Labor Studies Journal* 26(1): 98–120.

Esbenshade, J. (2004). *Monitoring Sweatshops: Workers, Consumers, and the Global Apparel Industry*. Philadelphia: Temple University Press.

Featherstone, L., and United Students Against Sweatshops (2002). *Students against Sweatshops*. New York: Verso.

International Labour Organization (1998). 'ILO Declaration on Fundamental Principles and Rights at Work'. Geneva. Available at www.ilocarib.org.tt/portal/images/stories/contenido/pdf/InternationLabourStandards/ILO%20declaration%20on%20fundamental%20principles%20and%20followup.pdf.

Keck, M., and K. Sikkink (1998). *Activists beyond Borders: Advocacy Networks in International Politics*. Ithaca, NY: Cornell University Press.

Ross, R. J. S. (2004). *Slaves to Fashion: Poverty and Abuse in the New Sweatshops*. Ann Arbor: University of Michigan Press.

Ross, R. J. S. (2006). 'A Tale of Two Factories: Successful Resistance to Sweatshops and the Limits of Firefighting'. *Labor Studies Journal* 30(4: Winter 2006): 1–21.

Worker Rights Consortium (2007). 'Model Code of Conduct'. Available at www.workersrights.org/university/coc.asp (accessed 9 April 2010).

Worker Rights Consortium (2009a). 'Mission'. Available at www.workersrights.org/about/ (accessed 29 December 2009).

Worker Rights Consortium (2009b). 'What Provisions Are Schools Required to Include in their Codes of Conduct?' Frequently Asked Questions. Available at www.workersrights.org/FAQ_11-11-05.pdf (accessed 29 December 2009).

Worker Rights Consortium (2009c). 'Russell Corporation's Rights Violations in Honduras'. Available at www.workersrights.org/Russell RightsViolations.asp (accessed 9 April 2010).

Worker Rights Consortium (2010). 'Progress Report re Implementation of Russell Athletic/Fruit of the Loom Remediation Agreements for Operations in Honduras Findings and Status Report. February 17, 2010'. Available at www.workersrights.org/linkeddocs/WRC%20 Progress%20Report%20re%20Russell%20Athletic%202%2017%2010.pdf (accessed 9 April 2010).

Zagier, A. S. (2009). 'Russell Shifts Course on Honduran Union Workers under Pressure from Anti-sweatshop Groups'. Associated Press. *Los Angeles Times* 18 November. Available at www.workersrights.org/press/ LA%20Times%20Russell%20Shifts.pdf (accessed 9 April 2010).

Part V
Finance Mechanisms

Introduction

Public goods cost money, and so a key question for global governance is how to raise the funds needed to confront transnational policy challenges (Kaul and Le Goulven 2003). Under the traditional model nation states volunteer funds to international organizations for specific purposes – a system that has proven fraught with difficulties. Promises often fall short of the need, funds can be suspended following the political whims of sovereign states, and the delivery of funds is often slow, or, with shocking regularity, less than what was originally pledged.

A number of institutional innovations have resulted. One idea has been to channel private money to public goods. This occurs, for example, with the Global Alliance for Vaccines and Immunizations, which draws donations not only from governments and international organizations, but also from private foundations and the private sector. Indeed, the Bill and Melinda Gates Foundation is the organization's largest funder (see also the section on multistakeholder initiatives).

A different way of bringing private funds to serve public purposes is to allow private actors to profit from activities with positive social externalities. A particularly developed example is the creation of markets for public and private carbon offsets. Because it does not matter to the climate where greenhouse gas emissions occur (so long as they are reduced and contained globally), making them a tradable commodity allows traders to buy emissions from places where reductions are cheap and sell them to places where reductions are expensive. In theory, this lowers the costs of reductions for all, though the process is not without technical difficulties.

Another strategy has been to attempt to bypass the nation state and bring funds directly to transnational public goods. UNITAID, a tax on airline tickets that funds the treatment of HIV/AIDS, is a particularly striking case of this approach, although it should be emphasized that, of course, the tax applies only in countries that have accepted the UNITAID tax. Following the 2008–9 financial crisis, there has been increased discussion of a global tax on financial transfers (named the Tobin tax, after the economist who proposed it), though the idea remains contested.

Given the pressing need for new funding sources for global public goods, it is perhaps striking that more innovative finance mechanisms do not exist. Of all the institutional forms presented in this volume, financing institutions are the least common. This scarcity reflects the firm control that traditional political institutions – the nation state and its intergovernmental organizations – retain on financial resources.

References

Kaul, I., and K. Le Goulven (2003). 'Financing Global Public Goods: A New Frontier of Public Finance'. *Providing Global Public Goods: Managing Globalization*, ed. I. Kaul. Oxford: Oxford University Press.

49

Carbon Offsets
Jessica F. Green

Carbon offsets are any activities that reduce greenhouse gas (GHG) emissions. They can be linked to national or intergovernmental regulations, or they may be voluntary. Carbon offsets are distinct from carbon trading, but the two are often coupled. In a carbon trading scheme, participants are allotted a certain amount of emissions. When a market participant – say, an energy company – emits less than its allotted amount, it may sell its excess permits – or credits – to others in the market. Alternatively, that energy company may also meet its reduction requirements through the purchase of carbon offsets. Offsets generate a net reduction in emissions, which are then credited against the overall reduction requirement. In other words, trading emissions rights and purchasing offsets are two distinct means of achieving emissions reductions.

Tradeable permits for pollution are a well-known and often-used policy instrument; the US acid rain programme is often touted as a successful trading scheme (see, e.g., Ellerman, Joskow et al. 2000). Carbon offsets, by contrast, are a relatively new market-based solution. This article therefore focuses on carbon offsets as an innovative contribution to the set of policy tools available to address climate change. It first describes the mechanics of carbon offsets. Second, it explains the role of carbon offsets in global regulation and in voluntary transnational private regulation. Third and finally, it discusses the challenges and problems associated with carbon offsets.

How Offsets Work

Offsets are generally organized as projects with discrete timetables and activities. Offset projects include building renewable energy capacity, capturing methane from organic sources, increasing the efficiency of energy generation systems, and planting or re-planting forested areas. Although any GHG-reducing activity can be considered a carbon offset, most offset projects aim to reduce emissions beyond a 'business-as-usual' scenario. This calculation is known as 'additionality': a carbon offset must show that any emissions reductions achieved are in addition to what would be emitted in the absence of the project. Estimating the additional reductions generated by a carbon offset project requires employing a counterfactual baseline to calculate how much carbon dioxide (or other GHG) would be generated in the absence of the project. There are accepted methodologies for calculating baselines and showing additionality, many of which have been created under the auspices of the Kyoto Protocol. Additionality also requires that the project is not causing 'leakage' – simply shifting the emissions from within the project boundaries to elsewhere.

Carbon offset projects usually include a complex landscape of actors, which vary by programme. However, there are three essential participants: the buyer, the seller and the monitor. The buyer is the actor in need of offset credits. This may be a country, a firm or an individual, depending on the nature of the regulation (mandatory or voluntary). In some cases, the buyer may re-sell the credits to another buyer. (Indeed, the re-sell rate of offset credits has increased markedly in the past three years (Hamilton et al. 2009).) The seller is the actor or actors who create the carbon offsets. They build wind turbines, reforest land, retrofit electricity generators and so forth. The monitor may be involved with the design of the project, to ensure conformity to accepted methodologies. It may also be charged with verifying the project activities at the end of the project, or another third-party monitor may be retained.

Carbon Offset Mechanisms

Carbon offsetting is permitted by the Kyoto Protocol via the Clean Development Mechanism (CDM). The CDM allows developed countries to purchase emissions credits for abatement activities undertaken in developing countries, and to apply these credits against their overall targets (developing countries have no targets under the Protocol). Thus, developed countries have the flexibility to decide whether to achieve their required reductions through domestic measures, by purchasing allowances on the open market through the emissions trading system, or by purchasing offsets. The logic behind the CDM is to produce emissions reductions in what is theoretically the most cost-efficient manner – by encouraging emissions reductions where they are most cheaply produced, i.e. in the developing world. Offsets under the CDM are required to demonstrate additionality, and there are lengthy planning, monitoring and review processes to ensure that this goal is met (for a helpful description of the CDM project cycle, see Wilkins 2002). Indeed, the CDM requires that each offset project be monitored by a third party, both at the beginning and at the end of the project. At the beginning, the third-party 'validator' is responsible for ensuring that the project meets the additionality requirement and uses acceptable measurement methodologies. At the end, a different monitor, called a 'verifier', must certify that the promised reductions have actually been generated. The Executive Board of the CDM has final say on whether to approve the credits. Thus, the additionality requirement involves several phases of regulatory oversight.

The market for carbon offsets under the CDM is now big business; in 2008, the value of the primary CDM market was estimated to be $6.6 billion (Capoor and Ambrosi 2008). The secondary market, where credits purchased directly from developing country projects are then re-sold, was valued at $26.3 billion (Capoor and Ambrosi 2008). The EU-Emissions Trading Scheme is the only other extant intergovernmental trading scheme (in addition to the CDM); it also accepts certain types of offsets generated via the CDM (European Parliament and European Council 2004). Some national level trading schemes, including the Japanese Keidanren Voluntary Action Plan, also accept CDM offset credits. Because of their requirements of additionality, and their connection to the two existing compliance-based markets, CDM offset credits are generally more expensive than the voluntary offsets described below (Kollmuss, Zink et al. 2008).

Carbon offsets are not restricted to intergovernmental regulation or so-called 'compliance-based' markets. There are several voluntary emissions reductions arrangements that also make use of carbon offsets. Perhaps the most noted is the Chicago Climate Exchange. Created in 2003, the Chicago Climate Exchange (CCX) is a voluntary but binding carbon trading market. Participants agree to reduce their emissions approximately 1 per cent per annum below a pre-established baseline. In addition to in-house reduction activities, participants may purchase carbon offsets to reach their targets. The CCX has developed its own criteria for the types of offset projects it will accept, and how the application, monitoring and verification processes must work (Chicago Climate Exchange 2009). It also accepts certain types of projects and methodologies from the CDM.

There are also a proliferating number of offset standards which are not explicitly associated with compliance-based markets like the Kyoto Protocol, or with voluntary ones like the CCX, though in some cases they are compatible. Since 2000, when the first rules related to emissions trading under the Kyoto Protocol were drafted, twenty different standards have been created to measure GHG emissions, and sixteen are devoted exclusively to measuring carbon offset projects (Green 2010). Using any of these standards, an individual or firm can purchase carbon offsets of varying types. Some project standards, such as the CDM Gold Standard or the Social Carbon Standard, provide environmental co-benefits in addition to offsetting GHG emissions. Other voluntary standards focus on offsetting emissions and ensuring additionality, much like the CDM methodologies. Interestingly, many of these voluntary standards – fully 75 per cent of them – recognize either rules or verification processes created by the CDM (Green 2010). The voluntary market is much smaller than the CDM, valued at approximately $400 million in 2008 (Hamilton et al. 2009).

Problems and Challenges

Though they have experienced steady growth since 2000, both the concept and practice of carbon offsetting have been the object of considerable critiques. The first objection to carbon offsets is normative: no one – person, firm or state – should be able to buy its way out of its individual responsibility to reduce GHG emissions. One non-governmental organization (NGO) report likened the practice of off-setting to 'carbon colonialism', whereby developed countries can continue their profligate consumption at the expense of developing countries, who must maintain a low-carbon economy (Martin 2008). Related to this critique is the concern that offsetting cannot be a permanent solution to climate change; a piecemeal approach to reducing emissions cannot substitute for a wholesale transformation of the way we produce and consume energy (Lecocq and Ambrosi 2007: 148).

Setting aside these larger concerns about the normative problems and efficacy of carbon offsets in combating climate change, there are three criticisms related to their implementation. First, there is a geographic imbalance of carbon offset projects. In 2007, 73 per cent of all CDM projects (as measured in metric tons of GHGs) were based in China; another 12 per cent were based in India (Capoor and Ambrosi 2008: 27). Fewer than 5 per cent of all projects were based in Africa. Since one of the stated goals of the CDM is to promote sustainable development, the disproportionate number of projects in relatively wealthy developing nations has been cited as evidence of a serious shortcoming of this institution (Ellis, Winkler et al. 2007). Even beyond the CDM, in the so-called 'over-the-counter' offset markets (which include all voluntary offsets not in the CDM or CCX), the vast majority of projects in 2008 were located in Asia (45 per cent) and the US (28 per cent) (Hamilton et al. 2009). A mere 1 per cent of over-the-counter offset projects were located in Africa (Hamilton et al. 2009). Thus, although the offset market may be funnelling some new money to the developing world, many of the poorest nations are not reaping the benefits.

Second, there is a critique about measurement of offsets. As pointed out above, most offsets require a demonstration of additionality, which in turn requires establishing a hypothetical baseline of the emissions that would have occurred in the absence of the project. Without a realistic evaluation of the baseline, the additionality of the project may be overestimated, and the credits earned may not correspond to actual emissions reductions, generating, in essence, 'fake credits'. However, as Gillenwater, Broekhoff et al note, '[n]o test for additionality can provide certainty about what would have happened otherwise' (2007). Some critics assert that fake credits not only are possible, but are being bought and sold constantly under the CDM (Victor and Wara 2008). Moreover, others point out how the additionality requirement has created perverse incentives. In the manufacture of industrial chemicals, producers in the developing world have created GHG emissions in order to receive credits for preventing the creation of more powerful GHGs (Wara 2007). These offset projects meet additionality requirements, but still represent a net increase in GHG emissions.

Third, there are problems with monitoring carbon offset projects. Most offsets require a third-party monitor to evaluate whether the project will produce the estimated reductions, and whether it succeeds in doing so. In some cases, one monitor performs both of these tasks; in others, two different monitors are required. One concern about this institutional configuration is that monitors are employed by buyers of offset credits, and, thus, may have a vested interest in producing a favourable evaluation of a project. This bias could include signing off on questionable projects, or overestimating the amount of credits generated (Green 2008). A second concern relates to transaction costs. The buyer and seller must contract with a monitor for each individual project. Then in some cases, such as the CDM, there is a monitor of the monitors, adding yet another layer of oversight – and costs. Some have argued that a project-based approach to offsets is overly costly to become a major component of regulation (Victor and Wara 2008).

Carbon offsets are a new twist on the traditional market approaches to pollution control. Instead of merely creating a limit on pollution and allowing participants to trade pollution credits, offsets provide another means to achieve reduction goals. In the context of compliance-based markets, this was a key contribution to forging political consensus. Offsets have also become widespread in voluntary markets, both as a way for buyers to demonstrate their climate-friendly proclivities, and in some instances, as a way to prepare for coming regulation (Kollmuss, Zink et al. 2008; Hamilton et al. 2009). Despite various critiques of the ethics and efficacy of carbon offsets, it appears that they will be a permanent fixture in future approaches to climate change.

References

Capoor, K., and P. Ambrosi (2008). *State and Trends of the Carbon Market 2008*. Washington, DC: The World Bank.

Chicago Climate Exchange (2009). 'General Offset Program Provisions'. Available at http://chicagoclimateexchange.com/docs/offsets/CCX_General_Offset_Program_Provisions_Final.pdf (accessed January 2011).

Ellerman, A. D., P. L. Joskow et al. (2000). *Markets for Clean Air: The U.S. Acid Rain Program*. Cambridge: Cambridge University Press.

Ellis, J., H. Winkler et al. (2007). 'CDM: Taking Stock and Looking Forward'. *Energy Policy* 35(1): 15–28.

European Parliament and European Council (2004). Directive 2004/101/EC, Amending Directive 2003/87/EC Establishing a Scheme for Greenhouse Gas Emission Allowance Trading within the Community, in Respect of the Kyoto Protocol's Project Mechanisms.

Gillenwater, M., D. Broekhoff et al. (2007). 'Policing the Voluntary Carbon Market'. *Nature Reports: Climate Change* 6: 85–87. Available at www.nature.com/climate/2007/0711/full/climate.2007.58.html#B13.

Green, J. (2008). 'Delegation and Accountability in the Clean Development Mechanism: The New Authority of Non-state Actors'. *Journal of International Law and International Relations* 4(2): 21–55.

Green, J. (2010). 'Private Actors, Public Goals: Private Authority in Global Environmental Politics'. Princeton University Ph.D. dissertation.

Hamilton, K., et al. (2009). *Fortifying the Foundation: State of the Voluntary Carbon Market 2009*. New York: Ecosystem Marketplace and New Carbon Finance. Available at www.ecosystemmarketplace.com/documents/cms_documents/StateOfTheVoluntaryCarbonMarkets_2009.pdf.

Kollmuss, A., H. Zink et al. (2008). 'Making Sense of the Voluntary Carbon Market: A Comparison of Carbon Offset Standards'. Stockholm Environment Institute and Tricorona. Available at http://assets.panda.org/downloads/vcm_report_final.pdf.

Lecocq, F., and P. Ambrosi (2007). 'The Clean Development Mechanism: History, Status, and Prospects'. *Review of Environmental Economics and Policy* 1(1): 134–51.

Martin, P. (2008). 'Beyond Carbon Neutral'. *CarbonSense* (London) May. Available at www.ictandclimatechange.com/USERIMAGES/Beyond_carbon_neutral.pdf.

Victor, D. G., and M. Wara (2008). 'A Realistic Policy on International Carbon Offsets'. PESD Working Paper, no. 74: Stanford, CA. Available at http://iis-db.stanford.edu/pubs/22157/WP74_final_final.pdf.

Wara, M. (2007). 'Measuring the Clean Development Mechanism's Performance and Potential'. *UCLA Law Review* 55(6): 1759–804.

Wilkins, H. (2002). 'What's New in the CDM?' *Review of European Community and International Environmental Law* 11(2): 144–58.

50

Financing mechanisms for climate change mitigation
Charlotte Streck

Focusing on the financing of greenhouse gas (GHG) emission reductions under the United Nations Framework Convention on Climate Change (UNFCCC or Convention), the aim of this chapter is to offer an overview of the existing and evolving structures of financing climate change mitigation.

Traditionally, international environmental governance, firmly based on treaty law, has been the arena of diplomats representing the interests of sovereign states. Over the last decades, it has however become obvious that traditional instruments of international law alone are unable to address the problems of an increasingly interconnected world. Recent years have witnessed the mushrooming of a variety of more or less formal alliances between public and private entities, which, because they are easier to create and more adaptive than traditional mechanisms of international cooperation, have spread around the globe (Streck 2005). In this context, the international debate on environmental governance has moved from a focus on governments to a focus on a multitude of partners; from governance at the international level to governance at multiple levels; and from a largely formal, legalistic process to a less formal, more participatory and integrated approach.

There are few regimes that have evolved as rapidly over the last years as the legal and cooperative framework of climate change. Whereas the 2009 UNFCCC conference at Copenhagen provides a case study more of blunt failure than of shining success, the various mechanisms adopted, implemented, discussed and considered highlight a number of new forms of global governance. The various proposed mechanisms and collaborations also show the tension between the traditional sovereignty that continues to dominate UN-led negotiations and the increasingly colourful picture around decision-making and implementation in climate policy.

International Climate Finance

Mobilizing investments for GHG reductions in developing countries has been a crucial issue under the UNFCCC and the Kyoto Protocol (KP). Since the adoption of the Convention in 1992, states have disputed how developed economies should assist developing countries in combating climate change. According to the principle of common but differentiated responsibilities enshrined in Article 3 of the UNFCCC, developed countries shall take the lead in reducing global emissions and help the developing world implement its own climate policies. This asymmetry inevitably influenced the design of existing finance mechanisms and will affect the structure of future ones under a post-2012 climate agreement.

There are two channels through which parties to the international climate regime provide financing for developing country mitigation activities. First, direct international funding to projects and programs in developing countries has been delegated to the Global Environment Facility (GEF), which also serves as a financial mechanism of three other multilateral environmental agreements: the Convention on Biological Diversity, the UN Convention to Combat Desertification, and the Stockholm Convention on Persistent Organic Pollutants.

Second, in addition to the administration of funds mandated by the Conference of the Parties (COP) of the UNFCCC, the Kyoto Protocol gave rise to a number of innovative 'flexible mechanisms' (Clean Development Mechanism, Joint Implementation, and International Emissions Trading) that opened the way to mitigation investments stemming from the market, rather than the usual bilateral or multilateral schemes.

The GEF and Its History

The UNFCCC requires a financial mechanism accountable to the COP, the supreme body of the Convention.[1] At its first meeting in 1995, the

---

[1] Note that the COP is named Conference of the Parties Serving as the Meeting of the Parties (CMP), when it comprises only Parties to the Kyoto Protocol.

COP appointed the GEF as the *ad interim* operating entity of the financial mechanism of the Convention. What began as a temporary solution has lasted over fifteen years, as its fund is cyclically replenished by donor states. Until very recently the GEF was the sole operating entity of the UNFCCC financial mechanism. Then, at the thirteenth session of the UNFCCC COP, parties appointed the Adaptation Fund Board as the operating entity of the Adaptation Fund established under the Kyoto Protocol. The GEF provides secretariat services to the Adaptation Fund Board, and is also entrusted with management of the Special Climate Change Fund and the Least Developed Countries Fund under the UNFCCC.

During the negotiations of the Convention, developing countries argued for a new financial mechanism that would provide support for developing country mitigation action. Developed countries, on the other hand, wanted to avoid a proliferation of separate funds for each environmental treaty, and envisioned the GEF as unified financial mechanism for all multilateral environmental treaties. Developed countries thus linked their financial commitment to the acceptance of the GEF as the operating entity of a UNFCCC financing mechanism. Developing countries eventually agreed to the GEF as an interim financial mechanism; the UNFCCC COP specified, however, that a permanent relationship between the GEF and the UNFCCC would be contingent on reforms that would ensure that the GEF would promote further transparency, democracy, and universality of participation (Boisson de Chazournes 2005). The result of intense negotiations is a restructured GEF that is 'an amalgam of UN and Bretton Woods traditional features' (Streck 2001). The GEF is the first global international fund whose policies and activities are decided on the basis of balanced representation of developing and developed states. The GEF has also been established with a minimum of formal arrangements, which has facilitated institutional learning over the years (Streck 2005). The GEF remains also among the most transparent of the existing international institutions. All documents are public and non-governmental organization (NGO) representatives are allowed to attend the GEF Council meetings not only as observers, but also as active participants. The GEF has increasingly reached out to the private sector to leverage financing and tap into private implementation capacity. These efforts culminated in the recent launch of the Global Earth Fund developed in strategic partnership between the GEF and the International Finance Corporation.

The GEF Trust Fund received $4.35 billion for the period 2010–14. This funding covers all operational areas of the GEF, including climate change. As this funding is too small to invest in large projects, the GEF focuses on removing market barriers to replicating demonstration projects and creating enabling environments (GEF 2006). The GEF plays a unique role as a mechanism that provides coordinated resources for projects and actions that promote the global environment. However, it is, at least in its current form, an unlikely candidate to serve as the sole operating entity for a scaled-up and enhanced UNFCCC financial mechanism. Despite the institutional innovations, the GEF is still struggling to solidify financing from donors and to endear itself to developing countries. Before its 1994 restructuring, these difficulties were largely due to the predominant role of the World Bank in the GEF decision process. Now, however, it is the cumbersome procedures required to obtain funds for GEF projects, at both international and national levels, that hinders trust among developing countries.[2] For these reasons, GEF funding and the current operational arrangements are inadequate to serve a more ambitious climate agreement (Porter, Bird et al. 2008). GEF disbursements are slow and limited in scale, procedures are cumbersome, and governance is burdened by an uneasy relationship between the COP and the GEF Council (Mueller and Gomez-Echeverri 2009). The GEF has recognized the need for reform in a recent publication that develops proposals for how the GEF can become a more substantial financial mechanism (GEF 2009). The call for reform reflects the increase in scope and complexity that will be required by a financial mechanism that responds to a more comprehensive post-2012 climate deal.

The Kyoto Protocol Flexible Mechanisms

The Kyoto Protocol is the first international agreement that develops a market-based compliance framework that actively involves the private sector. Through the so-called 'flexible' mechanisms the Protocol foresees the creation of markets for GHG emission reductions through project-based emission crediting or emission trading. Two of these mechanisms are available only to countries with qualifying targets: Joint Implementation and International Emission Trading. In addition, the Kyoto Protocol defines in Article 12 a Clean Development Mechanism (CDM), which aims to enhance cooperation among industrialized and developing countries to achieve sustainable development and reduce emissions. The flexible mechanisms in general, and the CDM in particular, are among the most innovative aspects of the existing climate change regime.

---

[2] For an empirical study on GEF financing in China, see Heggelund, Andresen et al. (2005).

The CDM, for instance, has been able to trigger investments for $15 billion in primary CDM transactions in 2007–8 (World Bank 2009). These transactions mobilized financial resources on emissions reduction projects in developing countries of $45.9 billion, mostly through participation of the private sector (UNFCCC 2008). In comparison with the money poured from thirty-two donor states into the GEF ($3.13 billion) for operations from 2006 to 2010, the CDM alone dwarfs the GEF in terms of financing (Figueres and Streck 2009).

The Kyoto mechanisms build a bridge between industrialized and developing countries, while establishing a platform for public and private entities to implement the treaty. They provide a framework under which new collaborative network structures consisting of nation states and non-state actors can evolve. Such cross-sectoral partnerships go beyond traditional concepts of special interest politics, giving non-state actors a variety of voluntary, semi-formal and formal roles in developing and implementing policy. The CDM governance structure in particular not only delegates to private entities part of the mechanisms procedures (Green 2007), but also empowers an international body, the Executive Board of the CDM, to undertake regulatory activities that have a *de facto* effect on states and private entities. This creates an intricate web of global entities, private actors and national administrations, which all have an indispensable part of the governance process (Kingsbury, Krisch et al. 2005; Streck 2005; Piñon Carlarne 2008). This complex governance arrangement has also led to relevant issues of accountability, legitimacy and democratic participation that have triggered multiple calls for CDM reform, including a reform of its governance to enable private actors to appeal decisions of the Executive Board and benefit from full legal due process rights (Meijer 2007; Streck and Lin 2008).

Renaissance of the State: COP-15 and NAMAs

The failure to reach a comprehensive climate agreement at the Copenhagen climate conference illustrates the difficulty of bridging the developed and developing worlds' interests. The most that could be agreed was a system of voluntary pledges of national reductions recorded in the annexes of the Copenhagen Accord, a non-binding agreement drafted during the last-minute negotiations.

While generally disappointing, the Copenhagen Accord includes promises for short- and long-term financing. Developed countries came to Copenhagen with clear promises to fund mitigation and adaptation actions in developing countries. According to the

Copenhagen Accord, $30 billion for the period 2010–12 will be provided, and long-term finance of a further $100 billion a year by 2020 will be mobilized from a variety of sources. The Accord also establishes two bodies to assist with the operationalization of the finance commitments: a High-Level Panel under the COP to study the implementation of financing provisions, and the Copenhagen Green Climate Fund.

The draft negotiation text that was not adopted in Copenhagen further envisages the establishment of a Finance Board for the finance mechanism under the Convention.[3] The Board would function as a supervisory body for the whole financing system; it would be accountable to the COP and would recommend rules for a balanced allocation of funds and guidelines to operational entities. A Green Climate Fund Facility would then be created by the COP as the main operational entity under the mechanism, assuring direct access to funds and with a membership representing developed and developing countries equally. It is unclear how this proposed governance structure would fit with the current one, especially regarding the GEF.

With regard to the mobilization of financial resources, the main emphasis of the text is on public sector funding. While there is limited recognition that the private sector will be essential to mobilize financing, transfer technology, and implement the infrastructure needed to effectively reduce global emissions, the discussions under the UNFCCC remain government-centric with little involvement of non-state actors. If anything, in the months that led to the Copenhagen climate conference in December 2009, governments played down market solutions, private sector finance, or implementation partnerships. The Copenhagen Accord states that 'funding will come from a wide variety of sources, public and private' but reduces the reference to markets to a single line. Private funding will, however, depend on incentives. If such incentives are not set internationally, they will have to be constructed around the national implementation of mitigation and adaptation action, in particular 'nationally appropriate mitigation actions' (NAMAs) by developing countries.

The experience gained with the Kyoto Protocol flexible mechanisms, especially with the CDM, proves how public–private partnerships can generate positive results in terms of mitigation investments. The governance structure supporting international mechanisms needs to be legitimate and effective, and in order to be so it has to rely on the participation of a multitude of stakeholders. However, state leadership is needed to create such a complex system and, at

[3] FCCC/CP/2010/2, 11 February 2010, Annex III.

the time of writing, it is certainly lacking due to the discrepant positions of states party to the UNFCCC. The recent climate negotiations have also seen a renaissance of the state and public finance, with the private sector playing little role in Copenhagen. Against this background and the absence of a strong international climate agreement, it is likely that single countries will enact financing schemes to reduce emissions on their territory, even in the absence of binding international commitments. Such a scenario might lead to a progressive polycentric approach in climate change actions, triggered not only by states but also by sub-state entities (Ostrom 2009). It is almost certain that local action rather than international mechanisms will provide a testing ground for new implementation arrangements that may give direction to international climate governance. This can create trust and examples that in the end will facilitate the ambitious climate regime needed to stabilize global temperature rise to not more than 2 degrees Celsius.

References

Boisson de Chazournes, L. (2005). 'The Global Environmental Facility (GEF): A Unique and Crucial Institution'. *Review of European Community & International Environmental Law* 14(3): 193–201.

Figueres, C., and C. Streck (2009). 'Enhanced Financial Mechanisms for Post 2012 Mitigation'. Policy Research Working Paper 5008. Washington DC: The World Bank. Available at econ.worldbank.org/external/default/main?pagePK=64165259&theSitePK=469372&piPK=64165421&menuPK=64166093&entityID=000158349_2009072108207.

GEF (2006). 'GEF Strategy to Enhance Engagement with the Private Sector'. GEF Council Meeting 6–9 June 2006, Agenda Item 23, GEF/C.28/.

GEF (2009). 'Future Strategic Positioning of the GEF'. GEF/R.5/7/Rev.1, 2 March 2009.

Green, J. F. (2007). 'Delegation to Private Actors: A Study of the Clean Development Mechanism'. Institute for International Law and Justice, New York University. Available at www.iilj.org/publications/ESP5-2007Green.asp.

Heggelund, G., S. Andresen et al. (2005). 'Performance of the Global Environmental Facility in China: Achievements and Challenges as Seen by the Chinese'. *International Environmental Agreements* 5: 323–48.

Kingsbury, B. (2007). 'Environmental Governance as Administration'. *Oxford Handbook of International Environmental Law*, ed. D. Bodansky, J. Brunnée et al. New York: Oxford University Press.

Kingsbury, B., N. Krisch et al. (2005). 'The Emergence of Global Administrative Law'. *Law and Contemporary Problems* 68: 1–15.

Meijer, E. E. (2007). 'The International Institutions of the Clean Development Mechanism Brought before National Courts: Limiting

Jurisdictional Immunity to Achieve Access to Justice'. *NYU Journal of International Law and Politics* 39.

Mueller, B., and L. Gomez-Echeverri (2009). 'The Reformed Financial Mechanism of the UNFCCC: A Brief History'. European Capacity Building Initiative Policy Brief, April.

Ostrom, E. 'A Polycentric Approach for Coping with Climate Change'. World Bank Policy Research Working Paper, no. WPS 5095. Available at http://econ.worldbank.org.

Piñon Carlarne, C. (2008). 'Good Climate Governance: Only a Fragmented System of International Law Away?' *Law & Policy* 30(4): 450–80.

Porter, G., N. Bird et al. (2008). *New Finance for Climate Change and the Environment*. Washington, DC: Heinrich Boell Foundation and WWF.

Streck, C. (2001), 'The Global Environmental Facility – A role model for global environmental governance', *Global Environmental Politics*, 1(2), pp. 71–94.

Streck, C. (2005). 'Governments and Policy Networks: Risks, Chances and a Missing Strategy'. *A Handbook of Globalisation and Environmental Policy*. Cheltenham, and Northampton (USA): Edward Elgar Publishing.

Streck, C., and J. Lin (2008). 'Making Markets Work: A Review of CDM Performance and the Need for Reform'. *European Journal of International Law*: 409.

UNFCCC (2008). *Update on Investment and Financial Flows, December 2008*. Bonn: UNFCCC.

World Bank (2009). 'State and Trends of the Carbon Market 2009'. Available at web.worldbank.org.

51

Global Alliance for Vaccines and Immunisation
Andrew Harmer and Carlos Bruen

The Global Alliance for Vaccines and Immunisations (GAVI Alliance) celebrated its tenth anniversary at the World Economic Forum in Davos on 29 January 2010, following a decade of vaccine provision and development, support for country-level immunization programmes and, since 2006, health systems strengthening (HSS). Launched on 31 January 2000, this innovative public–private partnership (PPP) was largely the creation of key global players working at the top level of the international health community.[1] It succeeded earlier international child health programmes – such as the Taskforce for Child Survival and the Children's Vaccine Initiative (CVI) – in the advancement of immunization.

GAVI's achievements are impressive. Between 2000 and 2008, GAVI disbursed approximately $2 billion to countries for vaccines, immunization programmes and HSS; it vaccinated 51 million children against diptheria, tetanus and pertussis; protected 213 million children with new and underused vaccines; and immunized 192 million, 42 million and 36 million children against hepatitis B, Haemophilus influenzae type b, and yellow fever, respectively.[2] How it has achieved these results is the subject of this chapter. In the following pages we review three innovations that distinguish GAVI from orthodox approaches to immunization: its governance structure; its cultivation of innovative financing for immunization; and its recent support for HSS. For each innovation, we synthesize findings from recent evaluations of GAVI to illustrate where the partnership is performing well and where further reform is necessary.

Innovation in Governance Structure

GAVI was initially an unincorporated public–private partnership hosted by UNICEF. Until 2008, it had a dual governance structure: an Alliance Board to steer the partnership, review country funding proposals and make recommendations to its financing arm, the GAVI Fund; and a Fund Board responsible for attracting tax-deductible

---

[1] Key actors advocating and driving the formation of GAVI included the Bill and Melinda Gates Foundation, the Programme for Appropriate Technology in Health (PATH), the International Federation of Pharmaceutical Manufacturers Association (IFPMA), the World Bank, the US Agency for International Development, World Health Organization (WHO) and the United Nations Children's Fund (UNICEF). Other bilateral donors, civil society organizations and low-income-country governments were either less prominent in the early stages of GAVI's formation or else became involved at a later point, though buy-in from relevant constituencies in some countries remains a problem. For a more detailed historical account, see Muraskin (2002, 2004).

[2] GAVI Alliance (2008) 'Achievements: 3.4 Million Future Deaths Prevented by GAVI since 2000'. URL: www.gavialliance.org/resources/15_EN_Achievements1_final_2.pdf (accessed 5 February 2010); GAVI Alliance (2009) 'GAVI Disbursements to Countries 2000-2008 as at 31 December 2008'. URL: www.gavialliance.org/performance/commitments/index.php (accessed 21 February 2010).

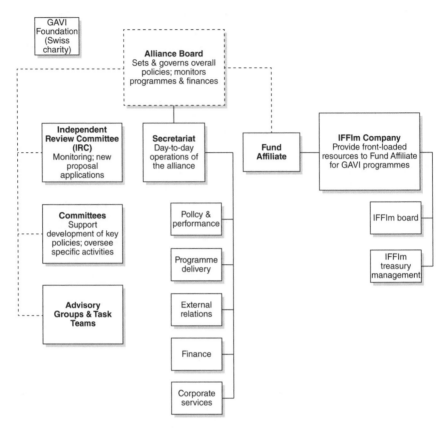

Figure 51.1   GAVI Alliance structure.

corporate donations. Confusion over responsibility and decision-making led to a governance redesign in 2008. The two Boards were merged but one-third of the new Board's members remained independent of the Fund's operations to ensure that a significant voice in strategic decisions remained free from potential conflicts of interest (see figure 51.1).

The redesign of the Board also took its inspiration from the private sector where, as GAVI's Director of Advocacy and Public Partnerships explained, 'corporate board membership is not based on representation but on individual qualifications' (Adlide, Rowe et al. 2009). GAVI describes its new, unified Board as 'a forum for balanced strategic decision making, innovation and partner collaboration', which comprises representatives from both public and private sectors. However, perhaps reflecting GAVI's preference for expertise over representation, and despite the partnership's claim to value input from civil society, it currently has just one representative from civil society on its Board, and one Alternate as of June 2008 (GAVI Alliance, 'The GAVI Alliance Board').

Unlike traditional multilateral or bilateral programmes for health, GAVI was established with a small Secretariat and lean supporting central administrative unit with no direct country presence. Instead, GAVI engages at the country level through Interagency Coordination Committees (ICCs) and Health Sector Coordination Committees (HSCCs). These are the primary coordinating bodies through which GAVI develops and implements proposals. GAVI also relies on partners with a country presence to coordinate technical inputs, and partially funds this through its work plan. Early evaluations of ICCs noted that they did not necessarily provide adequate technical support to implementers in all countries, and transparency issues and other weaknesses sometimes contributed to reduced partner involvement and policy dialogue (Chee, Fields et al. 2004). Despite these initial difficulties, ICCs have been shown to function well in some regions and countries, for instance with regard to information sharing and coordination of country partners for GAVI applications. Yet challenges continue with respect to evaluation and the coordination of immunization technical cooperation (Grundy 2009).

Cultivating Innovative Financing for Immunization

GAVI owes its existence to, and has received continued financial support from, the Bill and Melinda Gates Foundation. The Foundation provided an unprecedented $750 million start-up donation in 1999, and a further $750 million in 2005. At the 2010 World Economic Forum, the Foundation pledged $10 billion over the next ten years to develop and deliver new vaccines. In addition to funding from the Gates Foundation, GAVI has successfully mobilized significant and sustained grant agreements from various public and private donors, with approximately $4.5 billion cash received between 2000 and 2009 (table 51.1)

Drawing on 'private-sector thinking' and partnering with other organizations, GAVI has developed two mechanisms substantially different from more traditional donor channels for raising finances for child immunization: the International Finance Facility for Immunization (IFFIm) and Advanced Market Commitments (AMC) (GAVI Alliance, 'Innovative Funding'). Established in 2006, the IFFIm outsources its principle administrative support functions to GAVI while the World Bank, as the IFFIm's Treasury Manager, provides treasury functions and related accounting services. The IFFIm attempts to ensure sustainable financing by issuing bonds on the capital markets, with the backing of long-term government pledges. For example, the British government has committed to paying $1.38

Table 51.1 Donor contributions to the GAVI Alliance – cash received 2000–2009 ($)[5]

Australia	20,000,000
Canada	148,727,565
Denmark	26,149,592
European Commission	57,868,884
France	18,659,114
Germany	16,929,780
Ireland	26,210,480
Luxembourg	5,389,905
The Netherlands	190,755,989
Norway	440,856,502
Spain	40,536,200
Sweden	86,048,871
United Kingdom	121,562,308
United States of America	568,725,000
Direct contributions from government donors + EC	1,768,420,190
IFFIm proceeds	1,555,683,284
The Bill and Melinda Gates Foundation	1,137,838,000
La Caixa Foundation	12,270,772
Other private	10,737,189
Private and institutions	1,160,845,961
Total contributions	4,484,949,435

billion over twenty years (IFFIm, 'Donors'). By 2009 over $5.3 billion had been pledged to the IFFIm for the 2006–26 period. The proceeds from each bond sale are then translated into immediately available cash resources for GAVI programmes.

In 2009 GAVI, the World Bank, WHO, UNICEF, the Bill & Melinda Gates Foundation, and five donor countries launched the first AMC to stimulate the late-stage development, manufacture and adequate supply of suitable and affordable pneumoccocal vaccines. By committing money in advance, donors guarantee the price of vaccines once they are developed, thus creating the potential for a viable future market. The aim is to lower the long-term price of pneumoccocal vac-

[5] GAVI Alliance, 'Cash received 2000–2009'. Available at www.gavialliance.org/resources/Cash_Received_1999_2009.pdf (accessed 21 February 2010).

cines from $70 per dose. Through the AMC, the price per dose paid by GAVI and countries is to be capped at $3.50, with six donors contributing a further $3.50 per dose (Schwalbe and El-Ziq 2010). As of spring 2010, this innovative financing mechanism is still in its pilot phase. It is too early, therefore, to determine whether critics of the AMC are right to argue that the final costs will be much higher than GAVI's total donor contribution estimate of $1.5 billion (Usher 2009).

By successfully cultivating numerous funding sources, GAVI has been able to develop innovative funding streams to support countries and the roll-out of child vaccine and immunization programmes. In its earliest years GAVI focused specifically on funding for immunization services, injection safety, and new and underused vaccine support. This was expanded in later years to include broader health systems support, and support for civil society organizations. A variety of funding channels have been made available through GAVI to increase immunization coverage and to strengthen health systems, including immunization services support (ISS).

GAVI ISS funding was made available to qualifying countries in 2000. Designed as a performance-based funding mechanism for the improvement of immunization coverage, receipt of continued ISS funding is based on evidence of improved performance, and hence was also adopted as a financial incentive for the improvement of monitoring and reporting systems. Funding is paid in instalments over the first three years, while additional funding after that is 'rewarded' for higher levels of child immunization, as reported by countries that have completed a data quality audit. By December 2003, $38 million had been disbursed to fifty countries, rising to $155 million among fifty-three countries in 2006 as GAVI concluded Phase 1 (2000–5) and entered its second phase of activities (Chee, Carlson et al. 2007).

Despite evidence of improving immunization rates in countries, there have been concerns about the appropriateness of some vaccines for low-income countries, along with delays in the roll-out of newer vaccines (Milstien, Cohen et al. 2007). Further, whilst GAVI has sought to lower the prices of vaccines such as the pentavalent shot (which protects against Hib (Haemophilus influenzae type b), diphtheria, whooping cough, tetanus and hepatitis B), this has come later than expected with average prices forecast to drop 22 per cent by 2012. GAVI announced a suspension of further ISS payments in December 2008 until a review and reassessment of the ISS programme and reporting system were completed (Lob-Levyt 2009). This was in response to numerous challenges identified in evaluations of ISS, for instance evidence of potential under- or over-reporting of immunization rates and related deficits in health information systems (cf. Chee, Fields et al. 2004; Chee, Carlson et al. 2007; Lim, Stein et al. 2008; Lu, Michaud et al. 2006). While payments resumed in early 2009, the GAVI Secretariat and its Programme & Policy Committee were tasked with developing proposals for performance-based funding, including the possibility of replacing or redesigning the ISS funding stream.

Innovative Financing for Health Systems

Such difficulties bring to the fore the health systems constraints faced by both low-income countries and vertical health programmes like GAVI when trying to achieve their health targets. Evaluations of GAVI in the early years highlighted a variety of challenges, including perceptions of GAVI pressuring countries to accept vaccines that had not been requested in country applications (when requested drugs were often in limited supply), and the need for increased and flexible systems support to deal with problems such as weak immunization and information systems in countries (see Brugha, Starling et al. 2002; Chee, Molldrem et al. 2008; Milstien, Cohen et al. 2007; Starling, Brugha et al. 2002).

Noted for a willingness to respond to identified problems, and coming around to the position that strong health systems are required for achieving extensive immunization coverage, GAVI and its partners conducted joint assessments of health service delivery and immunization barriers and updated its work plan accordingly in 2004. The GAVI Board approved financing for HSS in December 2005, funds were made available from 2006 supported by the IFFIm, and processes to mitigate against HSS fiduciary risks were put in place, including internal and external review, monitoring and evaluation systems (Naimoli 2009). Between 2000 and 2008, GAVI has disbursed $240 million for HSS, with $800 million available to countries to help them overcome health systems bottlenecks (GAVI Alliance, 'Health System Strengthening').

Within the context of GAVI HSS activities, and recognizing the role civil society organizations (CSOs) play in country health systems, the GAVI Alliance also sought to formalize that role and developed proposals to provide support to CSOs. This was approved in late 2006, with two types of funding made available in 2007: a ten-country pilot supporting CSOs to help implement GAVI immunization programmes or HSS proposals (2007–9); and funding to strengthen the coordination and representation of CSOs in GAVI-eligible countries at national, regional and global levels. CSO funding, while additional to other

GAVI funding awarded to a country, is integrated within GAVI HSS support mechanisms.[3]

While still in its early days, GAVI funding for strengthening health systems has begun to have an impact. There is some evidence suggesting a stronger alignment between country proposals to GAVI and existing national health plans and in-country planning processes (Galichet, Goeman et al. 2010). Despite efforts to include a wide range and large number of diverse actors, however, problems of inadequate representation within countries, including late or no involvement of key stakeholders, continue to arise, while partner support for application development has been uneven (Naimoli 2009). While HSS funding is reflected in the national budget and additional to the government allocation to the health sector, in some cases either funding has been disbursed off-cycle with national fiscal year planning or countries have not had the required structures and mechanisms in place to absorb these funds, resulting in a delay in disbursement from national to sub-national levels (Plowman and Abramson 2009). Technical support for HSS grants has also been found to be inefficient, which may require institutional changes within the Secretariat, for instance the establishment of an HSS unit to enhance GAVI capacity to respond to and engage with countries (HLSP 2009).

Broader evaluations of the effects of global health initiatives, including GAVI, have long pointed to problems and transaction costs at the country level associated with parallel and duplicative processes, including non-alignment with countries' priorities and planning, budgets, and review cycles (e.g. Biesma, Brugha et al. 2009; WHO MPS Collaborative Group, 2009). In March 2009 the Chief Executives of both GAVI and the Global Fund to Fight AIDS, Tuberculosis and Malaria released a statement declaring their intention to begin a joint programme for HSS and to align resources and funding processes (Lob-Levyt and Kazatchkin 2009). From May 2009 the GAVI Alliance, the Global Fund and the World Bank, with technical support from the WHO, began a process of consultations and establishing a common HSS platform, with initial implementation in four or five countries taking place in 2010.

The Joint Funding Platform for Health Systems Strengthening represents a transformation in inter-organizational health financing and governance, and a reorganization of global efforts to coordinate,

---

[3] It is encouraging that GAVI is beginning to recognize the importance of CSOs for delivering health services, but it is questionable whether the $5.3 million that it has disbursed to this sector since 2000 (representing just 0.3 per cent of total disbursements) meets need ('GAVI Disbursements to Countries 2000-2008 as at 31 December 2008').

mobilize and channel resources to support health systems strategies. This evolving platform, while welcomed for shifting activity toward the principles of aid effectiveness agreed in the Paris Declaration and Accra Agenda for Action, is not without its critics (England 2009; Levine 2009). It has refocused attention on the definition, scope and attributes of HSS and, significantly, who determines and influences it. The process of establishing a joint HSS programme has opened debate regarding the respective roles of the three lead partners, and some have questioned the suitability of allowing these organizations to implement a broad and far-reaching HSS strategy for developing countries.[4] Either way, the current transformation in the financing and governance of global health is but one example of the vigorously contested nature of global health processes.

References

Adlide, G., A. Rowe et al. (2009). 'Public–Private Partnership to Promote Health: The GAVI Alliance Experience'. *Realizing the Right to Health*, ed. A. Clapham and M. Robinson. Zürich: Rüffer& Rub Verlag.

Biesma, R. G., R. Brugha et al. (2009). 'The Effects of Global Health Initiatives on Country Health Systems: A Review of the Evidence from HIV/AIDS Control'. *Health Policy & Planning* 24: 239–52.

Brugha, R., M. Starling et al. (2002). 'GAVI, the First Steps: Lessons for the Global Fund' *Lancet* 359: 435–8.

Chee, G., R. Fields et al. (2004). *Evaluation of GAVI Immunization Services Support Funding*. Cambridge, MA: Abt Associates, Inc.

Chee, G., N. Hsi et al. (2007). *Evaluation of the First Five Years of GAVI Immunization Services Support Funding*. Cambridge, MA: Abt Associates Inc.

Chee, G., V. Molldrem et al. (2008). *Evaluation of the GAVI Phase 1 Performance (2000–2005)*. Cambridge, MA: Abt Associates Inc

England, R. (2009). 'The GAVI, Global Fund and World Bank Joint Funding Platform'. *Lancet* 374(9701): 1595–6.

Galichet, B., L. Goeman et al. (2010). 'Linking Programmes and Systems: Lessons from the GAVI Health Systems Strengthening Window'. *Tropical Medicine & International Health* 15: 208–215.

GAVI Alliance. 'Health System Strengthening'. Available at www.gavialliance.org/support/what/hss/index.php (accessed January 2011).

GAVI Alliance. 'Innovative Funding'. Available at www.gavialliance.org/about/in_finance/index.php (accessed 19 March 2010).

GAVI Alliance, 'The GAVI Alliance Board'. Available at www.gavialliance.org/about/governance/boards/index.php (accessed 19 March 2010).

[4] See, for example, the Joint Statement by Civil Society Organisations (2009).

Grundy, J. (2009). 'Country-level Governance of Global Health Initiatives: An Evaluation of Immunization Coordination Mechanisms in Five Countries of Asia'. *Health Policy & Planning*. Advance Online access published 19 November 2009.

HLSP (2009). *GAVI Health Systems Strengthening Support Evaluation 2009*, Vol. II: *Full Evaluation Report*. London: HLSP.

IFFIm, 'Donors'. Available at www.iff-immunisation.org/donors.html (accessed January 2011).

Joint statement by civil society organizations (2009). 'Comments on the Proposed Joint Platform for Health Systems Strengthening'. October. Available at www.actionforglobalhealth.eu (accessed February 2010).

Levine, R. (2009). 'Wedding Bells for GAVI, the Global Fund and the World Bank'. Centre for Global Development. Available at http://blogs.cgdev.org/globalhealth/2009/07/wedding-bells-for-gavi-the-world-bank-and-the-global-fund.php (accessed February 2010).

Lim, S. S., D. B. Stein et al. (2008). 'Tracking Progress towards Universal Childhood Immunisation and the Impact of Global Initiatives: A Systematic Analysis of Three-dose Diphtheria, Tetanus, and Pertussis Immunisation Coverage'. *Lancet* 372(9655): 2031–46.

Lob-Levyt, J. (2009). 'Vaccine Coverage and the GAVI Alliance Immunization Services Support Initiative'. *Lancet* 373 (9659): 209.

Lob-Levyt, J., and M. Kazatchkin (2009). Joint Letter to Prime Minister Gordon Brown and World Bank President Robert Zoelick, from Julian Lob-Levyt (GAVI) and Michel Kazatchkin (TGF), 10 March. Available at actionforglobalhealth.eu/content/.../file/GAVI and GFATM letter.pdf (accessed 9 April 2009).

Lu, C., C. Michaud et al. (2006). 'Effect of the Global Alliance for Vaccines and Immunisation on Diphtheria, Tetanus, and Pertussis Vaccine Coverage: An Independent Assessment'. *Lancet* 368(9541): 1088–95.

Milstien, J., J. Cohen et al. (2007). *An Evaluation of GAVI Alliance Efforts to Introduce New Vaccines via the Accelerated Development & Introduction Plans (ADIPs) and the Hib Initiative*. London: HLSP.

Muraskin, W. (2002). 'The Last Years of the CVI and the Birth of GAVI'. *Public–Private Partnerships for Public Health*, ed. M. Reich. Cambridge, MA: Harvard Centre for Population & Development Studies.

Muraskin, W. (2004). 'The Global Alliance for Vaccines and Immunization: Is It a New Model for Effective Public–Private Cooperation in International Public Health? *American Journal of Public Health* 94: 1922–5.

Naimoli, J. F. (2009). 'Global Health Partnerships in Practice: Taking Stock of the GAVI Alliance's New Investment in Health Systems Strengthening'. *The International Journal of Health Planning and Management* 24: 3–25.

Plowman, B., and W. Abramson (2009). *Health Systems Strengthening Tracking Study – Final Synthesis Report*. Boston, MA: JSI Research & Training Institute.

Schwalbe, N. and I. El-Ziq (2010). 'GAVI's Advance Market Commitment'. *Lancet* 373: 638–9.

Starling, M., R. Brugha et al. (2002). *New Products into Old Systems: The Initial Impact of the Global Alliance for Vaccines and Immunisation (GAVI) at Country*

Level. London: London School of Hygiene & Tropical Medicine/Save the Children UK

Usher, A. D. (2009). 'Dispute over Pneumococcal Vaccine Initiative'. *Lancet* 374: 1789–880.

WHO Maximising Positive Synergies Collaborative Group (2009). 'An Assessment of Interactions between Global Health Initiatives and Country Health Systems'. *Lancet* 373: 2137–69.

52

UNITAID
Anna Holzscheiter

UNITAID is the official name chosen in 2006 for the International Drug Purchasing facility that aims to reduce prices for quality drugs and diagnostics, particularly with regard to HIV/AIDS, tuberculosis and malaria. It funds the development and procurement of drugs in developing countries, primarily by means of a solidarity tax on airline tickets. UNITAID has been in existence since 2006 and has, through its collaboration with other influential actors in the global health area, contributed to significant changes in drug availability and access, for example with regard to paediatric HIV/AIDS. In 2009, UNITAID became more visible in public debates through the launch of its patent pool, an approach that seeks to significantly broaden access to newly developed HIV drugs. Despite the growing visibility of UNITAID, its work and impact have, so far, attracted rather limited academic interest and have rarely seen a systematic assessment in terms of their legitimacy and effectiveness.

History of UNITAID

UNITAID was launched in the context of the 2004 Global Action against Poverty and Hunger. In that year, a group of forty-four countries took on the idea of raising additional funds for development via a small solidarity tax on airline tickets that would be channelled into global activities to combat hunger, illness and poverty. The creation of the International Drug Purchase Facility – later called UNITAID – was initiated by the governments of France, Brazil, Norway, Chile and the United Kingdom in 2006 and officially established the same year at the United Nations General Assembly. It was felt that the global governance of particularly critical health issues such as HIV/AIDS, tuberculosis (TB) and malaria lacked an innovative drug purchasing mechanism which would allow low-income countries to effectively deal with these severe health problems. UNITAID was created with the hope that such a new financing partnership between donor governments, international organizations, existing multistakeholder initiatives and private foundations would ensure greater sustainability of funds provided for tackling HIV/AIDS, TB and malaria.

UNITAID raises funds for products (i.e. drugs, testing kits) that are required to strengthen crucial health services offered to people suffering from HIV/AIDS, TB and malaria. Since 2006, UNITAID has committed around $730 million to support sixteen projects in ninety-three countries (UNITAID 2010). The funds for drug purchase are primarily raised through the airline tax, though some governments (UK, Norway) make direct contributions to the UNITAID budget. UNITAID's funds thus represent a sustained, renewable and long-term source of development aid. Nine countries have imposed the airline tax at present, among them France, Chile, Congo and Mauritius. Fifteen more countries are in the process of implementing a taxation scheme, the majority of them African countries. However, since many countries that signalled their willingness to introduce an airline tax have not yet done so, France to date remains the single largest contributor to UNITAID's $364 million budget, accounting for $US226 million or 62 per cent (UNITAID 2008).

Since it was created, UNITAID has focused on a number of niche areas such as care and treatment of children infected with HIV/AIDS, the prevention of mother-to-child transmission of HIV, and access to second- and third-line antiretroviral treatments (ARV). Most projects funded by UNITAID started between 2006 and 2008 and remain in development.

In July 2008, UNITAID's members agreed to establish a patent pool that allows a number of institutions and companies to share their patents for the production and development of drugs amongst each other and, thereby, to significantly lower the prices for these drugs even before the twenty-year-long patent protection has run out (Morris 2008). The pool was launched in 2009.

The patent pool aims to encourage patent owners (pharmaceutical companies, universities, government institutions) to share their HIV drug patents on a non-exclusive basis, in order to make cheaper drugs available to generic manufacturers even before the twenty-year patent term has ended. The body administering the pool licenses the use of patents to any party interested in production or further development of the drug. This initiative represents an important tool for wider access to life-saving drugs in low-income countries and, potentially, a way to circumvent the much-debated TRIPS agreement that protects patents internationally and, in certain cases, obstructs wider access to essential medicines (Cullet 2003). UNITAID is also the main stakeholder in the Affordable Medicines for Malaria Facility (AMFm), an initiative that aims to make artemisinin-based combination therapies for malaria (taken to be the best treatment for the disease) widely available.

In return for the sharing of their patents, patent owners reduce the costs and risks involved in patent development – any royalties collected for the licensing will go back to the original patent owner (Zakus, Kohler et al. 2010). The patent pool approach has been widely promoted by civil society organizations striving toward enhanced access to essential medicines, and major pharmaceutical companies have, to date, declared their willingness to consider contributing their HIV drug patents to the pool. Following the positive response of a broad range of actors and agencies to the idea of such a patent pool, UNITAID decided in late 2009 to establish and fund the licensing agency that will be responsible for the pool. Following the set-up of this institution, formal negotiations with pharmaceutical companies began, and the pool started operating in 2010. However, considering that the contribution to the pool is voluntary, it remains to be seen to what extent the pool as a new strategy in widening access to medicines will be a successful instrument.

Structure and Operation of UNITAID

UNITAID's governance structure is composed of three distinct bodies: the executive board, the secretariat, and the consultative forum. The executive board acts as the decision-making body of the organization. It consists of eleven members who are chosen according to the following ratio: one representative nominated by each of the five founding countries, one representative of African countries, one representative of Asian countries, two representatives of civil society, one representative of foundations, and one representative of the WHO. The structure of the consultative forum aims to be equally representative of all relevant constituencies. According to the by-laws of UNITAID, the consultative forum is responsible for, *inter alia*, voicing the concerns of those stakeholders who are not represented in the governance structure. The secretariat, as the bureaucratic 'spine' of UNITAID, is hosted by the WHO in Geneva and is composed of only fifteen people, with the aim of keeping UNITAID's administrative costs at a minimal level. UNITAID operates through a UN Trust Fund.

UNITAID has been described by its Executive Secretary as an 'operational unit' that relies heavily on the technical and medical expertise of its institutional host, the WHO (House of Lords 2008: 32). Of UNITAID's budget, which exceeded $320 million in 2007, 82 per cent is derived from the airline tax. More than 85 per cent of the organization's funds are allocated to low-income countries. Middle-income developing countries can receive only up to 5 per cent of UNITAID's budget, provided that they co-finance projects and show high disease prevalence.

UNITAID acts as an institution both independent from and complementary to existing actors operating in global health governance. Its funds are not directly disbursed to countries, but always through partnership agreements with other international actors (companies, public–private partnerships, international organizations). The Executive Secretary of UNITAID has described his organization as 'manufacturer-attractive', due to its predictable, sustainable, and long-term financing source (Bermudez 2008: 182). UNITAID envisages having an impact on market dynamics in order to reduce current prices for medicines and increase the number of people who have access to drugs through increasing health budgets for low-income countries. It also promotes better-quality control for existing drugs, as well as an improvement of the logistics by which drugs are delivered (Bermudez 2008: 183).

Impact of UNITAID – Effectiveness and Legitimacy

Both in terms of its legitimacy and with regard to output and effectiveness, UNITAID must be considered as an important component of the global health governance architecture, particularly taking into account its short existence. The agency has set ambitious goals such as, for example, to have reached around 400 million children with paediatric HIV treatment by the end of 2010. UNITAID's governance structure and standard operating procedures suggest that it aims toward the most efficient, transparent and democratic governance possible for a global institution – following excellent examples such as the Global Fund in this regard. Minutes of board meetings and all other relevant information on decision-making procedures are made available to the wider public via the Internet. A statement on ethics and conflicts of interest has been endorsed by UNITAID's members in 2007. Conflicts of interest are dealt with by the Director-General of the WHO, who may decide that an individual within UNITAID with conflicting interests may not be allowed to participate in critical decisions. In terms of both input and output legitimacy (Scharpf 1999),

UNITAID therefore seems to strive toward global standards of transparency, accountability and fair representation of interests and stakeholders.

In terms of the effectiveness of UNITAID, the very few studies that have looked at the effect of UNITAID's funds and policies suggest that it has strongly contributed to reductions in drug prices – such as, for example, in prices for paediatric antiretroviral drugs (ARV). In this field, UNITAID has worked closely with the Clinton foundation (CHAI) to lower prices of existing ARV (Bowen, Palasanthiran et al. 2008: 531). The CHAI/UNITAID collaboration has resulted in a reduction of prices for paediatric ARV formulas from initially $200 to $60 per year per child. The Joint United Nations Programme on HIV/AIDS (UNAIDS) considers UNITAID as occupying a 'major role' in scaling-up treatment programmes and the prevention of mother-to-child transmission (UNAIDS 2008: 136). It is still uncertain whether the patent pool will be an effective tool for enhancing and accelerating access to essential medicines. Even though several large pharmaceutical companies have confirmed their willingness to consider joining such a pool, statements by individual companies clearly express their reluctance and scepticism as regards such an instrument. Merck, for example, stated that 'patent pools may play a role in accelerating the development of combination therapy in specific areas' but that 'they will not solve the problem of access to medicines' (Merck 2009). Even though many see the UNITAID initiative as an important step toward closing the 'accessibility gap to life-saving drugs', they admit that UNITAID 'is still a promise' (Zakus, Kohler et al. 2010: 25).

In general, both academic literature about UNITAID and policy documents assessing the governance or impact of UNITAID are very sparse (Simon and de Lemos 2006). This might be related to UNITAID's character as a funding rather than policymaking institution, whose main responsibility is to liaise with existing actors in disease governance and disburse funds for their operations. However, considering that other financing facilities such as, most notably, the International Finance Facility (IFF) for Immunisation have attracted much more scholarly interest, there appears to be an acute need to analyse UNITAID's work in the context of and in comparison to other global health financing institutions.

References

Bermudez, J. (2008). 'UNITAID: Innovative Financing to Scale up Access to Medicines'. *Global Forum: Update on Research for Health*, ed. OGFo Development. Paris: OECD.

Bowen, A., P. Palasanthiran et al. (2008). 'Global Challenges in the Development and Delivery of Paediatric Antiretrovirals'. *Drug Discovery Today* 13(11/12): 530–5.

Chee, G., R. Fields et al. (2004). *Evaluation of GAVI Immunization Services Support Funding*. Cambridge, MA: Abt Associates, Inc.

Cullet, P. (2003). 'Patents and Medicines: the Relationship between TRIPS and the Human right to Health'. *International Affairs* 79(1): 139–60.

House of Lords (2008). 'Diseases Know No Frontiers: How Effective Are Intergovernmental Organisations in Controlling Their Spread?' *1st Report of Session 2007–2008*, ed. ScoI Organisations. London: House of Lords.

Merck (2009). 'Statement on UNITAID Patent Pool'. Available at merck.com/about/views-and-positions/unitaid_patent_pool_statement.pdf (accessed 25 February 2010).

Morris, K. (2008). 'Global Initiatives to Promote Wider Access to Medicines'. *Lancet Infectious Diseases* 8(9): 535.

Scharpf, F. W. (1999). *Governing in Europe: Effective and Democratic?* Oxford: Oxford University Press.

Simon, C., and G. de Lemos (2006). 'UNITAID: Innovative and Collective Financing System for the Fight against Malaria, ADS and Tuberculosis'. *Medicine Tropicale* 66(6): 583–4.

UNAIDS (2008). *2008 Report on the Global AIDS Epidemic*. Geneva: UNAIDS.

UNITAID (2008). '2008 Annual Report'. Available at www.unitaid.eu/images/news/annual_report_2008_en/pdf (accessed 25 February 2010).

UNITAID (2010). 'Achievements'. Available at www.unitaid.eu/en/Achievements.html (accessed 25 February 2010).

Zakus, D., J. C. Kohler et al. (2010). 'Achieving a Dream: Meeting Policy Goals Related to Improving Drug Access'. *Open AIDS Journal* 4: 25–7.

Index

Page numbers in *italics* refer to tables, *n* indicates footnote.

Aarhus Convention 317
Abbott, K. W. and Snidal, D. 20, 22, 39
accounting *see* International
    Accounting Standards Board
    (IASB)
Adlide, G., et al. 386
Africa
    conflict diamonds and Kimberley
        Process (KPCS) 302–3, 305,
        306–7
    environmental compliance
        (INECE) 99–100
    health initiatives 164–5, 192–3
    multinational enterprises (MNEs)
        319–20
African Development Bank
    (AfDB) 123–4, *131–6*
AIDS/HIV *see* Global Fund; UNITAID
Albert, M. 144
Alexander, D. 190
Alexander, K. R., et al. 39
Anheier, H. K., et al. 8
Annan, K. 350
antitrust agencies *see* International
    Competition Network (ICN)
arbitration bodies 14, *15–16*, 115–16
    see also commercial arbitration;
      specific bodies
Asian Development Bank (ADB/
    AsDB) 72*n*, 123–4, *131–6*, 205
Asian financial crisis (1997/8) 51, 52,
    53, 56, 275, 278
Asmal, K. 202
Auld, G. L., et al. 271
Aylward, R. B., and Linkins, J. 170

bank regulation *see* Basel Committee
    on Banking Supervision (BCBS);
    Financial Stability Board (FSB);
    independent accountability
    mechanisms (IAMs): regional
    development banks; Joint
    Forum on Financial
    Conglomerates
Banktrack 231–3, 234
Basel Committee on Banking
    Supervision (BCBS) 39–44
    governance 40–1
    history 39–40
    impact and criticisms 42–3
    and Joint Forum 42, 101, 102,
      103–4
    OECD 275
    structure and activities 41–2
Betsill, M. M. and Corell, E. 9
Bill and Melinda Gates
    Foundation 190, 387, 388
bribery *see* corruption: regulation and
    governance initiatives
Brinkerhoff, J. M. 206
Brown, D. 337
Bush, G. W. 56, 63, 64
Business Principles for Countering
    Bribery (BPCB) 323–4

Caldwell, L. K. 196–7
Cameron, M. A. and Tomlin, B.
    W. 118
Canada
    chemical industry (CCPA)
      328

Forest Stewardship Council
    (FSC) 267
International Competition Network
    (ICN) 85, 90, 91n
Joint Forum 103
Partnership Africa Canada 303, 305,
    306
see also North American
    Commission for Environmental
    Cooperation (CEC): citizen
    submission process
Carbon Disclosure Project
    (CDP) 213–18
  effectiveness 216–17
  function 214
  operation 214–16
  overall assessment 217–18
carbon offsets 371–7
  mechanisms 372–4
  operation 371–2
  problems and challenges 374–6
CEC see North American Commission
    for Environmental Cooperation
    (CEC): citizen submission
    process
Chakrabarty, S., et al. 337–8
chemical industry see Responsible
    Care
Chicago Climate Exchange (CCX) 373
child labour see Rugmark
child vaccination see Global Alliance
    for Vaccines and Immunisation
    (GAVI); Global Polio Eradication
    Initiative (GPEI)
China
  chemical industry regulation 330
  Global Fund 162–3
  labour standards 341
  toy industry 344, 346–7
  World Bank Inspection Panel
    (IP) 150, 151
civil society organizations (CSOs) see
    nongovernmental
    organizations (NGOs)
Clean Clothes Campaign see Swedish
    Clean Clothes Campaign (SCCC)
Clean Development Mechanism
    (CDM) 372–4, 375, 378, 380–1,
    382
climate change mitigation
  compliance network (INECE) 97–8
  financial mechanisms 377–84

Copenhagen Accord and state
    role 381–3
  Global Environment Facility
    (GEF) 378–80
  international 378
  Kyoto Protocol flexible
    mechanisms 380–1, 382
  see also Carbon Disclosure Project
    (CDP); carbon offsets
Codex Alimentarius Commission
    219–28
  history 219–20
  standard-setting process 221
    consumer representation 224–5
    developing countries 225–6
    future of 226
    WTO SPS-Agreement 220, 221–4, 226
  structure 221
commercial arbitration 138–47
  academic perspectives 142–4
    economic 143
    historical 142–3
    political science 143–4
  cases 140
  criticisms 141–2
  history 139–40
  operation 140–1
competition agency, EU see
    International Competition
    Network (ICN)
competition between interests 19–21
Conca, K. 205, 208
Conroy, M. E. 267, 271
Conway, S. A., et al. 191, 192, 194
Copenhagen Conference/Accord 213,
    381–3
coral reefs see International Coral Reef
    Initiative (ICRI)
corporate governance 273–80
  OECD principles 274–8
  World Bank Report on the
    Observance of Standards and
    Codes (ROSCs) 277–9
corporate social responsibility see
    Global Reporting Initiative
    (GRI); International Council of
    Toy Industries (ICTI) Code of
    Conduct; Social Accountability
    International (SAI); UN Global
    Compact; Voluntary Principles
    (VPs) of Security and Human
    Rights

corruption: regulation and
        governance initiatives 322–7
    Transparency International
        (BPCB) 323–4
    UN Global Compact 325
    World Economic Forum
        (PACI) 324–5
crime see policing
Cutler, A. C. 142, 144
    et al. 5, 9, 10, 19

Davies, H. and Green, D. 52, 103–4,
        105
democracy 28–9
developing countries 25–6
    business and finance issues
        banking supervision (BCBS) 42–3
        corruption: regulation and
            initiatives 322
        OECD Guidelines for
            MNEs 319–20
        offshore accounts 61
    environmental issues
        carbon offsets 374–5
        chemical industry 328, 330
        climate finance 378, 381–2
        forest certification
            scheme 269–70
        ISO 14001 certification 298–300
        Marine Stewardship Council
            (MSC) 313–14
        'nationally appropriate
            mitigation actions'
            (NAMAs) 382
    extractive industries
        conflict diamonds and Kimberley
            Process 302–3, 305, 306–7
        transparency initiative
            (EITI) 236–7, 239–40, 242
    health issues
        disease burden 173
        food standards (Codex) 225–6
        Global Fund 162, 164–5
        IHP+ 189, 190, 192–3
        pharmaceuticals (ICH
            guidelines) 92–3
        polio 170–5
        tobacco control process 159
        see also specific health initiatives and
            organizations
    labour issues
        child see Rugmark

toy industry (ICTI) 346–7
    Worker Rights Consortium
        (WRC) 366–7
    see also Fair Labor Association
        (FLA); entries beginning fair trade
security and human rights
    (Voluntary Principles) 357–8,
    360, 362
Dezalay, Y. and Garth, B. 141
diamond industry see Kimberley
        Process Certification Scheme
        (KPCS)
DiMento, J. F. and Doughman, P.
        M. 120
Dingwerth, K. 206, 207
    and Pattberg, P. 22
domestic politics 6–7, 30
Dorn, J. 110–11, 121
Dubash, N. K. 204, 205, 207, 208
    et al. 204, 206, 207
Dyson, E. 180–1

Earth Summit (Rio de Janeiro) 198,
        268
effectiveness of innovative
        mechanisms 23–4
emerging economies (BRIC) 27, 53, 362
    see also China; India; Russia
enforcement of regulations 10–11
environmental issues see Carbon
        Disclosure Project (CDP);
        carbon offsets; climate change
        mitigation; Earth Summit (Rio
        de Janeiro); Forest Stewardship
        Council (FSC); Global Reporting
        Initiative (GRI); International
        Coral Reef Initiative (ICRI);
        International Network for
        Environmental Compliance and
        Enforcement (INECE);
        International Organization for
        Standardization (ISO) 14001;
        Marine Stewardship Council
        (MSC); North American
        Commission for Environmental
        Cooperation (CEC): citizen
        submission process; OECD
        Guidelines for Multinational
        Enterprises (MNEs); Responsible
        Care; World Summit on
        Sustainable Development
        (WSSD)

Equator Principles 229–36
    institutional characteristics and
        consequences 230–2
    limits to effectiveness 232–3, 234
European Bank for Reconstruction
        and Development
        (EBRD) 123–4, *131–6*
European Investment Bank:
        complaints mechanism 128
European Union (EU) 9, 99
    Codex Alimentarius
        Commission 221–3
    competition agency *see*
        International Competition
        Network (ICN)
    diamond industry and Kimberley
        Process Certification Scheme
        (KPCS) 304, 306
    Emissions Trading Scheme 373
    International Accounting Standards
        Board (IASB) 66, 67, 68
    pharmaceutical regulation (ICH) 89,
        90, 91
    World Commission on Dams
        (WCD) 205
Europol 108
export credit and guarantee agencies
        (ECAs) 205
Extractive Industries Review 232, 237
Extractive Industries Transparency
        Initiative (EITI) 236–43
    aims 236
    history 236–8
    impact 240–2
    operation 238–9
    struggle for compliance 239–40

Fair Labor Association (FLA) 243–51,
        263, 341
    accountability to
        stakeholders 249–51
    Central American Ombudsman
        initiative 250
    effectiveness 247–9
    history 244–5
    legitimacy 251
    structure and activities 245–7
    Workplace Code 246–7, 248
Fair Trade Centre (FTC) 260–2, 263,
        283
fair trade system (Fairtrade Labelling
        Organizations / FLO) 252–9

    activities 253–4
    democratic decision-making 255–6
    effectiveness 256–7
    history 253
    legitimacy 257–8
    organization 254–5
Fair Value accounting 69–70
finance mechanisms 15, 17, 369–70
    see also specific mechanisms
Financial Action Task Force
        (FATF) 45–50
    compliance mechanisms 46–7
    concerns 48–9
    history 45–6
    strengths 47–8
financial crises
    Asian (1997/8) 51, 52, 53, 56, 275,
        278
    global (2008/9) 52, 53, 54, 56–7, 64,
        105, 276
Financial Stability Board (FSB) 50–5,
        67, 105
    governance 53–4
    and IAIS 73
    origins and structure 51–3
Financial Times (FT) Global 500
        companies 215, 216–17, 354
Fingleton, J. 85, 86
fisheries protection *see* Marine
        Stewardship Council (MSC)
Food and Agriculture Organization
        (FAO)
    fisheries management 309, 310
    and UNECE 270
    and WHO: Codex 219, 221, 226
food commodities *see* Codex
        Alimentarius Commission
Forest Stewardship Council
        (FSC) 265–73
    certification scheme 266–7, 269–71
    emergence of voluntary
        regulation 267–8
    evaluation 268–71
        effects on government policies
            and global timber
            corporations 270–1
        environmental impacts 269
        North/South dimension 269–70
    and WWF 309, 310
Fox, J. A. 150, 151–2
Framework Convention Alliance
        (FCA) 157–61

Framework Convention Alliance (FCA)
(cont.)
  civil society participation and
    negotiation 158–9
  current focus 159–60
  development 157–8
  significance 158
Framework Convention on Tobacco
    Control (FCTC) 157, 158, 159,
    160
Friedman, E. J., et al. 198
Friends of the Earth (FOE) 319
functionalist theories of
    change 18–29

G-7 48, 51, 58, 104, 278
G-8 58, 64
G-10 40–1
G-20 55–60
  critiques 57–8
  financial regulators 40, 43, 47, 53,
    63
  future directions 58
  and G-8, relationship between 58
  history and structure 55–7
  Joint Forum 104, 105
  members 56n
garment industry see Fair Labor
    Association (FLA); Swedish
    Clean Clothes Campaign
    (SCCC); Worker Rights
    Consortium (WRC)
Gates Foundation 190, 387, 388
Germany
  fair trade initiatives 334–5, 348–9,
    366
  financial regulation 39–40, 41, 67,
    103
  forest stewardship (FSC) 266, 268,
    269
Gillenwater, M. D., et al. 375
Global Alliance for Vaccines and
    Immunisation (GAVI) 384–94
  donor contributions 388
  governance structure 385–7
  health systems funding 390–2
  immunization funding 387–90
global capitalism 21
Global Compact see UN Global
    Compact
global credit crisis (2008/9) 52, 53, 54,
    56–7, 64, 105, 276

Global Forum on Transparency and
    Exchange of Information for
    Tax Purposes (GFTEITP) 61–6
  crisis and innovation 64
  future reforms 64–5
  legitimacy and inclusion 62–3
  role of state and intergovernmental
    organizations 63–4
  structure 61–2
Global Fund 161–6
  challenges and financing 163
  and GAVI Alliance 391
  Global HIV Initiatives Network
    (GHIN) 164
  history 161–2
  and IHP+ 193
  impact 163–5
  structure and operations 162–3
Global Polio Eradication Initiative
    (GPEI) 166–76
  assessment 172–5
  funding 170–4
  guidelines and standards 170
  history 167
  as solution to transnational
    cooperation problem 168–72
  structure and accountability
    mechanisms 167–8
Global Reporting Initiative
    (GRI) 281–9
  activities
    and actors 285, 286
    and structure 283–5
  history and goals 281–3
  impacts 285–7
Global Witness 236–7, 241, 303
Green, J. 8, 9, 10, 373, 374, 381
greenhouse gas (GHG) emissions see
    Carbon Disclosure Project
    (CDP); carbon offsets; climate
    change mitigation, financial
    mechanisms
Gulbrandsen, L. H. 312, 313
Gullison, R. E. 269, 270
Gurría, A. 61, 62

Hale, T. N. 11, 22, 119, 120, 121,
    152
  and Mauzerall, D. L. 198
  and Slaughter, A.-M. 119, 152
  Slaughter, A.-M. and 37, 55
Hasbro 347, 348

hazardous waste: Seaport Environmental Security Network (SESN) 99
healthcare *see* Framework Convention Alliance (FCA); Global Alliance for Vaccines and Immunisation (GAVI); Global Fund; Global Polio Eradication Initiative (GPEI); International Health Partnership and IHP+; UNITAID
Held, D. 195
  et al. 5, 6
  and McGrew, A. 3
  and Young, K. 27
historical theories of change 22–3
HIV/AIDS *see* Global Fund; UNITAID
Hülsse, R. 49
human rights
  UN Declaration 263, 358
  UN Global Compact principles *352*
  UN Special Representative 318, 319, 360
  see also Voluntary Principles (VPs) of Security and Human Rights
Human Rights Watch 242
hydropower *see* World Commission on Dams (WCD)

ideational theories of change 21–2
immunization *see* Global Alliance for Vaccines and Immunisation (GAVI); Global Polio Eradication Initiative (GPEI)
independent accountability mechanisms (IAMs): regional development banks 122–38
  comparative overview 130–6
  critical appraisal 127–9
  first- and second-generation 125–6
  functions 124–6
India 53, 127, 148, 328
  see also developing countries; Rugmark
Institute for International Finance (IIF) 275, 276
institutional innovations 1–4, 12–13
  implications 23–9
  research agenda 30–1
  rise and evolution of non-state governance 5–12
  theoretical explanations 17–23, 29–30

and traditional intergovernmental processes 3, 18, 30
types 14–15, *15–17*
insurance regulation *see* International Association of Insurance Supervisors (IAIS); Joint Forum on Financial Conglomerates
Inter-American Development Bank (IDB) 123–4, *131–6*
InterAction Alliance 340
International Accounting Standards Board (IASB) 66–70
  competition over standards 68–9
  development 67–8
  and IAIS 73
  impact 69–70
International Association of Insurance Supervisors (IAIS) 71–9
  history 72–3
  impact 76–9
  Insurance Core Principles (ICPs) 75, 77–8
  Joint Forum 73, 101, 104
  membership 72
  Multilateral Memorandum of Understanding (MMoU) 76
  operation 75–6
  structure 73–4
International Chamber of Commerce (ICC): Court of Arbitration 140
International Competition Network (ICN) 80–8
  founding members 80
  future community of governance 83–6
  objective 82–3
  structure 81–2
International Conference on Harmonization (ICH) of Technical Requirements for Registration of Pharmaceutical Products 88–94
  criticisms 92–3
  impact 91–2
  structure and operation 90–1
International Coral Reef Initiative (ICRI) 182–9
  analytical observation 186–8
  history and mandate 183–5
  monitoring network (GCRMN) 186, 188
  scientific cooperation 186
  structure 185

International Corporate Governance
Network (ICGN) 275
International Council of Toy
Industries (ICTI) Code of
Conduct 344–50
CARE Foundation 344–5, 348, 349
development 346–8
incentive for cooperation 345–6
legitimacy 348–9
International Drug Purchasing
Facility see UNITAID
International Electrotechnical
Commission (IEC) 290, 292–3
International Federation of
Accountants (IFAC) 67
International Finance Corporation
(IFC) 123–4, 125
& Multilateral Investment
Guarantee Agency (MIGA) 131–6
International Framework Agreements
(IFAs) 262–3, 264
International Health Partnership and
IHP+ 189–95
effectiveness and legitimacy 192–4
history and signatories 189–90
structure and operation 190–1
international interactions:
definition 4, 12
International Labour Organization
(ILO) 340, 341, 342, 344, 365
International Monetary Fund
(IMF) 25, 39, 42
accountability mechanisms
(IAMs) 128
corporate governance
principles 275, 278
extractive industries (EITI) 239–40
financial regulation (FATF) 47, 49
insurance regulation (IAIS) 73,
77–8
International Network for
Environmental Compliance and
Enforcement (INECE) 94–101
awareness raising 97
capacity building 97–9
climate 97–8
seaport security 99
training 98–9
impact 100
objectives and structure 95–6
regional networks 99–100

International Organization of
Securities Commissions
(IOSCO) 67, 69, 73, 101, 104
International Organization for
Standardization (ISO) 289–95,
300
cooperation and competition
292–3
implementation 291–2
legal pressure 292
market pressure 291
issues 293–4
and Social Accountability
International (SAI) 342
standard-making process 290
International Organization for
Standardization (ISO)
14001 295–302
background 296–7
impact 298–300
operation 297–8
and Responsible Care 330–1
Internet Assigned Numbers Authority
(IANA) 177
Internet Corporation for Assigned
Names and Numbers
(ICANN) 176–82, 199–200
development 177–8
governance 178–80
technical vs political role 180–1
Internet crime 107
Internet Domain Name System
(DNS) 176–8
Internet Governance Forum
(IGF) 178–9, 199–200

Jacquet, J. L. and Pauly, D. 312, 313,
314
Japan 41, 373
pharmaceutical regulation (ICH) 89,
90, 91
Japanese Bank for International
Cooperation (JBIC) 128
Jesover, F. and Kirkpatrick, G. 275
Johnson, J. and Lim, Y. C. D. 49
Joint Forum on Financial
Conglomerates 101–6
bank regulation (Basel Committee)
42, 101, 102, 103–4
governance 104–5
history (Tripartite Group) 102–3

insurance regulation (IAIS) 73, 101, 104
securities commissions (IOSCO) 73, 101, 104
structure 103–4

Kantor, M. 120–1
Karl, J. 316, 317
Keck, M. E. and Sikkind, K. 8
Kenchington, R. 187–8
Keohane, R. O. 3, 6, 27
  et al. 213
  and Nye, J. S. 6, 20
  Nye, J. S. and 8, 37
Khagram, S. 206, 207
  and Ali, H. 208
Kim, E. and Lyon, T. 218
Kimberley Process Certification Scheme (KPCS) 302–8
  controversies 306–7
  governance 303–5
  history 302–3
  impact 305
Kockan, T. 260
Koenig-Archibugi, M. 3n, 6
Kolasky, W. 85
Kolk, A. D., et al. 217, 218
Kolliker, A. 18
Krasner, S. 11
Kyoto Protocol mechanisms 372–4, 375, 378, 380–1, 382

labour rights
  Global Compact 352
  see also Fair Labor Association (FLA); Social Accountability International (SAI); Swedish Clean Clothes Campaign (SCCC); Worker Rights Consortium (WRC); entries beginning fair trade
law enforcement see policing
learning process 22
legitimacy of institutions 28–9
Leigh Taylor, P. 255
Lewis, D. 84, 86
Lichtinger, V. 120
Locke, R., et al. 247–8

malaria see Global Fund; UNITAID
Mansbach, R., et al. 8, 10

Marine Stewardship Council (MSC) 308–14
  controversies 313–14
  effectiveness 312–13
  governance and participation 311–12
  operation 310–11
    certification 311
    standards 311
    origin 309–10
Martin, P. 56
Mattel 347, 348
Mattli, W. 143–4
Mazey, S. and Richardson, J. 9
Merck 398
Mexico 61, 62, 271, 313
  see also North American Commission for Environmental Cooperation (CEC): citizen submission process
Millennium Development Goals (MDGs) 163, 189, 191
Milner, H. 6–7
mining industries see Extractive Industries Review; Extractive Industries Transparency Initiative (EITI); Kimberley Process Certification Scheme (KPCS)
money laundering see Financial Action Task Force (FATF)
Moravcsik, A. 7, 9
Morgera, E. 317–18, 319, 320
multilateral development banks (MDBs) see independent accountability mechanisms (IAMs): regional development banks
multinational enterprises see OECD Guidelines for Multinational Enterprises (MNEs)
'multiple jurisdictions' 129
multistakeholder initiatives 14, 16, 155–6
  see also specific initiatives
Murphy, C. 23
  and Yates, J. 289–90, 291, 293
Murphy, D. F. and Bendell, J. 266

Naylor, R. T. 49
neoliberal institutionalism 6, 7, 8

neorealism 5–6
Netherlands 96, 259, 260, 334
New York Convention on the
    Recognition and Enforcement
    of Foreign Arbitral Awards 141
nongovernmental organizations
    (NGOs) / civil society
    organizations (CSOs)
  business and finance issues
    Banktrack 231–3, 234
    Global Reporting Initiative
        (GRI) 281, 284
    OECD Guidelines for MNEs 317,
        318, 319, 320
    Transparency International 323–4
    World Bank Inspection Panel (IP)
        151
  environmental 9, 95, 96
    carbon emissions 214, 374
    CEC citizen submission
        process 119, 121
    coral reef protection (ICRI) 183–4,
        187
    dams 204, 206–7
    fisheries protection 310
    forest stewardship 266, 267,
        268
    Global Environment Facility (GEF)
        379
    ISO 289, 296
    UN Conferences 198
  extractive industries 236–7, 238,
      239, 241–2
    conflict diamonds and Kimberley
        Process 302–3, 304, 305, 307
  food standards (Codex) 225
  health 170–1, 189, 190, 191, 390–1
  Internet regulation 178
  labour issues
    Clean Clothes Campaign
        (SCCC) 259–62, 263, 264
    Fair Labor Association (FLA) 243,
        244–5, 246, 250
    Social Accountability
        International (SAI) 338–9, 343
    toy industry 346–7, 348–9
    Worker Rights Consortium
        (WRC) 366
  security and human rights
      (Voluntary Principles) 357, 360,
      363
  see also specific organizations

non-state actors 7–9, 12
non-state governance, rise and
    evolution of 5–12
North American Agreement on
    Environmental Cooperation
    (NAAEC) 118–19, 120
North American Commission for
    Environmental Cooperation
    (CEC): citizen submission
    process 117–22
  compliance mechanisms 118–21
  effectiveness 121
  origin 117–18
  Secretariat 119
North American Free Trade
    Agreement (NAFTA) 117,
    118
North–South governance gap 25–6
Nye, J. S. 28
  and Keohane, R. O. 8, 37
  Keohane, R. O. and 6, 20

OECD
  corporate governance
      principles 274–8
  Financial Action Task Force
      (FATF) 45–6
  health partnerships (IHP+) 191
  tax information (GFTEITP) 61–3, 64,
      65
OECD Council 62, 64, 318
OECD Guidelines for Multinational
    Enterprises (MNEs) 314–22
  background 315–16
  governance
    and implementation 318–20
    and standard-setting 316–18
  national contact points
      (NCPs) 315–16, 318–19, 320
OECDWatch 317, 318, 319
oil industry see Extractive Industries
    Review; Extractive Industries
    Transparency Initiative (EITI)
organized crime see policing

Panagariya, A. 337
participation of global South 25–6
Partnering Against Corruption
    Initiative (PACI) 324–5
Partnership Africa Canada 303, 305,
    306
Pereira, J. 193

pharmaceuticals *see* International Conference on Harmonization (ICH) of Technical Requirements for Registration of Pharmaceutical Products; UNITAID

Polanyi, K. 22–3

policing 106–13
  globalization of crime 107–9
  strategies 109–11

polio *see* Global Polio Eradication Initiative (GPEI)

Postel, J., et al. 177–8

power shifts and governance mechanisms 26–8

private governance 9–10

Publish What You Pay (PWYP) campaign 236–7, 239

Putnam, R. D. 7

Raustiala, K. 9
  and Victor, D. G. 11

regional development banks *see* independent accountability mechanisms (IAMs)

regulations, enforcement of 10–11

Reinicke, W. H. and Deng, F. 206

Responsible Care 328–33
  and American Chemical Council (ACC) 331, 332
  Global Charter (RCGC) 329–30
  history 328–9
  impact 332
  Management System (RCMS) 331
  and other self-regulation programmes 330–1
  recent activity 330
  structure 329

Reuter, P. and Truman, E. M. 49

Rio (Earth) Summit 198, 268

Risse-Kappen, T. 8

Rugmark 333–8
  history 334
  impact 335–8
  structure and activities 334–5

Russia 47, 57
  Chemists Union 330
  diamond industry and Kimberley Process (KPCS) 304–5

Seaport Environmental Security Network (SESN) 99

security forces *see* Voluntary Principles (VPs) of Security and Human Rights

Shiffman, J. 170, 172
  et al. 167

Slaughter, A.-M. 14, 37, 55, 95, 104
  and Hale, T. N. 37, 55
  Hale, T. N. and 119, 152
  and Zaring, D. 14, 37

Smouts, M.-C. 270

Social Accountability International (SAI) 338–44
  background 339
  SA8000 model 340–1
  structure 339–40

sportswear companies *see* Fair Labor Association (FLA)

Summers, L. 56

'surveillance assemblage' 110–11

Swedish Clean Clothes Campaign (SCCC) 259–65
  development and activities 260–2
  DressCode project 261–3, 264
  rules vs bargaining 263–4
  union responses 262–3

Synnott, T. 268

tax issues *see* Global Forum on Transparency and Exchange of Information for Tax Purposes (GFTEITP)

Taylor, P. 197

terrorist financing *see* Financial Action Task Force (FATF)

Tesauro, G. 84–5

Tietmeyer Report 51

timber industry *see* Forest Stewardship Council (FSC)

tobacco industry *see* Framework Convention Alliance (FCA); Framework Convention on Tobacco Control (FCTC)

toy industry *see* International Council of Toy Industries (ICTI) Code of Conduct

Trade Union Advisory Committee (TUAC) 275, 317

trade unions 262–3, 267, 276, 323, 340, 366

traditional intergovernmental processes 3, 18, 30

transborder interactions: definition 4
transgovernmental networks 14, *15*,
37–8
see also specific networks
transnational interactions:
definition 4, 12
transparency approach 11
Transparency International: Business
Principles for Countering
Bribery (BPCB) 323–4
tuberculosis *see* Global Fund; UNITAID

Ugarte, F. S. 82
UK *see* United Kingdom
UN
Convention Against Narcotic Drugs
and Psychotropic
Substances 45
Copenhagen Accord 381–3
Declaration of the Rights of
Indigenous Peoples 205–6
Economic and Social Council
(ECOSOC) 196, 198
FAO *see* Food and Agriculture
Organization (FAO)
and International Coral Reef
Initiative (ICRI) 184
Internet Governance Forum
(IGF) 178–9, 199–200
labour norms 340, 341
New York Convention on the
Recognition and Enforcement
of Foreign Arbitral Awards 141
Security Council 302–3, 319–20
Special Representative (human
rights) 318, 319, 360
Universal Declaration of Human
Rights 263, 358
UN Conferences: multistakeholder
involvement 195–202
history 196–8
World Summit on the Information
Society (WSIS) 199–200
UN Global Compact 350–6
criticisms 355–6
effectiveness 354–5
governance structure 353
healthcare (IHP+) 190, 191, 192–3, 194
history and purpose 350–1
operation 351–3
principles *352*
anti-corruption 325

scope 354
and Voluntary Principles (VPs)
363
UNAIDS 398
UNCED 268
UNCLOS 309
UNCTAD 254, 319
UNECE 270, 317
UNEP 95, 184, 204, 285
UNFCCC 377–80, 382–3
UNICEF 166, 174, 385, 388
Unilever 309–10
UNITAID 394–9
effectiveness and legitimacy
397–8
history 394–6
structure and operation 396–7
unitary actor assumption 6–7
United Kingdom (UK)
financial regulation 67, 103
International Health Partnership
(IHP+) 189, 190
mining industries (EITI) 238
Rugmark 335
security and human rights
(VPs) 357
United States (US) 27
Californian Public Employees'
Retirement Service
(CalPERS) 213
chemical industry and Responsible
Care 331, 332
Chicago Climate Exchange
(CCX) 373
Codex Alimentarius
Commission 219, 220, 221–2
Coral Reef Conservation Act
(2000) 187
Financial Action Task Force
(FATF) 48–9
and G-20 56
International Competition Network
(ICN) 81–2
and Internet regulation
(ICANN) 177–80, 199–200
labour issues
'anti-sweatshop' campaigns 244,
364, 366–7
Rugmark 335
toy industry (ICTI) 348
Overseas Private Investment
Corporation 205

pharmaceutical regulation (ICH) 89, 90, 91

President's Emergency Plan for AIDS Relief (PEPFAR) 191, 193

Securities and Exchange Commission (SEC) 68

security and human rights (Voluntary Principles) 357, 363

tax information (GFTEITP) 61, 63, 64

World Bank Inspection Panel (IP) 150

see also North American Commission for Environmental Cooperation (CEC): citizen submission process

United Students Against Sweatshops (USAS) 364, 366–7

university logo clothing *see* Worker Rights Consortium (WRC)

vaccination *see* Global Alliance for Vaccines and Immunisation (GAVI); Global Polio Eradication Initiative (GPEI)

Veggeland, F. and Borgen, S. O. 223

Voluntary Principles (VPs) of Security and Human Rights 357–63

content 358–60

private security forces 359–60

public security forces 359

risk management 358

criticisms and required reforms 361–3

impact 360

voluntary regulations 14–15, *16–17*, 211–12

see also specific regulations

von Finckenstein, K. 81, 83, 85

Warner, K. E. 159

Willets, P. 196

Worker Rights Consortium (WRC) 364–8

governance and approach 364–5

impact and challenges 366–7

operation 365–6

World Bank 25

accountability mechanisms (IAMs) 127

climate finance 380, 381

coral reef protection (ICRI) 184, 186, 187

extractive industries (EITI) 232, 237, 238

health issues

GAVI 391

IFFIm 387–8

IHP+ 190, 191

insurance regulation (IAIS) 73, 77–8

International Financing Corporation (IFC) 229–30, 232

Report on the Observance of Standards and Codes (ROSCs) 277–9

World Commission on Dams (WCD) 204, 205

World Bank Inspection Panel (IP) 123–4, *131–6*, 148–53

evaluation 151–2

operation 148–50

origins 148

politics 150–1

World Commission on Dams (WCD) 202–10

effectiveness and legitimacy 206–8

impact 204–6

origin and objective 203–4

World Diamond Council 303, 304

World Economic Forum: Partnering Against Corruption Initiative (PACI) 324–5

World Health Organization (WHO)

disability-adjusted life-year (DALY) 172*n*

food standards (Codex) 219, 226

International Health Partnership (IHP+) 190, 191

Maximizing Synergies Consortium 165

pharmaceutical regulation 89

tobacco control (FCTC) 157, 158, 159, 160

UNITAID 396, 397

vaccination programmes

GAVI 388, 391

polio (GPEI) 166, 167, 168, 169, 174

World Health Assembly (WHA) 157–8, 168, 169, 174

World Social Forum 254

World Summit on the Information Society (WSIS) 199–200

World Summit on Sustainable
    Development (WSSD) 198, 199,
    236–7
World Trade Organization (WTO) 83,
    254, 292

food standards (SPS-Agreement)
    220, 221–4, 226
World Wide Fund for Nature
    (WWF) 268, 309–10,
    313